Silke Braselmann
The Fictional Dimension of the School Shooting Discourse

Buchreihe der ANGLIA/ ANGLIA Book Series

Edited by
Lucia Kornexl, Ursula Lenker, Martin Middeke,
Gabriele Rippl, Daniel Stein, Hubert Zapf

Advisory Board
Laurel Brinton, Philip Durkin, Olga Fischer, Susan Irvine,
Andrew James Johnston, Christopher A. Jones, Terttu Nevalainen,
Derek Attridge, Elisabeth Bronfen, Ursula K. Heise, Verena Lobsien,
Laura Marcus, J. Hillis Miller, Martin Puchner

Volume 65

Silke Braselmann

The Fictional Dimension of the School Shooting Discourse

Approaching the Inexplicable

DE GRUYTER

For an overview of all books published in this series, please see
http://www.degruyter.com/view/serial/36292

ISBN 978-3-11-076605-9
e-ISBN (PDF) 978-3-11-064901-7
e-ISBN (EPUB) 978-3-11-064762-4
ISSN 0340-5435

Library of Congress Control Number: 2019937333

Bibliographic information published by the Deutsche Nationalbibliothek
The Deutsche Nationalbibliothek lists this publication in the Deutsche Nationalbibliografie;
detailed bibliographic data are available on the Internet at http://dnb.dnb.de.

© 2021 Walter de Gruyter GmbH, Berlin/Boston
This volume is text- and page-identical with the hardback published in 2019.
Printing and binding: CPI books GmbH, Leck

www.degruyter.com

Für Alva Nora
und meine Eltern

Acknowledgements

Spending years researching harrowing mass murder frequently left me speechless and, at times, incredibly sad. I could not have finished this book without the support of my family, friends, colleagues and supervisors.

First and foremost, I want to thank the supervisors of my dissertation: Wolfgang Hallet at the University of Gießen, who provided me with invaluable support and incredibly constructive feedback on my writing and research, as well as Jörn Ahrens, who supported me in all the ways a young researcher could possibly ask for. Thank you!

Further, I want to thank the members of my dissertation committee: Marion Gymnich, without whom I would not have pursued an academic carreer, and Joanna Rostek. Also, I want to thank Lauren Greyson and Madeleine LaRue for their thorough editorial support.

At the *International Graduate Centre for the Study of Culture* and the *International PhD Programme Literary and Cultural Studies*, I was able to develop my own research embedded in a network of brilliant researchers from all over the world. I do not only thank the GCSC and its entire staff – in particular its director Ansgar Nünning – but also my fantastic colleagues and friends that fill the Graduate Centre with life. Special thanks go out to Alexander Scherr at the English Department and Thomas Linpinsel at the Department of Sociology for countless hours of inspirational talks in the office, for beers and coffee and many shared meals.

At DeGruyter, I want to thank the editors of the Anglia Book Series, as well as my in-house editors Ulrike Krauß and Katja Lehming. I am thankful for receiving financial support through a stipend by the *Konrad-Adenauer-Stiftung*, and further want to express my gratitude to everyone at the *Dr.-Herbert-Stolzenberg-Stiftung* and, especially, to the *Körber-Stiftung* for awarding my work with the *Deutscher Studienpreis 2018*.

This book could not have been realized without my fantastic family and my friends. Above all, I want to thank my parents, Doris and Frank Braselmann, for always supporting me and believing in me, and Daniel Ziesche – my partner, best friend, brilliant colleague, and father of our wonderful daughter – for being the fantastic, loving, funny and smart person that he is. Special thanks go out to Daniela Wawrzyniak, who is always there for me – be it for a good laugh, a good talk, or emergency proof-reading –, to my sisters Anke and Kerstin, to Christoph Ermert for his friendship and a place to crash during all those years in Gießen, and to Hendrik Stoppel for mastering the art of formatting. And, last but not least, I am deeply thankful for all my friends in Cologne and Leipzig who watched school shooting films with me on Saturday nights or dragged me out of my study to talk about the more life-affirming topics: you know who you are.

Contents

1	**Introduction — 1**	
1.1	Society, Media and School Shootings as "the Inexplicable" — 1	
1.2	School Shootings and Fiction: Research Questions and the State of Research — 6	
1.3	Overview: Structure, Corpus Design and Key Concepts — 10	

Part I: Narrative, Fiction and Fact in the School Shooting Discourse

2	**We Need to Talk About *Amok*: Tracing the Narratives of School Shootings — 19**
2.1	Describing the Traditions of Rampage Violence: Ancient *Amok* and School Shootings — 22
2.1.1	The Discursive Dynamics of *Amok* and the School Shooting Phenomenon — 22
2.1.2	Popular Explanations for School Shootings and the Challenges of the School Shooting Debate — 39
2.2	Playing the 'Blame Game': Media Violence and the School Shooting Discourse — 53
2.2.1	The Debate about Media Violence in the Aftermath of School Shootings — 55
2.2.2	Prevalent Approaches to Fictional Representations of Excessive Violence — 61
2.3	Meaning-Making in the School Shooting Discourse — 77
2.3.1	The Necessity of Narrative in the Face of Excessive Violence — 77
2.3.2	Outlining the Basic Components of the School Shooting Narrative — 82

3	**Blurred Boundaries: The Role of Fiction in the School Shooting Discourse — 90**
3.1	Observations of Reciprocity: Illustrating the Relationship of School Shootings and Fiction with Matt Johnson's *The Dirties* (2013) — 94
3.1.1	The 'Look of School Shootings': Authenticity and Remediation — 95
3.1.2	The Reciprocal Relationship of School Shootings and Fiction — 106

3.2 Shifting Perspectives: New Understandings of Fictional Representations of School Shootings —— 124
3.2.1 Outlining the Fictional Dimension of the School Shooting Discourse —— 125
3.2.2 Functions of Literature and Film in the School Shooting Discourse —— 133

Part II: Discursive Functions of School Shooting Literature and Film

4 **Multimodal Representations of the School Shooting Narrative in *Give a Boy a Gun* (2000), *Shooter* (2004) and *Big Mouth & Ugly Girl* (2002) —— 149**
4.1 High School Lifeworlds: Multimodality, Remediation and Authenticity in Young Adult School Shooting Novels —— 153
4.1.1 Multimodality in Young Adult Fiction —— 153
4.1.2 Aesthetic Experience and the Adolescent Act of Reading —— 167
4.2 Lessons from Columbine: Functions of Multimodal Fictionalizations of the School Shooting Narrative —— 175
4.2.1 Remediation and Modes of Remembering —— 175
4.2.2 Processes of Marginalization in the School Shooting Narrative —— 189
4.2.3 Friendship, Complicity and the Position of the Adolescent Reader —— 196
4.3 Conclusion: The Young Adult School Shooting Novel as a Tool for Prevention —— 207

5 **Experiencing the 'Rashomon-Effect': Functions of Multiperspectivity in *Violent Ends* (2015), *This is Where It Ends* (2016) and *Elephant* (2003) —— 210**
5.1 Taking Perspectives, Picking Sides: Multiperspectivity in Young Adult School Shooting Novels —— 213
5.1.1 Perspective Structures and Perspective Taking in *This is Where It Ends* and *Violent Ends* —— 215
5.1.2 Functions of Literary Multiperspectivity for the School Shooting Discourse —— 226
5.2 A Labyrinth of Explanations: Multiperspectivity in Gus Van Sant's *Elephant* —— 236
5.2.1 Describing Multiperspectival Representation in *Elephant* —— 238

5.2.2	Functions of *Elephant*'s Aesthetics —— **250**	
5.3	Conclusion: The Aesthetic Experience of Polyvalence, Complexity and the Denial of Closure —— **261**	

6	**Unsettling Narratives: The Inexplicability of School Shootings in *We Need to Talk About Kevin* (2003) and its Film Adaptation (2011) —— 265**	
6.1	Inexplicability, Insolvability and Social Taboos: Lionel Shriver's *We Need to Talk About Kevin* —— **268**	
6.1.1	Epistolarity, Subjectivity and Unreliable Narration —— **269**	
6.1.2	Representations of Motherhood, Responsibility and Accountability —— **282**	
6.1.3	Remembering, Forgetting and the Cultural Memory of School Shootings —— **292**	
6.2	Modes of Interpretation in Lynne Ramsay's Adaptation of *We Need to Talk About Kevin* —— **301**	
6.2.1	Adaptation as Product and Interpretation —— **302**	
6.2.2	Representations of the 'Bad Mother' and the 'Monstrous Child' —— **308**	
6.3	Conclusion: Unreliability in the School Shooting Narrative —— **312**	

7	**Conclusion —— 315**	
7.1	The Relevance of Fiction to the School Shooting Discourse —— **316**	
7.2	Potential Functions of School Shooting Novels and Films —— **320**	
7.3	Contributions, Limitations and Topics for Further Research —— **326**	

Referenced School Shootings and Mass Shooting Incidents —— 330
 School Shootings Referenced by Name of Perpetrator(s) —— **330**
 School Shootings Referenced by Place —— **331**
 Other Mass Shooting Incidents Referenced by Name or Place —— **331**

Bibliography —— 332
 Primary Works —— **332**
 Novels —— **332**
 Films —— **332**
 TV Productions —— **333**
 Secondary Literature —— **333**

Index —— 351

> Well here is a fuckin' news flash for you stupid shits, everyone is a follower! Everyone who says they aren't followers and then dresses different or acts different... they got that from something they saw on TV or in film or in life. No originality.
> – Eric Harris

> Among other things, you'll find that you're not the first person who was ever confused and frightened and even sickened by human behavior. You're by no means alone on that score, you'll be excited and stimulated to know. Many, many men have been just as troubled morally and spiritually as you are right now. Happily, some of them kept records of their troubles. You'll learn from them – if you want to. Just as someday, if you have something to offer, someone will learn something from you. It's a beautiful reciprocal arrangement. And it isn't education. It's history. It's poetry.
> – J.D. Salinger, *The Catcher in the Rye*

> Crazy killers are always obsessed with *Catcher in the Rye*.
> – Matt Johnson, *The Dirties*

1 Introduction

What is so remarkable about the subject of this book, about excessive, apparently unmotivated and sudden acts of violence at educational institutions, is that these events are incredibly rare. In fact, compared to other deadly crimes, the so-called *school shootings* that have prompted western societies to install metal detectors at high schools, dispatch armed officers at elementary schools or pass legislation that allows the concealed carry of weapons at universities hardly ever happen. But despite their rarity, school shootings are deeply engrained in the collective memory, the images of grieving students and crime scene tape on school campuses all too familiar. The grainy images from surveillance cameras in high school cafeterias, and even yearbook pictures of 'normal' adolescent boys, can now be associated with mass murder.

This discrepancy between the prevalence of this phenomenon and the societal reaction to it gave rise to one of this books's central questions: if school shootings hardly ever happen, how can it be that they receive so much media, scholarly and public attention? This volume does, of course, contribute to the body of existing research. However, as it connects the phenomenon with its fictional representations, it approaches the topic from a decisively different angle. In this short introduction, I outline my basic approach, the structure, research questions, corpus design and the basic concepts to be employed. A thorough overview of the state of the research as well as the theoretical background for studying school shootings and school shooting narratives is presented in Chapter 2. My own theory about the school shooting phenomenon and its relationship to school shooting fiction is explained in Chapter 3. Since the author is well aware that this book is itself a contribution to the discourse it seeks to analyze, this dynamic interweaving of theory and my research contribution and observations about the topic appeared to be a reasonable way to go.

1.1 Society, Media and School Shootings as "the Inexplicable"

Even though some scholars have admitted that researching an event as rare as school shootings poses many challenges for empirical studies (cf. e.g., Muschert 2007, Böckler/Seeger 2010), these acts have been researched extensively by criminologists, sociologists and psychologists, especially in the United States, but also in Germany and Scandinavia, where a number of tragic high-profile school shootings have occurred over the last fifteen years. As James Alan Fox and Jack

Levin (1999: 166) observed in relation to serial killers in the U.S., there may by now be more researchers who study school shootings than there are cases or perpetrators to be studied.

School shootings have garnered even more attention from the media than they have from academia: in America, both the Columbine High School shooting in Littleton, Colorado on April 20, 1999 and the Sandy Hook Elementary School shooting in Newtown, Connecticut on December 14, 2012 were leading news stories of their respective years (cf. Muschert 2007, Fox/De Lateur 2014). By now, the media and public reaction to school shootings or comparable acts of rampage violence appears to be almost reflexive. Studies have shown that politicians use similar words to express shock and grief, while the media employs recurring frames.[1] Media coverage, along with social and political reactions, seems to follow carefully constructed and rehearsed rituals, even though the aspects emphasized in the aftermath may differ (cf. Ahrens 2015: 151f.).

These rituals became quite obvious in one of the rather recent cases of a shooting committed by an adolescent, and involving mainly adolescent victims, at a mall in Munich in July 2016. After this horrible mass shooting at the *Olympia Einkaufszentrum*, it was unclear who the shooter was or if he had acted alone. Because the possibility of a terrorist attack could not be excluded, panic spread across the city and in the mass media. As soon as the police confirmed that the shooter had acted alone and that the event was not connected to a terrorist organization, however, the media immediately resorted to its rhetoric of school shooting coverage in order to reintegrate the event, even though the shooting was not committed at a school (cf. Braselmann/Ahrens 2017). The shooter was described as lonely, sad, bullied and most likely mentally ill. His media consumption and the time he spent on the Internet were commented on by experts and journalists. In the end, helplessness and the diagnosis that nothing could explain why this normal, unsuspicious boy turned into a mass murderer dominated coverage until, finally, bullying was singled out as the motive for the shooting in the final report in March 2017.[2] Here, the constructedness of the school shooting discourse could be very well observed.

Unease grew among media studies scholars, however, when a connection between school shootings and their media representations was observed. "In the contemporary world", school shooting researchers Glenn W. Muschert and

---

[1] For analyses of media coverage in America, see e.g., Muschert (2007); for Canada, see Howells (2012); for Germany, see Verhovnik (2015), Ahrens (2015).
[2] cf. "Amoklauf in München: Mobbing als Motiv." *Spiegel Online*. 17 March 2017. Online: http://www.spiegel.de/panorama/justiz/amoklauf-in-muenchen-ermittler-sehen-mobbing-als-motiv-a-1139327.html.

Johanna Sumiala note, "modern mass media and the Internet have become key sites of and for symbolic performance of school shootings. Media are part of school shootings and school shootings are part of the media" (Muschert/Sumiala 2012: xvii). In the 1990s, when a 'miniepidemic' (cf. Newman/Fox 2009, Kellner 2008) of school shootings shocked America, "the public perception of school shootings as an emergent and increasing social problem" (Muschert 2007: 65) took shape.

The notion of a new, uncontrollable threat reached its peak with the Columbine shooting in 1999. Even though it was not the first mass shooting committed by students at their own school, Columbine can be seen as prototypical in two respects. First, Columbine was the first school shooting to attract extensive international media attention. It marked, in Stanley Cohen's words, the "cognitive shift from 'how could it happen in a place like this?' to 'it could happen anyplace'" (Cohen 2002 [1972]: xiii). Secondly, the perpetrators Eric Harris and Dylan Klebold planned and staged their attack in a way that established a connection between school shootings and media consumption that alarmed parents, politicians and educators alike. Harris and Klebold were the first school shooters to present themselves as violent killers at their school in a fictional film they made for a school project, and the first to leave behind a number of home videos in which they documented their planning and explained themselves. Further, they famously referenced various forms of media content and cultural artifacts before and even during the shooting.

While the Columbine shooters' affinity for violent films and video games gained much attention, the fact that the phenomenon itself, due to its spectacular nature, was rather quickly mediatized in many different ways (cf. Muschert/Sumiala 2012) was not reflected upon until much later. But the link between school shootings and their media representations goes beyond the genesis of the shooting itself: as school shootings are such a rare phenomenon, most people only experience such events through these media representations. Douglas Kellner (2008) has powerfully argued that school shootings are "media spectacles", which he defines as "technologically constructed media events that are produced and disseminated through the so-called mass media" (cf. Kellner 2008: 3). However, this alone cannot explain the disproportionally large presence of school shootings in the cultural imaginary and social discourse.

After Columbine, it became clear that school shootings "could generate questions that address both the lasting problem of violence within the social realm and the seemingly ubiquitous representation of violence through cultural artefacts" (Ahrens 2015: 137). Contrary to what the emphasis on the number of school shootings and the rather morbid rankings of the deadliest school shootings in the news suggest, the effect that these incidents have on society cannot be reduced to the severity of the attacks alone. After all, even in societies that define themselves as civilized and peaceful, other events or processes claim many more lives than school shootings and yet are not scandalized in the same way. The many victims of gang violence in urban areas, for example, attract only a fraction of the attention that school shootings at suburban or rural schools do, as scholars have rightfully criticized (cf. Ferguson/Ivory 2012, Linder 2014).

School shootings inherently question the societal narrative of peacefulness; in their excessiveness, by being carried out in public and appearing to be directed at no one in particular, they have the potential to remind society of the ubiquitous possibility of violence. While violence is accepted in some parts of society and an integral part of popular culture, it cannot suddenly interrupt societal normalcy without calling into question the very stability of that society.

School shootings, by proving that violence can happen any time, at any place, to any one, and by appearing to be unpreventable, signal a loss of control (cf. Heitmeyer et al. 2013). As a reaction to this loss of control, so as to "avoid having to engage with the causes of structural loss of control and to provide reassurance, the dominant public discourse aims to disassociate such phenomena from normal society" (Heitmeyer et al. 2013: 27f.). Confronted with recurring acts of public violence, society's attempt to restore the civilized notion of peacefulness requires considerable effort. This attempt shapes all discursive elements – media coverage, cultural artifacts like literature and film, scholarly works and the way that school shootings are understood and talked about.

The notion of 'excessive violence' is extremely helpful for understanding the dynamics of the school shooting discourse, as it connects the act of violence with the reactions it triggers in society. 'Excessive violence' thus does not refer to the number of victims or the severity of the act, but aims to highlight the disproportionality of the violent act and the way in which it exceeds any possible rational end (cf. Gerster/Krämer/Ziegler 2015). In its disproportionality, excessive violence resists all strategies for normalization, which can usually be achieved by creating causal narratives. An act of excessive violence appears to be meaningless. In this respect, it is closely linked to Jan Philipp Reemtsma's notion of 'autotelic violence' – violence for the sake of violence.[3] Autotelic violence "seeks to damage or destroy

---

[3] Reemtsma differentiates between three forms of violence: locative, raptive and autotelic, which he "distinguishes based on their phenomenological relation to the body" (Reemtsma 2012: 56). Locative violence wants "to eliminate the body as an obstacle or relocate it" (ibid.: 60) and thus signifies a form of violence that forces a body to be in a certain place (e.g., kid-

the body" (Reemtsma 2012: 56) in an act of "senseless cruelty" (ibid.: 63) – which problematically implies that something like "sensible cruelty" exists (cf. ibid.: 64). As autotelic violence defies causal narratives, processes of 'othering', as well as notions of evil and monstrosity, are commonly employed. In Terry Eagleton's words: "The less sense it makes, the more evil it is. Evil has no relations to anything beyond itself, such as cause" (Eagleton 2010: 3). As understandable as this reaction to the inexplicable and senseless may be, with reference to Paul Ricœur (cf. 1988: 188) it can be pointed out that the notion of the 'monstrous' belongs to the realm of the fictional rather than the description of real, historical events. In the school shooting discourse, which has to cope with the notion that presumably innocent children are capable of committing unspeakable crimes, employing the notion of evil or monstrosity is a common strategy for circumventing the necessity of causality. If all strategies of creating causality fail due to the sheer disproportionality and excessiveness of the violent act, as this volume shows time and again, the public discourse can still resort to notions of evil. Even though it "does so only at the cost that this kind of malignant behaviour is here to stay" (Eagleton 2010: 5), evil can serve as an explanation that does not require causality.

Even though they are rare and have garnered disproportionate scholarly attention, school shootings remain a highly relevant topic for analysis because the dynamics of the school shooting discourse can provide profound insight into the constitution of modern societies, the relevance of narratives and, as this book shows, the important role of fiction. School shootings are tragic and they are chaotic. They question societal notions of peacefulness and control, and they raise questions of preventability, of nature and nurture, of childhood and parenting, of guilt and accountability, of institutional and structural failure. Finding answers to these questions, which affect almost every member of society in one way or another, and coming to terms with an act that defies rational explanations is what propels most efforts made in the school shooting discourse. However, as I show in the next chapter, the attempts "to explain the school-shooting phenomenon through a myriad of convergent causes, whether psychological, social, cultural or historical" (Paton/Figeac 2015: 233) in fact constructed what I am referring to as the school shooting discourse. This concept is based on the Foucauldian understanding of discourse as the entity of sequences and signs as statements (cf. Foucault 2002 [1972]: 90ff), which is constructed by various discursive elements that deal with school shootings. The school shooting discourse, in my understanding, therefore includes the predominant understanding

---

napping, slavery, political violence). Raptive violence uses a body, mostly for sexual acts (i.e., rape, sexual slavery) and autotelic violence seeks to destroy the body.

and way of describing, representing and perceiving school shootings in different forms of communication – spoken, written, or, at times, performed. Thus, I focus not only on the media discourse, but also understand scholarly works (such as my own), fictional and non-fictional representations, video games, music lyrics and various forms of multimodal communication on the Internet as elements of discourse formation. In this volume, I focus mainly on the fictional representations of school shootings as specific discursive formations and on their contribution to the construction of the discourse. Understanding the dynamics and relations of the school shooting discourse and its discursive formations, I believe, is essential for understanding the school shooting phenomenon at all. School shootings "turn out to be the effect of a negotiation of cultural patterns" (cf. Ahrens 2015: 151). These cultural patterns that can also be shaped by cultural artifacts, as I will show, connect the construction of the school shooting discourse to the realm of the fictional.

1.2 School Shootings and Fiction: Research Questions and the State of Research

This connection, I posit, can be observed on various levels of the school shooting discourse: in past school shootings, their media coverage, the public and scholarly discourse in their aftermath and in their fictional representations. In order to describe this connection and the blurred boundaries between the fictional and the real in the school shooting discourse, I argue that it possesses what I call a *fictional dimension*. With this notion, I want to show that not only does the phenomenon refer to and incorporate a multitude of fictional elements – observed in the way that school shooters have staged their attacks or in the communicative processes and performative acts they engaged in – but that the social discourse that attempts to make sense of the disruptive act of violence consciously uses fictionalizations and dramatizations for approaching or making sense of the events. These discursive functions of the fictionalizations have, surprisingly, been largely neglected thus far.

Fictional representations are an established and extremely apt cultural practice for dealing with any form of conflict and violence (cf. Ahrens 2017b). Fictional representations, with their aesthetic means and possibilities, can help societies to deal with the challenges that these events pose to processes of meaning-making. It is thus not surprising that most fictional representations of school shootings clearly emphasize or illustrate the struggle of coming to terms with these events. Fictional representations of school shootings are approaches to the inexplicable – they, too, create narratives, but, unlike news media coverage, which fulfils specific social functions (cf. Luhmann 2000), fictional artifacts have the aesthetic freedom to create counter-narratives that disturb, disrupt and confront their readership or audience.

Furthermore, they contribute to the cultural imaginary of school shootings in a way that images and narratives from mass media cannot. The "cultural imaginary" is a term that was coined by Winfried Fluck, who draws upon Wolfgang Iser's notion of the imaginary. For Iser, the imaginary is a "featureless and inactive potential" (1993: xvii) that depends on the fictive, as it "compels the imaginary to take up form at the same time that it acts as a medium for its manifestation. What the fictive targets is as yet empty and thus requires filling; and what is characteristic of the imaginary is its featurelessness, which thus requires form for its unfolding" (ibid.). Based upon this notion, the cultural imaginary in Fluck's definition, in short, provides the stock of images that is available for articulating and representing cultural processes and events. At the same time, however, the cultural imaginary is itself dependent on finding articulation in fictional works. As Fluck points out, "[w]e can only speak through the linguistic signs and cultural patterns that are available to us, but these will never completely express the range of associations, images and affective states that seek articulation" (2002: 270). As a result, the cultural imaginary must be understood as highly dynamic and constantly changing. As the school shooting discourse is dependent on the cultural patterns at its disposal, I argue that fictional representations of school shootings have powerful means to assume relevant social and discursive functions via their contribution to the cultural imaginary.

From these briefly outlined observations about the school shooting discourse, the relevance of narratives for meaning-making and the close connection between school shootings and fiction – observations that will be scrutinized further in the following chapters – this book derives its two major research questions, which aim to describe the different levels of the fictional dimension of the school shooting discourse.

The first question concerns the school shooting narrative and its relation to fictional artifacts: if school shootings are understood as events that exist in a close, presumably reciprocal interrelation with their narratives, how and by what means are these narratives themselves influenced by fictions? This question aims to show the various levels on which the boundaries between the actual event of the school shooting and its fictionalizations are constantly blurred.

The second question then zooms in on fictional representations of school shootings as one element of the school shooting discourse. However, instead of asking how school shooting literature and film can influence school shootings as individual events, or the perpetrators' motivation or inspiration, I want to know how school shooting fiction can shape and influence the school shooting discourse. How do fictional works depict and describe school shootings? Which aspects of the narrative and what imagery of the events and perpetrators do they disseminate, question or reinforce? This is based on the assumption that, while the media discourse has to focus on explanations, cause and effect, fictional artifacts can employ narrative techniques that prompt the reader or audience to reflect upon or even question the dynamics of the school shooting discourse.

As a very brief overview of school shooting research in Germany and the anglophone countries can show, the connection between the construction of the school shooting discourse and its fictional representations has not been investigated in detail. Understandably, most of the research on school shootings clearly focuses on explaining the events and finding modes for prevention – especially in criminology, psychology, education, and American sociology. Furthermore, media scholars, most notably Glenn W. Muschert (e.g., 2007, 2007a, 2012), have analyzed the role of the media in the construction of the school shooting discourse. However, as I show in this volume, most school shooting research clearly contributes to what I argue is the prevalent school shooting narrative, i.e., those explanatory attempts that are deeply rooted in the school shooting discourse and are reflexively revisited whenever a school shooting occurs.

To this day, the most seminal and influential work on school shootings remains *Rampage: The Social Roots of School Shootings* by Katherine S. Newman and her colleagues, first published in 2004. Backed by extensive and thorough field work in the communities of Westside, Arkansas and Heath, Kentucky, where school shootings occurred in the late 1990s, the researchers comprehensively describe "five necessary but not sufficient conditions" for the emergence of school shootings (cf. Newman et al. 2005), which I will return to at a later point. A special issue of *American Behavioral Scientists* in 2009 also included substantial research – as part of the issue, Katherine S. Newman and Cybelle Fox revisited their theories from the early 2000s in light of the school shootings that had occurred since the publication of their monograph.

In Germany, school shootings have also received some scholarly attention, and German and American researchers have at times concentrated their efforts in internationally edited volumes (e.g., Muschert/Sumiala 2012, Böckler et al. 2013, Ziegler et al. 2015). Some German approaches that have not yet found their way into the anglophone sphere come from cultural studies and cultural sociology. These approaches focus on the media and social construction of the school shooting narratives and imagery and stress how the phenomenon can only be understood in relation to its discourse. Instead of focusing on what 'really happened' and what the 'real motives' for the attacks could be, these scholars investigate the societal construction of rampage violence and the social, historical and cultural circumstances in which the events were received. These ap-

1.2 School Shootings and Fiction: Research Questions and the State of Research

proaches are not meant to create means for prevention, but rather to describe and understand the social constitution from which these events emerge and the larger societal questions that they raise. Jörn Ahrens exemplifies this approach in a number of recent publications that have substantially influenced my approach (e.g., Ahrens 2011, 2015, 2017, 2017a). Other publications that clearly shaped and influenced the constructivist approach to excessive violence are earlier works by media studies scholar Heiko Christians (2005) and literary studies scholar Joseph Vogl (e.g., 2003, 2014), whose work includes the construction of narratives and the role of media representations. A fairly recent study by Marco Gerster (2016) thoroughly analyzes the social narratives for coping with the questions that school shootings raise.

School shooting research concerned with fictional representations of violence will be thoroughly addressed in Chapter 2. But, as it will be seen, the connection between fictional representations of violence and school shootings has mostly been analyzed in regard to its potential influence on the perpetrators (cf. e.g., Robertz 2004, 2013). In contrast to these traditional approaches to media violence, André Grzeszyk (2012), whom I introduce in Chapter 3, provided a comprehensive analysis of the reciprocal influence of school shootings and their filmic representations based on a more complex understanding of media dynamics and reception processes. Literary representations of school shootings, however, are widely neglected and have only been examined sporadically, for example, in regard to their strategies for authentication or their representation of the event and the perpetrators in articles by Philipp Hubmann (2012) and Isabella von Treskow (2015, 2017).

A substantial part of anglophone research focuses on risk factors and possibilities for prevention (cf. e.g., Verlinden et al. 2000, Meloy et al. 2001, Vossekuil et al. 2002) or the social, psychological and political backgrounds of specific cases (cf. e.g., Larkin 2007). Studies by Douglas Kellner (2008, 2012) and Karen L. Tonso (2009) have further analyzed the link between school shootings and images and scripts that connect masculinity to violence, as Newman et al. (2005) already noted.[4] This notion has been particularly influential for the few, very recent publications that are concerned with fictional representations

---

[4] The connection between school shootings and concepts of masculinity is most evident in the observation that school shootings are hardly ever committed by female teenagers. It is also for this reason that, in this book, I refer to the school shooter only in masculine – this is not to be understood as a generic masculine, but, in fact, refers to the male shooter. Studying the few cases of excessive violence committed by female teenagers or the cases in which female school shooters did not go through with their plan but rather looked for help would be the subject of a different research project.

of school shootings and the role that these fictional works play in the school shooting discourse. Using two of the works also analyzed here, an article by Richard T. Evans (2016) asks how authors and directors of fictional representations of school shootings use the phenomenon to address notions of heteronormativity, teenage sexuality, masculinity and homophobia. Kathryn E. Linder's monograph on fictional school shooting narratives (2014) also focuses solely on issues of race, class and gender. Linder contrasts fictional representations of excessive youth violence in urban and rural settings, and states that these representations mainly reinforce existing civic hegemonies and images of masculinity and heteronormativity. Even though she acknowledges the relationship between news media and fictional representations (cf. Linder 2014: xxvi), Linder's rather brief analysis does not manage to clearly establish *how* the various works gain the potential to actively influence and shape the public discourse. While her focus on the issues of race, class and gender provides valuable insight into the establishment of 'normality' in regard to excessive violence in American culture, she does not reflect upon the fictional representations' status as discursive elements, nor on how their reception can serve as commentaries on those very processes.

In sum, although the rather obvious connection between fiction and school shootings has gained some attention, at least in Germany, the role of fictional representations of school shootings for the construction of the school shooting discourse has not yet been investigated. Studies stressing the constructedness of the discourse, the relevance of narrative or the way in which perpetrators include fictional artifacts in their subject formation have not been published in English. Especially since America is still by far the country with the most school shootings (cf. Böckler et al. 2013), this can be seen as scholarly desideratum, which I aim to address by drawing on both German and anglophone research in my approach to fictional representations of school shootings. Moreover, by connecting the phenomenon with its discourse via the 'fictional dimension', I want to present a comprehensive understanding of the overarching relevance of fiction to school shootings.

1.3 Overview: Structure, Corpus Design and Key Concepts

This book can be divided into two major parts: the first part consists of Chapters 2 and 3 and provides the theoretical background to the school shooting phenomenon and its discursive dynamics. Further, this part explains the relevance of fiction and of studying fictional representations of school shootings for understanding the school shooting discourse. The second part, comprising Chapters

4 through 6, consists of analyses of novels and films: Todd Strasser's *Give A Boy A Gun* (2000), Joyce Carol Oates' *Big Mouth & Ugly Girl* (2002), Walter Dean Myers' *Shooter* (2004), *Violent Ends* (2015) – written by seventeen authors and edited by Samuel Hutchinson –, *This is Where It Ends* (2016) by Marieke Nijkamp, Lionel Shriver's *We Need To Talk About Kevin* (2003), the filmic adaptation of Shriver's novel by Lynne Ramsay (USA 2011) and Gus Van Sant's *Elephant* (USA 2003). Narratological concepts support my functional approach to these works.

As these introductory pages have merely presented a brief overview of the most basic assumptions and presuppositions of this book, Chapter 2 can be understood as the theoretical foundation of my approach to school shootings, which focuses on and illustrates various discursive practices and processes of narrative meaning-making. Here, I trace the connection between school shootings as a form of excessive violence and their narratives of causality and explanation both diachronically and synchronically. Drawing upon approaches from German cultural studies and cultural sociology (cf. e.g., Christians 2008, Vogl 2014, Ahrens 2015), I aim to link school shootings to its ancient predecessor: a Malayan form of excessive violence that is called *amok*, which will we be thoroughly scrutinized in Chapter 2. Based on studies that analyze the media coverage of school shootings, I outline the predominant attempts at explanation, highlight the discursive preoccupation with media violence and present existing approaches to the relationship between school shooting and fictional representations of violence.[5] Chapter 2 also provides an overview of the theoretical basis and the key concepts for my understanding of the relevance of narrative, and outlines the basic constituents of the school shooting narrative: its setting, characters and plot.

Chapter 3 explores the connection between school shootings and their fictional representations and provides the theoretical background to a decisively functional approach to fictional works. The reciprocal relationship between school shootings and their fictional representations, this chapter posits, can be observed in five stages that exist in a cyclical structure: subject formation,

---

[5] While I do not present a thorough discourse analysis, I do draw upon existing school shooting research and analyses of media coverage after the most infamous school shootings in order to outline what the prevalent explanatory attempts in the discourse are. In doing so, I not only present an overview of existing school shooting research, but also highlight the role that this research plays in the construction of the school shooting narrative. As I focus on the relationship between the discursive elements and the construction of the school shooting narrative, I have not limited the number of cases that I refer to in this volume. A list that provides the basic facts about all cases of school shootings and other mass shooting incidents that are referenced here can be found in the Appendix.

school shootings as a performative act, discourse formation, fictionalization and the reception process. These observations are based on the analysis of accessible video material, case files and fictional representations, as well as on research on selected school shootings in the U.S. and in Germany (e.g., Böckler/Seeger 2010, Grzeszyk 2012, Paton 2012, Schildkraut/Muschert 2014, Ahrens 2015). In order to illustrate the complex reciprocal relationship between school shootings and their fictional representations, I include Matt Johnson's *The Dirties* (Canada 2013) as a point of reference. Matt Johnson's film thematizes and illustrates this reciprocity and cyclical relationship and can thus help to make the rather abstract notion of reciprocal influence more accessible. The fact that *The Dirties* thematizes the blurred boundaries between school shootings and fictions on the level of both its filmic and narrative structure further emphasizes the extent to which school shootings and their fictional representations are inextricable interwoven. Furthermore, by using the film as an example, I can also introduce the concepts of remediation and premediation (cf. Bolter/Grusin 2000; Grusin 2010) as they have been employed for cultural memory studies by Astrid Erll (e.g., 2007, 2010). After having shown the relevance of fictional artifacts to the phenomenon, I then move away from the actual events and perpetrators and focus on the construction the social discourse and the role of school shooting literature and film. As I want to support this observation with functional approaches to fictional works in Chapters 4, 5 and 6, I also introduce the key concepts that allow for the formulation of functional hypotheses in the following analysis. Alongside concepts from cultural memory studies, I introduce Wolfgang Iser's (1989) concept of the aesthetic experience and the ways in which Winfried Fluck uses Iser's reception aesthetics for his concept of the history of the changing functions of literature (cf. Fluck 2002) and his notion of the cultural imaginary (cf. Fluck 1997).

The second part of this volume consists of three chapters that analyze fictional representations of school shootings. While non-fictional works such as Michael Moore's documentary film *Bowling for Columbine* (USA 2002) and Dave Cullen's journalistic book *Columbine* (2009), which both create causal narratives to explain the events in Littleton, played a great role in the dissemination of the Columbine story and its images, fictional representations of Columbine have not gained comparable attention.[6] However, over the last fifteen years, the body of

---

6 While I will refer to Dave Cullen's book as an example of the construction of a causal school shooting narrative, I have decided to not include Moore's film in my study. Not only has it been researched extensively (recently, for example, by Benson/Snee 2015), but including a non-fictional film in a study concerned with fictional representations of school shootings did not seem beneficial.

fictional representations of school shootings has grown considerably. Even though this corpus is still rather small, many of the works have gained notable popularity. Some, like Jodi Picoult's novel *Nineteen Minutes* (2007) or Jessica Knoll's *Luckiest Girl Alive* (2015), were on the *New York Times* Best Seller list. Others won prizes, like the highly controversial *Vernon God Little* by D.B.C. Pierre (2003), which won the Booker Prize, or Lionel Shriver's *We Need To Talk About Kevin* (2003), which received the Orange Prize for Fiction and was later adapted into a critically acclaimed film. Both works will be analyzed in Chapter 6 of this book. Richard Russo's *Empire Falls* (2001), which also thematizes the impact of a school shooting on a suburban community, was awarded the Pulitzer Prize for Fiction in 2009, and Gus van Sant's film *Elephant* received the Palme d'Or at the Cannes Film Festival in 2003. In theatre, noteworthy plays that are concerned with school shootings include William Mastrosimone's *Bang Bang You're Dead* (1999), which was later adapted into a film, Simon Stephen's *Punk Rock* (2009) and Steven Soderbergh's *The Library* (2014). In television, high school series such as *One Tree Hill* ("With Tired Eyes, Tired Minds, Tired Souls, We Slept", dir. Greg Prange, USA 2006), *Buffy the Vampire Slayer* ("Earshot", dir. James Espenson, USA 1999) or, more recently, an episode of *American Horror Story* ("Piggy Piggy", dir. Michael Uppendahl, USA 2011) come to mind. As far as films are concerned, works that represent the aftermath rather than the shooting are more common. Examples are *Beautiful Boy* (dir. Shawn Ku, USA 2010) and *April Showers* (dir. Andrew Robinson, USA 2009). In literature, the emergence of the subgenre of Young Adult (YA) school shooting fiction could be observed, as ever since the early 2000s, a growing number of books have thematized school shooting, frequently in multiperspectival or multimodal narratives.

The selection of the works for my analysis of discursive functions of school shooting fiction is based on my observations regarding the relevance of narrative for the social understanding of and coping with school shootings. Fictional representations always refer to real school shootings, as they actualize the cultural imaginary of school shootings. Due to their aesthetic constructedness, I want to show, they have the possibility to employ various narrative strategies in their creation and representation of the school shooting narrative. Because of this, they can question and disrupt the societal attempts for creating causality and foster reflection on the discourse as such. I want to support these general observations by studying a few selected fictional works and describing the potential functions of particular narrative techniques.

The school shooting narrative, as it is constructed in media and scholarly discourse, focuses on creating causality. Thus, this book examines novels and films that use particular narrative strategies or modes that have the potential to disrupt the semantic coherence of this causality. By focusing on multimodality

(Chapter 4), multiperspectivity (Chapter 5) and unreliable narration (Chapter 6), I show how the fictional works can offer alternative approaches to 'the inexplicable'. These narrative strategies are inherently connected to each other, as multimodal narratives are always multiperspectval (cf. Nünning/Nünning 2000a), and multiperspectival narratives can prompt the reader to question the reliability of the different perspectives in the fictional work (cf. Menhard 2009).

In designing the corpus, I have decided to focus on novels and films for both practical and conceptual reasons. Including films in the analysis is the most obvious choice, since the medium is already closely connected to the school shooting phenomenon. Films have been hotly debated in the aftermath of school shootings because they are frequently referenced by actual school shooters. Moreover, in its techniques of repetition and variation of image, movement, plot and sound, film is considered the prime medium for the representation of societal processes (cf. Ahrens 2017b: 22ff.). Including school shooting novels, on the other hand, suggests itself because of the manifold possibilities of the reception processes and because literature is the medium in which school shootings are thematized and represented most frequently. Despite this, school shooting novels have received hardly any scholarly attention. Even though films and novels are received differently and have different ways of assuming similar discursive functions, I want to point out how their respective narrative techniques can work towards similar ends. For this reason, two of the chapters include analyses of both media. Considering plays and TV shows, while highly interesting, would have raised theoretical issues of performance and seriality that would have gone beyond the scope of this volume.

The particular novels and films were chosen according to three major considerations: first and foremost, the plot had to be centered around a school shooting and/or its aftermath. While Chapter 2 shows how difficult the issue of defining 'school shootings' is, here, I used a heuristic definition of the phenomenon that required the novels and films to thematize an (attempted, averted or allegedly planned) attack committed by one or more adolescents at an educational institution with the intention of killing people because of their actual or symbolic role in the perpetrator's life.

The second decisive aspect that served to narrow down and order the corpus is the way in which the works are narrated – their narrative strategies. My basic assumptions about the various potential functions of literature and film, which I postulate in the different chapters, draw upon theories from reception aesthetics, functional approaches, cultural memory studies and narratology. By using tools and concepts from (intermedial) narratology, I focus on the narrative structure of the fictional works and analyze how this influences the perception of the text. Each chapter thus focuses on a different narrative strategy. Drawing upon approaches and concepts from (intermedial) narratology allows for a systematic and thorough analysis of the fictional works and makes it possible to formulate functional hypotheses that are firmly based on those works. As the potential functions of a fictional work can only be activated during the reception process and can thus hardly be proven empirically, my analysis concentrates on the various possibilities of the different narrative strategies within the discourse.

The third criterion for the choice of works is the date of publication, which also serves as a structuring device. Most importantly, all fictional works had to be published or released after Columbine (April 1999). Columbine, as the first chapters explain, has significantly shaped and influenced the public understanding of school shootings. Only if the works appeared after Columbine can they build upon the same discursive knowledge and cultural imaginary.

Chapter 4 analyzes three multimodal novels for young adults from the early 2000s: Todd Strasser's *Give a Boy a Gun* (2000), Joyce Carol Oates' *Big Mouth & Ugly Girl* (2002) and Walter Dean Myers' *Shooter* (2004). Even though multiperspectivity is inherent to multimodal novels, I analyze the multimodal novels before the multiperspectival ones due to their dates of their publication. In Chapter 4, I show that the Young Adult novel is an extremely apt genre for approaching school shootings, as it draws upon and aims to represent the lifeworld from which the phenomenon emerges. Multimodal novels have an exceptionally great potential to engage the readers in an active reading process. Thus, the aesthetic experience that the young adult readers can have is intensely vivid. Here, I will ask whether or how this reading experience can make the young adult readers reflect upon their position in the school shooting discourse. Chapter 4 also deals with the question of authenticity, aiming to determine how the YA school shooting novels communicate the school shooting narrative and whether they reinforce or question certain aspects or dynamics of that narrative.

The two multiperspectival YA school shooting novels analyzed in Chapter 5 were published much more recently. The appearance of *Violent Ends*, published in September 2015, and *This Is Where It Ends* from January 2016 reflects how contemporary and topical the phenomenon remains, especially for young adults. While I had originally only planned to analyze Gus Van Sant's *Elephant* (USA 2003), my decision to include the two YA novels indicates the flexibility that dealing with a still-emerging research topic requires. The choice of the novels can also highlight potential differences between fictional works that were published shortly after Columbine and still very much under its influence, and fictional representations that include knowledge of the Virginia Tech massacre at a U.S. campus and the Sandy Hook massacre, committed at an elementary school. Chapters 4 and 5 can thus show which aspects and elements of the school shooting narrative have lasted over a more than a decade and which aspects may have become dated. Furthermore, the inclusion of these recent works may underline the intense historicity of the phenomenon as well as the rapidly changing lifeworlds of teenagers.

Furthermore, in analyzing Gus Van Sant's critically acclaimed, award-winning independent film *Elephant* (USA 2003), Chapter 5 shows how narrative techniques can unfold their valuable potential across the media. By drawing upon findings from inter- and transmedial narratology (e.g., Kuhn 2009, Schlickers 2009, Ryan 2014), I want to show how the multiperspectivity in *Elephant* can confront its audience with the inexplicability of school shootings in a unique way and serve as meta-commentary of the extrafictional school shooting discourse.

Chapter 6 also include a novel and film – in this case, a novel and its filmic adaptation: Lionel Shriver's *We Need to Talk About Kevin* (2003) and Lynne Ramsay's adaptation from 2011. By including both works, I am able to investigate whether and how the narrative strategy of unreliable narration can be transferred from one medium to another. What is also of particular relevance in this chapter is how both works focus on and thematized the question of nature versus nurture and the discursive practice of 'othering' a school shooter as 'monstrous' and evil from birth. Shriver's novel raises questions of motherhood, the role of the family and particularly the mother and the possibility of a child born bad, all of which are well known from the school shooting narrative as outlined in Chapter 2. Here, I will show how and to what end the unreliable narration can prompt readers to actively engage with the text and to come to their own conclusions, and how this can prompt a reflection upon the school shooting discourse. As adaptations are always interpretations of the original text (cf. Hutcheon 2006), the analysis of Ramsay's film focuses on its interpretation of the textual ambiguities and asks if and how the film has tried to include the intense subjectivity and unreliability of the homodiegetic first-person narrative of Shriver's novel.

These analyses are strictly functional and always ask a) how the works represent the school shooting phenomenon, the perpetrators and the reaction to the event, as well as which aspects from the school shooting narrative they reinforce or question, and b) how the aesthetic experience of the reader or spectator is shaped by the respective narrative technique and how this experience can influence readers' or spectators' understanding of the school shooting phenomenon and its discourse. Through these questions, I want to highlight the constructedness of the school shooting discourse, and of the phenomenon itself, and thus contribute to a more comprehensive understanding of the various potential functions of fictional representations in a contemporary and still emerging discourse.

Part I: **Narrative, Fiction and Fact in the School Shooting Discourse**

2 We Need to Talk About *Amok:* Tracing the Narratives of School Shootings

School shootings cannot be understood separately from the discourse surrounding them, the narratives and images of the phenomenon that circulate, the perpetrators and victims and the public debate about why these events can happen. In fact, "[a]ny examination of school shootings is intimately linked to the discourse of school shootings. Indeed, in a society dominated by mass media, images of crime and crime control become as 'real' as the events themselves" (Muschert/Ragnedda 2011: 346). In this book, school shootings will be discussed primarily with regard to their discursive dynamics. Including the media, public and scholarly discussions, the role of narratives in the emergence of the school shooting discourse will form the center of the analysis here.

School shootings are inexplicably cruel crimes that inflict unimaginable pain on individuals, families and communities. Even though this suffering is very real, the 'event' of the shooting always exists in and is constructed out of the cultural imaginary – the cultural inventory of images, narratives, affects, and human desires (cf. Fluck 1997: 21). As this volume shows, the way in which the perpetrators plan and stage their attacks, how the victims, witnesses and observers perceive them, and how the public understands the school shooting phenomenon is inextricably connected to the juxtaposition of narratives of excessive violence and the narratives of a peaceful society. Both narratives draw upon and are constructed from the cultural imaginary, which is, by definition, shaped and defined by fictional elements (cf. Fluck 1997). So as to find a suitable way to describe the complex interwovenness of real, gruesome events and the fictional dimension of the narratives from which they emerge and in which they are constructed, this chapter will approach school shootings from an angle that takes the different narratives of this form of excessive violence into consideration. The relevance of narratives for the societal understanding of school shootings and the narrative constructedness of the school shooting discourse as such is rooted in the debate about what can be classified as a school shooting: "Classifying events as school shootings", as Harding et al. point out, "often depends on the question that is being asked" (2002: 177).

The attempt to define what school shootings actually are, occupied the rather small but active circle of scholars engaged in school shooting research ever since the phenomenon first attracted large-scale interest in the late 1990s. Various studies have attempted to delineate the phenomenon from other forms of excessive violence such as serial killings, spree killings and workplace violence (cf. Böckler et al. 2013: 4ff., Muschert 2007a: 63ff.). Others have focused on categorizing it according to the shooters affiliation to the targeted school or the number of victims (e.g. Newman et al. 2005). These definitions, however, have often been challenged by the *modus operandi* of following attacks; whenever a new school shooting happens, so it seems, at least one of the factors included in previous definitions simply does not apply.

The difficulty of creating a clear-cut definition of school shootings becomes obvious in the case of the school shooting in Newtown, Connecticut in December 2012, where Adam Lanza shot his mother and then proceeded to kill 20 first-graders and six educators at Sandy Hook Elementary School before taking his own life. The media, public and politicians quickly reached the consensus that he had committed a school shooting. However, if one chooses to strictly follow predominant definitions of these events, Lanza's assault does not fulfill one of the most basic and most widely accepted requirements for being defined as a school shooting, since he was not "a member or a former member of the institution" (Newman et al. 2005: 231). As a result, a factor previously considered essential to the definition of school shootings was swiftly cast away and the Sandy Hook Massacre, both in media and scholarly publications, is now referred to as a school shooting. It is not only the typologies but also the terminology used for describing school shootings that has frequently been contested and by now covers anything from a school rampage, to school shootings, to severe targeted school violence or, in the German context, to *amok*. The terminological idiosyncrasy in German will be of particular interest in this chapter; *amok* does not only signify rampage killings, but has a very complex and far-reaching history of its own, dating back to 15th century Malaysia and India (cf. Adler 2000: 11ff., Spores 1988: 11ff.).

Instead of describing past events and cases of school shootings, I will use the narratives of the phenomena as the vantage point for analysis. While it has frequently been argued that school shootings and other cases of rampage violence need to be analyzed separately, I want to investigate the *similarities* between the discursive dynamics of different forms of excessive violence in section 2.1.1. In doing so, I want to draw attention to the societal reactions to these events rather than the events as such. As this volume will carve out what I call the *fictional dimension of the school shooting discourse*, I will begin by investigating the unique narrative elements of these events and with analyzing the various ways in which these narratives incorporate fictional elements. While I do not want to contest the importance of clear-cut typologies for empirical study in criminology or other disciplines, I believe that examining the diachronic relation between school shootings and their ancient predecessor in Malayan and Indian forms of excessive violence will allow for insights into the underlying dynamics and anxieties that can be found in the school shooting discourse. Thus, instead of delineating the school shooting from similar violent phenomena, I will investigate what the narratives about the phenomena hold in common. Drawing upon these similarities, I will present an overview about the contemporary phenomenon and the narratives and debates in which it is constructed as a "media spectacle" (Kellner 2008). As this book is critical of simplifying definitions and typologies, I will use a very broad and heuristic definition of the school shooting phenomenon, which is based on existing studies and includes societal reactions and cultural narratives. The definitions in 2.1.1 serve to emphasize the relevance of narratives in the emergence of the school shooting phenomenon.

The relevance of narratives for societal reactions to school shootings will also be central of 2.1.2, where I will present the state of school shooting research so as to point out the particularities and ambiguities that can be observed within the field as well as in the general school shooting discourse. Here, I will not only investigate the debate surrounding school shootings and present recent shifts in perspective observable in international scholarship, but I will also aim to challenge some of the lines of argumentation that are still prevalent in discussions by the media, the public and scholarly communities. Throughout this section, the focus will remain on the narratives that are created in these approaches to the phenomenon; I will also ask what role school shooting research plays in the constitution of the fictional dimension of the school shooting discourse. In the first part of this chapter, I will not attempt to settle the question of what school shootings are, and thus contribute to an ongoing debate about definitions and terminology, but rather attempt to trace how society *perceives* school shootings, meaning how the school shooting narrative has been spelled out, refined and disseminated. Especially with regard to public perception, the mass media and its role in the discourse are of crucial importance.

The frequent reliance on reductive explanations or singular causes, as I will point out, stems from a societal longing for control that manifests itself in the creation of coherent narratives. Within the scope of this project, the role of media and media representations of violence in providing explanatory frameworks is of particular relevance. Debates surrounding fictional representations of violence and school shootings in particular are often prone to point fingers, engaging in a kind of "blame game" (Lohr 2012), and frequently focus on the effects of media violence on delinquent youths. In a book that deals with representations of school shootings that are by nature also representations of violence, the heated debate about the possible dangers of these representations cannot be simply glossed over.

Section 2.2.1 will critically examine the media representation of the school shooters, the assault itself and the victims. Here, I will outline the different positions in school shooting research so as to position my research within the debate. Section 2.2.2 will then move on to outline the most common scholarly approaches to fictional representations of excessive violence, which are often suspected to contribute to the creation of the perpetrator's fame and to imagery of hypermasculine violence. I will present two approaches that can or have been used to include fictionalized school shootings in the debate about media violence in order lay the groundwork for my own approach to fictional representations of school shootings.

After having outlined the discursive dynamics of the school shooting discourse, I want to underline the relevance of narratives for meaning-making and for establishing causality and coherence in the face of a disturbing phenomenon. Chapter 2.3 will address the most important aspects of the social need for narratives in order to show how the fictional dimension of school shootings is established. School shootings disrupt the societal narrative of peacefulness (cf. Reemtsma 2012 [2008]) in such an extreme way that they require a cultural narrative of coherence to reintegrate them into the self-understanding of civilized societies. This last subchapter will show how important narratives are for making sense of and approaching the inexplicable. Here, I will also outline the basic components of the predominant school shooting narrative, which will be revisited in analyses of the literary and filmic approaches to the phenomenon that follow in the later chapters.

2.1 Describing the Traditions of Rampage Violence: Ancient *Amok* and School Shootings

2.1.1 The Discursive Dynamics of *Amok* and the School Shooting Phenomenon

School shootings, and cases of lethal violence at schools in general, are extremely rare events. Even though the presence of school shootings in the media may suggest otherwise, researchers across disciplines agree that schools come close to being the safe space desired by society – at least if compared to the students' home or neighborhood environments (e.g., Harding et al. 2002: 174, Muschert 2007: 60). Nevertheless, mass killings at schools have received disproportionate amounts of media, scholarly and public attention. While the community of international researchers debates their findings about the social, psychological or educational reasons behind these acts of excessive violence, the media publishes almost constant speculations about the perpetrators and their motives, desperately attempting to create explanations for these mass killings. Especially in the United States, public and political initiatives aim to either ban weapons from school or encourage the arming of guards or teachers.

Naturally, all violent crime is shocking and tragic. But, as the societal reaction to these events suggests, school shootings "touch a nerve in the public conscience" (Ferguson/Ivory 2013: 48). Inarguably, the fact that school shootings are so closely linked to discourses of childhood, innocence and hope for the future contributes to the effect that these events have on the public: In modern Western societies, there is still a "universal consensus about the positive value of schools as centers of local communities and of schools and children as symbols for collective hope for the future and cultural reproduction" (Muschert 2011: 353) and schools are ascribed a very central role in society. The positive value and collective hopes invested in schools are actively threatened by attacks on these institutions:

> Mass school shootings violate school campuses, environments that are typically considered idyllic and insular havens. They also strike down victims who are youthful achievers in the early stages of promising careers, along with educators who have dedicated lifetimes of service to the ideals of learning and scholarship. Lastly, their perpetrators are often also youthful members of the schools' communities, students whose decision to murder their peers sadden, enrage, worry and puzzle us. (Ferguson/Ivory 2013: 48)

In addition to the shock provoked by what adolescents are capable of, school shootings seem to affect everyone within highly developed Western societies, where these events normally take place (cf. Böckler et al. 2013: 10). In these countries, everybody has a direct relation to the institution under attack, as nearly everyone who lives in the United States, Canada, Finland or Germany – to name some of the countries that have witnessed these attacks – has gone to school themselves or even has children or other relatives who still go to school. As a result, the threat that school shootings express becomes tangible for everyone who hears or reads about a school shooting.

This, as researchers have pointed out, is not coincidental. School shooters choose the targeted institution not only for an individual revenge plot, but also for its symbolic power (cf. Newman et al. 2005, Muschert 2007), as schools are the center of communities, especially in small towns or suburbs. Equally important is the symbolic quality of the social structures and hierarchies at schools: These social structures often represent the "social arrangements" that exist in the community on a smaller scale (Muschert/Ragnedda 2011: 355):[1]

---

[1] While the structure and dynamics of the German and American school system differ signifi-

> Schools are both the location of their adolescent social failures and the center of community life, not just for students but for everyone in these small towns. [...] It is the only public stage with strong connections to the entire community, and by opening fire randomly at school, shooters issue a public expression about how they have been treated in their communities and about the way they want to be remembered. (Newman et al. 2005: 152f.)

The symbolic power of the attack, however, at times even seems to transcend the shooter's direct frame of reference (cf. Muschert/Sumiala 2012: vxii); while the perpetrators may pick an educational institution to which they are or have been affiliated so as to find a target that symbolizes the alleged reason for their perceived suffering, their actions are understood as a threat to society as such (cf. Vogl 2003). This aspect can be understood as one of the points around which the public reaction to shootings assembles, but cannot fully explain the dynamics of the school shooting discourse during the past two decades. This cultural dynamic, as this book shows, essentially revolves around the school shooting narratives that have emerged from more general societal fears and anxieties, as well as around narratives of social peacefulness (cf. Reemtsma 2012).

When dealing with phenomena of excessive violence, it quickly becomes obvious that it is not easy to find the right term to describe what has happened. In Germany, school shootings are frequently referred to as *Schulamoklauf* – *school amok*. *Amok* is a term for any kind of rampage and, metaphorically, for almost every form of unexpected outburst of aberrant, normatively unacceptable and usually violent behavior, or even idiomatically used to describe extreme forms of irritability and anger.[2] In the anglophone context, the metaphorical usage of "running amuck"[3] or, nowadays, of "running amok", and the synonymous phrases *going berserk* or *going postal* is rather common (cf. Kellner 2008: 13f.), whereas the term *amok* for rampage violence is only seldom used in the context

---

cantly, utterances by school shooters and previous research suggests that schools are a kind of microcosm for the community in both countries.

2 German scholar Heiko Christians goes as far as to say that Germans even have become accustomed to *amok* as a phenomenon of violence because of its excessive use in everyday language and in the media (Christians 2008: 19ff.).

3 The divergent spelling *amok* and *amuck* most likely dates back to 1886, when *A muck, To run* had been introduced by Henry Jule and Arthur Coke Burnell into the anglophone world (cf. Christians 2008: 68), at that time still referring to the ancient Malayan phenomenon of excessive violence. The original Malaylan word is *Amuk*, which translates as *furious*. *Mengamuk* indicates a spontaneous and murderous attack, and *pengamuk* refers to a perpetrator (cf. Adler 2000: 9, Spores 1988). *Amok*, however, has become the more prevalent spelling over the last years (cf. e. g., http://grammarist.com/spelling/amok-amuck).

of mass killings.[4] In Germany, however, *amok* now serves as an umbrella term for all kinds of rampage killings. It is only in the academic context that the use of the terms has become more differentiated: The English term *school shooting* has become prevalent in German scholarship over the past years and is now used to distinguish the phenomenon from similar acts of excessive violence such as rampages committed by adults in public places, or from the phenomenon of workplace violence, which is still frequently subsumed under *amok* (cf. Brumme 2011: 11ff., Bondü 2012: 21ff.).[5] In the public or media discourse, however, this differentiation is usually not made. While German scholars from various disciplines agree that *amok* is in fact an entirely different phenomenon than school shootings and plead for terminological precision, a small number of German scholars from the cultural studies have stressed the similarities between these two phenomena (cf. e.g. Gerster 2016, Grzeszyk 2012). Here, too, I want to emphasize that similarities in the discourse, as well as the societal reactions to the events, allows for certain continuities to be drawn between ancient *amok* and contemporary school shootings. Analyzing these similarities can help to reach an understanding of the importance of narratives – fictional as well as non-fictional – and the more general dynamics of the school shooting discourse.

Exploring *Amok*
Amok, a term that is used here to describe a particular form of rampage killings, is by no means a Western or even a contemporary phenomenon. A passage from the of the earlier reports of *amok* can serve as a good entry point for exploring what the historical phenomenon can add to an understanding of the discursive particularities of the school shooting discourse.[6] Written in the colonial tradition, this short passage from a very graphic and detailed description of a case

---

[4] The noteworthy exceptions within rampage and violence research are Fox and Levin (2003), Douglas Kellner (2008).
[5] The problems that come with the definition and labeling of *amok* and school shootings will be further examined below.
[6] A comprehensive analysis of the historical *amok* discourse would go beyond the scope of this chapter. I merely want to draw attention to similar phenomena of excessive violence so that school shootings are not seen as an isolated, contemporary phenomenon that has emerged out of nothing. The parallel between *amok* and school shootings that has been denied by most criminologist and psychologists will be established here via the narrative dynamics and what I argue to be the fictional dimension of these discourses. To do this, I will draw upon documents presented and analyzed in studies by John C. Spores (1988), Lothar Adler (2000) and Heiko Christians (2008), despite the fact that our approaches and understandings of the phenomena differ in various regards.

of Malayan *amok* reported by J.W. Brewster in 1891 shows how rampage killings in the colonies were reported and framed for the colonizers:[7]

> SIR, – with reference to the recent 'amok' case at Pulau Tiga, I have the honour to submit the following report to you. On Thursday ... I received a letter from the Penghulu of Palau Tiga stating that ... the previous evening an Imam Mamamt had run 'amok' at Pasir Gram, killing four persons and wounding four others, and that the culprit was still at large [...]. There was no reason whatever for this 'amoker's' action, he being on most friendly terms with every one, and he himself said he did not know what he was doing, only his head went round and the devil told him to do it. He also stated he had been living on remnants of food, etc.,...that he heard the people searching for him, also that he had hidden two of the spears near the scene of the murder, and pointed out the spot and the boat came down stream, and on landing Inspector Evans found the spears. (J.W. Brewster in *The Perak Government Gazette*, qtd. in Spores 1988: 1, 5f.)

This account of an individual act is only indicative of the general understanding of *amok* at the time: In the 19th century, *amok* signifies the act of one man who, for no apparent reason, kills many people with a spear, and afterwards states that he has no recollection of what happened. Interestingly, this definition is still frequently used to describe or define rampage killings. *Amok* was a phenomenon reported by colonizers in areas that are now the modern states of Malaysia, Indonesia, Brunei, Singapore, Thailand, the Philippines as well as parts of South India (Adler 2000:9) at least from the 18th century onwards, with the earliest reports dating back to the early 15th century (ibid.: 12, Vogl 2003: 211). In their observations, the colonizers used their reports of *amok* to underline their notion of the murderous savage – and the accounts of random mass killings were indeed met with great curiosity from the recipients. German scholar Heiko Christians, one of the first cultural studies scholars to analyze the specific dynamics of the phenomenon, emphasizes the difficulties that reports such as Brewster's may pose for the contemporary reader:

> Especially when approaching the early history of amok, it must be taken into account that amok, as a rule, is only known from reports or messages. The media packaging plays a cru-

---

[7] It should be noted that Spores' approach to and understanding of *amok* is very different from the one that is used in the present book. For Spores, *amok* "represents a behavioral constellation unique to the Malay context and distinguishable from similar patterns occurring in other cultures. It is a culture-specific syndrome wherein an individual unpredictably and without warning manifests mass, indiscriminate, homicidal behavior that is authored with suicidal intent. Curiously, this frightful act of violence is marked by an element of cultural sanction and legitimacy" (Spores 1988: 7). While the last aspect makes *amok* fundamentally different from other, especially contemporary and Western, phenomena, the ways in which Malayan *amok* have been perceived and found their way into Western consciousness are of interest here.

cial role. [...] The more one moves back in time, not only the events, but their principles, their forms and proceedings become all the more strange. (Christians 2008: 60, transl.)[8]

This hints at the first unlikely similarity between the ancient cases of *amok*, to which one has no direct access, and the contemporary and mediatized phenomenon of school shootings, to which every inhabitant of our mediatized world has very direct access: Phenomena of excessive violence then and now cannot be understood as isolated from their various representations. From the beginning of the *amok* discourse, these phenomena generated a discourse that, in turn, brought forward similar events in different cultural settings and times (cf. Ahrens 2015: 151). Since the phenomenon reached Europe, both "the events themselves and the public perception of them [have been] intimately tied to media logic" (Muschert 2013: 266). Despite the continuities in the narratives of *amok* and contemporary school shootings, it should to be stressed that what drove the societal reactions to *amok* was completely different from the modern reactions to school shootings; after all, *amok* took place in countries that were far away and could be observed from a safe distance. The spectacle of *amok* and the curiosity it generated were largely due to colonial sensationalism and the fascination with the 'wild', 'savage' and allegedly brutal world far away from home. Imagining the threat faced by the men and women living in the colonies served to emphasize the sense of purpose and, consequently, the support for the politics of colonialization. The mediatized spectacle of school shootings, on the contrary, garners attention because it happens so close to home. Repeated reports of school shootings result in "a cognitive shift from 'how could it happen at a place like this?' to 'it could happen anyplace'" (Cohen 2002 [1972]: xiii). School shootings are not far away; they appear to be an imminent and growing threat. Therefore, while both phenomena are closely linked to the media logic of their time and generate similar discursive dynamics, the driving forces behind these dynamics diverge considerably.

Travelling Narratives of Excessive Violence

Arguably, the most defining aspects of the school shooting discourse are the societal attempts to deal with the inexplicability of the act. As a consequence of the

---

[8] "Gerade bei einer Annäherung an die Frühgeschichte des Amok gilt es zu berücksichtigen, dass wir den Amok in der Regel nur als Bericht oder Nachricht kennenlernen. Die mediale Verpackung spielt eine entscheidende Rolle. [...] Je weiter man sich auf der Zeitachse zurückbewegt, desto fremder werden einem nicht nur die Geschehnisse, sondern auch die Prinzipien, Formen und Verfahren ihrer Überlieferung" (Christians 2008: 60).

initial inability to clearly define what exactly happened and what led to the events there is a lot of confusion about what school shootings actually are. The narratives, typologies and terminology varies; school shootings seem not to adhere to any clear framework, but rather to follow their own dynamics, which are closely interwoven with the publicly and medially transported narratives about them.[9] School shootings, and this is the underlying assumption and vantage point of this book, cannot be understood as separate from the narratives constructed around them. As a result, the seemingly simple and deliberately casual question of *"what are we even talking about?"* proves to be rather difficult to answer.

Even though the differences in the respective culture and the reasons for the reactions to the phenomenon need to be kept in mind, approaching the discursive dynamics of school shootings from the descriptions of *amok* can be highly instructive. When looking at accounts of the ancient phenomenon, a tradition of framing the events in order to come to terms with the problems they pose can be noticed.

Scholars have struggled with the diversity of the cultural and historical backgrounds that gave rise to cases of *amok*. In his seminal study about *amok*, German psychologist Lothar Adler writes:

> The wide dissemination over an area that encompassed extremely diverse ethnic, religious and political bonds, and the dynamic, only vaguely documented historical development do not let *amok* appear a distinct and consistent phenomenon, especially since the historical sources are fragmentary and for the most part consist of reports by diversely motivated travelers, clerks of the colonial governments and, only since the middle of the last century, also occasional colonial doctors. (Adler 2000: 9, transl.)[10]

The 'trustworthiness' of the reports and descriptions about the phenomenon give rise to another problem. Starting with early reports about Malayan *amok*, narratives that were constructed to frame and explain the events have always had a fictional dimension. The diverse nature of early Western reports about Southeast Asian *amok* make it difficult to reconstruct the phenomenon and reveal the interwovenness of the phenomenon with fictional narratives. Travelogues, a fa-

---

9 This will be elaborated in Chapter 3 of the present volume.
10 "Die weite Verbreitung über ein Gebiet mit sehr verschiedenen ethnischen, religiösen und politischen Bindungen und die dynamische, wenig präzise dokumentierte historische Entwicklung läßt Amok nicht als ein klar umschriebenes und einheitlich bezeichnetes Phänomen erscheinen, zumal die historischen Quellen lückenhaft sind und im Wesentlichen aus Berichten sehr unterschiedlich motivierter Reisender, von Beamten den Kolonialregierungen und erst seit der Mitte des letzten Jahrhunderts auch vereinzelter Kolonialärzte bestehen" (Adler 2000: 9).

mous genre in 17th century Europe in which the earliest accounts of *amok* were transported, had a strong affinity for the spectacular and sensational. Cases of *amok*, of men who picked up a spear and indifferently killed friends, family and random strangers in a frenzy before they were finally killed or overpowered (cf. Adler 2000: 13), were exciting and suspenseful stories to tell. So as to make their experiences overseas a worthy read, many reports most likely 'spiced up' the reports by adding *amok* or exaggerating the violence (cf. Christians 2008: 102ff.). With these reports, *amok* quickly became the epitome of the savage and exotic world of the colonies in Southeast Asia. It was a manifestation of the supposed dangerousness and wildness of countries and their uncivilized inhabitants and injected a certain amount of adventure into the eastern imaginary concocted by the educated classes in Europe. Because of its spectacular nature, the phenomenon of *amok* gained immense popularity among travelers and readers of travelogues, which were published *en masse* in Europe (cf. Christians 2008: 108ff.). It is important to bear in mind that travelogues constituted a genre that traditionally combined facts and observations with subjective evaluations and experiences, as well as legends, regional myths and hearsay; reading them was therefore a much more entertaining pastime than one would imagine it to be. In the 17th century, reports by travelers from the colonies became even more popular after travelers were encouraged by scientific societies to collect as much data as possible on their journeys. Originally, their findings were meant to convey data from the ship's instruments back to the traveler's respective home countries and companies (cf. Andree 2006, Christians 2008). The boundaries between scientific texts and entertainment, however, were rather blurry: As the distinction between *history* and *romance* was not yet established, travelers casually enriched their travel reports with dramatizing and spectacular stories and rearranged the narratives of their journeys to reach a broader audience (Andree 2006: 222).[11] A phenomenon of excessive violence was clearly suited to this purpose. Thus enriched, these reports were entertaining rather than informative, and so the genre of the *voyage narrative* emerged and became

---

[11] In *The Reality of Mass Media* (2000), Niklas Luhmann stresses the importance of the rise of the novel with regard to developing the distinction between fact and fiction and points out the direct link between the need to mark publications as fictional and the technological development of the printing press. However, elaborating on the emergence of fictional texts and the history of their reception over the course of the 17th, 18th and 19th century would go far beyond the scope of this project. However, understanding how the reports of *amok* were influenced by the general interest in spectacular and sensational stories from the travelers is of great value for understanding the dynamics behind the narrative of contemporary phenomena of *amok* and their parallels to school shootings.

immensely popular: In 18th century England alone, the number of published travel reports has been estimated to no less than 2000 publications (Andree 2006: 216ff). Reports from the remote parts of the Empire and beyond, which thrilled their readers with 'news' from hitherto unknown parts of the world, were extremely popular among the urban educated classes.

By means of these travel reports, the term *amok* made its way to Europe, where it eventually gained popularity. The exotic phenomenon thus traveled via its narratives, and – now termed rampage violence, workplace violence, or school shootings – was detached from the ancient Malayan form and eventually understood as a phenomenon that was understood as 'symptomatic' for certain individuals' inability to deal with the modern Western world, as Joseph Vogl points out:[12]

> *Amok* and its history is not only manifest in the reports, narratives and logs of European witnesses. Moreover, it is the result of a movement that, over the course of centuries, turned strange incidents among the indigenous peoples of a restricted cultural region into a rather symptomatic event within Western societies. (Vogl 2003: 211, transl.)[13]

In the 20th century, rampage violence had become an event of violence that was understood as rare but very typical for societies that struggled under the challenges of modern life (cf. ibid.). Considering that word of *amok* spread over centuries and continents, it is remarkable that most studies seem to agree that historical *amok* was by no means and at no time a frequent phenomenon. Despite this, the term quickly began to appear with disproportionate frequency in media and literature, as sources from the late 19th century observe (cf. Adler 2000: 16f). This attention created the rather false impression of *amok* as a commonplace behavior of the Southeast Asian peoples.

Here, a comparison to the school shooting discourse can be drawn, as both the ancient and the modern phenomenon appear to be a much more frequent event than they actually are, due to the disproportionate media attention they generate (cf. Muschert 2007, Braselmann 2016). Naturally, media dynamics in the 15th to 19th century can hardly be compared with media dynamics in the

---

12 In Western societies, *amok* discourses differ in terms of their starting points and general development. Especially in America, which the news of Malayan *amok* reached only indirectly, a public rampage discourse is often said to have started with Charles Whitman (cf. Grzeszyk 2012).
13 "Der Amoklauf und seine Geschichte haben sich also nicht nur in den Berichten, Erzählungen und Akten europäischer Beobachter verfertigt, er ist vor allem auch das Ergebnis einer Bewegung, mit der über einige Jahrhunderte hinweg die seltsamen Vorfälle unter dein Eingeborenen eines begrenzten Kulturraums zu einem durchaus symptomatischen Ereignis westlicher Gesellschaften geworden ist." (Vogl 2003: 211)

time of the Internet, cable networks and new media. Nevertheless, the continuities in rampage violence discourses over centuries are helpful in coming to grips with how excessive violence prompts societies to reinforce their narratives of peacefulness and normalcy by juxtaposing them with narratives of an allegedly increasing threat asserted in the form abnormal or pathological behavior. By briefly looking at the way in which the *amok* narrative travelled to Europe and how rampage violence in the Western world developed, the effect of early narratives and images of *amok* on contemporary perceptions of acts of excessive violence, such as school shootings, can be explored.

After the "discovery" of *amok* and its entrance into the European imaginary, the readers of the reports struggled to find reasons and motivations for these violent attacks, while colonizers in Southeast Asia tried to find solutions for dealing with the *amoucos*. These attempts at explanation changed over the course of the years, according to the prevalent perception and scientific trends of the time. From the 19th century onwards, the *amoucos* in Southeast Asia were not simply punished, but hospitalized and analyzed by psychiatrists (cf. Adler 2000: 23). As a result of the general shift in the European perception of crime and the criminal, as described by Foucault (e.g., 1995 [1977]: 19f.), the perpetrator of a rampage killing was now seen as both guilty and mad – "guilty certainly, but someone to be put away and treated rather than punished" (Focault 1995 [1977]: 20).

However, the explanations for Malayan *amok* incidents varied significantly: European travelers linked the phenomenon to a primitive and uncivilized psyche, to drug and alcohol abuse, to the influence of Islam and later to psychiatric diseases such as schizophrenia, psychosis or paranoid personality disorders (cf. Spores 1988: 98ff., Adler 2000: 23ff.). Many of these explanations can still be found in the contemporary discourses on rampage violence.

The speculations about the motives for or direct triggers of these attacks were even fuzzier: Many observers seemed to agree upon the fact that the triggering factor for *amok* was often related to "a loss of love, a loss of money, or a loss of face" (Pinker 1997: 364)[14]. And this notion, too, found its way into the modern school shooting and rampage discourses, in which the experience of 'loss' is widely accepted as the last 'triggering cause' (cf. Böckler/Seeger 2010: 65).[15] Be-

---

14 For discussions of 'triggerging causes', see Vossekuil et al. (2002), Heitmeyer et al. (2013), Böckler/Seeger (2010).

15 In the school shooting discourse, some influential studies (e.g., Heitmeyer et al., 2013) have commented on the loss of control that is often linked to experiences of rejection and the resulting loss of stable relationships (e.g., Robertz 2013). These feelings of loss are often understood to be a direct result of the bullying that many perpetrators described prior to their attacks. Jonathan Fast's polemic yet widely received book *Ceremonial Violence* has been rightfully criticized

sides this general assumption that loss was the ultimate trigger, however, "[t]he motives for individual *amok* were and are obviously diverse and affect all imaginable problematic aspects of life" (Adler 2000: 18, transl.).[16]

In fact, the wide range of possible motivations is one of the main challenges of the *amok* discourse and can be found in both the ancient, medially imported and transmitted phenomenon and school shootings, its modern descendant. The crux of the matter and one of the predominant reasons for the public reaction to these attacks is the fact that, ever since the phenomenon of *amok* has reached Europe, no consequential mode of explanation has been provided for rampage violence. The modern shift towards judging the 'soul' of the criminal rather than his or her crime, towards asking what kinds of causal processes might be assigned to the production of the crime (cf. Foucault 1995 [1977]: 19), was and still is radically subverted by rampage violence. Thus, these acts defy the human understanding of an existing causality which would explain the event and make it somehow understandable.

In the face of 'senseless' violence (cf. Reemtsma 2012: 64), the public needs to construct these explanations; this was the case in the early reports of *amok* incidents, and this is still the case with modern forms of rampage killings such as school shootings. Interestingly, however, this quest for explanations or even justification[17] cannot be separated from the definitions of the phenomenon as such.

---

for establishing a monocausal link between the effects of bullying and school shootings (cf. Diehl 2014).

16 "Die Motive für individuelle Amokläufe waren und sind offenbar sehr vielfältig und betreffen alle denkbaren problematischen Aspekte des Lebens" (Adler 2000: 18).

17 While murder can hardly be justifiable, Mary Ellen O'Toole argues that society still tries to frame school shootings as somehow justified, but ultimately fails to even partially understand what has motivated the perpetrator: "Justification is what the public want to know in order to make sense of the crime. They want to be able to say, 'Ok, I understand now why someone would go into a school and shoot and kill ten people.' There will never be a reasonable justification for what Jeffrey Weise did that day. However, the motive for a crime is entirely different. The motive is the offender's emotional and psychological reasons for committing the crime, which can be either conscious or subconscious. We may not understand these motives, agree with them, or believe them. We most likely will find them to be repulsive or offensive. But the point is that motives are the offender's unique reasons for his or her behavior. It has nothing to do with our ability to be able to reconcile their behavior" (O'Toole 2013: 185).

Definitions of School Shootings

Traditionally, definitions of rampage violence beginning with the early reports of *amok* are based on the assumption of a lack of a clear or somewhat sufficient motive – and definitions of school shootings are no exception. It is commonly argued that the two major differences between regular rampage violence and school shootings are the age of the perpetrator and the way in which their attacks have been planned. In most of the common definitions, school shooters are juveniles and have a direct connection to the school or institution that they attack. If the shooter is a teacher, janitor or employer of the educational institution, however, the attack is most commonly referred to as a rampage killing or massacre (cf. e.g. Newman et al. 2005). It is only if the school shooter is indeed an adolescent that the attack is labeled a school shooting. The other difference is in the eruptive nature and the suddenness of the attack: *Amok*, it is the common assumption, is never planned, while school shootings verifiably take months of meticulous and clandestine planning, which mostly also involves leaking. This difference, however, has been contested by a number of researchers: Ancient *amok* (cf. Spores 1988: 104ff.) and modern forms of rampage violence (cf. Adler 2000) are both mostly meticulously planned and only appears to have been an eruption of violence (cf. Fox/Levin 2003, Adler 2000, Fox/DeLateur 2014: 126f.).

While these possible differences are important for a working definition of school shootings, contemporary rampage killings can be understood as a form of *amok* on the discourse level, as I have shown earlier. As a very specific subcategory of a rather general phenomenon, both the school shooting phenomenon and its discourse can be understood as part of a longer tradition. Naturally, if one wants to talk about phenomena of violence, even with a focus on the discourse rather than the crime, working with definitions and categories is unavoidable and indeed helpful.

As I have pointed out earlier, defining school shootings is a difficult task.[18] One of the most common and useful definitions of school shootings is by Katherine S. Newman, Cybelle Fox, David J. Harding, Jal Mehta and Wendy Roth and has been widely adopted. According to Newman and colleagues, school shootings must take place at a school or a school-related[19] place before an audience,

---

18 I will further explicate what Glenn W. Muschert (2007) has called the 'Rashomon-effect', so as to stress the perspective-dependency and the struggle with the case-definition-problem of school shooting definitions in Chapter 5.
19 In this definition, Newman and colleagues use the term school, while others speak about 'educational institutions'. This small difference has a great impact with regard to the cases included in the studies, as shootings at universities and other institutions of higher education,

must involve multiple victims – some of them chosen for their symbolic relevance or at random – and must involve one or more shooters who go or went to the school (Newman et al. 2005: 50).[20] These perhaps unrealistically clear-cut definitions are needed for sociological examinations of the phenomenon and are essential for empirical research. The attacks themselves, however, do not always adhere to the definitions set out by researchers. The category 'school shooting' has to remain an artificial subcategory, created and often modified *a posteriori*, within the homicide-suicide-spectrum (cf. Muschert 2007: 62ff.). The resulting definitions vary significantly and cause major discrepancies in research findings and meta-observations because of the fact that "researchers are left to define the subject of analysis largely according to their own standards and subjective preferences" (Böckler et al. 2013: 3).[21] Here, drawing mostly upon the definition by Newman et al. (2005), and including aspects from Böckler/Seeger (2010), Muschert (2007) and Vossekuil et al. (2002), the school shooting is broadly defined as a phenomenon that a) takes place at a school or an institution of higher education because of either its personal or symbolic meaning for the perpetrator, b) are committed by an *adolescent* perpetrator with the goal to hurt and kill more than one person, with the intention and plan being of greater relevance than the actual number of victims, and c) the attack takes place during everyday life, in front of witnesses. The victims of the attack can be a) chosen before the shooting because of either their personal or their symbolic role, b) random victims that were at the wrong place at the wrong time or c) perceived as standing in the way of the perpetrator, either before, during or after the shooting, e.g., parents at home, police or people who are shot during the attempt to flee the scene.

---

such as the Virginia Tech Massacre, have also occurred in the US, with an increase since 2002 (Newman et al. 2009). Interestingly, Charles Whitman's shooting in Austin, to which school shooting research frequently refers, was technically a *college rampage shooting* (cf. Newman/Fox 2009) or *IHE shooting* (cf. Bondü/Beier 2015). There are, however, major differences in both offender and offense characteristics between attacks at institutions of higher education and at schools (for comprehensive studies, see Newman/Fox 2009; Bondü/Beier 2015). As the dynamics of the college rampage shooting discourse function in similar patterns as the school shooting discourse (and can also be understood in the tradition of amok phenomena in general), I will sometimes refer to college rampage shootings such as Seung-hui Cho's shooting at Virginia Tech. My main focus, however, remains on school shootings.

20 As mentioned earlier, the case of Adam Lanza and the Sandy Hook massacre calls for alteration of this definition, as he had no direct affiliation with the school he attacked. Generally, for informative explanations and alterations of the prevalent definitions, see Böckler et al. (2013: 4ff).

21 This is most commonly referred to as the "case-definition-problem" (Harding et al. 2002, Muschert 2007) and will be also be commented on in Chapter 5.

As mentioned earlier, creating a typology of the stereotypical school shooter's characteristics and background is tempting when describing a crime, as this suggests a certain degree of preventability. While the creation of profiles appears to be an indispensable tool for criminologists (e.g., Bannenberg 2010), I will not include the perpetrator's characteristics or background in the definition of the phenomenon. Instead, I will focus on some of the school shooters' representations of themselves, on the personae they have actively created before the school shooting, and on the ways in which these aspects are related to the school shooting narrative and the cultural script of school shootings. The school shooter, as I will further elaborate in Chapter 3, is a constructed persona rather than a set of characteristics and experiences that can be described or listed. I locate the similarities between different school shooters in their references to the shared cultural script and to the school shooting narrative, not in their personality or character. I will, however, subscribe to one commonly accepted definition of school shooters by only referring to the male school shooter. This is not only due to the fact that there are, in fact, very few female school shooters (cf. Langman 2012), but also because I am approaching the phenomenon in terms of its discourse. The school shooting discourse and the fictional dimension of its narratives and imagery (see Chapter 3) is closely bound up with images of violent masculinity, as a number of studies have shown (cf. e.g., Newman et al. 2005, Kellner 2008, Tonso 2009). How these notions and images of masculinity may have influenced or could potentially influence female school shooters would be the subject of different study.

What is particularly interesting about many definitions of the school shooting is that they are closely linked to the assumed motivation behind the attacks. In my working definition, these aspects can also be found in the inclusion of the intention and the personal or symbolic meaning of the setting and the victims. Frequently, definitions of school shootings go hand in hand with the attempt to find explanations for the attack in the perpetrator's character. Certain characteristics and predispositions that seem to be evident in more than one school shooter are then included in typologies of typical perpetrators prone to excessive violence. These typologies have quickly found their way from academic research into media discourse, and have thus given rise to the image of the stereotypical school shooter. Moreover, perpetrators are stereotypically characterized as ordinary, inconspicuous loners, which makes the event all the more unexpected.[22]

---

[22] Jan Philipp Reemtsma states that the meaning of term 'ordinary' does in fact vacillate and is highly dependent on the frame of reference (Reemtsma 2012: 4). The manner in which *amoucos* and later school shooters or other rampage killers were and are characterized as 'ordinary' there-

These typologies are meant to approach the inexplicability of the attack by highlighting its disproportional severity and by creating the image of an abnormal perpetrator (cf. Langman 2009). These descriptions of the perpetrators and the attempts to find characteristics the attackers hold in common are highly informed by the culturally constructed narrative surrounding the events.

Societal reactions to Rampage Violence

As has become clear, the relating of school shootings and rampage violence is subject to similar discursive dynamics. An apparently sudden outburst of extreme violence that indiscriminately affects peers, random victims and sometimes even family – as with Newtown's Sandy Hook Elementary School-shooter Adam Lanza or the shooter of Springfield, Kip Kinkel – rampage violence confronts society with profound fears and insecurities. Acts of excessive violence, whether or not they occur schools, painfully reveal the fragility of society (cf. Reemtsma 2012). As the attacks are committed from the inside of society, community and social group or class, they point the subjects toward their own violability as well as that of the social environment. This shock to the witnesses' and bystanders' understanding of safety and society's regulating power is one of the main characteristics of the school shooting discourse and stems from the fact that societies define themselves by their ability to institutionalize, monopolize and regulate violence. This, as Jan Philipp Reemtsma shows with reference to Thomas Hobbes, is closely linked to trust, as it serves as one of the binders that keep the societal construct intact: "Practices of social trust", Reemtsma writes, "proved as criteria for normality, reliability, and predictability" (2012: 21). But even though trust is necessary for any society to remain stable, it is also extremely fragile. It is constantly at risk of being temporarily or fundamentally undermined or destroyed. Acts of excessive violence can be understood as posing a danger to trust in society and as a threat to the understanding of society as a peaceful and non-violent zone. This understanding of social normality, of course, is itself constructed and, as Jörn Ahrens writes: "what presents itself as a given set of routines, institutions, symbolizations etc., is equipped with a massive fictional dimension" (2011: 77). This fictional dimension consists of, and is shaped by, social narratives that are established to construct and preserve social norms Narratives in society, especially those that frame violence that calls social norms and values into question, assume a highly important function: They

---

fore serves to underline the bewilderment caused by an attack *from within a society* (see also Gerster 2016).

create order and help to make sense in a world that is otherwise chaotic. They transmit norms and values and thereby lend stability (as I will discuss further in section 2.3).

However, one of the prominent narratives about excessive violence within the public discourse is that these acts of violence are quite frequent, when in fact they are not, and that they are on the rise. Especially in the school shooting discourse, the public perception is that the number as well as the severity of these incidents has been increasing over the past decades. In 2001, only a couple of years after the archetypical Columbine school shooting, Meloy and his colleagues begin an article by reassuring the reader that "[d]espite the sensational reporting of the commercial media, a plethora of data indicates that homicide among juveniles has substantially decreased during the past decades" (2001: 719) and further stress that the cause of death for adolescents was statistically "least likely to be an intentional killing in school" (ibid.). These statements can be understood as a scholarly reaction to the observation that the USA, following "an apparent spate of incidents occurring between 1997 and 2001 [...], was on the brink of a moral panic" (Muschert 2007: 60). The notion of moral panic, frequently invoked in the school shooting discourse, was coined by Stanley Cohen in his study about youth culture and delinquency. He observes:

> Societies appear to be subject, every now and then, to periods of moral panic. A condition, episode or group of person emerges to become defined as a threat to societal values and interests; its nature is presented in a stylized and stereotypical fashion by the mass media; the moral barricades are manned by editors, bishops, politicians and other right-thinking people; socially accredited experts pronounce their diagnoses and solutions; ways of coping are evolved or (more often) resorted to; the condition then disappears, submerges or deteriorates and becomes more visible. Sometimes the object of the panic is quite novel and at other times it is something which has been in existence long enough, but suddenly appears in the limelight. Sometimes the panic passes over and is forgotten, except in folklore and collective memory; at other times, it has more serious and long-lasting repercussions and might produce such changes as those in legal and social policy or even in the way that society conceives itself. (Cohen 2002 [1972]: 1)

Moral panics have not been uncontested: instead of happening "every now and then", they seem to have become a regular state of panicked reaction, and instead of being the unintended outcome of journalistic practice, as described by Cohen, they seem to have become its goal. "Used by politicians to orchestrate consent, by business to promote sales in certain niche markets, and by media to make home social affairs newsworthy, moral panics are constructed on a daily basis" (McRobbie/Thornton 2012: 560).²³ In the foreword to the third edition of his study, Cohen himself uses school shootings as a contemporary example for a moral panic: While bullying and other forms of school violence are usually normalized, Columbine was the event that signaled the shift to the state of a moral panic, as the notion that 'it could happen anyplace' began to take over the school shooting discourse (cf. Cohen 2002 [1972]: xiii).

Whether or not one chooses to use the term 'moral panic', in the late 1990s, school shootings went from being local news to national tragedies (cf. Muschert 2002: 6ff.). The climate of fear and the perception of school shootings as an epidemic (cf. Newman et al 2005: 49f.) may be statistically unfounded (cf. Böckler et al. 2013: 9) but can be understood as a logical reaction to the media dynamics following these attacks (cf. Newman et al. 2005, Heitmeyer et al. 2013, Muschert 2007). Muschert and Ragnedda stress that, as with the disproportionate presence of historical *amok* in travelogues and voyage narratives, school shootings are also assigned much greater significance than they actually have:

> The mass media contribute to a culture of fear, by continually returning to and emphasizing the motif of school violence, creating a discrepancy between public fear and the real risks of victimization, fusing the perception of fear with the real event, and soliciting an emotional response divorced from its context. (2011: 346)

This fear of victimization and a vague sense of a new threat for society and community is based on excessive violence erupting from within society, but is inarguably fostered by the media discourse that perpetuates what I have elsewhere called a 'discourse of emergency' (cf. Braselmann 2016). This can especially be observed at times when school shootings have been perceived as a social rather than a local or national problem – a perception that is closely linked to the media attention received by the shooting.²⁴ Here, too, a parallel between historical *amok* and the contemporary phenomenon of school shootings can be observed: Although statistically extremely rare, spectacular and excessive acts of extreme violence from within a self-proclaimed non-violent society or an intact community gain public attention via the media and, as a consequence, are per-

---

23 Considering contemporary media dynamics and the ongoing commercialization of media outlets, this glosses over to an extent to which 'media' and 'business' are no longer to be separated.

24 For example, while the shooting in Bethel, Alaska did not attract national media attention in 1997, the shootings that followed did, and since 1999 "school shootings have been recognized as a social phenomenon rather than a set of isolated incidents" (Muschert/Ragnedda 2011: 352).

ceived as social problems that are then diagnosed as symptoms of a 'broken' society.

Moreover, the climate of fear and the vague sense of an indistinct threat to society, as sociologists have pointed out, results in a desire for control (cf. Heitmeyer et al. 2013, Muschert/Ragnedda 2011). This leads to reactions that aim to reduce the complexity of the phenomenon and to deflect from the far-reaching societal issues on which these phenomena might touch. Consequently, narratives that aim to frame school shootings with a consistent story and causality are prevalent in the discourse. The societal reactions to school shootings and the dynamics of the school shooting discourse, which will be further elaborated in the next subchapters, are therefore not unprecedented. Rather, they assume dynamics similar to those that were already established centuries ago in the *amok* discourse. In this respect, this ancient discourse, which derived its particular dynamics from the changes in the penal system and understanding of crime in general (cf. Foucault 1995 [1977]), has effectively shaped the Western understanding and approach to rampage violence.

2.1.2 Popular Explanations for School Shootings and the Challenges of the School Shooting Debate

In the school shooting discourse, like in the *amok* discourse preceding it, a shift from monocausal towards multicausal explanations of the attacks can be observed not only in the scholarly debate but also in media coverage and public perception. Yet, even when multiple factors are considered, they are incorporated as part of a coherent and consistent narrative.

By exploring, analyzing and closely examining various risk factors, media as well as scholarly analyses have sought rational and causal explanations for these events. Finding single or clear explanations suggests the possibility of a simple means of prevention and thereby reestablishes the sense of control that society has been temporarily robbed of by these acts. These dynamics, which could be observed especially in the late 1990s and early 2000s, follow a compelling logic: the simpler the explanation, the simpler the prevention method. Most of these causal explanations focus either on individual risk factors and motives or on larger, abstract security issues. Individual explanations focus strongly on bullying and view school shootings as a revenge plot directed against the perceived or real tormentors[25], or the focus is put on substance abuse or men-

---

25 Or against symbolic persons in a 'death by proxy' situation (cf. Fox/Levin: 56f.).

tal illness. There is certainly an incentive to find individual explanations within a complex discourse that is concerned with disproportionate and unreasonable acts of misguided individuals; after all, it "places responsibility with individuals and suggests that individual treatment could solve the problem" (Muschert/Ragnedda 2011: 354). However, this reaction is also highly problematic, as it frequently deflects from the underlying social problems that foster and enable adolescents to plan and eventually commit such an unspeakable crime. When emphasis is put on the idiosyncrasies of the particular school shooting, more sustained investigation of the broader nexuses at play are made redundant.

Further, in reacting to school shootings, the media and public frequently revert to monocausal explanations that reveal more about general societal developments than the motivation behind the crime Single risk factors, such as excessive consumption of violent media content or familiar neglect, are often sought out to provide the fodder for debates about controversial social developments, youth culture and the state of modern societies as such. The selection of risk factors, however, also fuels dangerous discursive dynamics, as has been the case with violent media content.[26] The so-called copycat effect, one of the hot topics in the school shooting discourse of the early 2000s, and most famously described in a polemic monograph by Loren Coleman (2004), combines well-founded observations about the reciprocal relationship between media and school shootings with claims about the 'real culprits'. The copycat effect seemed to be just what cultural pessimists had been waiting for. While the media dynamics of school shootings are extremely complex, the copycat effect, or "the dirty little secret of the media" (Coleman 2004: 1), simply points the finger at films, music, computer games and even literature, and Coleman explores this using individual cases as examples (cf. Böckler/Seeger 2010: 71).

As the copycat effect and the debate about the role of the media will be discussed in greater detail in section 2.2, for now I will return to the tendency to choose individual motives or the select risk factors in way that reduces complexity. Instead of simply pointing out the shortcomings or aberrances of the public and scholarly discourse, I will focus on the ongoing differentiation of the discourse that can be observed over the last decade. By presenting a short overview of the predominant strategies for explaining and, consequently, for coping with the school shooting phenomenon, underlying mechanisms within the school

---

[26] 'Dangerous' may seem at first to be an extreme choice of words, but if the stigmatization that has followed members of the Goth culture and consumers of certain film or musical genres as well as the cries for strict censorship of this content are considered, the 'security measures' – such as systematic locker searches of 'suspected groups' – have in fact been a danger to individual as well as artistic freedom.

shooting discourse will become clear. In the process, I want to make way for a better understanding of the discussion of the role of the media and, especially, of violent media content, as this will be of special interest in the further course of this book.

When examining popular explanations, it is striking that they have all been observed in single or even multiple school shooting cases, but that each fails to serve as a sufficient explanation because of the disproportionate severity of the shooter's action. While all of these explanations may have played a role in past school shootings, their capacity to work as isolated explanations or justifications for the attacks must, by their very nature, falls short. The following section will examine explanations related to mental illness, eruption of violence, family problems, bullying, and gun availability.[27] Naturally, there have been many more attempts at explanations, but the aspects mentioned in the following pages are the ones that best illustrated the public need to establish causality and the way that incomplete and insufficient information is constructed into a coherent narrative.

Mental Illnesses

One of the common attempts to explain school shootings relies on the diagnosis of mental illness. This, especially seen in the tradition of historical *amok*, is not surprising at all, as *amok* is still understood as "a bona fide, albeit antiquated, psychiatric condition" (Saint Martin 1999: 66) by some psychiatrists and researchers. The historical understanding of *amoucos*, the Malayan attackers, as 'crazy' in the common sense, thus served as an explanation for what could not be explained in other terms. This technique involves the common strategy of pathologizing what defies rational explanation in order to render it 'other' and can be observed in most approaches to rampage violence and school shootings. A more recent definition of rampage violence in the *Diagnostic and Statistical Manual of Mental Disorders (DSM IV)*, however, classifies *amok* as a dissociative episode that is sometimes linked to psychotic episodes (cf. Gaw/Bernstein

---

27 Within the scope of this project, the list of predominant and popular attempts at explanations can only be a short and selective overview about some of the most prevalent themes of the school shooting discourse. For comprehensive synopses of the most important aspects approached from various disciplinary backgrounds in English see Muschert (2007) and Böckler et al. (2013). For comprehensive overviews in German and comparisons of German and American findings see Robertz (2004), Bondü (2012) and Böckler/Seeger (2010).

1992).²⁸ The psychiatric understanding of rampage violence and school shootings is thus linked to the history of a discipline: Outdated diagnoses have been supplanted by more contemporary diagnoses such as depression or psychosis. Frequently, as in Dave Cullen's journalistic bestseller on the Columbine school shooting (Cullen 2009), the contested diagnosis of psychosis is also included in the description of a school shooter's mental health; here, Eric Harris serves as a paradigmatic example.²⁹ In Germany, the early and striking example of the connection between rampage violence and mental illness was the school teacher Ernst August Wagner, who killed his family, set a village on fire, shot nine people and wounded eleven more. His horrific crime was followed by a whole series of psychiatric diagnoses – most prominently paranoia (cf. Adler 2000: 31) – and is still included in many new studies on rampage violence and school shootings.

The American prototype for rampage violence at an educational institution is Charles Joseph Whitman, who carried out his crime from the tower of the University of Austin, Texas in 1966. Because of its relation to an educational institution, this case is directly linked to the school shooting discourse. Additionally, its relation to psychiatric discourse is interesting in several regards. In a confessional letter, Whitman himself demanded to have an autopsy performed on his body after his attack because he was concerned that his killing spree had been caused by mental health issues. He even wanted all his money donated to a mental health foundation so that further attacks like his own could be prevented (cf. Grzeszyk 2012: 82). Already in 1985, a study compared Whitman's attack with other acts of excessive violence, such as the 'Calgary-Mall-Sniper' or the 'Memorial-Day-Man'. In this study, these attacks were then compared to cases of Malayan *amok* (cf. Adler 2000: 40) and various mental health problems were discussed. By this time, the heated debate about mental illness has become a standard element in the discourse surrounding rampage violence:

> The question of the mental illnesses of the perpetrators is one of the most important and most controversially discussed topics there is with regard to amok. All essential syndromes from psychiatry, from socially induced, normal stress disorders to psychosis, were most

---

28 Like Spores (1988), Gaw and Bernstein refer to the Malayan form of *amok* as a "culture-bound syndrome".
29 While aware of the differences between the individual shooters, Peter Langman uses psychiatric categories – diagnoses and categories – in his own attempt to create a typology of school shooters. He divides the perpetrators into three types: psychopathic, psychotic and traumatized. In this way, he implies all school shooters suffer from severe mental health issues (cf. Langman 2009a: 79ff). This is a prime example of the quest to provide consistent explanations and the need to create coherent narratives and a sense of causality, as well as universal typologies.

likely understood to be typical or at least especially frequent at some point. (Adler 2000: 72, transl.)[30]

In the attempt to approach the inexplicable, debates about mental illnesses are among the first media reactions to school shootings. In the case of the Sandy Hook Massacre in 2012, even years after the attack, new *post mortem* diagnoses of the shooter were published – especially by sensationalist media. In 2014, for example, the *Daily Mail* published an article titled: "Anorexic, unmedicated and obsessed with a murder-mad cyber world: Adam Lanza's mental issues went untreated". (Oliveira 2014). The article further blames Lanza's mother, who was a victim of the attack herself, for allegedly having refused psychological treatment for her son.

This reaction clearly shows the need for consistent and, in the best case, 'curable' explanations. With adequate treatment, the mentally ill – as media reports about disturbed shooters suggest – are not dangerous. And the very fact that they are dangerous is framed as abnormal, as no healthy, 'normal' boy would commit a crime of this nature. Naturally, these reactions derive from the need to feel in control and the societal necessity to develop mechanisms for prevention. While this is understandable, these dynamics have recently been challenged by researchers, as a quote from Fox's and DeLateur's quite polemic publication against prevalent myths in the school shooting discourse illustrates:

> It would certainly be a fitting legacy to the tragedy in Newtown if mental health services were expanded and improved. However, greater access to treatment options may not necessarily reach the few individuals on the fringe who would seek to turn a school, a shopping mall, or a movie theater into their own personal war zone. [...] In the aftermath of high-profile mass shootings, political leaders often rally to address the needs of the mentally ill. Unfortunately, this timing tends to stigmatize the vast majority of people who suffer from mental illness as if they too are mass murderers in waiting. (2014: 135)

This is especially important to bear in mind, as the direct relation between mental illness and phenomena of excessive violence such as school shootings has not been clearly established (cf. Meloy 2001). Quite the contrary: Adolescent school shooters show fewer signs of mental illnesses than adult perpetrators

---

30 "Die Frage nach der psychischen Gestörtheit der Täter gehört sicher zu den wichtigsten und am kontroversesten diskutierten Themen im Zusammenhang mit Amok überhaupt. Von sozial bedingten, normalen Belastungsreaktionen bis hin zu Psychosen dürften alle wesentlichen Syndrome der Psychiatrie als typisch oder doch zumindest als häufig angeschuldigt worden sein." (Adler 2000: 72)

of rampage violence (cf. Bondü 2012: 111), and only "[f]ew school shooters are diagnosed with mental illnesses before their crimes. Yet many are discovered afterwards to be mentally ill" (Newman et al. 2005).[31] In any case, the mental health issues from which many of the perpetrators suffered, such as depression, do not suffice to explain violent acts (cf. Brumme 2011: 43). Even though the pathologizing of a perpetrator is one of the most common societal reactions towards acts of violence (cf. Foucault 1995 [1977]: 20), especially when it comes to autotelic and excessive violence (cf. Reemtsma 2012: 152), this attempt to create a causal narrative is particularly problematic: Not only does it actively 'other' the perpetrator in an attempt to reinforce social normalcy, this 'othering' actively allows for the dangerous stigmatization of already marginalized adolescents who suffer from mental illnesses. While the relationship between certain kinds of mental illness and behavior theoretically suggests a comparatively easy way to detect a school shooter before the crime, linking illnesses like depression to excessive violence further stigmatizes anyone who suffers from these illnesses.

'Sudden Eruption' of Violence

"When we are at loss to explain something", Newman et al. point out "we look for the most proximate or immediate potential cause" (2005: 60). In the school shooting discourse, this often results in discussions about bad break-ups, punishment by the principal, a teacher, the parents or any other reason for an adolescent boy to 'snap'. These immediate explanations, however, indicate that hitherto 'ordinary' adolescent boy suddenly becomes an unpredictable mass murderer.[32]

These explanations, as news media is bound to realize as the story of the shooting unfolds, fall short in every case, as school shooting research has shown: As described earlier, school shootings are usually planned well in advance and mark the peak of an adolescent's impression of growing hopelessness

---

31 While evaluating the perpetrator's mental health is often difficult, either because the attackers take their own lives or because their diagnoses are confidential, the mental health issues of Michael Carneal, who killed three and injured five people in his shooting at Heath High School in West Paducah, Kentucky, in 1997, were discovered after his attack. After the shooting, a history of mental health issues in his family was uncovered and forensic psychiatrists attested to his mental illness as part of his defense. Later, he developed schizophrenia in jail. Because his appeals for a re-trial based on his mental health issues were rejected, he was still serving his sentence at the time this book was written.

32 Adam Lanza's 'ordinariness', for example, was emphasized by descriptions that are highly emblematic of the perception of many school shooters; he was described as "smart, introverted and nervous" and had "gone out of his way not to attract attention" (Barron 2012).

and a perceived lack of alternative solutions for their problems. As some studies suggest, the various social and psychological predispositions of the perpetrator lead to a feeling of extreme vulnerability and social instability, most likely resulting from a highly complex and individual accumulation of problems such as low self-esteem, insufficient coping mechanisms and social incompetence (cf. Robertz 2013: 110). Together with this emotional development, rejections and humiliations may lead to the experience of a loss, real or perceived, that does not seem to be compensable in the perpetrator's subjective reality. The notion of the loss of control underlines the fact that school shootings are the result of various processes in the perpetrator's life and development; despite "the existence of triggers in close proximity to the crime, school shootings are not fundamentally situative events. Rather, they occur against the background of a lengthy developmental sequence" (Robertz 2013: 110). Heitmeyer et al. therefore relate the loss of control "to the situation of the perpetrators and their loss of control over their own lives. This is (a) evoked through negative recognition and *erosion of recognition* in families, schools, and peer groups as agents of socialization, which (b) raises issues of *social disintegration*" (ibid.).

What Heitmeyer et al. call the *double* or 'systematic loss of control' on both the individual perpetrator's as well as the societal level relates this individual experience to the dynamics of the school shooting discourse. This double loss of control results from the failure to accurately respond to the "*crucial factors influencing* the scientifically known setting of the act" (Heitmeyer et al. 2013: 28). The unexplained systematic relation of the processes that trigger the attack and a general lack of knowledge about these triggers causes further exacerbates societal insecurity in dealing with these events. Recognizing the reactions to the 'double loss of control' can help to reflect on the discursive dynamics of attempts to regain control.

Family Problems

Heitmeyer et al.'s notion of systematic loss of control suggests growing social disintegration, can be understood in the context of a lack of attention by the family and the general dissolution of social bonds (cf. Robertz 2004: 126ff.). The media has always been quick to seek blame within the families of the shooters. In the aftermath of school shootings, in Germany as well as the United States., the situation at the shooter's home was analyzed in various newspaper articles centering around the question "How could the Harrises and Klebolds not have realized that something, everything, was seriously awry?" (Belluck/Wilgoren 1999).

Assigning blame to the direct surrounding of the perpetrators is a very common reaction in the aftermath of school shootings, as one of the most unbelievable aspects of these attacks is the fact that the meticulous planning always went completely unnoticed by friends and family. Parental neglect is the accusation that mostly results from these observations, frequently resulting in statements that create a direct causal link between the family situation and other explanations for the attacks. Due to "the lack of parental support", as one of the common lines of argument goes, "offenders found solace and company in their favorite television program or barbaric video game" (Kidd/Meyer 2002).

Stressing apparent parental neglect can be understood as yet another reaction of a community under attack: Although school shootings happen mostly in close-knit communities and small towns, where the intact family is one of the core values (cf. Newman et al. 2005), the public, especially those within the community, is completely blindsided. One of the ways to approach the tragedy is to assume that the family circumstances of the shooters must have been much more complicated and their parents more negligent than schools or neighbors suspected.[33] When the narrative of the close-knit community suddenly appears unreliable, suggesting that information was deliberately hidden is a way of restoring trust in the communal structures by implying that 'nobody could have known' (cf. Newman et al. 2005: 179ff).

Yet, the findings from school shooting research do not suggest that school shooters come from dysfunctional families in the traditional sense. Rather, the shooters come "from a variety of family situations, ranging from intact families with numerous ties to the community, to foster homes with a history of neglect", as Vossekuil et al. point out in their governmental report (2002: 19). Here, too, school shootings and the perpetrators defy simple typologies and the easy logic of causality. Following what can almost be called a rare consensus among international scholars, it can be assumed that the shooters must have had a lack of social and personal resources (cf. Böckler/Seeger 2010: 62). This lack of resources, however, cannot be easily blamed on the shooter's surroundings, but has sometimes been initiated by the shooters themselves, who withdrew from their existing and previously intact relationships prior to the attack (cf. Brumme 2011: 40).

---

33 The assumptions about the shooter's families must remain speculative because of the difficulties gathering any information about the families, as the parents of school shooters often face civil lawsuits, public shaming and exclusion from their community and therefore mostly remain silent about their son's actions or publish short apologies. Only years after the attacks of their son did the family of Columbine shooter Dylan Klebold openly talk about their side of the story (cf. e.g. Klebold 2009, 2015).

Bullying

School shootings and bullying are inextricably connected in attempts to approach and understand the inexplicable, in media, public and scholarly discourse alike.[34] Many of the fictional representations of school shootings present bullying as a central motif, which makes this aspect especially interesting within the scope of this volume (see Chapters 4 and 5). It is crucial to understand how this very prominent problem in schools has been discussed as the prime explanation for excessive violence in the discourse. The attention that bullying has received in the aftermath of school shootings is not at all surprising, as a number of school shooters have referred to their experiences with bullying in suicide notes, diaries and videos that they left behind. Bullying is a pressing problem that can turn time at school into an ordeal for many young people in America as well as in Germany. The personal suffering that results from being bullied should be underestimated.[35] In fact, the bullying problem suggests underlying social and institutional problems in school systems, and should therefore not be trivialized or overshadowed by other aspects of the school shooting discourse (cf. Muschert/Ragnedda 2011).

However, even though school shootings are frequently framed as acts of revenge (cf. Fox/Levin 2003: 56) – especially by the perpetrators themselves – bullying does not suffice to explain school shootings. Even though the shooters go to great lengths to explain their suffering at school and attempt to justify their actions, their experiences fail to explain why they choose to indiscriminately kill their peers.[36] Jonathan Fast's *Ceremonial Violence* presents its readers with narratives about the suffering of school shooters and establishes a clear link between their marginalization at school and the revenge that follows (Fast 2008). A passage from Pearl High School shooter Luke Woodham's suicide note is quoted, for instance, which reads: "Throughout my life I was ridiculed. Always beaten, always hated. Can you, society, truly blame me for what I do? [...] I have no mercy for humanity, for they created me, they tortured me until I snapped and

---

[34] As I will show, the vast majority of fictional representations of school shootings – especially those for young adults – also pick up the bullying problem in one way or another.
[35] Even though school systems in the US and Germany cannot be compared in terms of social hierarchies, bullying is a problem in German schools as well. Especially in terms of verbal harassment and abuse, studies did not find remarkable differences between both countries. Physical abuse and the use of weapons in schools, however, is more a problem in the US than in Germany (cf. Brumme 2011: 46f).
[36] On the internet, however, an entire community of fans of school shooters hails their heroes and the revenge they took on the school and the people that cause so much suffering (cf. Paton 2012).

became what I am today" (Luke Woodham, qtd. Fast 2008: 156).[37] Similar statements were made by the German school shooter Sebastian Bosse from Emsdetten, who states: "They punched me, they spit on me, they knocked me down, they laughed on me [sic]" (Bosse, qtd. in Grzeszyk 2012: 133).[38] Virginia Tech campus shooter Seung-Hui Cho's utterance seem to echo Bosse when he asks: "Do you know what it feels [sic] to be spit on your face and to have trash shoved down your throat?" (Cho, qtd. ibid.). And Eric Harris, as one of the prototypical avengers of the bullied, writes in his diary: "Everyone is always making fun of me because of how I look, how fucking weak I am and shit, well I will get you all back, ultimate fucking revenge here" (Harris, qtd. Langman 2014: 7).

Here, the interwovenness of school shootings and fiction becomes apparent on the level of the perpetrator's self-portrayal, which I will discuss in detail in the next chapter. Perceiving themselves as the avengers for the suffering of all those who have been or are bullied, the shooters themselves attempt to establish a causal narrative. Interestingly, school shooters who described themselves as victims of bullying and who identified revenge for being picked on as their motive, like the shooters from Westside and Heath, were said to "have given as good as they got" (Newman et al. 2005: 64) by fellow students and teachers. Jens Hoffmann, too, warns against generalizing the perpetrator's social standing, pointing out that not all school shooters were bullied or could even be described as 'loners' (Hoffmann 2007: 28). However, as Heitmeyer et al. stress, "one must consider the possibility that [...] such peer relations are only superficially unremarkable and are experienced by the young people themselves as inadequate, fragile, and insufficiently functional" (Heitmeyer et al. 2013: 38). Without doubt, perceived marginality is one of the 'necessary but not sufficient conditions'[39] for school shootings. Even though "[s]chool shooters are not all loners and they are not all bullied, [...] nearly all experience ostracism and social marginality. For some of these boys [...] exclusion takes the form of bullying bordering on torture. Others [...] are invisible. For still others [...] it's the perception of marginalization, despite evidence to the contrary, that matters most" (Newman et al. 2005: 242).

This marginalization, whether real or perceived, has to be considered a real and pressing problem for adolescents and should serve as a starting point for

---

[37] Fast's monograph can be seen as typical of the relationship between school shootings and their narratives.
[38] Bosse, for reasons that will become clear throughout the next chapters, talked English in his self-explanatory videos.
[39] As Newman's study will be dealt with in greater detail in the next subchapter, the other four conditions are not of importance at this point.

debates about physical and verbal violence and abuse in schools instead of further normalizing it (cf. Cohen 2002 [1972]: xiii). The "ideological blindness" regarding bullying (Larkin 2013: 170f.) can be seen as the result of a "hegemonic interpretation of reality" (ibid.: 171). The complex cultural system within institutions justifies hierarchical arrangements and functions in order to present existing social organizations as more cohesive than they really are, often resulting in conflict being downplayed (ibid.). This can even happen in the face of continuous violence. Students who suffer from harassment and violence at school are therefore often left alone with their problems and have no one to turn to.[40] This is relevant whenever bullying is debated in the context of school shootings; while it might fail to serve as a causal explanation for these gruesome acts of violence, downplaying the effect that perceived marginalization and experiences of bullying have on adolescents can ultimately reify the questionable and dangerous power structures and hierarchies at schools.

Gun Availability

There is no denying that gun availability is a crucial factor when it comes to school shootings. Without guns, school shootings either would not happen or they would have fewer fatalities, as the very few events in which an axe or knife was used have shown (cf. Bondü et al. 2011: 23f.). However, the increasing availability of guns in the US does not necessarily account for the spike in rampage violence at schools (cf. Newman 2005: 260), as "[h]unting communities have always kept guns at the ready, but school shootings began to occur fairly recently" (ibid.: 70). Thus, even though the connection is an obvious one, it falls short as a monocausal explanation for school shootings. Easy access to guns is only another factor in the amalgamation of elements that may lead to a school shooting. In the quest for effective prevention strategies, the public outcry for stricter gun laws is understandable. However, in the political debate that swiftly follows every school shooting, it seems that the media is quickly used by both sides of the political spectrum to push their agendas, all too often at the expense of respect for the victims. "If one thing is predictable of mass shootings, it is that they will spark heated debate over gun control" (Fox/DeLateur 2014: 135). A good example of the dynamics of the gun availability debate is the shooting at Sandy Hook Elementary School in Newtown in December 2012. The Sandy Hook shooting was one of the most shocking attacks on a school thus far, mostly because the many dead and wounded children were all five to ten years old,

---

40 See also Newman et al. (2005: 155ff.) and Chapter 4 of this study.

which was much younger than the victims of most other shootings. In a televised address after the shooting on December 14, 2012, President Barack Obama already hinted at the debate that this attack would spark:

> As a country, we have been through this too many times. Whether it's an elementary school in Newtown, or a shopping mall in Oregon, or a temple in Wisconsin, or a movie theater in Aurora, or a street corner in Chicago – these neighborhoods are our neighborhoods, and these children are our children. And we're going to have to come together and take meaningful action to prevent more tragedies like this, regardless of the politics.[41]

In the following months and years, several actions were taken by the White House, advocacy groups and Congress. However, all of the proposed bills, including enhanced background checks and the ban on assault weapons, failed. President Barack Obama, however, anticipated this struggle when he asked in another speech after the Sandy Hook shooting: "Are we prepared to say that we're powerless in the face of such carnage, that the politics are too hard? Are we prepared to say that such violence visited on our children year after year after year is somehow the price of our freedom?"[42]

The reaction of the conservatives, "the progun lobby and right-wing pundits", as Douglas Kellner calls them (2008: 43), did not come as a surprise, as statements such as "[g]uns have little or nothing to do with juvenile violence [...]. The causes of youth violence [...] are daycare, the teaching of evolution and working mothers who take birth control" (Tom DeLay, qtd. Kellner 2008: 43), made by a former House Republican majority leader, can still be heard in American political discourse. The gun lobby, most famously the National Rifle Association, uses school shootings to reinforce their well-known rhetoric: 'The only thing that helps against a bad guy with a gun is a good guy with a gun.' This is echoed in the debate about concealed carriage of firearms at schools und university campuses, which is hashed out time and again in some states that prohibit concealed carriage.[43] By invoking the rhetoric of crisis, emergency and imminent threats at schools, pro-gun lobbyists add to a discourse of emergency that suggests school and campus shootings are a much more frequent phenomenon

---

[41] The White House. "President Obama Makes a Statement on the Shooting in Newtown Connecticut." December 14, 2012. https://obamawhitehouse.archives.gov/photos-and-video/video/2012/12/14/president-obama-makes-statement-shooting-newtown-connecticut

[42] The White House. "Remarks by the President at Sandy Hook Interfaith Prayer Vigil." December 16, 2012. https://obamawhitehouse.archives.gov/the-press-office/2012/12/16/remarks-president-sandy-hook-interfaith-prayer-vigil

[43] In September 2016, a Virginia Tech student went on a hunger strike, demanding a review of the University's gun policy (cf. Manch 2016).

than they actually are. While lobbyists do so in order to push their political agenda, the discussion about gun availability and the right to bear arms also affects the general public perception of school shootings. Only a fortnight after Adam Lanza's shooting, the NRA's executive vice president Wayne LaPierre stated that "our society is populated by an unknown number of genuine monsters" and asked: "[D]oes anybody really believe that the next Adam Lanza isn't planning his attack on a school he's already identified at this very moment?" (qtd. in Farrell 2016: 360). In this way, LaPierre deliberately stoked societal fears and the sense of emergency in order to further advocate for the right to carry guns even at school and campuses.

The discussion about gun control and the power of the gun industry and its lobby in the debate is highly complex. An adequate treatment of the topic would go beyond the scope of this project and would also not contribute significantly to my argument. However, it should be pointed out that, while strict gun laws may not prevent school shootings, they most likely reduce their frequency: A list by Böckler and colleagues, which includes school shootings that occurred between 1925 and 2011 worldwide, shows that the occurrence of school shootings is more than ten times higher in the US than in Germany – or any other country, for that matter (cf. Böckler et al. 2013: 11). A study by German criminologist Britta Bannenberg (2010) shows that almost all weapons used in German school shootings belonged to immediate family members. They were therefore not stored according to German security standards, or the shooters observed where the keys to the weapons and ammunition were kept and gained access to the weapons (Bannenberg 2010: 86).[44] Interestingly, Bannenberg observes that adolescents who wanted to attack their school but did not have access to weapons in their home failed to acquire guns elsewhere (cf. ibid.). Attacks in German schools that were committed with other weapons, such as axes or knives, show that strict gun control cannot completely prevent school shootings, but may help to reduce their frequency as well as the severity of the attack (cf. Bondü et al. 2011: 23). Within the school shooting discourse, the connection between is easy access to weapons and school shootings is easily made. . However, access to weapons still does not explain why school shootings happen. Rather, the frantic debate about gun control and access to guns is emblematic of society's need for control, as it strives for clear methods of prevention that rely on regulations and security measures.

---

[44] The father of the German school shooter from Winnenden was convicted of negligent homicide for not having stored his gun according to German legislation (cf. *Der Spiegel*, February 1, 2013. Online: http://www.spiegel.de/panorama/justiz/amoklauf-von-winnenden-tim-k-s-vater-zu-bewaehrungsstrafe-verurteilt-a-880882.html).

Attempts to Explain the Inexplicable

After this very brief overview of the most popular and widely discussed attempts to explain and define school shootings, three observations can be made that will serve as the groundwork for this book:

First, the debate about school shootings is thoroughly contemporary and cannot be understood separately from contemporary media logic. Almost all of the popular explanations mentioned thus far have in some way been related to the debate about violent media content and the role of the shooters in a mediatized world. At the same time, however, the dynamics of the school shooting discourse – both in scholarly works and the media – closely resemble the discourse of historical *amok* and other phenomena of excessive violence, as section 2.1.1 has shown: Strategies for explaining, simplifying and establishing causality have been employed in the school shooting discourse ever since the 1990s. Especially in academic discourse, a shift from monocausal to differentiated approaches to the phenomena can be observed. Media coverage, on the other hand, still primarily pursues a narrative of causality. In this narrative, the event is embedded in a continuous line of events. This continuity, as presented by the media, seems inevitable. As a result, the event itself does not have to be seen as a sudden rupture in everyday life; in these narratives, it is not an isolated act that defies any rationale, but can be understood in terms of cause and effect.[45]

Second, the school shooting discourse is dominated by attempts to find consistent explanations and causal links in order to explain the act of extreme violence or to at least help society understand it in terms of abnormalities that can be explained. As Ferguson and Ivory put it:

> When mass homicides occur, politicians, scholars, and the general public sift about for clear explanations. It is understandable that people would look for an answer as to what could cause such awful events. For some, finding such an answer would provide an illusion of control over the events and the notion they might be prevented in the future. (2013: 48)

These frequently speculative and reductive explanations are mostly circulated by the mass media in the direct aftermath of a school shooting, and a vigorous scholarly debate then ensues to validate or refute the public assumptions. This, too, is understandable, as the search for effective methods of prevention is and should be one of the main goals of sociological, criminological and psychological examinations of the phenomenon. Oversimplifications, however, have

---

45 For further comments on this particular dynamic, see Bartz (2007).

failed to foster a better understanding of the dynamics of school shootings. Many challenges have crept up in the scholarly debate as well as the public and media discussion, resulting in the development of new and more differentiated approaches over the last years, which are now examined by media scholars (cf. Schildkraut/Muschert 2014).

Third and lastly, one of the great problems of the school shooting discourse, as with the *amok* discourse, is the fact that it remains impossible to characterize the typical school shooter. As pointed out earlier, almost all findings point towards the fact that most school shooters share the feeling of marginalization, as a result of which they chose to commit an unspeakable act of violence as a way of coping with their perceived position in society. Apart from this observation, however, the various attempts to classify 'the school shooter' are necessarily vague and reliant on stereotypes (cf. Vogl 2014, Adler 2000: 28). Therefore, these models have to be adjusted after a new mass shooting adds another factor to the list or fails to meet one of the previous criteria, as in the case of the Sandy Hook Massacre.

One aspect that I have deliberately left out is the aspect of media violence, which has prompted heated debates across disciplines. However, as this aspect is of particular relevance for this book which essentially focuses on violent media and the fictional representations of excessive violence, the issue of media violence as explanation for school shooting will be thoroughly examined in the following pages.

2.2 Playing the 'Blame Game': Media Violence and the School Shooting Discourse

In the struggle for explanations and the establishment of a clear cause-and-effect-scenario, violent media content has traditionally been one of the most common culprits. When approaching the role of violent media content, it is of great importance to distinguish between two separate discourses and the context in which these are debated. On the one hand, there is the debate about violent media content's effect on readers and audiences; this can be traced back all the way to ancient Greece. As the diachronic approach to school shootings and the continuity between societal reactions to school shootings and the historical *amok* discourse has shown, school shootings may be a contemporary phenomenon, but the discursive dynamics of the phenomenon are best understood when examined alongside similar phenomena preceding it. On the other hand, there is a more recent debate about the portrayal of actual school shootings, especially in media coverage after a school shooting and the representation of the perpetrators.

Because these two heated debates offer important vantage points for this book, they will be discussed at greater length than the other explanatory approaches. From examining how the school shooting discourse includes media content – whether in fictional representations or in mass news media – I will move on to the examination of the fictional representation of school shootings. This focus, it will become clear, is a logical consequence of the debate about violent media. Naturally, fictional representations of school shootings are always representations of extreme and excessive forms of violence. Additionally, they may convey a certain image of the school shooter, journalistic depictions of which have been heavily criticized in the past few years (cf. Regener 2017).

This leads to the next important factor that needs to be considered when approaching the debate about school shootings and their relation to violent media: One of the few points of consensus among school shooting researchers is that these acts of violence can be regarded as a thoroughly contemporary phenomenon that cannot be understood outside of the context of mediatization. Mediatization here "refers to the idea that social and cultural life has become heavily influenced and shaped by the media on all levels: private, public, social and even international" (Muschert/Sumiala 2012: xiv).[46] In the special case of school shootings, mediatization can be observed on two levels: not only the school shooting a phenomenon, but also the public perception of the events can be understood as highly dependent on modern media logic:

> As a cultural phenomenon school shootings have high symbolic value. Although carried out in relatively small numbers, school shootings images and meaning are widely spread around the world, and thus have potential to nurture the collective imagination of destruction and fear much beyond their physical power. (Muschert/Sumiala 2012: xvi)

While school shootings are only experienced by very few people, they are witnessed and experienced by millions via mass media. Initially, images of school shootings are distributed via news media channels. Later, debates about the images conveyed by the media and their possible effects are held on the same channels; in an observation of second order (*sensu* Luhmann), the public is

---

[46] When I refer to a consensus, I do not mean to insinuate that all scholars necessarily agree to the concept of mediatization as proposed by Muschert and colleagues in their edited volume (2012). However, a broad variety of scholarly (and media) approaches do refer to the role of the media and the complex interplay between school shootings and media content in various ways; for more on this, see section 2.2 and Chapter 3.

thus actively engaged in the discourse about media effects, which explains the prominent role of this particular aspect in the school shooting discourse.

On the level of the school shooting as an event, mediatization has also proven to be a fertile concept for approaching the complex interaction between school shootings and media. It acknowledges that school shooters themselves do refer to media content and must be influenced by certain content, as they are participants in a global age that is essentially defined by the role of the media. The concept can therefore be used to examine the representation of school shootings in mass media and the reception of these representations, as well as media consumption by school shooters and the larger effects of violent media. On the following pages, I will approach the highly complex relationship between school shootings and media starting with the debate about media violence and school shootings. I will then focus on the scholarly debate about fictional representations of excessive violence, which will serve as groundwork for my approach to fictional representations of school shootings in the following chapters.

2.2.1 The Debate about Media Violence in the Aftermath of School Shootings

It is not surprising that media violence is one of the hot topics in the aftermath of every school shooting. 'Violent media' is indeed one of the easier and more abstract scapegoats. Moreover, the evidence of a causal relationship between school shootings and media use is compelling, as a number school shooters have shown great interest in violent media, ranging from film and video games to music and even journalistic or scholarly works on violence. But while "violent people are often attracted to violent entertainment, the ability to document a direct causal link indicating that consuming violent entertainment leads to violent behavior has eluded social science researchers for years" (Fox/DeLateur 2014: 132).

Indeed, the attempt to establish a clear causal link between consumption of certain media content and violent behavior 'in real life' has been debated heatedly not only for decades but for centuries now. In fact, the debate about the possible effect of representations of violence and the resulting need to protect humans from violent content can be traced back all the way to Plato, who famously warned his contemporaries about the negative effects of fairytales and theater. Those interested in the historical dimension of the debate about media violence, especially in terms of *imitatio*, can retrace a passionate discussion that tends to repeat itself whenever a new art form emerges: Art forms that are now regarded as high culture, such as drama or the novel, were once feared to make the reader blindly adopt and re-enact what they had seen or experienced while consuming the fictional works. While these accusations may seem preposterous now, newer forms of art and entertainment are now imputed to have the same effect: "The longer the author is dead, the more likely the violence is considered to be art" (Kunczik/Zipfel 2006: 28, transl.).[47] But even in the old days, not everybody was opposed to the representation of violence in art: In antiquity, it was Aristotle who countered these statements with the idea of catharsis, claiming that media violence keeps the audience from actually wanting to commit violent acts in real life. These two positions form the opposite ends of an immensely broad debate and can only begin to give an idea of the intensity of the discussion that has been held in the public as well as the scholarly discourse ever since. The emerging field of media effects studies, which often combines psychological and sociological methods and has yielded a variety of empirical findings, has often contributed to the public discourse with polemic statements about the effects of media violence.[48] However, by and large, years of media effects research have not yet yielded any definitive evidence of the effects of media violence (cf. Otto 2008: 25f.).

The desire for this empirical evidence is especially strong after spectacular acts of violence such as school shootings. Unsurprisingly, quite a number of seminal works in media effects research begin with references to school shootings, as these events quite reliably serve to reboot the debate about the negative influence of media violence on today's youths. Kunczik and Zipfel state that the media itself frequently contributes to the propagation of reductive understandings of media violence and its effects. Spectacular acts of violence such as school shootings seem to provide proof of the dangers of media violence – ironically, however, they are also covered extensively because of the massive news value they hold for the news stations (cf. Kunczik/Zipfel 2006: 15ff.).

In a discourse that is overwhelmed by the lack of rationale and that appears to be stumbling over the shortcomings of the simple explanations that are repeated after every new school shooting, discussing media violence is a convinc-

---

[47] For German overviews about the debate, see Kunczik/Zipfel (2006) and Otto (2008). For an overview from a German cultural studies perspective, see Andree (2006a). For an overview about the reception of film with regard to media violence in the US, see Philipps (2008).

[48] As Isabell Otto points out in her seminal study, the term 'media violence' is already highly suggestive: 'Media violence', she shows, only *pretends* to be referring to (mostly fictional) *depictions* of violence. Implicitly – and sometimes even explicitly – this term implies a direct causal link to a specific form of actual violence, such as school shootings. The term, she points out, is a simple condensation or a formula that already implies and imputes actual effects of these media representations on real-world violence (cf. Otto 2008: 33f.).

ingly logical reaction: School shootings are a contemporary phenomenon and their connection to changes in media culture can hardly be denied. Most of school shooters take advantage of new media forms – they purchase weapons via the internet, upload videos on YouTube (cf. Paton 2012, Grzeszyk 2012), and in some cases have their own websites. Additionally, the intensity of the debate is fueled by the fact that everyone involved in the discourse can directly relate to the subject of discussion, since everyone has their own experience of media consumption and can therefore take a stand for or against media violence – often, so it seems, according to personal preference and taste. Reductive ideas and rather crude arguments relying on cause and effect can consequently be found in commentaries, popular scientific texts, and TV documentaries. As Kunczik and Zipfel criticize, these widely spread assumptions about media effects are an impediment to the dissemination of scientific facts, which may be less spectacular or clear-cut, but are empirically proven according to more scientific standards (Kunczik/Zipfel 2006: 19).

Infamous, too, are the findings about certain school shooters' affinity for video games such as *Doom* or *Counter-Strike*; years down the line, the debate about the effects of these very graphic and interactive forms of media violence has not yet come to rest.[49] Ferguson and Ivory relate this disproportionate reaction to violent video games – and media violence in general, for that matter – to the dynamics of moral panic, drawing upon Stanley Cohen's concept.[50] "Moral panics are commonly understood as the manufacture of exaggerated fears toward a 'folk devil', against which there is moral repugnance" and often focus on issues that involve youth and crime (Ferguson/Ivory 2012: 59).[51] In most cases, "it is the elite or powerful of society itself that 'spins' the moral panic wheel, with preexisting moral beliefs setting the stage for the rest of the process. This may take the form of expressed disgust, offense, or devaluation ('Why would anyone want to play that?')" (ibid.: 60).

Once the wheel has started to spin, research findings are frequently collected in accordance with the preexisting and predominant beliefs and ideas (ibid.: 61). In the case of the media violence debate, this can clearly be observed: Otherwise inconclusive evidence, such as reports about the hours spent with certain video games or a preference for a certain film or music genre, is widely assumed to be the causal factor for the gruesome acts of violence committed by a miniscule

---

[49] For a concise overview, see Ferguson/Ivory (2012).
[50] This concept has become essential for research on phenomena of youth violence and was introduced in Cohen's seminal work *Folk Devils and Moral Panics* (2002 [1972]).
[51] See also Muschert (2007).

number of adolescents.[52] As a result, as with most of the popular explanations mentioned above, measures to regain control – or at least the feeling of control – over these gruesome events are then taken. This has frequently led to debates about stricter censorship methods, outcries to restrict control over who purchases violent media, and even calls to ban media with graphic violence altogether.[53] These outcries, too, can be put into perspective by turning to the historical debate about media violence.

Kendall Philipps points out that, while the tension between the regulation of depictions of violence and the human desire to watch or to hear about graphic violence predates film, the depiction of violence in moving images on screen has endowed the debate with a new dimension (cf. Philipps 2008: 53). While Goethe's *The Sorrows of Young Werther* even led to the coinage of the term *Werther Effect* to describe the increased suicide rates after the release of popular media artifacts depicting suicides,[54] the emergence of violent films gave rise to even more heated debate about copycat crimes. This was especially the case with regard to juveniles, who were traditionally thought to consume these violent fictions more excessively than adults. Violence in film has been blamed for the theft and train robberies in the early 20th century, the increase of violence

---

[52] Ferguson and Ivory further point out that the evaluation of this alleged evidence also contains a dimension of stereotyping that is related to race and class of the shooters. While youths from minorities consume much more violent media (i.e. video games) than white middle-class youths, violence committed by adolescents from minorities is only seldom connected to their media consumption. "The tendency for people to look to violent video games as a cause for high-profile crimes committed by middle-class white youth despite the proportionally greater prevalence of video game among non-white youth may be a result of some people's stereotypical associations between racial minorities and violent crime. This type of stereotyping may lead to a tendency for people to accept violent crime with little explanation when it is perpetrated by those stereotypically associated with it, but seek explanations (such as violent video games) for the crimes when they conflict with our stereotypical perceptions or where violent criminals come from and look like." (Ferguson/Ivory 2012: 59f.). This critique had previously been levelled by Kidd and Meyer (2002), who state that "[m]edia portrayals of youth violence often depict African-American males as the offender. As a result, the expectation that juvenile violence was only a problem for minority youths created a false sense of security among many majority status communities" (Kidd/Meyer 2002).
[53] In Germany, for example, the school shootings in Erfurt and Emsdetten, where both perpetrators turned out to be passionate gamers, sparked heated debates about the availability of violent video games and outcries for stricter laws from politicians and scholars. Mosel and Waldschmidt (2010) present an informative comment on these rather frantic reactions.
[54] Regarding youth violence, hordes of savage juveniles were said to roam the German woods in murderous manner to 'realize' Schiller's play *Die Räuber* in 1785 (cf. Andree 2006: 182ff.).

after the emergence of the gangster film genre in the late 1920s and, consequently, mass murder in the 1990s (cf. Philipps 2008: 49ff).

Further, film has been blamed for sexual immorality and a general decline in values, and the reaction to the debate about violence in film has been led with not only a moral but also a regulatory impetus. The debate, Philipps points out, follows similar patterns

> [I]ssues of criminality and violence have long been conceptualized in relation to social scientific or medical discourses. Whereas concerns over sex were often articulated through a discourse of religion and morality, violence and criminality, with their behavioral definitions, have consistently been understood as medical, sociological, or psychological issues that require a 'solution'. (2008: 52f.)

Supposed sexual immorality may present a challenge to society and confront the public with changing value systems and norms. Violence, however, is seen as "threat to the very fabric of society" (Philipps 2008: 52), and therefore needs to be controlled and directed into the right, i.e. regulated, channels. As mentioned earlier, in a society that understands itself as non-violent, acts of excessive violence or a subjectively perceived sudden increase in violence must be the result of some outside influence. Because copycat crimes adhere to this striking logic, they receive considerable public attention: These adolescents simply re-enact what they have seen on screen. While the public has applied these notions most prominently to cultural products, scholarly works have recently begun to debate the journalistic depictions of school shooters and their attacks.

One of the ideas that has emerged within the school shooting discourse with regard to the media depiction of school shootings and the perpetrators is the notion of the 'Superstar Killer', as coined by German researcher Frank J. Robertz (cf. Robertz 2004: 183). This notion encompasses both the depiction of actual school shooters in the news and in media coverage of school shootings. Media coverage has often been criticized for focusing disproportionally on the perpetrators and for neglecting the victims of the shooting. As a result, scholars have pointed out, the media may make it easier for other troubled adolescents to relate to the school shooters, as school shootings are presented as an actual opportunity to gain fame and notoriety (cf. e.g., Muschert 2007, Sitzer 2013, Böckler et al. 2012).[55] The 'Superstar Killer', by which Robertz means the fantasized prototype of an infamous and violent avenger, is comprised of various media depictions of hypermasculine killers and, naturally, of school shooters.

---

[55] For the role of fame and notoriety will further be explicated in Chapter 3 of this study.

Because auf the way in which school shooters are portrayed, Böckler et al. warn, "the perpetrators, who often find themselves in the role of powerless outsiders and losers, believe that a school shooting is their *only* chance of breaking out of their marginal status and attaining control, power and popularity" (Böckler et al. 2012: 37). With Eric Harris and Dylan Klebold, a "new brand of perpetrator" emerged, which quickly reached the status of the "perfect villain" and, as Muschert puts it, the "juvenile superpredator" (Muschert 2007a: 363). This should be viewed critically in the conglomerate of factors that may lead up to school shootings. The popularity of former school shooter is a spectacular 'way out' for juveniles who may have already pondered the idea of committing an act of violence.

The perception of some school shooters to be part of an infamous 'gang', part of a 'tradition' of school shooters, and members of network of like-minded people, must be seen as highly problematic (cf. Böckler et al. 2012: 38).[56] Media coverage may help to establish school shooting tropes that can be picked up by future school shooters in their planning, self-understanding and justification of their attack. Because of this, researchers have been debating the effect of perpetrator-centered news coverage of school shootings for years, suggesting that granting the attackers the status of infamous villains could be a factor that motivates crime. It is only in the past few years that increasingly victim-focused news coverage has emerged (cf. Schildkraut/Muschert 2014). Through this shift in focus, the shooters' carefully planned "strategy for media attention" (Kellner 2008: 118) is foiled, which can be seen as reaction to a growing awareness of the dynamics of school shootings as mediatized phenomena.[57]

As this volume focuses on how closely school shootings and media are connected and seeks to show the various potential functions and effects that fictional works can have on society, it cannot be denied that media content has an impact. Culture is not only transmitted by but also constructed in cultural and media artifacts, and the cultural imaginary is essentially constructed out of fic-

---

[56] As Böckler et al. point out, the perception of Dylan's and Klebold's deed as a "subversive act of rebellion" (2012: 38) mostly came from the shooters' portrayal of themselves as avengers of the bullied and the weak, "acting in the name of a greater collective" (ibid.).
[57] Schildkraut and Muschert compared the news coverage and the moral discourse about school shootings that followed the Columbine shooting and the Sandy Hook shooting in Newtown. They found not only that little information was released about Adam Lanza in the media, but that the focus was on telling the stories of the victims and educators. However, this can also be understood in relation to the victims of the shooting, who were considered particularly newsworthy due to their race, age, socioeconomic status and the way they were killed (Schildkraut/Muschert 2014: 36ff).

tions. Individuals engage in processes of lifelong learning that transcend early childhood and even adolescence, as their imaginary is continually expanded. These learning processes, of course, may also include the 'learning' of violent behavior (cf. Kunczik/Zipfel 2006: 14). While one position in media effects research maintains that the correlation between media violence and actual violence is inconsequential, many scholars agree that consuming vast amounts of violent media content might make some people prone to violent behavior, when they incorporate a variety of other risk factors.[58] In extreme cases, school shootings as medially transmitted strategies for problem solving may seem like a possible solution to individual struggles,[59] as "our culture offers copious illustrations of this solution. Not only are fictional models for violent action provided by films, music, and books etc., but the simplified portrayals in the news media also create concrete templates for identification" (Robertz 2013: 122). This notion can be supported by similarities in school shooters' attire, taste in music and films, choice of weaponry, the *modus operandi* of the attacks and statements made by the perpetrators.[60] While these similarities can be understood in relation to a complex interplay between medially transmitted images of school shooters and dynamics of idolization that I will elaborate on in Chapter 3, they can also be used to support the thesis that a school shooting trope exists and validate concerns that a violent prototype has been established.

2.2.2 Prevalent Approaches to Fictional Representations of Excessive Violence

School shooters have traditionally referred to media depictions of acts of violence; they have quoted previous perpetrators and have referenced the style, self-perception and self-representation of their fictional as well as real idols. Even the fact that school shooters began to kill themselves or had themselves killed by the police after their attacks can be understood as a reference or trend set by prototypical shooters – namely Harris and Klebold. All these observations suggest a causal relation or at least a link between media consumption and school shootings.

---

[58] For one concise and insightful description of possible risk factors, see Robertz (2013).
[59] In this regard, the oversimplifying causal explanations that are disseminated via mass media prove to be highly problematic. If school shooters are constantly represented as victims of bullying and their behavior as thereby justified, for example, other bullied adolescents may in very rare cases relate to the strategy applied by previous school shooters.
[60] For the shooter's shared preferences in music and film, see Kiilaakosi/Oksanen (2011).

As a result, the media violence debate has gained become even more heated in the school shooting discourse, as fictional representations of violence are often suspected to provide 'templates for action'. Previous studies have reinforced the notion of school shootings as clear-cut copycat crimes. Along with the explanatory attempts mentioned before, fictional representations of excessive violence can in fact been seen as a central culprit in the 'blame game', which insists that acts of excessive violence, which are perceived as unprecedented in their cruelty, nihilism and degree of premeditation, cannot come out of nowhere. While this is an assumption that the present volume shares, the simple conclusion that is frequently drawn from this observation must be criticized for constituting another reductive explanation. As with the other modes of explanation, the causal argument clearly falls short: If the shooters had not consumed representations of excessive violence, the crime would not have been committed. Loren Coleman, who promoted the term of the copycat effect in relation to school shootings, states:

> Suicide clusters of the 1980s would be replaced by the school shootings of the 1990s, almost all conducted by suicidal male youth. The copycat-effect had merely shifted its target as the media had shifted its focus. School violence has been around for a long time, but the media-driven contagion of modern school shootings dates back to Feburary 2, 1996, when Barry Loukaitis, a 14-year-old boy in Moses Lake, Washington, killed two students and a math teacher. He ended his rampage by saying, 'This sure beats algebra, doesn't it?' Loukaitis had taken the expression directly form the Stephen King novel, *Rage*, which he had really liked and which was about a school killing. Loukaitis said his murderous loss of control was inspired by *Rage*, Pearl Jam's music video *Jeremy* and the movies *Natural Born Killers* and *The Basketball Diaries*. Unfortunately, the explosive media attention to Loukaitis's school shooting triggered a series of similar events. Today, Stephen King says he wishes he had never written *Rage*. (2004: 4)[61]

In this quote, three of the most discussed references to fictional representations of excessive violence are mentioned: *Natural Born Killers* (Oliver Stone, USA;

---

61 While opinions differ as to the actual similarity of Loukaitis' quote to any dialogue in *Rage*, Stephen King himself stated: "There are factors in the Carneal case which make it doubtful that *Rage* was the defining factor, but I fully recognize that it is in my own self-interest to feel just that way; that I am prejudiced in my own behalf. I also recognize the fact that a novel such as *Rage* may act as an accelerant on a troubled mind; one cannot divorce the presence of my book in that kid's locker from what he did any more than one can divorce the gruesome sex-murders committed by Ted Bundy from his extensive collection of bondage-oriented porno magazines. To argue free speech in the face of such an obvious linkage (or to suggest that others may obtain a catharsis from such material which allows them to be atrocious only in their fantasies) seems to me immoral" (King 1999). For a discussion of *Rage* and its connection to school shootings, see also Burger (2016: 73ff.).

1994), *The Basketball Diaries* (Scott Kalvert, USA 1995) and Steven King's novel *Rage* (1977). Because the references to these two works of fiction are among the most obvious, alongside *The Matrix* (Lana and Andrew Wachowski, USA 1999) and later *Elephant*, they have become emblematic of the effects that depictions of rampages and killing sprees may have on misguided adolescents. This has been discussed in media, scholarly and even legal discourse to varying degrees. While the Moses Lake shooting did not receive international media attention, Eric Harris's and Dyland Klebold's attack on Columbine High School in Littleton, Colorado, in April 1999 did. Somehow, this particular school shooting "struck deep psychic blows, not only in citizens' individual psyches, but also in the collective sentiment" (Schildkraut/Muschert 2014: 24).

Columbine did not only become a prototype of a hitherto unimaginable dimension of cruelty (Harris and Klebold had actually planned to blow up the school, but failed to build the time bombs correctly), it became the most researched school shooting and received the most media coverage (cf. Schildkraut/Muschert 2014). Because of the rise of the internet and omnipresence of cable television and live coverage, news about Columbine spread quickly, not only in America, but the whole Western world. Up until this day, Columbine is regarded as one of the biggest stories of its time, even though other school shootings (such as the shooting in Moses Lake) had occurred before it and did not receive comparable media attention (cf. Muschert/Ragnedda 2011: 352). The debates that were sparked by the Columbine shooting were further pushed by the unprecedented access to the shooter's personal statements: As families of the Columbine victims mistrusted the Jefferson County Sherriff's Office, which was in charge of the investigation, a lawsuit forced the officials to release all the files about Columbine one year after the shooting. Both Harris and Klebold left behind journals, which also were released.[62] Of their infamous videotapes, the so-called *Basement Tapes*, only transcripts are available (cf. Langman

---

[62] Pages from the journals and other Columbine documents can now be found and accessed at http://www.acolumbinesite.com. The author of the site, C. Shepard, collected information when it became accessible and even archived writings from Harris's personal website, still online at the time. As for his motives, he states: "I knew the true story was lurking out there somewhere so I started digging around, online and off. I put up a website on a free web host: A single site with a list of the known names of the dead, updated as they became available, and information about where the event had happened. [...] I suppose what continues to hold my interest the most – apart from having a digital horde of information left to post – is that I'm waiting to see whether Jefferson County will ever release the infamous Basement Tapes to the public. That, I think, represents the final chapter in this tragic book of history. It's the last episode left to be seen. It won't offer much closure but it might provide a little more insight and understanding." (Shepard n.d.)

2014b). However, images from the shooter's videos and writings from their journals and personal websites have by now become infamous.

The insights into a shooter's psyche and the meticulous planning made the event all the more shocking and brought forward new issues for debate. Particular artifacts of popular culture became suspicious, sparked especially by the fact that Harris and Klebold named the day of their attack 'NBK', a reference to *Natural Born Killers:*

> When I go NBK and people say things like, 'oh it was so tragic' or 'oh he is crazy!' or 'It was so bloody.' I think, so the fuck what you think that's a bad thing? Just because mumsy and dadsy told you blood and violence is bad, you think it's a fucking law of nature? Wrong. (Harris, qtd. in Langman 2014: 3)

But not only Harris and Klebold were fans: Michael Carneal, who came before them, and later Finland's shooter Pekka Erik Auvinen from Jokela, too, were admirers of Oliver Stone's feature film (cf. Kiilakoski/Oksanen 2011: 261). Orange High School shooter Alvaro Castillo can allegedly be heard in a video he took of himself while watching it, in which he "laughs loudly at the most gruesome parts, and at other times narrates the scene or demonstrates his familiarity with the dialogue by chiming in, word for word, with the actors" (Lieberman 2008: 210).[63] As a result of these observations, public attention was drawn to popular culture as one of the culprits, with Oliver Stone at the center of criticism. A number of journalists and authors of popular science works, such as Joseph Lieberman, claimed to have found a way of explaining and preventing school shootings and used the shooters' open affinity for Stone's work to craft a clear cause-and-effect argument:

> One can appreciate the experimental cinematic elements in Natural Born Killers that made it so appealing to film critics of its day [...], but those same innovative techniques – psychedelic special effects, segues into animation and sitcom sequences, facial distortions, alternating color with black and white – also pushed its popularity among a small but growing demographic of youth partial to gratuitous violence, hallucinogenic drugs, casual sex, and semiautomatic weapons. (Lieberman 2008: 211)

---

[63] As Castillo also films himself while watching footage from the Columbine shooting and openly refers to Harris and Klebold in his videos, his fandom can best be understood as relying on the cultural script of school shootings, on which I will elaborate later, which enabled school shooters to feel connected and have a sense of community, as Kiilakoski and Oksanen (2011) have argued.

Passages like this reveal another discursive particularity of school shootings: the general and very traditional (cf. Cohen 2002 [1972]) distrust of younger generations or particular subcultures within youth culture. Combined with the incredibly rapid cultural changes brought about by the internet in the 1990s, an air of misunderstanding and distrust permeated the school shooting discourse (cf. Kellner 2008: 76ff). Naturally, this only helped to facilitate the finger-pointing at popular cultural artifacts. However, the artifacts that had been debated bore a rather symbolic value, such as Marilyn Manson, who was blamed for having influenced the killers and the Goth culture in general. Neither Harris nor Klebold, however, were fans, and the links to the local Goth culture were limited as well (cf. Kiilakoski/Oksanen 2011: 253).[64] *Natural Born Killers* must also be understood as a symbolic representative for a variety of fictional representations of excessive violence. Up until this day, it is used to explore the relationship between school shootings and popular culture.[65]

As mentioned earlier, the idea of the copycat effect quickly began to dominate the debate. The *Werther effect* became prominent all over again, but with a new urgency, as Katherine S. Newman and colleagues observe:[66] "Exposure to violent media has increased dramatically among our youth over the last decade, pushing media influence forward as a prime explanation for the string of school shootings in the mid- to late 1990s" (2005: 70). This focus on media violence quickly developed a dynamic of its own, for example when Michael Carneal, who had mentioned *The Basketball Diaries* as inspiration for his shooting later said that he only referred to the film because police officials directly asked him "whether he had seen or read anything reminiscent of what he had done" (ibid.: 71). Of course, like most adolescents in this day and age, he had. And that is exactly where the 'prime explanation' falls short, as "[m]illions of young people play video games full of fistfights, blazing guns, and body slams. Bodies litter the floor in many of our most popular films. Yet only a minuscule fraction of the consumers become violent. Hence, if there is an effect, children are not all equally susceptible to it" (ibid).

---

64 See also Larkin 2007: 181ff. and Chapter 4 of this study.
65 For a thorough analysis of *Natural Born Killers* and its relation to school shootings, see Grzeszyk (2012: 222ff.)
66 For Loren Coleman, the direct links are obvious, as the following quote shows: "Trench-coat-clad Leonardo DiCaprio's use of a shotgun to slaughter his classmates in a scene in *The Basketball Diaries* and Keanu Reeves's (also in black trench coat) use of high-powered firepower in *The Matrix* have both been directly linked to the school shooting in Paducah, Kentucky, and at Columbine, in Littleton, Colorado" (2004: 222).

While it can be assumed that certain risk factors may make a small percentage of adolescents more susceptible to these influences, the question then remains how this 'miniscule fraction of consumers' can be understood as directly influenced by having seen or read about acts of excessive violence. Most research on media violence surrounding school shootings does not clearly differentiate between media violence in general and depictions of excessive, rampage-like attacks or killing sprees in particular. If it is assumed, however, that media content does provide templates for action or inspires troubled boys to pick up a gun and imitate what they have seen on screen or read in a book, it quickly becomes clear that instead of there being a simple causal link, greater cultural dynamics are likely at play. Only very few studies have discussed the relevance of fictional depictions of excessive violence and, consequently, of school shootings. As a point of departure for my analyses, it is imperative, then, to elaborate on the two most prevalent approaches that have included fictional artifacts, namely German scholar Frank J. Robertz's understanding of the relevance of phantasy for school shooters and Katherine S. Newman and colleague's concept of the cultural script of school shootings.

The Relevance of Fantasy and Over-Identification to School Shooters

In his problematic yet influential approach to school shootings, Frank J. Robertz understands fantasy (and the fictional elements included in a shooter's fantasy) as a crucial aspect in the genesis of school shootings. He operates with the idea of the 'typical' school shooter, which is deduced by taking into consideration a broad variety of studies about school shootings from various disciplines. His framework is based on theories of control that assume that deviation from norms is not an exception but rather the rule of human behavior; only intact relationships and a strong bond to society and its values make a human want to pursue their own goals *within* a given society (Robertz 2004: 126ff).

In Robertz's approach, typical school shooters come from dysfunctional families in which the adolescent perpetrators "felt out place, abandoned, and lonely" (Robertz 2013: 107f.) and usually perceive themselves as "objects of victimization, threats, and exclusion" (ibid.: 108). As established earlier, this is not always the case, and Robertz is well aware of the difficulties in evaluating the perpetrator's experiences from the outside. Yet, as mentioned before, it is important to bear in mind that it is not the actual marginalization that affects the adolescents, but rather the *perception* of oneself as being marginalized or ostracized by their peers, family and within the existing (educational) system.[67] A striking number of scholars from different disciplines, including media effects researchers, prevention experts and sociologists, have agreed that this perceived marginalization is one of the most crucial risk factors for violent behavior in an adolescent. Robertz stresses another aspect of special importance: the deterioration of social bonds.[68] This erosion, he argues, is perceived as highly dramatic by the adolescents and this perceived lack of control and social rejection that result from it are a recipe for volatility: The adolescent does not see any positive prospects for his life. As Luke Woodham stated: "I didn't really see my life go any further. I thought it was all over with...I couldn't find a reason no to do it" (qtd. in Robertz 2004: 180).

The situation for the adolescent becomes unbearable. For Robertz, one means of escaping this unbearable state is to "take refuge in violent phantasies which become more intense, more specific, and more detailed as the time of the shooting draws closer" (Robertz 2013: 110). "Phantasies", he points out, "are such powerful tools that they enable us to remain functional even in the most extreme situations. [...] In situations that are difficult to endure, the experience of reality can be softened by means of mitigating phantasies" (Robertz 2013: 112).

---

[67] A number of school shooters therefore publish statements and manifestos against the system, positioning themselves within a rather crude mixture of political ideologies and utterly antidemocratic views; their ideologies, however, are mostly too incoherent to be taken seriously. Regarding the self-images and self-narratives of school shooters and the reception by their devotees on the internet, see Böckler/Seeger (2010), Böckler et al. (2013).

[68] Social bonds, as defined by Travis Hirschi, comprise of a variety of factors, namely "*attachment* (emotional bonding to other people), *commitment* (a feeling of obligation), *involvement* (participation in conventional activities), and *belief* (faith in conservative values)" (Robertz 2013.: 108). Attachment refers to the totality of emotional bonds to family, peers and groups of friends that lead to a feeling of dependence on other people's opinions, commitment to the idea that adolescents consider the consequences of their actions and would not do anything to endanger their status-quo – given that they believe it is worth sustaining. Involvement, on the other hand, signifies the inclusion of a person in socially accepted, conservative activities that reinforce a feeling of belonging and achievement and may also keep an adolescent busy enough to not become deviant. Belief describes the acceptance "by the adolescent of a conventional system of norms and values that is shared with the social environment" (Robertz 2013: 108f.). Here, Robertz clearly stresses a preventative effect: If a student, he suggests, shows weak social bonds, i.e. withdraws from social activities or expresses disagreement with social values or norms, adults should make an assessment of the social bonds and, if need be, strengthen them. This, however, is extremely difficult, as this theory implies that adolescents who choose not to subscribe to this rather normative understanding of social interaction are in danger of being judged prematurely. As pointed out earlier, suspecting juveniles who live outside the conservative norm are deviant or even to be prone to lethal violence may only intensify the feeling of marginalization for those who already feel that they "do not fit in".

For school shooters, as many of their journals and other writings show, everyday life is perceived as insufferable. The question remains, however, how one can withdraw into fantasies and how the fictional representations of excessive violence might play a role within these dynamics.

Elaborating on this, Robertz draws upon a theory by Reinhart Lempp, who coined the term 'secondary reality' to describe a subjective reality originating in early childhood and existing next to the shared 'pimary reality' (cf. Lempp 2006: 22f.). After some time, children learn to distinguish between these two realities so as to communicate adequately with adults and other reference persons, but maintain the secondary reality in order to compensate for the shortcomings of 'reality' by withdrawing into daydreams and fantasies (Robertz 2004, 190ff.; 2013: 113f.). While fantasies of revenge, wishful thinking, and even violence are not automatically harmful or dangerous, the school shooters' fantasies are here understood to be particularly vivid. Robertz's assumption is that school shooters have a very specific fantasy, which is extraordinarily active and filled with 'especially violent content' (cf. Robertz 2007: 14; see also Robertz/Kahr 2016: 40f.).

Fantasies, Robertz is well aware, are almost impossible to study empirically due to their individual nature. They can, however, be traced in an individual's creative output, writing and drawings (cf. Robertz/Wickenhäuser 2007: 74f.). The creative output by shooters like Eric Harris and Dylan Klebold or Seung-Hui Cho, which is frequently extremely violent, can therefore be understood as evidence of the extraordinarily violent fantasies that the shooters engaged in during the planning of the attack. In the worst case, Robertz and Wickenhäuser (2007: 76) argue, the experience of their fantasies may become so intense that it may even leads to a short-term loss of control of their own imagination. Consequently, the shooters may believe to be acting in their secondary reality, while they are actually acting in their primary reality, thereby affecting and hurting other people directly, maybe without even realizing it.

For this fatal failure to distinguish between a primary and a secondary reality to happen, Robertz insists, the adolescent must be extremely vulnerable and suffering from a lack of both social and personal resources to help them cope with hurtful experiences of rejection and a perceived loss of control over their lives (Robertz 2004: 222, Böckler/Seeger 2010: 62ff.). This extreme vulnerability and a possibly dangerous accumulation of risk factors are also frequently understood to be the basis for the negative effects of media violence (cf. Kunczik/Zipfel 2006, Robertz/Kahr 2016: 48f.). For Robertz, media violence, particularly representations of extreme violence, plays a crucial role in the genesis of school shootings, as he assumes that the gradual withdrawal into the secondary reality can be induced by the consumption of violent media, especially video games and films. In the case of medially induced withdrawal into a secondary reality, the process is the result of a gradually growing identification with a heroic role model, i.e. a character from a movie or the avatar of a video game.

The adolescent begins to identify with this role model, which Robertz identifies as a hypermasculine male, who does not experience but causes fear (Robertz 2004: 193). In his fantasy, the adolescent begins to go through scenes that hurt and humiliate him in his primary reality – only that in secondary reality he can solve them the way his hypermasculine role model would. Following Lempp, Robertz emphasizes that some partial transmissions of these fantasies do not necessarily motivate the adolescent to act out the entire violent fantasy, i.e. the school shooting. However, if the primary reality becomes more and more unbearable, the adolescent may fixate on the much more glorious secondary reality and, at some point, may not be able to return from there but remains in the fantasy of the heroic hypermasculine character.[69] In cases of lethal violence such as school shootings, the consequences of this assumed failure to distinguish between wishful thinking and real life are extreme. This is also one aspect of Robertz's concept that is criticized, as the issue of responsibility becomes rather difficult to work with: The shooter may have acted within a fantasy world, but the victims are real persons who are robbed of their lives. Moreover, while in the case of historical *amok* amnesia has been reported much more frequently (cf. Spores 1988), there is no compelling evidence that a majority of school shooters did not know what they were doing at the time of the killing spree or later could not remember what they had done.

Robertz's approach has influenced a number of studies, especially in cultural studies, where Heiko Christians (2008) and Martin Andree (2006a), among others, have drawn upon the idea of over-identification with a fictional role model caused by the excessive and highly repetitive consumption of fictional representations of excessive violence. This excessive consumption has been reported in the case of Orange High School shooter Alvaro Castillo with *Natural Born Killers* and later with Jeffrey Weise, who was said to have repeatedly watched Gus van Sant's *Elephant* before his shooting at Red Lake Senior High School (cf. Newman/Fox 2009: 1290). From a cultural studies perspective and, consequently, within the scope of this volume, this is of special interest, as this argument is based on an understanding of the effects and functions of fiction that suggests a very direct and even causal effect of a certain mode of reception of

---

[69] Reinhart Lempp subscribes to the thesis that especially fictional moving images lead to over-identification with what is seen on the screen; the adolescent really believes that she or he has become the role model seen in the film or video game. However, Lempp admits that it is unknown why and how certain adolescents over-identify and others do not (2006: 24).

fictional works. Fiction, as this understanding suggests, allows a human being to 'disappear', to be submerged in a work of fiction to such a degree that the fictional world can no longer be distinguished from the extratextual or 'real' world. However, this shall be discussed in greater detail in section 3.2, where I will turn to the concept of function of fiction in general and fictional representations of school shootings in particular. According to Robertz's approach, these representations contribute to the fantasy prototype of the 'superstar killer' outlined above, which is akin to Kellner's, Newman's or Linder's notion of the hypermasculine 'macho villain' (cf. Kellner 2008, 2012; Newman et al. 2005, Linder 2014). Through representations of school shootings in fictional works, Robertz criticizes, the school shooter has become a 'subcultural icon' (cf. Robertz 2007/Wickenhäuser: 81) in and of itself. Instead of gathering role models from more general representations of excessive violence, as in *Natural Born Killers*, the consequence may be that school shooters can now feed their fantasy with depictions of real-live as well as fictionalized school shooters as heroic villains and can hope to become famous as the protagonist of a blockbuster themselves.

The question that remains unanswered is why a small minority of adolescent consumers of certain fictional works are prone to withdrawing themselves from their primary reality to the extent that they slowly lose the ability to return to 'real life'. In this regard, apart from referring to a perceived loss of control and a lack of sable relationships, Robertz's approach does not offer compelling arguments (cf. Robertz/Kahr 2016: 47ff.). Nevertheless, considering the media consumption of previous school shooters, assuming that these fictional artifacts could have shaped the shooter's fantasy which is then merely 'acted out' could serve as rather simple explanation. School shooters' intense engagement with hypermasculine characters and fictional content cannot and should not be denied. However, this observation does not point to an easy explanation nor does it allow blame to be assigned to any fictional works consumed by the perpetrators. Rather, Robertz's observations can serve as the groundwork for a broader observation of cultural dynamics that may help to understand why an adolescent may feel the desire to identify with the hypermasculine ideal of a man. This leads to another approach that considers the role of fictional representations in excessive violence and school shootings: Katherine S. Newman and colleagues' concept of the cultural script, which directly refers to the role of fiction, but redirects attention to broader cultural problems in which these fictions are only one of many elements.

The Cultural Script of School Shootings

Katherine Newman and her colleagues have developed an elaborate, highly acclaimed and widely received approach to understanding what they call 'the social roots of school shootings'. Relying on extensive field research conducted in the towns of Heath and Westside, which both witnessed a school shooting in the late 1990s, they were able to carve out "five *necessary but not sufficient conditions*" (Newman et al. 2005: 229): the shooter's self-perception as marginalized, psychological problems, a failure of surveillance systems that should have identified the adolescents as highly troubled, gun availability and the *cultural script* that suggests an armed attack as a possible solution to problems (ibid: 229f). With these factors, Newman and colleagues have created a comprehensive approach to understanding the genesis of school shootings and state that "[a]cknowledging that school shootings are the product of a combination of factors moves us away from futile discussions about the explanatory power of any single cause" (ibid.: 230). As the previous subchapters have shown, popular attempts to find explanations have always failed to establish a clear chain of causality and convincing motive for school shootings. The multicausality in Newman and colleague's approach is a far more differentiated view that considers shortcomings of society as such and locates the cultural and social factors that can lead to these acts of excessive violence without assigning blame to a single institution, law or industry. At the same time, they stress that these factors are never sufficient to "predict which communities will be next or which students will explode" (ibid.) and admit that at least one of their factors can hardly be tested: The notion of the cultural script, they point out, has to remain rather abstract. In the scope of this project, however, the cultural script provides a very fertile approach to understanding how fictional representations of excessive violence relate to school shootings.

Newman and colleagues use the term 'cultural script' in a highly specific way, as a brief look at the general understanding of scripts shows: The notion of 'scripts' is frequently used synonymously with the term 'schemata' (Gavins 2005: 520), while schema theory uses the term schema more as a "superordinate label for a broad range of knowledge structures, including frames, scenarios, scripts and plans" (Emmott/Alexander 2014). These notions have been of particular interest for research in artificial intelligence (AI), where knowledge storage needs to be organized, but is also used to various ends in psychology, linguistics and in the study of ways of worldmaking and cognitive narratology in the cultural studies. While literary studies use the idea of schemata and scripts mostly in the context of how texts are understood and gaps are filled in by the readers (cf. Nünning 2014: 153), the notion of 'script' more generally refers to organizations of knowledge about what to expect and how to handle everyday life situations (cf. Schank/Abelson 1977: 41). Drawing upon findings from AI, Roger Schank and Robert Abelson (1977) have developed a widely acknowledged theory of knowledge scripts from the perspective of cognitive psychology, which Abelson summarizes as follows:

The casual definition of a script is a 'stereotyped sequence of events familiar to the individual'. Implicit in this definition are two powerful sources of constraint. One is the notion of an event sequence, which implies the causal chaining of enablements and results for physical events and of initiations and reasons for mental events [...]. The other constraint generator comes from ideas of stereotypy and familiarity. That an event sequence is stereotyped implies the absence of fortuitous events. Also, for events to be often repeated implies that there is some set of standard individual and institutional goals which gives rise to the repetition. (Abelson, qtd. in Quinn/Holland 1987: 19f.)

Scripts, as temporally-ordered schemata, are "basic building blocks of our everyday understanding" and, as "standardized sequences of events [...] fill in our understanding of frequently recurring experiences", as Naomi Quinn and Dorothy Holland put it (1987: 19). Quinn and Holland introduce the term 'cultural model', which draws upon Schank and Albeson's definition, but stresses the culturally specific nature of knowledge. Very similar to the idea of the script, their model deals with "how knowledge is organized in culturally standardized and hence familiar event sequences [...]. These 'stories' include prototypical events, prototypical roles for actors, prototypical entities, and more. They involve, in effect, whole worlds in which things work, actors perform, and events unfold in a simplified and wholly acceptable manner" (Quinn/Holland 1987: 20).[70] This definition includes an aspect that is especially interesting for understanding cultural scripts, which signify a broad, simplifying and culturally accepted manner.

School shootings, of course, are by no means acceptable. They can, however, be understood as *based* on a widely accepted script, which Katherine Newman and colleagues include in their theory – the script that connects manhood with violent behavior: "Journalists and social critics have suggested that exposure to violent films, television, and videos is at the heart of rampage shootings in school. We believe that the media plays a role, but not quite the one that has been assigned to it" (2005: 153). Instead of simply blaming gory films and violent video games for causing school shootings, they raise a very important question: Why are school shootings highly gender-specific and tied to certain images of

---

[70] As it will become clear in Chapter 2.3, however, scripts and narratives cannot be confused: While the script designates the cognitive aspects of understanding and approaching school shootings, narratives establish causality by ordering the events.

masculinity? Indeed, one of the most obvious characteristics of school shooters is their gender, as nearly all school shooters who actually went through with their attack have been male.[71] With this in mind, the authors ask why girls who consume the same violent media do not seem to understand a school shooting as a valid solution to their problems. This leads them to the notion of the cultural script of school shootings, which delimits the adolescent's options for reacting to marginalization and individual vulnerability and provides the 'masculine exit', a manly solution to their problems and a possibility of improving their status, which is perceived as inferior and unacceptable. A cultural script provides an escape from an unbearable situation, in which the perpetrators die to end their torment but do not do so quietly.[72] Instead, they choose a notorious, a "gutsy and daring" (Luke Woodham, qtd. Newman et al. 2005: 249) end to their story; one that also grants them fame; here, Robertz's notion of the 'superstar killer', the subcultural icon and deviant pop cultural hero of the school shooter, comes to mind.

The notion of the cultural script, too, can be linked directly to cultural artifacts, and Newman and colleagues clearly underline the crucial part that fiction plays in the distribution of a certain image of manliness: "When we see films featuring macho heroes or villains who shoot their way to greater notoriety, we are looking at the traces of a cultural script that links manhood and public respect with violence" (ibid.: 230). However, as Douglas Kellner, who draws upon Newman's concept of the cultural script for his own examination of a culture of 'guys and guns amok', points out, "the media are just part of the mix that creates problematic conceptions of hypermasculinity and contributes to societal violence" (Kellner 2008: 24) – a fact that the authors of *Rampage* are aware of:

> Are violent video games, lyrics, and movies to blame for the recent spate of rampage school shootings? Or, as the movie *Scream* suggested, is it that movies just make killers more creative? Watching and listening to violent media doesn't brainwash otherwise happy and healthy teenagers so that they murder teachers and peers. That is why millions of youths ingest countless hours of bloody films and come out none worse for wear. But for school

---

[71] Two noteworthy exceptions are the infamous case of Brenda Spencer in 1979, who killed two people at the Cleveland Elementary School in San Diego, CA (cf. Fast 2013), and the campus shooting committed by Latina Williams, who killed two students at the Louisiana Technical College in 2008 (cf. Newman/Fox 2009).
[72] At least since Columbine, most school shooters have committed suicide or provoked a police officer in order to be shot during their escape, suggesting that a cultural script of school shootings that includes suicide has emerged: "Virtually no one ever gets away with a rampage shooting, and almost everyone who commits this type of crime is aware of that" (Newman et al. 2005: 248).

> shooters – whose social status is marginal and who are beset by vulnerabilities such as mental illness, depression, or difficult home lives – scripts that connect manhood to guns, domination, and the power that comes from terrifying the innocent, offer a template for action. Books, TV, movies, and song lyrics influence decisions that direct their anger outward instead of inward; they provide the justification for random attacks. They are a set of stage directions. (Newman et al. 2005: 252f.)

As a 'set of stage directions', fictional representations of violence can serve as a "prescription for behavior" (ibid.: 230), offering templates both for the course of action itself and for the *modus operandi* of the attack. Both levels, as Newman and colleagues show, are highly influenced by the artifacts that represent a culture of violence. When violence – and even excessive forms of violence, such as mass killings – is presented as a legitimate strategy of asserting a hypermasculine, infamous and threatening identity, a masculine exit from a world perceived as tormenting can be seen as a good option by vulnerable juveniles (cf. Kellner 2008). When media discourse in the aftermath of school shootings additionally promises – and, as discussed above, often grants – fame and public recognition, committing an act of excessive violence can seem a valid way of establishing the identity for which the adolescent has been striving.

The importance of cultural artifacts should be stressed when it comes to cultural scripts: As cultural scripts are shared, mediated and elaborated through images, narratives and actions, many school shooters consume the same cultural products. These include music, films, books, blogs, fashion and even popular cultural idols, both from works of fiction and flesh-and-blood persons (cf. Oksanen/Kiilakoski 2011: 264). As a consequence, school shooters also use a similar vocabulary in their self-narratives and apply similar strategies for framing their them. School shooters, it seems, are not only aware of the cultural script but use it: They "actively construct, edit and re-edit it, combining performance violence, fame-seeking and extreme forms of oppositional masculinity" (Sandberg et al. 2014: 281).

Narrative criminologist Sandberg and his colleagues, who analyze the importance of narratives in acts of terrorism and other forms of extreme violence, stress the relevance of the cultural script of school shootings with regard to their performativity and perception:

> The concept of a cultural script further illuminates the relationship between story and action. In much the same way as narratives, cultural scripts concern temporality and causality. A cultural script refers to schema that organizes a person's understanding of a situation, creating expectations about the nature of the event and its subsequent media reception. [...] Cultural scripts are narratives acted out, and thus a fruitful way to capture the stories that action tells. (Sandberg et al. 2014: 282)

Furthermore, cultural scripts underline the complex interwovenness of cultural artifact and school shootings demonstrated by Newman and colleagues: School shooters in the early 21st century, as opposed to in the late 1990s, do not necessarily need to look for 'inspiration' in films or video games but rather refer to the cultural script of shootings as it has been shaped by previous attacks. While the Columbine shooters referred to a variety of cultural products in their planning, school shooters can now borrow from the widely distributed cultural script elaborated by previous offenders (cf. Newman et al. 2005: 252). School shooters, most notably Harris and Klebold, "were active on the Internet, made videos of themselves and detailed their thoughts in a way not seen in previous school shootings. They developed their plan as if it was a movie script" (Sandberg et al. 2014: 281). In this 'movie script', the shooters did not only construct identities in which they could already see themselves as notorious, they also presented a *modus operandi* that was later adopted by the school shooters that followed.[73] What seemed like a combination of fragments from a variety of films, video games, subcultural attire and attitudes after the Columbine attack is now deeply ingrained in the cultural imaginary in popular culture: "The Columbine shooters thus contributed significantly to what has been termed the cultural script of school shootings" (Sandberg et al. 2014: 281).

Today, the imagery and the perpetrator's mode of planning and communication as shaped by the Columbine shooting is an essential element in any representation of school shootings, as I will show. The cultural script of school shootings has long had a life of its own and exists in a relationship of close-knit, reciprocity with popular culture that draws upon a variety of narratives about school shootings (see Chapter 3.2), as Kathryn E. Linder observes: "Popular culture influenced early school shootings, which influenced more school shootings to the degree where it is no longer clear which is the primary influence. Fact and fiction have merged" (2014: xvi). This merging of reality and fiction "within a larger media spectacle of rural school violence serves to distort what the public can define as the real in narratives of school shootings" (Linder 2014: xvi). Linder points out that these narratives of school shootings have further contributed to the existing cultural script, especially when considering the perception of school shooters with regard to gender and images of masculinity as well as race. Here, the importance of images of masculinity and the notion of a 'culture of violence' gains additional importance, as these images as they circulate in popular culture reveal prevalent ideas of race, class and gender that dominate

---

[73] The relevance of notoriety and fame for the process of identity formation will be explicated further in Chapter 3 of this study.

the school shooting discourse and its cultural perception and modes of representation.

This leads to the discursive level of the cultural script, which cannot only be observed on the level of the shooter's imagination, planning and staging of attacks, but also on the level of the highly medially prefigured, i.e. 'scripted', school shooting discourse. While this will be discussed in greater detail in the next section and Chapter 3, it is important to note yet again how closely interwoven the phenomenon itself is with the discourse that surrounds it. When it comes to the cultural script of school shooting, there is a double logic or function: Not only does the script inform and, as the findings of school shooting research suggest, influence the *modus operandi* of school shootings, it also shapes and prefigures the cultural – the public, scholarly and media – discourse. German philosopher Hans Lenk, who has worked extensively on modes of interpretation, has pointed out that scripts are in fact essential to grasp what is happening in the world around us. Everything that humans as conscious and acting subjects can conceive and, in fact, represent, is dependent on the formation and creation of schemata (cf. Lenk 2004: 56). Humans, Lenk maintains, are 'schematizing animals', since all thinking, conceiving and behavior consists of acts of structuring (cf. ibid: 57).

Hans Lenk's use of schemata is not entirely equivalent to script, as he stresses that 'script' is mostly used for describing prefigured structures of *action* rather than 'mere' conception. While the cultural script of school shootings has mostly been discussed in terms of the school shooter's application of the script as a template for action, considering the public's schematization of school shootings as a rather immediate act of structuring, interpretation and, eventually, representation, is central for understanding the dynamics of the school shooting discourse. The specific function of schemata is that they include or represent every detail of a given situation, but leave space for the adjustment of certain variables, so they can be applied to several recurring events or encounters; schemata help humans to classify, subsume and recognize (ibid: 67). In doing so, they transcend the singular phenomenon and help to connect several events; they present a 'bridge' from the singular phenomenon and the singular experience to something more general (ibid: 89).

When school shootings occur, as extremely seldom, yet radical, singular events, they immediately require schematization. According to Lenk, this is a human necessity for the individual. In the cultural effort to grasp this chaotic event, it is integrated into an established and, by now, well-known schema of processing experience. In this schema, as Lenk also points out, the singular event can always be integrated and processed as such: A schema is like the script for a play or a movie, and the 'instantiation' or activation of this script can be understood as the actual staging of the play (cf. Lenk 2004: 92). In this comparison, the importance of narrative for the concept of schemata or scripts becomes clear: While a schema or script is necessary for the conception of school shootings, the creation, formation and representation of this schema are ultimately dependent on narratives. Narratives, in turn, make use of existing scripts and schemata in the process of meaning-making, as it will be further explored in the following sections.

2.3 Meaning-Making in the School Shooting Discourse

2.3.1 The Necessity of Narrative in the Face of Excessive Violence

School shootings are a phenomenon that cannot be understood separately from the discourse surrounding them and the various narratives that society has constructed to approach the inexplicable. In this regard, school shootings illustrate that there is, in fact, no 'real event' and no 'real thing' that is unmediated. As I have stressed earlier, the death and devastation wrought by school shootings are very real and extremely tragic. By no means do I want to imply that school shootings are merely constructions and did not 'actually happen' – a balancing act which any study that focuses on the social, narrative or symbolic construction of violence has to master. However, the 'real events' of excessive violence, ever since the archetypical Malayan *amok*, have always been and still are phenomena of perception (cf. Ahrens 2015): What has happened and what characterizes the phenomenon and the perpetrator is only ever defined *a posteriori* in carefully constructed narratives of description, explanation and re-integration (ibid.). These narratives draw upon knowledge, images and narratives from the cultural imaginary, which is, according to Fluck, the 'inventory' of images, affects, desires that determine, challenge and shape the perception of reality (cf. Fluck 1997: 21). This imaginary is always articulated and, as a result, redefined by its fictional representations. Thus, while the death brought about by school shootings is tragically real, the events that lead up to it are constructed out of the cultural imaginary and are essentially shaped, defined and re-defined by the fictions that express and articulate the cultural imaginary. Here, the fictional dimension of the school shooting discourse can be observed, as all of the attempts to describe, define or characterize the event and the perpetrators draw upon a constantly growing image repertoire, which includes fictionalized images and narratives. Before describing this complex interwovenness in greater detail in the next chapter, however, I want to elaborate on the very specific and important role of the construction of narratives in the discourse.

School shootings exert most of their effect on society through their suddenness. They undermine the public perception of society as non-violent and thereby disrupt notions of safety and the prevalent and necessary narratives of societal peacefulness. Rampage violence appears to simply erupt, and the main efforts of the public discourse in the aftermath are directed at containing or re-integrating these events into the way that society understands itself (cf. Ahrens 2011, 2017; Gerster 2016). In this respect, creating narratives is the most important and most basic strategy of meaning-making in a chaotic world: "In order to live in that world, we must find ways to grasp it, establish some sort of order in it" (Bal 1994: 4). And, to quote Richard Bauman's seminal study on oral narratives, "[i]t is the structure of signification in narrative that gives coherence to events in our understanding" (1986: 5). To establish and reinforce this order and coherence and to create meaning from events, humans resort to narrative as a "basic human strategy for coming to terms with time, process, change" (Herman 2009: 2).[74] Even without having to subscribe to radical constructivism, narratives can easily be seen as the most important way of making sense of the world, and surely "one of the most powerful ways of worldmaking" (Nünning 2010: 191); narratives "evoke, generate or make worlds" (ibid.: 196) through processes of selection, deletion, configuration and textual representation.[75]

School shootings are a 'phenomenon of radical terror' (Ahrens 2011: 73) because they confront society with the instability of the concept of peacefulness. This concept, however, is needed for a culture to perceive itself as *civilized*, as a civilized society believes "it imposes reasonable and coherent restrictions on

---

[74] The relevance and ubiquity of narrative has long been acknowledged in various disciplines and has shaped discourses on historiography and psychology over the last decades – especially since the emergence of cognitive narratology, "the study of mind-relevant aspects of narrative" (Herman 2013), which highlights the relevance of narrative for sense-making, understanding events and approaching lived experience.

[75] As Nünning points out, the qualification of a certain historical incident as 'event' is already an act of worldmaking, as it results from procedures of selection, deletion and 'weighing' (in the sense of Goodman), procedures that "reflect, but arguably also yield or even generate, cultural hierarchies" (2010: 198). Comparing narratological criteria for eventfulness that were developed for the analysis of fictional texts with discussions of 'events' in social history, Nünning points out that "events tend to unsettle the experience, expectations, and the imagination of the contemporaries" (ibid: 200), that this surprising or shocking effect is a collective one, and that they have consequences that can be noticed by contemporaries (ibid.). As chaotic events "can only be made accessible and communicated in society after having been transferred into comprehensible stories and pictures" (ibid.: 202), the particular importance of narrative becomes obvious here.

violence" (Reemtsma 2012: 103). Civilization and culture are therefore closely linked to the way in which a society deals with violence:

> [A] civilization's form is characterized by its zones of violence – the areas in which it prohibits, permits, or mandates violence, alone or in combination. No rigorous study of violence can ignore these zones, for they are the backdrop against which all talk about violence takes place. Every legitimation (or delegitimation) of violence seeks to reinforce (or change) presumed zones of permitted, prohibited, and mandated violence. These zones share a fundamental link with the type of social trust that characterizes a civilization. Indeed, social trust rests on the stability of these zones. (ibid.: 103f.)

The notion of a peaceful society, however, is a narrative in and of itself and the established zones of legitimate and illegitimate violence existing in modern civilizations are cultural constructs that need to be upheld by means of narratives that provide stability. Phenomena like school shootings violate the zones of legitimate violence, requiring the construction of narratives that make sense of the event and create coherence. As a result, the narrative of the peaceful society is contrasted with a narrative of disruption. The school shooting narrative as a narrative of disruption focuses on making sense of the events by constructing them as disruptive and abnormal. And only through the existence and construction of these narratives of abnormality is the narrative of a societal norm of peacefulness upheld.

A narrative that tries to make sense of school shootings as an otherwise inexplicable form of violence can thus be understood as an essential element in the overarching narrative of a peaceful, civilized society. By effectively 'othering' the school shooter and the school shooting as a transgression of normatively acceptable behavior and by pathologizing or dehumanizing the perpetrators, society can reassert what it perceives as 'normal' or acceptable behavior. Narratives of explanation and of causality, as I will show in the next chapters, frequently establish causal explanations that emphasize the disruption caused by the event.

In these processes, narrative is as ubiquitous as it is fundamental for the stability of society. Roland Barthes, a structuralist who anticipated some aspects of cognitive narratology, famously stated that narrative is "international, transhistorical, transcultural" and that it is "simply there, like life itself" (Barthes 1975: 237). Taking this ubiquity of narrative even further, Hayden White states that narrative is a "panglobal fact of culture" (1980: 5) and more than just another code "for endowing experience with meaning" but rather a "metacode" (ibid.: 6). White, in his approach to historiography, states that "narrative might well be considered a solution to a problem of general human concern, namely, the problem of how to translate *knowing* into *telling*, the problem of fashioning human experience into a form assimilable to structures of meaning that are generally human rather than culture-specific" (ibid.). Moreover, narratives help to structure events and can

> reveal to us a world that is putatively 'finished', done with, over, and yet not dissolved, not falling apart. In this world, reality wears the mask of a meaning, the completeness and fullness of which we can only imagine, never experience. Insofar as historical stories can be completed, can be given narrative closure, can be shown to have had a plot all along, they give to reality the odor of the ideal. (White 1980: 24).

The more disturbing a historical event is, the more it disrupts the existing human strategies of narrativization, of reasoning and moralizing, the more clear-cut the counter-narrative for explanation and causality has to be. The narrative and rhetorical strategies that are used in the transformation of a chaotic and shocking event into a comprehensible story, however, "are by no means inherent in the events as such, but are imposed on the actual events by the narrative discourse which functions as a shaping pattern" (Nünning 2010: 202).

The narrative components used in the construction of the culturally predominant school shooting narrative will show the patterns and elements that are involved in the narrative construction of these events. When it comes to school shootings, setting, character and plot[76] – to use the three most basic components of a story – are highly relatable and recognizable. Drawing upon Fludernik's concept of experientiality,[77] they have a high emotional relevance, which further en-

---

[76] These components are by no means a reflection on the current narratological debates about narrativity and shall not serve as an answer to the question of what the basic elements of narrative are or what a narrative is. This discussion has been held at great lengths by a number of scholars. I use the terms setting, plot and character here solely to structure my brief outline of the *story* of school shootings – well aware that this does not represent the complexity of the term 'narrative' or the various approaches to school shootings. However, this oversimplification shall serve for now as a means of approaching the role and importance of narratives for the discourse and will be further elaborated on and differentiated in the following chapters.

[77] While for Monika Fludernik 'experientiality' and 'narrativity' are interchangeable terms (cf. Fludernik 1996), I understand experientiality – "the ways in which narrative taps into readers' familiarity with experience through the activation of 'natural' cognitive parameters" (Caracciolo 2014) – as one of the *necessary but not sufficient conditions* of narrativity. However, especially in the scope of this project, it is clear that the experientiality of a narrative is highly important: "Yet, the fact that experientiality cannot be taken as a sufficient condition for narrativity does not mean that stories can be devoid of experientiality. No matter how distant from the laws and conventions of what we consider to be our real world, stories are always bound up with human experience: they speak to human concerns and help us negotiate values that are part of our everyday reality" (ibid.). In this study, I will employ the term narrativity not only to ap-

hances the disproportionate sense of emergency and urgency. Because of this experientiality and recognizability, any representation or narrative of school shootings has a high degree of "perceived realism" (Nünning 2015a: 95) for the contemporary reader.[78] In order to approach these events,

> [t]he first functionality of discourse formation concerning events of rampage is thus the production of a particular narrative. By that process, what has happened is integrated into both an individual biography that eventually leads to mass murder and the continuity of social life and normality which has been severely disrupted by this phenomenon. (Ahrens 2015: 153)

This narrative is constructed in 'natural' narrative settings, such as conversations, as well as in fictional narratives. However, the popular explanations and (mis-)conceptions about school shootings that are most established are the ones that have been presented by the media and later adapted in fictional representations. In the immediate aftermath of a school shooting, the media coverage follows clear patterns:

> The first task of media coverage, then, is to attempt such a reconstruction of the offender's motives and intentions, for which reason he apparently dominates media coverage and public interest. Not without reason, any media coverage following such incidents starts with two attempts of reconstruction: first, the chronological reconstruction of the incident itself; second, the reconstruction of the offender as a person with a history, an intention and, if possible, a serious problem or psychological disorder that made him act in such a shockingly violent way. (Ahrens 2015: 151)

This reaction makes perfect sense for individuals in modern societies, where autotelic violence has no legitimate place and defies explanation, and where, "when instrumental explanation fails, we pathologize; when that fails, we mystify" (Reemtsma 2012: 152).

The predominant school shooting narrative focuses mainly on the instrumental explanation as a first approach. However, as autotelic violence (cf. Reemtsma 2012: 56), school shootings defy this sort of explanation; the narrative is bound to fail and pathologizing and mystification are needed in order to uphold a coherent narrative.

---

proach and understand fictional narratives but rather to the school shooting narrative as a whole.

78 In this regard, even school shooting narratives that include fictional elements and fictional representations of school shootings gain much of their disturbing quality from the fact that they are extremely realistic in the way that they represent the school shootings (cf. Bode 2011: 46f).

2.3.2 Outlining the Basic Components of the School Shooting Narrative

Besides the basic human need to cope by adhering to explanatory narratives, the fact that school shootings and excessive violence are so deeply engrained in the cultural memory can be traced back to the high degree of tellability that the phenomenon possesses. The tellability of an event "is dependent on the nature of specific incidents judged by storytellers to be significant or surprising and worthy of being reported in specific contexts" (Baroni 2014: 836). Because of the fact that school shootings touch upon so many aspects of everyday life, the story behind the event is of great interest. The fact that the school shooting narrative has come to develop such a particular discursive dynamic with such great prominence, however, is not only rooted in the somewhat grim fascination with violence, but also stems from the fact that school shooting narratives have a highly relatable and recognizable setting (the school and suburban family homes), interesting yet strangely relatable characters (the 'nerd' or the 'weird loner'), and a suspenseful plot ('loner developing radical issues and going on a killing spree'). While this summary sounds cruel in the light of all the suffering that school shootings have brought upon individuals, families and communities, recognizing these basic constituents of the school shooting discourse helps to understand the way that society deals with this phenomenon and even helps to explain how school shooters situate themselves within these narrative structures. How this narrative structure has been shaped can be seen in the example of the Jefferson County Sherriff's Office documents, commonly referred to as the JCSO documents, which exemplify the construction of the school shooting narrative in the wake of the Columbine High School shooting. The JCSO documents and their journalistic and academic reception have laid the groundwork for the creation of a prototypical school shooting narrative, which is activated and (re-)told after every new school shooting.

The JCSO documents were released following a lawsuit filed against the Sherriff's Office in the wake of the Columbine High School shooting (cf. Schildkraut 2012: 240). They consist of tens of thousands of pages – transcripts of witness statements, memos, descriptions of evidence, evidence files and the diaries and letters written by Harris and Klebold. Most of it is accessible to anyone who is interested and can be easily downloaded.[79] Thousands of legal documents present the work and findings of the JCSO, and they can either be sorted by date and

---

[79] Most parts of the documents can be found online in various forms, e.g., as a whole (cf. Anonymous: *The 11.000 Page Report*, n.d..), indexed by names (cf. Langman n.d) or organized by theme (cf. Langman 2016).

document number or by constructing a narrative out of the information that the fragments present. While some of the documents possess a high degree of narrativity – such as the diary entries and short stories written by the perpetrators or some of the scans of the officer's note pads – other document pages remain opaque, such as lists of items apparently found in classrooms, or unintelligible sketches and drawings. Together with the infamous "Basement Tapes", a morbid video-diary recorded by Eric Harris and Dylan Klebold prior to their killing spree, the JCSO documents have been used many times to create narratives, which have established the basic elements and, indeed, the tone for the school shooting narrative retold and remediated after every new tragedy.

Naturally, the media has a leading role in the creation of the narrative, but I will use the example of Dave Cullen's journalistic book *Columbine* to briefly outline the basic narrative patterns and elements that will be encountered throughout the following chapters. Cullen, who has a background in journalism, has written the prime example of a coherent narrative that arises from the process of making meaning. Out of a massive amount of material, he has crafted the story of two vulnerable, lonesome, mentally ill young men, who go out on a killing spree for revenge. In accessible prose, he presents the reader with thorough analyses of the killers, the victims, the exact chronology of the crime and its preparation and the aftermath as experienced by a shocked and traumatized community. Cullen has collected various explanatory narratives from the media and public discourse and endows his own version of the Columbine story with the air of 'truthfulness' by debunking various myths that the news media created in the direct aftermath of the school shooting; these include rumors about the 'Trenchcoat Mafia', victims such as Cassie Bernall and the shooters' sexual orientation, to name only a few examples. Revealing the media dynamics that led to these myths about Harris and Klebold and some of their victims suggests that Cullen has gotten to the 'bottom of it' and has found 'the truth' – a claim that makes his widely received book a perfect example for outlining the components and functions of the school shooting narrative.

Character
Journalists over the past decades have found that school shootings make for a *great story*, worth being told and reported, and therefore endowed with great tellability. The 'protagonists' of the school shooting narrative are classic villains and, on the other side, there are either innocent victims or heroes, as Muschert (2007a) has explained. The shocking effect of the narrative partially stems from the fact that the victims and heroes of the school shooting narrative since Columbine are always highly relatable: They are children or teenagers, often presented

in a rather glorified fashion and praised for their virtue and innocence. Cullen uses this fact when he writes about the "bright, smiling faces" of the students at a gathering before the prom night of 1999 at the very beginning of his book (2010: 4).

Only a few pages later, Dave Sanders, the only teacher who died during the shooting, is introduced as an all-American guy who cares about "friendliness, honest effort, and sincerity" (ibid.: 19). In the pages between, as a contrast, the readers are introduced to Eric Harris and Dylan Klebold through their problems finding dates for the prom. The first descriptions of the shooters, which are refined with insights into their thoughts and struggles inspired by their carefully crafted diaries, suggest that they are just 'normal' teenagers. This impression shifts radically when he contrasts the struggles of any regular adolescent before prom night with what is represented as the abnormality and monstrosity of their planned attack in the simple statement "Eric wanted ammo and a date for prom night" (ibid.: 16).

Even in these brief introductions, the basic narrative strategy concerning the representation of this story's main characters becomes obvious: As in most media coverage, Cullen draws upon clearly "good victims" (Muschert 2007b: 363) to serve as a foil for the two shooters, who are "perfect villains" (ibid.). As perfect villains, Klebold and Harris hide their monstrosity behind a carefully crafted façade, and – especially in Harris's case – disguise their cold-blooded abnormality with fake normality. Cullen creates causal links mainly through a depiction of Harris as the psychopathic mastermind behind the school shooting, who coldly exploits the weaknesses of his depressed friend Dylan. In contrast to their victims, whose lives, struggles and aspirations are vividly described, the two perpetrators are presented as a *duo infernale*. By pathologizing Dylan and Harris, Cullen draws upon the very common strategy of 'othering' the perpetrator. The pathological, by nature, resists explanation; the existence of the pathological disrupts social normalcy but, by being termed pathological, can reinforce societal notions of what is normal. Applying the uncanny and scientifically contested category of the psychopath to one of the villain reinforces clear definitions of good and evil, normal and abnormal.

While not all representations and reports of school shootings resort to these clear-cut juxtapositions, one of the main components of the overarching school shooting narrative is the fact that school shootings involve a disturbingly high degree of premeditation directed against victims who can either be perceived as innocent because of their youthfulness, or, in the case of the teachers, as heroic. Especially when it comes to the depiction of characters, the categories of race, class and gender have great relevance in school shooting narratives. While the young, white, middle-class male shooter is frequently pathologized or 'othered' by being placed "in direct comparison with male characters who embody hegemonic masculinity" (Linder 2014: 34), white saviors are frequently encountered; Cullen's depiction of Dave Sanders as the all-American hero exemplify this dynamic. The victims and heroes in the school shooting narrative are usually more than just an individual story; they reinforce societal notions of normalcy and serve as a contrast to the disruption caused by an inexplicable attack on this normalcy. Thus, when Cullen describes Coach Dave Sanders as a man who "personified the community" (2010: 19), the heroic victim of the Columbine shooting comes to symbolize the victimization of the whole community. Heroes who stand up against the shooters and display bravery in the face of a sudden threat also "stand-in as sources of long-term hope for the community's restoration to a sense of normalcy that was present before the act of violence took place", as Linder points out (2014: 16). This sense of normalcy is also one of the most important factors in the next element of the school shooting narrative: setting.

Setting
The setting of school shootings is, as much as the characters, highly relatable and generates a high degree of experientiality in school shooting narratives. American high schools and suburban or rural communities present a familiar setting for a huge audience. Because of a myriad of American TV shows and films, the images of hallways with lockers and the clean, broad streets of American small towns are a familiar sight even outside of the United States. The cultural imaginary of the setting from which school shootings emerge is transnational and is continually enriched with new images and narratives. The images of schools as crime scenes, of ambulances, stretchers and grieving students and parents have become international symbols of mass killings at schools. These images derive their shock value from the inexplicability that results from the juxtaposition of a setting normally associated with notions of peace and safety and its disruption by a school shooting. Schools, as mentioned earlier, also symbolize a solid and thriving society and the allegedly tight-knit community of a smaller town serves as an antithesis to more dangerous and violent urban areas. When this safe haven is under attack, it appears as an attack on the core of modern civilization.

The same dynamic can be applied to the middle-class family home from which the school shootings gain part of their inexplicability; the predominant logic that only a broken home can bring forth a murderous child.[80] Here, the aspect of class is most notable. The naturalized myths about white middle-class families that are circulated within Western societies are disturbed by the actions of the adolescent offspring of these families. Curiously, the notion that school shooters frequently come from stable middle-class families has clearly been established by the Columbine narrative, but evidence suggests that the perpetrators come from various family backgrounds (cf. Newman 2005: 244f). Nevertheless, this background has been integrated into the predominant narrative and underlines the inexplicability of the events as well as the monstrosity of the deed.

"Something about those incidents provoked me, and activated my imagination", Lionel Shriver, the author of the school shooting novel *We Need to Talk About Kevin* once stated in an interview, "because they scream *story*. And they scream stories that newspapers never completely reveal: what was going on in these kids' heads, what was really happening in their families" (Shriver 2005). The middle-class nuclear family is usually associated with the ideal of the caring and loving home that provides everything a child needs to grow up to be an upstanding citizen. Frequently, as a reaction to this notion, school shooting narratives go to great length to depict the family as dysfunctional behind a functional façade. Much like with the depiction of the killers, this serves as reassurance that 'nobody could have known'. Because the families of the killers in the predominant school shooting narrative are regular middle-class families, they provoke the question of 'what was really going on', prompting investigators to dig deeper and find the 'true story' underneath.[81] In this particular attempt to approach the inexplicable, the fictional dimension of the juxtaposition of the peace narrative and the narrative of disruption becomes clear. In the construction of the recognizable setting as standing for social normality and of the perpetrator and his actions as abnormal, normality is yet again reinforced.

Plot

This juxtaposition is fundamentally constructed and upheld in the plot of the school shooting narrative: "To make up a plot is already to make the intelligible spring form the accidental, the universal from the singular, the necessary or the probable from the episodic" (Riceour 1984: 41). Here, the plot of the school

---

80 This aspect will be analyzed at greater length in Chapter 6 of this study.
81 Here, Cullen choses a different approach, as he focuses more on the clandestine nature of the planning, even though he points out shortcomings of the parents, especially in the Harris family.

shooting narrative is not 'made up', but it is constructed from various elements, the singular pieces that need to be 'grasped together' (cf. ibid.: 66). Plot schematizes "the intelligible signification attached to the narrative taken as a whole" (ibid.: x). It can therefore be seen as the most important constituent of the school shooting narrative, as it is the most crucial aspect of the process of sense-making.[82] School shootings, of course, are not fictional events in that they are 'made up'; they belong to the 'discourse of the real'. The construction of a plot endows these events with a beginning, middle and an ending and presents a clear line of causality by means of narrative explanation.[83]

Even though each school shooting is different, and every perpetrator has his own biography, the plot of the predominant school shooting narrative has a clearly recognizable structure. As mentioned earlier, despite the fact that there had been school shootings before April 1999, the massacre at Columbine High School and its media representation has established the basic elements of this plot that has not only been retold, but even reenacted, ever since. Columbine "has itself become a script: an icon for notoriety and antisocial defiance conducted in the name of upending conformist pecking orders" (Newman/Fox 2009: 1294). School shooters, the plot suggests, might be inconspicuous and may appear normal. They might hail from regular families in normal communities, but at some point, their otherwise regular development derailed. As a result, they go out on a killing spree, fueled by hatred and the irrational desire for revenge. In this narrative, the popular explanations for school shootings (as outlined in section 2.1.2) are taken up to explain the exact point at which they became derailed and used to create a consistent narrative. The contingencies that every school shooting and each school shooter's biography naturally exhibit are endowed with clear patterns of cause and effect, and the development of the adolescent into a villain is laid out *a posteriori*. Mental illnesses are used to 'other' the shooter and make his actions appear abnormal and inexplicable. In the 'triggering causes', such as hidden family problems, the shooter's allegedly 'normal' background is set apart from the recognizable setting of suburban or rural communities. Here, Dave Cullen's depiction of the development of Eric Harris can again serve as an example of the dynamics of the school shooting narrative and its plot: "[E]ven before adolescence, he was exhibiting telltale signs of a

---

[82] However, any approach to plot in the school shooting narrative in either fictional or discursive representations must remain partial and overly generalized. Each school shooting as a singular tragedy, when talked or written about, is provided with its own attempt of sense-making.
[83] Hayden White's criticism of plot in historiography cannot be ignored here. For White, plot equates to *narrative closure* and therefore *artificially* imposes a narrative structure on the flow of events and time (cf. White 1980: 24f).

particular breed of killer. The symptoms were stark in retrospect, but subtle at the time – *invisible to the untrained eye*" (2010: 111, my emph.).

Because Eric Harris was a psychopath, this quote suggests, his ability to hide 'what was really going on' was not the failure of his social environment, but rather a logical effect of his illness – a symptom of psychopathy. Nobody could have known, and, consequently, the path that his 'monstrous' biography took to a tragic end was inevitable. To cope with the shock and the disruption of peace, narrative strategies for coherence and causality are applied and serve as modes of explanation or even 'justification' (cf. O'Toole 2013: 185). They make the perpetrator's actions appear inevitable because of clearly defined factors such as psychopathy or other forms of abnormality that can be detected in the *post mortem* construction and analysis of their behavior.

Summary

On all levels of the school shooting discourse, understanding its underlying narratives is of special relevance for understanding the school shooting phenomenon as such. The definition of the school shooting phenomenon, as I have shown, is solely based on and constructed by narratives, but the shooters also subscribe to pre-existing narratives of rampage violence that are then put into action. Here, the notion of the cultural script as being performed and actively edited and re-edited is of special importance.

Furthermore, as this chapter has shown, the public discourse is dominated by the explanatory, pathologizing narrative. Neither school shootings as a phenomenon nor the school shooting discourse can therefore be understood separately from its narratives. In the juxtaposition of the societal narrative of peacefulness and the narrative of disruption and abnormal behavior, school shooting narratives acquire a fictional dimension. So as to uphold the notion of a peaceful society despite the fact that violence clearly has occurred, contrasting this narrative with clearly outlined notions of abnormality and deviance is paramount. Only by recognizing a counter-narrative, the predominant narrative of peacefulness – which is necessary for social stability – can prevail in the face of unspeakable crimes such as school shootings. As the construction of these narratives always draws upon the cultural imaginary, including its fictional elements, there is a fictional dimension that can be seen even in non-fictional narratives such as *Columbine*. In this respect, a non-fictional book like Cullen's and a fictional work, such as the ones analyzed in the following chapters, are not substantially different. However, due to their aesthetic constructedness and their fictionality, they actively provide the cultural imaginary with new elements, which are then included in school shootings as well as their public perception. Here, a reciprocal and reciprocal relationship between fictional artifacts and the construction of the school shooting discourse emerges.

As this chapter has shown, even in the earliest accounts of rampage violence, fiction and real events are inextricably interwoven in the narratives. What was understood as *amok* centuries ago and what still influences the public perception of rampage violence today, has its roots in fictionalized, sensational narratives and early forms of 'media spectacle', and is not too different from the media dynamics that can be witnessed in the aftermath of school shootings today (cf. Kellner 2008). Nowadays, what is seen as a school shooting cannot be said to rely on clear-cut definitions of the event or a typology of the perpetrator, as these are highly difficult to create, but rather on fictionally pre-mediated notions of what a school shooting is. As a result, these narratives also shape the fantasy of the school shooters. But they also influence and shape the cultural script of school shootings, which is constituted mainly by the culturally prevalent and widely distributed narratives of what school shootings are and look like. Based on culturally prevalent scripts of masculinity and violence, these narratives can present a masculine 'way out' for adolescent boys that have a variety of risk factors, as Katherine Newman et al. have shown. That narrative is a strategy for meaning-making, for explaining and for creating coherence is a widely accepted notion across the disciplines. The public reaction to school shootings and the way that public discourse repeatedly subscribes to prevalent narratives of causality and coherence is only natural in any struggle to understand and reintegrate events that defy any inherent logic. That these narratives have a *fictional dimension* that is highly informed by fictional representations of excessive violence, however, requires that they be scrutinized in more detail. Thus, the following chapter will describe the complex interwovenness of fact and fiction in the school shooting discourse, considering both fictional narratives of school shootings and the way that these narratives shape the public perception of school shootings.

3 Blurred Boundaries: The Role of Fiction in the School Shooting Discourse

The school shooting narrative, as described in the previous chapter, incorporates various influences that shape the cultural imaginary of these rare events. It combines the representation of previous school shootings in the media, their public and academic discussion and fictional representations of excessive violence. The shooting at Columbine High School in April 1999 has been a defining event for the emergence of this narrative. Not only has Columbine "come to characterize the problem of youth violence and the general understanding of youth social problems" (Muschert 2007: 351), the event as such, the self-representations of the perpetrators, and the notions and ideas circulating in the emerging school shooting discourse have contributed to the cultural imaginary by providing images of the events and a narrative of causality. These images and narratives are rife with references and allusions to works of fiction. As the notion of the cultural script of school shootings has shown, the various ways in which school shooters have referred to cultural artifacts and have used fictional role models and depictions of school shootings to inspire the *modus operandi* and the planning of their own deeds is only one of the indicators of the relevance of fictional representations in the genesis of a school shooting. But this reciprocity does not only exist on the level of the individual perpetrator and the planning and staging of a school shooting. It can also be observed on the level of this reciprocal relation between fact and fiction, which has taken on references and allusions originally found in fiction in the effort to approach and understand the emerging phenomenon.

To describe the various ways in which fictional artifacts and the school shooting discourse are inextricably connected and the different levels on which the interwovenness of the fictional and the factual can be observed, I rely on the notion of the *fictional dimension of the school shooting discourse*. The school shooting discourse and the cultural imaginary of the phenomenon, as I will further explicate in this chapter, is influenced by fictional representations of school shootings and by the ways in which real school shooters have interpreted and received these fictional representations. Moreover, it has allowed for the creation of a narrative that both draws upon and creates attempts for explanation that are further established in works of fiction. Fiction has thus permeated all levels of the complex school shooting discourse and thereby become an integral part of the contemporary phenomenon of school shootings itself. In order to describe and analyze this fictional dimension, I will examine the processes in which fictional elements enter and shape the discourse by describing the reciprocal relationship between fictional representations and school shootings. This reciprocal relationship can be seen in various discursive notions that can help to model the history of school shootings "as a history of circulations of images, narratives, a history of staging and self-staging and re-staging. Every new deed quotes its predecessors, both on the level of cultural processing and mediation, and on the level of the concrete acts, thoughts and feelings of the perpetrators" (Grzeszyk 2012: 13, transl.).[1]

This reciprocity, I will show, can be broken down into a cyclical model of reciprocal influence consisting of five stages: In the first stage, the school shooter's persona as well as the performance in the staging of the attack is highly informed by fictional elements, as he incorporates fictionalized elements in the process of identity formation of the shooter as well as the planning and staging of the attack; here, the perpetrator's references to fictional works and representations of violence are of particular relevance. In the second stage, the school shooting as a performative act connects the mediatized and the social reality, 'transporting' these fictional elements into the real world with the act of the shooting. As a result, these fictional elements influence the representation in the media and the public perception of the particular shooting. Here, the performative aspect of the second stage overlaps with the next stage: As school shootings are a phenomenon that is defined entirely *a posteriori* and primarily on the basis of representations and accounts in the media, these fictional elements are automatically included in the definition and thus in the general understanding of the individual event and the phenomenon itself. It is in the third stage that discourse formation can be located, as the school shooting narrative is re-told and modified in the process of defining and attempting to explain what happened.[2]

The fourth and fifth stages concern the fictional representations of school shootings as a discursive element. The fourth stage describes the process in which the fictional representations either draw upon and reinforce or, converse-

---

[1] "Anhand der verfügbaren diskursiven Äußerungen lässt sich die Geschichte der school shootings als Geschichte einer Zirkulation von Bildern und Erzählungen, als Geschichte von Inszenierung, Selbstinszenierung und Reinszenierung modellieren. Jeder neue Fall zitiert die vorangegangenen, sowohl auf der Ebene der kulturellen Vermittlung als auch im konkreten Handeln, Denken und Fühlen der Täter" (Grzeszyk 2012: 13).

[2] A simple example of the dynamics of these first three stages could be: When a school shooter refers to a fictional movie before and during his shooting, by choice of words or clothing, this is noticed, communicated and interpreted in the media and public discourse after the event. Because school shootings are so rare but have an enormous presence in the media, this reference is then picked up in the interpretation of the event and used to attempt to make sense of the particular school shooting, as well as the definition of the phenomenon as such.

ly, challenge and disrupt the school shooting narrative. Last but not least, the fifth stage considers the reception of these fictional narratives and the way in which the narrative can transform the recipient's understanding of the school shooting phenomenon. Here, the potential functions of fiction come into play. This relationship between actual school shootings and their fictional representations comes full circle when examining how school shooters, too, actively engage in the public discourse prior to their attack and, as consumers and recipients of the fictional representations of school shootings, draw upon the school shooting narrative as a form of cultural script.

To explicate this observation, the following chapter is divided into two larger sections. In the first part, the different stages of the reciprocal influences are explained and illustrated with the help of Matt Johnson's *The Dirties* (Canada 2013). Using a fictional film's approach to the phenomenon instead of only focusing on the references that actual shooters have made to different films and fictional idols makes sense on two levels: On the one hand, the film thematizes the way in which school shootings and artifacts from popular culture are interwoven by using multifarious references, allusions and quotes – as such, *The Dirties* is a fictional film that fictionalizes the relevance of other films for the genesis of a school shooting. On the other hand, Johnson's film can be understood as a paradigmatic example of the fictionalization of the school shooting discourse, as it does not only thematize the complex relationship between fact and fiction by showing the genesis and staging of school shooting, but it also illustrates these blurred boundaries by taking the form of a pseudo-documentary. Moreover, illustrating the theses presented here with a work of fiction underlines and shows the relevance of fiction for the school shooting phenomenon as well as the approach to cultural artifacts taken up in this book.

By employing a genre that disrupts the neat categorization of fact and fiction, the audience might be prompted to question the nature of the 'real' school shooting, as well. As a pseudo-documentary, *The Dirties* is an embodiment of the fact "that the categories between documentary and reality, fact and fiction, defy hard and fast definition", as film scholar Bill Nichols writes (1994: xiii). Examining this idea on the level of the film might help to elucidate the way in which the boundaries between fictional and actual events are interwoven in the real-world phenomenon.

After presenting an overview of the plot, structure, conventions surrounding genre and narrative strategies[3] used in *The Dirties*, I will focus on the cultural

---

[3] I deliberately use the term 'strategy', using the definition provided by Valerij Tjupa: "Narrative strategy is a use of certain narrative techniques and practices to achieve a certain goal. The ap-

3 Blurred Boundaries: The Role of Fiction in the School Shooting Discourse — 93

script of school shootings as both depicted and directly thematized in the film in sections 3.1.1. and 3.1.2. When outlining the dynamics of reciprocity at work in the film and its relation to the school shooting discourse, the concept of remediation will be applied. Remediation allows aspects of inspiration through cultural artifacts and the notion of the (fictional) school shooting as a performative act to be approached, as well as the way in which school shootings are publicly perceived. I also investigate how the school shooter's identity formation and the allegedly 'popular figure' of the shooter are intertwined; here, the questions of fame and notoriety, as raised by *The Dirties*, will be of importance. Building upon these findings, section 3.2 moves on to the level of the school shooting discourse and the way in which literature and film can be regarded as relevant elements within it. Before pointing out the very specific roles and functions of the texts analyzed in the second part of the present volume, *how* fictional works can assume their potential discursive functions and *why* they are important subjects for analysis must be established – especially, in the face of 'inexplicable' violence.

Exploring the functions of fiction is of particular importance for a discourse in which fictional representations of violence have been thematized to such great extent and in which the direct effect of fictional representations of violence on the audience and readership is discussed so controversially, often with little theoretical argumentation. Here, instead of simply assuming that fiction can have certain social functions and effects, I want to elaborate on possible ways to describe and approach them.

Drawing upon the observations regarding reciprocity made in section 3.1, the second part of this chapter then provides the theoretical framework for exploring how fictional representations can assume potential functions for the reader and society, as it will be done in the second part of this book. By combining concepts from reception aesthetics (Wolfgang Iser), functional approaches to fiction (Winfried Fluck) and cultural memory studies (Astrid Erll), this part elaborates on how the fictional dimension of the school shooting can be described and how the role of literature and film can be approached.

---

proach adopted and the intended goal, which presuppose certain competences (creative, referential, and receptive), characterise the author of the artistic text" (Tjupa 2014: 564). As this book analyzes film as narrative, the notion that film is the result of collective authorship rather than one single flesh-and-blood author is as important to bear in mind here as the fact that film "derives its impact from a number of technical, performative and aesthetic strategies that combine in a syncretizing, largely hybrid medium, establishing interlocking conventions of storytelling" (Kuhn/Schmidt 2014: 387). This will be considered in the analysis of *The Dirties* as well as other films throughout this volume..

3.1 Observations of Reciprocity: Illustrating the Relationship of School Shootings and Fiction with Matt Johnson's *The Dirties* (2013)

What makes Matt Johnson's rather unknown film so relevant for this book is the fact that the film does not only represent but also openly thematizes the role of fiction and its complex interwovenness with real events in the school shooting discourse. The film tells the story of two adolescents who are bullied and ostracized until one snaps and carries out a school shooting. This otherwise rather conventional school shooting narrative focuses especially on the role of fiction and popular culture in the development of the shooter. With its frequent commentary about cultural artifacts, its various references to popular films and music, and its open discussion about the role and power of fiction, *The Dirties* has been called "a big bowl of meta", and "a movie within a movie, a story by a film obsessive about a film obsessive, a character suffering an identity crisis played by an actor getting lost in his own performance" (Godfrey 2014). Matt, played by director Matt Johnson himself, and Owen, played by Johnson's friend Owen Wilson, are two film-obsessed boys at a Canadian High School. While producing a film that is highly reminiscent of Columbine shooter's video project *Hitmen for Hire*[4], Matt and Owen are filmed by an unknown cameraperson.

When they screen their project about their personal vendetta against a bullying group of jocks called "the Dirties" in class, they are bullied even more fiercely. As a reaction to the increasingly unbearable situation at school, Matt withdraws into yet another film project and plans a live killing of his tormentors, staged for and captured by his camera. While Owen is trying to resolve his status as a marginalized student by finding new hobbies, making new friends, and falling in love, Matt frantically works towards the ultimate dissolving of boundaries between fiction and reality, between imagined and real violence, and wonders: "What if we'd actually just gone and killed all the Dirties! Imagine if we showed that movie to class!" *The Dirties* traces a gradual blurring of boundaries between the real and the fictional, beginning in Matt's imaginary and extending into the 'reality' of the fictional world, culminating in the ultimate mediatization of violence by capturing the actual murder on film.[5] In the next pages, I will show how the film's structure and narrative strategies represent the fictional dimension of

---

4 The film that Eric Harris and Dylan Klebold produced for a school project before their shooting and which shows them as killers who shoot jocks at Columbine High School.
5 In this book, all quotations from the various films are transcribed to the best of my abilities and as concisely and precise as possible from the soundtrack of the film. Any errors are my own.

the school shooting phenomenon and operate as a fictional commentary on discursive modes of explanation.

3.1.1 The 'Look of School Shootings': Authenticity and Remediation

In the depiction of Matt's transition from a very likeable, funny film-geek into a confused killer on a mission to avenge himself, his best friend and every victim of bullying, *The Dirties* assumes a film-within-film structure with a pseudo-documentary style: The film serves as a frame for the genesis of a school shooting in which a fictitious school video project, named "The Dirties", emerges. The project depicts Matt and Owen as heroes who set out to avenge a vendetta against their actual bullies and is riddled with references to Hollywood cinema and their personal stylization as heroes. Naturally, their revenge fantasies have consequences and their teacher forces them to edit the first version of "The Dirties" into a less violent one; after a painfully awkward screening in class, it is met with bewilderment and further bullying by their peers.

As a result, Matt begins the intense planning phase for his own project "The Dirties II", which – in his mind – is simply a harmless a film about a shooting but which, consequently, involves an actual school shooting. Only gradually does Matt's friend Owen – and with him the audience – realize the dimension of Matt's meticulous planning and his growing identification process with school shooters like Eric Harris and Dylan Klebold. "The Dirties II" is presented as the simultaneous planning of a school shooting, which is, very much in the sense of Katherine Newman and colleague's "template for action" (2005: 71), staged according to a carefully crafted script. The school shooting itself is captured by various cameras planted in the hallways of his school, as well as by the handheld camera of the unknown cameraperson. The film-in-film structure and the low-budget documentary style have two major effects: On the one hand, the structure allows for the inclusion of an enormous amount of references and meta-commentary on the role of fiction in the evolution of a school shooting. On the other hand, the pseudo-documentary style, itself a reference to other existing filmic representations of school shootings, gives the impression of a high degree of authenticity, closing the gap between audience and film and thereby illustrating the relevance of fiction for school shooting discourse. *The Dirties* is filmed completely in the fashion of an amateur film – a stylistic choice that is relatively common in fictional representations of school shootings. The most obvious predecessor of a school shooting film employing this filmic style is Ben Coccio's *Zero Day* (USA 2003). Like *The Dirties*, Coccio's film is comprised almost exclusively of amateur footage that appears to be taken by two school shooters and is reminiscent of the popular genre of fake found footage, or 'discovered footage', films (cf. Bordwell 2012). Much like *The Dirties*, *Zero Day* refers and remediates well-known footage from the actual shooting at Columbine High School taken from YouTube. *The Dirties* can also be seen to operate in the same tradition as Gus Van Sant's *Elephant* (USA 2003), which is the most famous school shooting film and is frequently praised for its innovative style.[6] While it is certainly no pseudo-documentary, *Elephant's* "sparse cinematography" (Rich 2012: 1314) alludes to elements of the documentary by shooting on location at a regular high school, filming actual students of the school rather than professional actors, and featuring highly improvised dialogue (cf. Nichols 2001: ix). *The Dirties* takes this even further and was filmed with very little equipment on location at a Canadian school during regular school activities. At times, students had no idea they were being filmed or for what purpose, and this was so that the behavior of the involuntary extras would come across as authentic as possible.

These strategies are known from other films that employ documentary aesthetics – one of the most famous ones in recent years being Sacha Baron Cohen's mockumentary *Borat* (Dir.Larry Charles, USA 2006), which purportedly also turned clueless bystanders into extras (cf. MacLeod 2011). As mentioned earlier, with its frequent use of footage from a handheld camera, *The Dirties* is also reminiscent of found-footage films, such as *The Blair Witch Project* (USA 1999). The low-budget production by Eduardo Sánchez and Daniel Myrick has frequently been discussed as the vanguard of the genre and has become infamous for its shock value, which was further enhanced by establishing a connection to the lifeworld of its audience via the Internet. However, even though films that blur the boundaries between fact and fiction have a long-standing tradition, the labels mockumentary, docufiction, docudrama and pseudo-documentary are frequently used interchangeably and the genres themselves confused. In order to avoid such confusion and to analyze how Johnson's film challenges the audience's understanding of categories of truth, fiction and authenticity, the genre of Johnson's film needs to be examined in greater detail.[7]

---

[6] For an analysis of *Elephant*, including its form and functions with regard to school shooting discourse, see Chapter 5.

[7] The fact that *The Dirties* exists in a line of films that have employed and established the use of filmic styles that suggest authenticity of the footage must by no means be understood as a flaw. Rather, keeping in mind what has been said about classic Hollywood cinema, it is yet another method of enhancing the authenticity and the realistic feel of the film: Observing clear filmic conventions in cinematography, cutting, etc. establishes a certain style, which allows the audience to become so accustomed to watching this particular style that they forget about stylistic devices and, instead, focus on what is being said (cf. Cavell 1979: 24).

Genre Confusion: *The Dirties* as Pseudo-documentary

Films like *The Dirties* rely on certain aesthetics and means of representation that suggest authenticity while openly displaying their fictionality through filmic or paratextual markers. In this way, they can "operate as if telling the truth even when we know it is not and the film is telling us" (Bishop 2013: 81). This strange amalgam of fact and fiction is the unique mode of representation that films such as *The Dirties* rely on to confuse and thereby draw in their audience.

Two genres are invoked most frequently in connection with films that use the aesthetics of the documentary: the mockumentary and the pseudo-documentary – both of which are sometimes confused with the genre of the docudrama.[8] Surely, both terms have a certain fuzziness about them and are sometimes used interchangeably, but this is also due to the fact that even the documentary itself has proven hard to pin down. In his seminal work *Introduction to Documentary*, Bill Nichols points out that documentaries "adopt not a fixed inventory of techniques, address no one set of issues, display no single set of forms or styles. Documentary film practice is an arena in which things change" (Nichols 2001: 21). Drawing upon the possibilities of the broad arena of the documentary genre and the expectations that the genre raises in its audience, fictional films that use the techniques, iconography[9] and aesthetics of documentaries frequently draw upon the most commonly accepted set of conventions of documentary film in order to simulate their own documentary nature.

Mostly, these conventions include the use of the handheld camera, low-budget editing or the impression that there has been no editing at all. Sometimes, voice-over narration or the use of talking heads is also included. All these stylistic devices are meant to enhance what Ryan Bishop has called the "aesthetic-truth-ratio" (2013: 70). This ratio refers to the nexus of perceived authenticity and imagery, and follows the simple logic: "the worse the image, the less slick the presentation, the higher the verity" (ibid.). Nichols, too, stresses that "[c]ertain technologies and styles encourage us to believe in a tight, if not

---

8 A genre that is very commonly used for the representation of school shootings is the so-called docudrama. In contrast to the mockumentary or pseudo-documentary, the docudrama mostly draws upon re-enactments of real-life events, mixes them with original footage and often includes talking head sequences that are sometimes – but not always – presented by actors. The re-enactments and the appearance of actors, however, are mostly clearly recognizable as such. The prevalence of this genre might be due to its most important generic qualities: 'relatability', with the depiction of ordinary characters, and 'rootability', by rooting themselves in well-known current events (cf. Paget 2012: 247). However, the docudrama in the school shooting context has all too often been used in a way that psychologizes, glorifies or is voyeuristic.
9 "A genre's iconography consists of recurring symbolic images that carry meaning from film to film" (Bordwell/Thompson 2008: 320), such as objects or setting.

perfect, correspondence between image and reality" (2001: xii). The effects that are commonly known from documentary film, such as "lenses, focus, contrast, depth of field, color, high-resolution media (film with very fine grain, video displays with very many pixels) seem to guarantee the authenticity of what we see. They can all be used, however, to give the impression of authenticity to what has actually been fabricated or constructed" (ibid.). Moreover, some films also use paratextual markers that suggest that the spectator is in fact watching a documentary and assert the truthfulness of the depicted events.[10] In the case of *The Dirties*, this last aspect can be observed in a very brief scene prior to the beginning of the actual movie. This scene, merely a few seconds long, can be seen as exemplary of the film's approach to its own fictionality: the spectator looks at a monitor, on which an editing program can be seen. The sound of a mouse click suggests an editing process. However, what the spectator does not yet know is that the sequences that are shown in the editing window could belong either to the fictional school project "The Dirties" or to the film that they are actually watching – *The Dirties*. There is no way of telling which editing process they are witnessing. To add to the confusion, a cross-fade into a black screen with a white text that warns the audience about the graphic imagery in the movie is followed by the statement: "Out of respect for the victims and the families the footage has not been altered in any way". The ironic opposition to the editing process shown in the previous frame openly communicates its own strategy as 'fiction that claims not to be fiction'.

The Dirties uses the genre conventions of the documentary film in its highly realistic representation of the genesis of a school shooting. Unlike the docudrama, a genre that uses actors to re-enact a historical event,[11] the events represented in Johnson's film are fictional. Even though they are clearly based on previous school shootings and are closely connected to actual events, the audience is aware of their fictionality. As film scholars Bordwell and Thompson point out, one of the most common distinctions between documentaries and fictional films is that fictional film presents "*imaginary* beings, places, or events" (Bordwell/Thompson 2008: 341, emphasis mine).

---

10 Or, like in the most famous example of mockumentary, *Borat*, or to a certain extent also *The Dirties*, some films go so far that even the people starring in the film are unaware of its fictionality (cf. MacLeod 2011: 112ff.).
11 Here, the BBC TV-production *Zero Hour: Massacre at Columbine High* (David Hickman, UK, 2004) is a good example of the use of this genre in the representation of school shooting. *Zero Hour* represents the events of the Columbine High School shooting via voice-over narration and commentary from talking heads such as Brooks Brown, while actors re-enact the events of the shooting. News footage from the real shooting is also included.

The audience's expectations surrounding a film that is marked as fictional by paratextual or other indicators govern the way in which the film is perceived and understood. Expectations about a film's actuality or fictionality even affect processes of understanding and interpretation when a fictional film is comprised almost completely of documentary footage. Conversely, when a documentary includes staged and prearranged events or re-enactments, as is the case with the popular genre of the docudrama the reception and understanding of these elements is still governed by the assumed purpose of the fictional work (cf. Bordwell/Thompson 2008: 341). Frequently, the creation of documentary and fiction film hybrids has served to confuse the audience and raise questions about authenticity, fictionality and "how fact and fiction may intermingle" (Bordwell/Thompson 2008: 342). When school shootings are considered, inviting the audience to reflect upon the relationship between fact and fiction is of particular relevance. In this way, *The Dirties* is a highly interesting example of a school shooting film, as it is not only its genre, but the way in which the events are told in the film, that complicate the boundaries between fact and fiction.

As has been shown, hybrid genres between documentary and fiction are often confused. The question of which genre Johnson's film might be assigned to, therefore, remains open. As the film plays with various genre conventions, precisely defining its genre will have some bearing on the approach to the film taken here.[12] The most famous term, the mockumentary, as the portmanteau of mock and documentary already suggests, has most commonly been used to describe pseudo-documentary films that are comedic or parodies of documentaries – the most famous examples being *This is Spinal Tap* (Rob Reiner, USA 1984) and *Borat*. Mockumentaries often "imitate the conventions of documentaries but do not try to fool audiences into thinking that they portray actual people or events" (Bordwell/Thompson 2008: 342). However, even though a mockumentary does not necessarily have to be comedic in nature, when a film fuses fiction and documentary in a less comedic way or uses a documentary style to represent dramatic events, the term may be misleading. In fact, *The Dirties* actively plays with the conventions of the mockumentary. It begins with highly comedic scenes and only reveals a more tragic story throughout the course of the film. By doing so, it plays with audience expectations: While the audience may expect to watch

---

[12] It needs to be pointed out, however, that the categorization of a film should be regarded critically. Following Peter Young, I am very aware that "[e]ach analysis is merely one expression of genre knowledge among many" (Young 2008: 232) and that, in the tradition of film scholar Rick Altman's pragmatic approach to film genres, discussions about genre should always include the question "For whom does a text 'belong' in a genre? For whom does a genre equal a definite set of semantics and a consistent arrangement – a syntax – of those elements?" (Young 2008: 231).

a comedic mockumentary rather than a dramatic pseudo-documentary fiction film, the way in which the story develops makes them realize that they are, in fact, watching a dramatic pseudo-documentary. Relying on the audience's expectations surrounding genre, the filmmakers are able to enhance the shock value of the film as the change in the film's tone mirrors the change in Matt, as the events proceed.

Keeping in mind the trajectory of the film, the broader term pseudo-documentary is the most appropriate genre in which to place it. According to Bordwell (2012), the formal framework of the "pseudo-documentary fiction film", which has a long-standing tradition, is used for both comedic and dramatic purposes and has its own conventions, such as "to-camera interviews and the occasionally awkward framing, most noticeable in the recurring image of a fallen camera" (ibid.) – both of which can be found in *The Dirties*. Pseudo-documentary film, whether comedic or dramatic, questions the "ontological and/or functional distinctions between fictional and nonfictional discourses" (MacLeod 2011: 111) and "signal Baudrillard's murder of the real, the degree to which the real and fictional have become interchangeable, and, consequently, the pointlessness of differentiating between the two" (ibid.). However, the pseudo-documentary film is not without its challenges, as Bordwell (2012) points out:

> The problem of the pseudo-documentary is to motivate the fact that someone is filming these dramas. Various solutions have been worked out. You might make the protagonist a filmmaker exploring a subject or creating a diary. Or you can pretend that the people being filmed are celebrities (as in *Spinal Tap*). Or make the act of filming an effort to document dramatic occurrences. Filmmakers face a second problem as well: motivating how the film has been made public. You can, for instance, present it as a TV or theatrical documentary, as *Spinal Tap* purports to be. More recently another solution has been found. You can suggest that this film has been discovered after the events were over.

The Dirties combines a number of possible solutions to legitimize its existence and publication as a pseudo-documentary film, but not without adjusting them to the specificities of the school shooting-discourse: The protagonist is a filmmaker, who is exploring the subject of bullying at his high school and the effect it has on his own life, and the film documents dramatic occurrences. Naturally, here, the school shooting as the main content of film already legitimizes both the filming and the publication: The act of filming is understood in the tradition of filmic self-representations of school shooters since Columbine (cf. Paton 2012), and the publication is explained by the public interest that the YouTube videos and diaries of real-live school shooters have received.

When this close connection to filmic elements of the school shooting discourse is considered, Johnson's film can be said to use documentary style to underline the importance of the topic that is being represented or to find a way to depict the otherwise 'unspeakable'.[13] By drawing on conventions from documentary film, the pseudo-documentary can, using genre conventions, pretend to be "a *representation* of the world we already occupy", as Nichols writes of documentaries (2001: 20). It can take on the highly complex topic of school shootings without resorting to comedy and without having to find or even create the aesthetic means to approach this topic. By employing realistic cinematography,[14] it can draw upon pre-existing imagery and thereby addresses the audience's experiences directly.[15] The frequent use of this strategy brings to mind Nichols's observation that "[f]ilmmakers are often drawn to documentary modes of representation when they want to engage us in questions or issues that pertain directly to the historical world we all share" (2001: xiv). But besides engaging the audience

---

13 While a pseudo-documentary at times fakes its documentary character and includes various signals that encourage the audience to believe that what they are watching is real (cf. Elias/Weber 2009: 182), it is important to note that this is not a matter of deception. The creators of these fictional works rely on and, simultaneously, challenge the audience's learned ability to differentiate between fact and fiction and play with the existing boundaries between the two. With literary scholar Wolfgang Iser's triadic understanding of fiction, reality and the imaginary in mind, fiction is always already 'known' and perceived as fiction, even without specific signals that explicitly reveal its fictionality, and thus cannot be deception (cf. Iser, 1996; 1993: 2ff.). Iser's understanding of fiction will be thematized to greater extent in section 3.2.

14 When I use the term 'realistic' or 'realism', I refer to a broad definition that "moves away from any ties to specific forms and takes 'realism' to refer to any work of art that is seen to capture reality". (Birke/Butter 2013: 2f.). In this sense, 'realistic' is "a positive adjective that denotes the adequacy of a representation" (Birke/Butter 2013: ibid. 2f.).

15 In doing so, the proximity of what is seen on screen and the shared reality of the audience is underlined and addressed directly. This is the most important aspect of the frequent recourse to documentary style when it comes to the representation of school shootings: it can thematized and illustrate the dynamics of the societal reaction to school shootings in a way that is relatable and understandable. As has been shown in Chapter 2, the school shooting phenomenon gathers much from its impact on society from its extraordinary shock value as an attack against society, which transcends its pure physical impact as an act of violence. Creating an overwhelming impression of authenticity and, thereby, a great proximity of the fictionalized event to the audience can be understood as both a reaction and an answer to the helplessness in the processing of these complex events. As a reaction, presenting highly authenticated and 'realistic' fictional works can be understood as a way representing these gruesome events without having to find or to invent an aesthetic language and imagery that corresponds to the social impact that they have. As an answer, the cinematographic and narrative strategies of authentication can be understood as a way of trying to cope via fictional representation; by showing a version of 'what really happened', films like *The Dirties* can be seen as very much in line with the societal desire for causal explanations. When these films are presented in a documentary style that is highly reminiscent of previous events, explanations presented within the fictional work may be used for re-integration and processing of the phenomenon in the extra-fictional world.

and addressing existing questions and issues regarding the phenomenon that is being represented, documentary modes also offer the possibility of avoiding the ethical dilemma that representations of violence involuntarily pose. By relying on pre-existing imagery and a documentary style, the controversy about artistic representations of phenomena of violence is at least partially avoided.[16] Here, it can already be seen that the genre of the pseudo-documentary has great impact on the function of *The Dirties* for the school shooting discourse, as the genre itself questions the distinction between the real and the fictional, and the film poses this question in relation to the school shooting phenomenon and its discourse.

Remediation and the 'Look of School Shootings'
Remediation is of great relevance for the school shooting discourse and fictional representations of school shootings, as well as the pseudo-documentary style. The concept was originally introduced by Bolter and Grusin to try to come to terms with the quickly developing and theoretically challenging dynamics of New Media (cf. Bolter/Grusin 2000) and to describe "the strategy by which designers in one medium (or media form or genre) position their work in relationship to other media (media forms, genres)" (Bolter 2008. 23). However, the authors underline that remediation has not emerged with the rise of new digital media, but can be observed in older media forms of visual representation at least since the Renaissance. For centuries, different forms of media have been "commenting on, reproducing, and replacing each other, and this process is integral to media" (1999: 55). Importantly, this process can work in two directions, as "a new medium can borrow from an older one, or an older medium from a newer one" (Bolter 2008: 23). This means that film, for example, can borrow from photography or the novel as much as the novel can borrow from digital media and film. Bolter and Grusin's concept of remediation has been adapted to cultural memory studies, most notably by Astrid Erll, making it especially pertinent to this volume.

"Just as there is no cultural memory prior to mediation there is no mediation without remediation", Astrid Erll and Ann Rigney argue, as "all representations of the past draw on available media technologies, on existent media products, on patterns of representation and medial aesthetics" (2012: 4). What Bolter and Gru-

---

16 However, cultural memory scholars Astrid Erll and Stephanie Wodianka rightfully ask whether or not all filmic representations of extreme violence are an aestheticization of the gruesome acts they show and ask how a film may use its potential to generate emotional responses with 'authentic' imagery (Erll/Wodianka 2008: 10).

sin call the 'double logic of remediation' – multiplying media and, at the same time, wanting to erase all traces of mediation (cf. Bolter/Grusin 2000: 53ff.) – can be observed in the dynamics of cultural memory, as Erll and Rigney point out:

> On the one hand, most memorial media strive for ever greater 'immediacy'. The goal is to provide a seemingly transparent window on the past, to make us forget the presence of the medium and instead present us with an 'unmediated memory'. On the other hand, this effect is usually achieved by the recycling and the multiplication of media. While 'immediacy' creates the experience of the presence of the past, 'hypermediacy', which reminds the viewer of the medium, points to the potential self-reflexivity of all memorial media. (2009: 4)

While school shooting-films cannot be fully compared with other memorial media,[17] it is interesting to observe how films that represent school shootings employ strategies of representation very similar to the 'memorial film' (cf. Erll/Wodianka 2008) and its filmic remembering (cf. Erll 2008). As in memorial films that thematize war, films that represent school shootings rely on remediation as a strategy of authentication and represent as well as shape the emerging cultural memory of these events.

In line with Harold Innis's differentiation between time-biased media that preserve their traditions and are durable, and space-biased media that are more ephemeral and rather serve a broad distribution of their content, Erll and Wodianka understand film as one of the central modern media that, as a space-biased medium, functions as a distributor of images and concepts of historical as well as contemporary events (2008: 4). For the distribution of images and concepts, remediation is one of film's possibilities to annex other forms of media, such as newspaper-headlines, news footage, other pre-existent fictional films or images from documentaries and thus process them for another audience. In the process, remediation also becomes a strategy for authentication and simultaneously serves as a self-reflexive element that underlines the medial character of memory as such (cf. Erll 2008: 141).[18]

---

17 Usually, memorial media is concerned with historical events of a greater scope – e.g., war, terror, and genocide – that have an impact on processes of cultural identity. However, I have pointed out that, even as a rare and highly specific phenomenon, school shootings touch the core of societal self-understanding. Therefore, these events of excessive violence can also be debated in terms of cultural memory and memorial media.

18 The extensively studied war film has a longer and much more influential tradition and addresses a much bigger issue than the school shooting film. Astrid Erll underlines that film and military are clearly interwoven in American culture and that films serve as a reference for the cultural expectations, experiences and memories of war (cf. Erll 2008: 143). While the war film functions on a different scale than the school shooting film, the dynamics of remediation

The example of war and war films helps to elucidate the concept and its relevance for the school shooting discourse: For most people, the 'reality' of war is only accessible by means of media representations, and yet war has an ongoing historical presence that is conveyed by news media of various kinds: newsreel, video footage, documentaries, night-vision shots, magazine photographs. "[T]he images of war we experience in film", film scholar Robert Eberwein points out, "have a built-in inflected valence of reality because of the indexical quality of the historical recorded images" (2010:54). Even if he does not employ the term, Eberwein, too, refers to remediations of preexistent media representations of war:

> Even if we are not at war in a given period, war's presence is felt through films which reinforce historical memory with our genre memory. These two memory banks not only support one another; the one has the effect of validating the sense of reality of the other. War films seem real, in part because they actually use material taken from battlefields, but also because the reality of the actualities bleeds into the reenactments. The authenticity of the one generates an ontological authority for the other. (ibid: 55)

The perceived 'presence' of war is thereby increased, even in times of peace or countries that do not actually experience war. This can be seen as analogous to the perceived presence of school shootings that are actually extremely rare: A sense of emergency and the resulting need for societal reactions to the problem is generated by disproportionate media presence (cf. Kellner 2008, Braselmann 2016) and can be enhanced further by remediation in filmic representations. By means of filmic representation, a 'look of warfare' (cf. Erll 2008: 148) has emerged, comprised of certain images taken from mass media as well as from the 'look of the time' in which the depicted events took place. Films like *Platoon* use the aesthetics of shaky handheld camera images for recreating the look of war journalism of the 1960s and 70s. When war films integrate these media representations via remediation, they increase the experientiality (*sensu* Fludernik) of the representation. At the same time, this ensures what Erll calls the film's 'historical saturation' (*Vergangenheitssättigung*): a historical correctness that helps to create a direct connection between the film and the actual historical event (cf. Erll 2008: 147f.). School shootings, too, are mostly 'experienced' or witnessed via mass media reports (cf. Linder 2013: xv) and fictional or non-fictional representations of past events that help to foster a high degree of experientiality of that which is represented. Considering the remediation that can be

---

as well as the medial character of the phenomenon that is being represented are strikingly similar.

observed in *The Dirties*,[19] the strategies for authentication employed by it are strikingly similar: by constant remediation of pre-existing imagery and mass mediated information about the actual events, school shooting films have in fact shaped what could be called the 'look of school shootings'.

The Dirties remediates media representations of school shootings on three levels, always referring to Columbine and thus reinforcing it as the prototypical event: First, on the level of the filmic narrative, it relates what has become the predominant school shooting narrative – the story of a loner who goes out to seek revenge. Within this story, the film also ascribes to a specific explanatory narrative, which, very much in line with its own self-reflexive stance, comments on the power of fiction and the loss of reality, as theoretically elaborated by Frank J. Robertz (see Chapter 2). On a second level, the film remediates aspects of Columbine and elements from the school shooting discourse by referencing them. Matt, for example, wears the same famous yellow shirt worn by the protagonist of Gus Van Sant's *Elephant*. Also, he is shown reading Dave Cullen's *Columbine* and even verbalizes a growing identification with the version of Eric Harris presented by the book. By wearing a *The Catcher in the Rye* t-shirt and borrowing all copies from the library, he simultaneously offers a meta-commentary on the influence of fiction.[20] Third, on the level of representation, the film remediates the 'look of school shootings' as it has been presented in the media. By relying on the shaky handheld camera aesthetic, the film does not only depict two students filming a school project that is clearly reminiscent of Harris's and Klebold's revenge phantasy *Hitmen for Hire*, it also refers to all other footage that is known of the two shooters and that can still be found on YouTube, activating the audience's memory of actual school shootings in order to establish a clear connection between or merging of the fictional and the real. This is most obvious in a scene where the boys go on a trip to a quarry and practice their shooting skills. Matt sits in the driver's seat in his cousin's truck and, in a very brief close-up, lifts his hand to form a gun while looking directly in the camera – a pose that clearly references the video *Dylan Klebold and Nate Dykeman going to Columbine*, which is one of the many self-representations of the shooters prior to their attack.[21]

---

[19] As well as in other school shooting films such as *Zero Day* or *Elephant*.
[20] Further, this mirrors the communicative aspect of clothes that has a particular relevance for school shooters, as the deliberate choice of clothing by several shooters has shown (cf. Kiilakoski/Oksanen 2011)
[21] The fact that many scenes in *The Dirties* are filmed in Matt's basement, where he lives, can be understood as a remediation of the infamous Basement Tapes, a number of confessional videos taken by Eric Harris and Dylan Klebold that have not been released by the JCSO, as well as Gus

This scene in the truck is embedded in an entire sequence that is highly reminiscent of videos showing Harris and Klebold shooting guns in the woods, which is also still available on YouTube. The videos of Harris and Klebold exert an uncanny effect mainly because the viewers know that the boys seen boisterously practicing their shooting skills commit a mass murder shortly afterwards.

In *The Dirties*, while the outcome of the story is not yet clear, the remediation of the Columbine videos already serves as a dark foreboding of what the boys are up to, and also infuses it with an element of suspense. In this sense, remediation serves as a means for authentication that helps to establish a 'look of school shootings'. Remediation thus plays a significant role as it links the process of discourse formation to the establishment of the cultural imaginary. The process of remediation does not only draw upon but, simultaneously, generates the imagery that informs and shapes the school shooting discourse, as will soon be shown. Remediation, as it is used in *The Dirties*, actively contributes to the image repertoire of school shootings – it increases the audience's idea of what school shootings are and, via enhanced experientiality, fosters a sense of their omnipresence.

The fact that *The Dirties* remains a fictional film and that, consequently, fictional imagery becomes part of the audience's understanding and idea of school shootings, shows the fictional dimension of the school shooting discourse. Before this is examined further, however, another aspect on the level of the school shooting phenomenon rather than its public discourse needs to be elaborated on: *The Dirties* depicts how the fictionally generated 'look of school shootings' is actively used by a school shooter in the planning and staging of his attacks and, at the same time, helps to establish the very look itself. This cyclical structure of reciprocity is paramount for understanding the relevance of fiction for the school shooting phenomenon and, consequently, for the public discourse.

3.1.2 The Reciprocal Relationship of School Shootings and Fiction

On the filmic level, it is rather obvious how fictional representations and actual school shootings influence one another. By means of remediation and 'authentic' representations of both the genesis of a school shooting and the deliberate inclusion of discursive elements (e.g., bullying, media violence, etc.) the film

---

Van Sant's *Elephant*, which also depicts the shooter's everyday life as well as the clandestine meticulous planning of the shooting.

displays and illustrates the close reciprocal relationship of school shootings and the media dynamics accompanying these events. Regarding school shootings as mediatized violence allows cultural artifacts and media representations of violence (including school shootings) to be understood as by no means isolated events, but rather caught up in recursive webs.

The reciprocal relationship of school shootings and their media representations can be described as a cyclical one. André Grzeszyk, as quoted earlier, has pointed out that school shootings exist in circular structures of representation, staging and (re-)staging (cf. 2012: 13), which is most obvious in the perpetrators themselves. As shown in Chapter 2.2, it can be observed that, in almost every case, school shooters refer back to previous shooters, their self-representations and the fictional and non-fictional representations of previous events (cf. Paton 2012). Shooters like Seung-Hui Cho, the Finnish school shooter from Jokela, Pekka-Erik Auvinen (2007) or the German school shooters Bastian Bosse from Emsdetten (2006) and Robert Steinhäuser from Erfurt (2002) went to great lengths to create explanatory videos and whole media packages. Their self-representations, frequently including grandiose statements about their self-understanding as either avengers of the tormented or god-like figures who simply implement the laws of 'natural selection',[22] have been uploaded to YouTube channels or, in Cho's case, handed directly to a cable network news station. In their self-representations, school shooters clearly display that they are well aware of the actions of their predecessors – from Harris to Bosse or Auvinen – and they are not shy to comment on their admiration as well as their desire to not be seen as mere copycat-killers, but as 'equals' within a perceived community of school shooters (cf. Böckler/Seeger 2010: 134ff.). And yet, contrary to what the copycat theories suggest, school shooters do not simply copy previous shooters. Rather, they locate themselves within the same cultural script of school shootings and consciously modify and extend it with their own self-representation and performance. By performing their school shooting as an act in the social sphere, they actively change this sphere; moreover, with their medially transported self-representations and the imagery that they actively cultivate before and during the shooting, they complete the transformation of their former selves into a school shooter – not only for themselves, but also with regard to their public image. Through this performative act, the school shooter's subject (trans-)formation and the perception of him changes the media representation and thereby

---

[22] This can be seen in the writings and video messages of Eric Harris or Pekka Erik Auvinen. Harris, on the day of his attack, wore a t-shirt that said 'Natural Selection', while Auvinen donned a t-shirt reading 'Humanity is Overrated' in one of his video clips prior to his attack.

refigures the public perception of school shootings. In the process, the imagery that is used by the shooter and by the media representations is either altered or reiterated, depending on the shooter's engagement with the available images and narratives.

What requires further examination is the how the 'fictional dimension' of this complex interplay can be described in terms of media prefiguration, self-staging and performance, i.e., how the fictional elements are integrated in the school shooting discourse and how the school shooter participates in this process.

Fiction and Identity Formation

The Dirties can help to illustrate existing studies and findings about identity formation of school shooters, as it fictionalizes these processes and comments on them while, at the same time, the film establishes and provides another fictional element of the school shooting-discourse. It has already been discussed how "school shooters have actively used cultural products in their identity construction. Furthermore, the shootings themselves have become material for creating further films, books and documents" (Kiilakoski/Oksanen 2011: 249). Also, it has become clear that school shooters consciously contribute to this script, which consists of various media products that are highly dependent on the availability and accessibility of certain media at certain times. However, what still needs to be approached is the aspect of identity formation – the fictional dimension in the transformation of a 'normal' young adolescent into a school shooter.

In *The Dirties*, Matt's transformation is described in a way that could be understood as the fictionalized representation of the Robertz's theory of fantasy (see Chapter 2.2): Matt, suffering from unbearable humiliations in his reality, is presented as obsessed with films and books, and as gradually disappears into a fictional world of his own creation in which he gradually becomes a fiction of himself. He and his friend Owen, who does not turn into a school shooter, 'devour' fictions; his room is plastered with posters from films, some of them altered so that they show Matt and Owen as the protagonists. Apart from films, the two friends consume media of all kinds: books, video games and music. While Owen at times seems to be bemused by his friend's obsession with consuming and, most importantly, producing films, Matt is portrayed as losing himself in a fictional version of his lifeworld. In a slow process, the film suggests, he gradually fails to differentiate between his life as a film that he is making and the reality that he shares with the people around him. He seems to experience his life as an ongoing movie that can be altered and scripted in any way that he likes.[23] In one scene in particular, Owen and the audience realize just how much Matt comes to think of himself as the director and producer of his life as a film: Matt is shown in a medium shot, practicing Kung Fu moves. As the camera moves to a full shot, the audience sees that he is dangerously close to the edge of a cliff. The handheld shot pans to the left, Owen is in the picture and nervously tries to convince Matt to move back. Medium close-ups of Owen shot from a low angle suggest the rising tension between the friends. When Matt refuses to step back from the cliff because his position 'looks better' when he is standing there, the argument begins:

Owen: "It doesn't matter how good it looks – it's just me!"

Matt: "Can you hear yourself 'It doesn't matter how good it looks'? – This is a movie!"

O: "This is not a movie right now! This is just you and me..."

M: "Trust me, this is a movie! Trust me! We'll go home, I'll show you the footage and you'll be like 'holy shit...'"

O: "This is sick- how you act like this all the time now! How it's always a movie for you, how you're always acting. It's pathetic!"

[Matt acts like he is almost falling down the cliff, followed by a description of a dialogue between him and Owen ending in Matt falling down the cliff while trying to reassure Owen that all is well]

O: "Listen, I don't care if this is a good shot in a film that you are making and that I am not making..."

M: "The scene is Danny Glover in *The Royal Tennenbaums!*" [Matt repeats dialogue from *The Royal Tennenbaums*]

O: "Shut up! Shut up. I don't think it's funny....so if I don't think it's funny, who is it for?" [...] "You're acting. You're always acting"

M: "I'm never acting!"

O: "You're acting even right now! I don't know what's real with you and what's not real with you" "This is real! I'm being real! Look, I am standing on a cliff saying I want to do a shot of us doing Kung-Fu. That's real!"

O: "It's not real when you're doing the Kung-Fu [...]"

[Owen leaves angrily]

---

23 For example, when Owen wants to get the attention of a girl he likes, Matt helps him by staging the perfect setting for a phone call that Owen receives. Generating an image of Owen as a popular guy, Matt, acting as Foley artist, creates the background noise of raging party – the plan works out, and Owen gets the popular girl's attention.

O: "Well, I guess this is a good time for you now to end the scene? Okay, Cut."

This scene is informative not only because it sets off the falling out between Matt and Owen – which, as the film suggests, is the trigger for Matt going through with his school shooting plan[24] – but also because it clearly demonstrates and underlines the film's understanding of the genesis a school shooter: Matt is depicted as the writer, director and editor of his life movie.

Here, the self-fashioning of the Columbine shooters is echoed. As Jennifer Rich writes: "There is no doubt that Harris and Klebold were aware of the 'filming' of their massacre by the school's security system. Even at the moment of suicide, they are directing. They remind each other to wait until they both count to "four" to pull the trigger, so that their suicide is timed perfectly—all for the sake of their future viewers" (Rich 2012: 1311).

One of the scenes that stand out against the dominant hand-held aesthetic of the film is shown to Owen at a later point as parts of "the latest shots". It is a montage of sequences that show Matt and Owen riding their bikes through the streets at night and scenes of Matt planning his school shooting, gathering information about the school and carefully creating a death list with the help of old yearbooks, highlighted with background music and slow motion effects. Only by seeing this footage does Owen seem to realize just how much Matt is already invested in the actual planning of the shooting. In this scene, again, the audience has been captured within the triple structure of the film: While the audience watches *The Dirties*, as the film made by Matt Johnson, they are simultaneously watching the protagonist Matt's film about his life and, now, they also watch Owen, who is turning from actor and director to witness and spectator of the events. Matt, the protagonist, seems to become detached from reality; when he is editing the footage of a scene in which he is bullied and beat up at school he says: "Funny, huh? You see something happen to you on camera, it's like it's not even...it's not even happening to you, it's like it's happening to a different person. It's...it's crazy".

However, Matt's development into a school shooter does not at all seem erratic or arbitrary. Instead, he is presented as consciously modeling his new school shooter persona. Subject formation in *The Dirties* is presented as a very overt process and Matt actively uses the floating imagery and ideas about how a school shooter has to be. For example, when he decides to borrow all copies of *The Catcher in the Rye* at once, "because it makes us look crazy!", he actively

---

[24] Studies have shown that school shooters frequently experience loss or loss of control shortly before they commit the shooting (cf. Böckler/Seeger 2010: 65f., Verlinden et al. 2000).

models himself after previous school shooters.[25] Matt depicts what Heiko Christians has described as the entirely non-hierarchical recourse to available role models that is characteristic of a school shooter's identity formation process: Role models from fictional and non-fictional representations, from the school shooter's personal encounters and long established general notions of role models (e.g. the hypermasculine avenger) have the same relevance and actuality (cf. Christians 2008: 39f). In Matt's identity formation, he draws on representations of previous school shooters (as the active reading of Cullen's *Columbine* suggests) as well as fictional representations of school shootings (his yellow t-shirt from Van Sant's *Elephant* suggest that he is very familiar with school shooting films).

These referencing of single or multiple discursive elements is well documented in actual school shooters: Jeffrey Weise was said to be a great fan of Van Sant's movie (cf. Newman/Fox 2009: 1290), and shooter who went on a mass shooting in Munich in July 2016 allegedly read Peter Langman's 2009 study *Why Kids Kill* (cf. Johnston 2016). Matt's construction of his new identity is embedded in a perception of the planned attack that is equally constructed from fictional as well as real 'templates' for action – Matt clearly uses the cultural script of school shootings. In the dress rehearsal for his shooting (shortly after he decided to plan 'The Dirties II'), he wears a t-shirt featuring the cover of *The Catcher in the Rye*, as "crazy killers are always obsessed with *Catcher in the Rye* – it's a *Catcher in the Rye*-themed school shooting. It's like we're planning a prom!"

The transformation of Matt is presented as slow but somehow predictable, as Matt's demeanor gradually grows more violent. The prospect of the impending shooting, of "The Dirties II" as an act of revenge seems to find its way into his lifeworld; when he is bullied at school, he begins to strike back and, like most real school shooters, leaks his plans (cf. Newman et al. 2005).

This development in *The Dirties* illustrates three important aspects of the role of fiction in the cyclical structure of school shootings. As a meta-commentary, *The Dirties* (as a fictional representation of a school shooting itself) illustrates the media prefiguration of the school shooting by cultural artifacts, the cultural script of school shootings and the active participation and re-modeling of this script, as well as the process of subject formation from a normal adolescent into a school shooter. Matt, like actual school shooters, does not only use and consume cultural artifacts of various kinds, but is also aware of how this

---

25 References to *The Catcher in the Rye* and its protagonist Holden Caulfield have become a theme in fictional representations of school shootings and can also be found in various works that thematize school shootings in different ways, such as Jessica Knoll's *Luckiest Girl Alive* (2015).

very consumption of cultural artifacts is publicly understood as 'necessary' in the genesis of a shooting, as the *Catcher in the Rye* references show. Actual school shooters such as Harris, Klebold and Cho have used fictional representation of extreme violence as inspiration for the *modus operandi* of their hypermasculine acts of revenge (cf. Kellner 2008, Newman et al. 2005, Schildkraut 2012, Grzeszyk 2012). Shooters such as Bastian Bosse and Pekka-Erik Auvinen have, in turn, referred to their predecessors as their idols and heroes. All shooters have staged their attacks as carefully planned and highly geared toward media attention, obviously anticipating the attention that a spectacular act of violence at a school receives.

In *The Dirties*, Matt as a fictional school shooter takes this script even further: He does not consider the security camera footage as good enough (cf. Rich 2012: 1311), but literally stages his shooting as a film – a logical next step in the evolution of school shootings as mediatized violence. Before his shooting, he plants cameras in the school, and sets them up carefully so they capture his murderous act from different angles. The audience of *The Dirties* witnesses the shooting partially through these set-up "GoPro" cameras and through the lens of the still involved cameraperson who follows Matt during the shooting.[26] The viewer, here, becomes a witness not only by seeing the footage from the static cameras, but also, through the perspective of the anonymous cameraperson, is even made an accomplice – a partner in crime, who is watching a mass murder through a camera.

The Fictional Dimension of a School Shooter's Identity

While the idea that a person might entirely loses himself within his phantasies is unsatisfying in various ways, it cannot be denied that the *modus operandi* of a school shooting is medially (and frequently fictionally) prefigured by representations of school shootings, and that the perpetrators also use the imagery of their new, notorious identity in their self-representations and identity formation. In his transformation into a school shooter, Matt is a good example for what

---

[26] The use of "GoPro" cameras once more stresses the historicity of school shootings: In the performance, shooters are not only dependent on the circulating media and the availability of images, but also on the availability of technical possibilities. In the shootings in the 1990s, for example, the fairly new accessibility of the internet did not allow for extensive self-representation on channels like YouTube. Live mediatization as is made possible by New Media today changes the perception of these events: E.g., during the massacre in Munich in July 2016, where witnesses posted videos from the crime scene and even of the alleged shooter while the massacre was still going on.

André Grzeszyk describes as the creation of an "Amok-Persona", the formation of the violent subject that is embedded in forms of media strategies (cf. Grzeszyk 2012: 59). The school shooter as a 'subject in search of roles' (cf. Christians 2008: 39), searching everywhere in his social-material or media surroundings for roles to take on and embody, slowly grows into the person that is able to kill his peers. Like Matt in *The Dirties*, Eric Harris created his *amok-persona* on a piece of paper in his diary and in short stories, in videos and in his own creation of a level of *Doom* before committing the actual deed (cf. Grzeszyk 2012: 59). In various media, shooters quite literally spell out their potential new identity. Seung-Hui Cho wrote brutal scripts for plays (cf. Berardi 2015: 66 f) and Adam Lanza allegedly created a short story of a grandmother running *amok* years prior to his attack (cf. Farrell 2016: 354).

The various media technologies that are available to the school shooter are the prerequisite of any kind of subjectivization; the transformation of the school shooter must be understood as a process in which the adolescent prepares to become a school shooter (Grzeszyk 2012: 59). In an effort to show the world around them what they want to communicate, school shooters use socially and medially available frames of representation and narration to create new images of themselves (cf. ibid.: 60). 'Image' here has an important double-meaning. As Jörn Ahrens shows, it is as a term for the socially accepted characteristics and features of the subject as well as a term for visual motive as a carrier of meaning – which corroborates the particular relevance of visual media and film for the formation and constitution of the modern subject (Ahrens 2015a: 294).[27] The school shooting is therefore medially prefigured and incorporates, interprets and expands upon the available imagery and narratives of the time, as is inevitable in today's media culture. By using cultural imagery and engaging in the creation of a consistent biographical and self-explanatory narrative, the shooter establishes his *amok-persona* and simultaneously prepares the reception of his attack.[28]

---

[27] In this study, I focus on narrative representations of school shootings and analyze filmic representations by means of narratology rather than visual analysis. Images in news media and fictional representations alike are therefore understood as highly relevant, as shown by Ahrens (2015, 2015a), Müller et al. (2012), Paton (2012) and Regener (2017).

[28] The randomness of the perpetrator's narratives has been analyzed by Sveinung Sandberg in an article about Anders Behring Breivik; while Breivik was not a school shooter, Sandberg has shown various similarities between the attacks in Utøya and school shootings (Sandberg et al. 2014). Of the self-representations of the Columbine shooters, Jennifer Rich writes: "Of course, this self-awareness is made up of typical adolescent detritus gone mad: they want a revolution, but for whom or what is never articulated. They hate country music. They hate 'stupid people'. They hate people who say that wrestling is real, and they hate Star Wars fans. They do, however, love their parents, and the tapes accordingly attempt to exonerate their parents from blame. The

This new and violent persona, however, does not make the 'real person' disappear. The subject is not dissolved in the media images and (fictional) idols of the evolving school shooter. "School shooters", as Grzeszyk underlines, "orientate themselves by their predecessors and media models, but they do not lose themselves in them. Their own personality (or what is left of it) has to remain as and within their image" (2012: 69, transl.).[29] The school shooter uses a variety of fictional components in his self-representation and the active modelling of how he is perceived, but he does not disappear within the realm of the fictional. He might only be able to communicate his real-life experience by using preexisting content taken from film dialogues and texts he has read and that he uses and quotes to make his own position clear, but the content does not dictate what he wants to communicate or express. His experiences, both medial and social, remain his own (cf. Grzeszyk 2012: 123). In contrast to what *The Dirties* suggests, the school shooter therefore does not lose himself within the fictions he receives or creates, but rather allows them to expand his own experiences and understanding of his life-world and himself. He creates ways for his reality to 'fade out', and for himself to become a liminal subject in a state in between fiction and reality (cf. Iser 1989: 244), by forming a fictionally enhanced version of himself and the world around him. In the subject formation of the school shooter, fiction and reality thus overlap and become interwoven and blurred by the adolescent. As the school shooters prepare themselves, they engage in what Heiko Christians has described as an 'autonomous and dynamic' process of 'self-programming' (cf. Christians 2008: 46).[30] The school shooter creates his identity as a conglomerate of his own personality and the medial prefiguration of himself – not the adolescent that he is, but as the perpetrator and killer that he will be.

After Seung-Hui Cho's campus shooting at Virginia Tech (2007), one psychologist is quoted saying regarding the self-representations of Cho in the videos he made prior to the attacks: "[T]hese videos do not help us understand Cho. They distort him. [...] This is a PR tape of him trying to turn himself into a Quentin Tarantino character" (qtd. in Berardi 2015: 63). Cho, Jaclyn Schildkraut argues,

---

content of their "revolution", then, is simply their passionately held prejudices without any ideological foundation" (Rich 2012: 1310f.).

29 The original reads: "School shooter orientieren sich an Vorgängern und medialen Vorbildern, gehen aber nicht in ihnen auf. Die eigene (Rest-)Persönlichkeit muss als und im Bild erhalten bleiben" (Grzeszyk 2012: 69).

30 However, where Christians sees this process as rather detached from the subject's conscious influence, Grzeszyk stresses that school shooters have a highly reflexive and differentiated relationship to their mediatized models and predecessors (cf. Grzeszyk: 70ff.).

thereby took the process of self-representation even further than the shooters before him:

> [U]nlike Harris and Klebold, who had speculated whether Spielberg or Tarantino would tell their story, Cho was unwilling to leave his story up to Hollywood producers. Instead, he constructed his own reality, and used the news media directly to his advantage to spread his story. It was a move that was as calculated as the massacre, and the results were beyond what Cho probably could have imagined. (2012: 233)

However, Cho's self-representations are not merely a PR stunt. The school shooter does not only present himself for others, but also performatively models his own identity. When in his videos Cho models his identity after his fictional heroes, more than simple acting is involved – the videos document a process of subject formation. This subject formation gains a fictional dimension where character traits, personality and a fictionally charged version of the shooter blur. While shooters like Harris, Cho or Lanza have occasionally 'practiced' their new violent identity in the creation of fictional works such as scripts for plays, short stories or essays in which their own experiences were fictionalized, visual artifacts in particular tend to be instruments of self-fashioning. Jörn Ahrens points out that visual media play an integral part in modern practices of subject formation, as they connect visual aesthetics as cultural forms of reproduction and representation with social discourses in a specific way (cf. Ahrens 2015a: 302; see section 3.2). With this fictionally modified and expanded identity, the shooter actively subscribes to the cultural script that his predecessors and the public discourse has presented him with; he can act upon this script, but he can also modify it, change it and re-write it. And he does so with the knowledge that, not only potential school shooters after him, but also the public discourse itself will partake in the modification of this script by understanding his actions and his carefully crafted *amok-persona* in line and in the tradition of previous events. The school shooter knows that his actions will have great impact – and the better his persona is stylized and his actions are staged, the greater the impact will be.

The Relevance of Notoriety and Fame

For Matt Johnson, fame is one of the central themes of *The Dirties*. In an interview with *The Guardian*, he says:

> It's the sickest malady of American culture that we inherited globally, [...t]his massive selfie generation that believes that it deserves fame, and that fame is the only achievement worth having. We tried to make a movie about how fame is more important for young people now than literally anything else: money, happiness, anything. We're a celebrity-obsessed society,

and young men especially can get completely twisted in the way that Matt does. (Godfrey 2014)

The Dirties does in fact portray an obsession with fame, even though the protagonist does not seem to care too much about being traditionally popular. While he is bullied, he is also depicted as having constructed an identity that builds on his very specialized interest in film and popular culture. And he is not alone in this. However, his constant production of film material and the staging of himself and his friend Owen as heroes and entertaining protagonists suggest a desire to be appreciated and recognized. As Johnson says elsewhere, this desire eventually takes over, as "Matt is trying to become a movie star of his own creation" (Johnson 2013). That his transformation into a sort of movie star is successful, can, according to Johnson, be observed in Matt's increasing references to his new persona. "There is a difference between constantly making reference to things and trying to somehow become the thing to which you're making reference", he states (Johnson 2013). While Johnson claims in *The Guardian* that he does not want to provide answers or even a reason for the school shooting his film depicts, Matt's gradual retreat into a fictional version of himself and of his life and his inability to 'pass the reality-test', in his mother's words, suggest that the protagonist has in fact lost himself in his quest for fame and recognition.

The suggestion that Matt has abandoned a shared reality for one of his own creation finds echoes in literature on school shooters, as well. In studying school shootings, various scholars have argued that fame or, more precisely, celebrity is one of the main goals of the perpetrators. "The only ideology that motivated them", Jennifer Rich writes about the Columbine shooters, "was the 'spectacle'. They wanted to be famous; they wanted to enter the exclusive club of serial killers and terrorists; they wanted to out-McVeigh Timothy McVeigh, and they wanted it all on film" (Rich 2012: 1311). As she observes, they were successful: As infamous founders of a new phenomenon of youth violence, they have become the protagonists of a number of books, films, TV series and plays. In a way, Harris and Klebold, and at least some of the shooters after them, have become celebrities and thus, following Larkin, have become part of the "royalty of the postmodern era" (2008: 181). While school shooters are infamous rather than famous, they do succeed in becoming celebrities. At least for some time after the attack, "[t]hey commandeered the attention of all Americans, including the president of the United States, every high school principal in this land, researchers such as this writer, pundits, the clergy, and every kid in America capable of watching the news" (Larkin 2008: 193).[31]

It should be pointed out that the aspect of fame and the shooter's anticipation of their notoriety are single aspects of a highly complex phenomenon. As this book promotes a multicausal approach to school shootings, I do not want to argue that fame is the central motivation for a school shooting and consequently will not assign blame or responsibility to medial representations of school shooters. However, what is remarkable about the celebrity status of school shooters – as it has been produced by news media, fictional representations, the Internet, and arguably even academic research – is that it is built upon a notion of 'notoriety', as it is deeply ingrained in the cultural script of school shootings. This notoriety, as Douglas Kellner (2008), Katherine Newman and colleagues (2005) and, more recently, Kathryn Linder (2014) have shown, is closely linked to masculinity and compulsory heterosexuality. This notorious new identity of the school shooter relies on becoming a celebrity, like the shooters before him, and this fame is modeled after notorious and infamous celebrities as they are presented in popular culture. Kiilakoski and Oksanen state:

> Popular culture offers exciting role models who use violence as a solution and sometimes glorifies powerful and destructive performances. Popular imagery offers role models of masculinity and, according to critics, produces a cult of fame which is an integral part of the script of school shootings. This impact of popular culture can be seen as public pedagogy [...]. To put it briefly, cultural products provide elements for the script and thus work as pedagogical forces in the media-centred modern existence. (Kiilakoski/Oksanen 2011: 251)

In an article about rampage violence and school shootings in popular culture, Brigitte Frizzoni states that the school shooter cannot be considered as a "pop-

---

[31] This culture of celebrities, Larkin points out, is also reflected in the American high school system and is thereby internalized by every student – whether they engage in it or protest it by deliberately positioning themselves at the margins of this system. This notion, it can be observed, has become part of the cultural script of school shootings, which is consequently often seen as highly 'Americanized'. German shooter Bastian Bosse writes about the 'jocks' at his school in his suicide note and videos (cf. Anonymous 2006). While bullying is a problem in German schools, there is no real equivalent to the high school system that includes groups like 'jocks' and 'nerds' to be found. However, by applying this term from the American high school system, which he only knew from cultural artifacts, Bosse shows that he has internalized the cultural script of school shootings, which always includes revenge-phantasies against the 'jocks' (see also the group known as "The Dirties" in the film) – apparently regardless of whether or not the school shooter has actually been victimized by bullies (cf. Anonymous 2006, Prokop 2015: 189).

ular figure". In order to become a popular figure, she argues, characters in popular artifacts develop lives of their own, beyond the artifact that has made them known. They have the ability to become focal points of broader public discourse; they are abstract and they are always the protagonists, mostly in an artifact belonging to a popular genre (cf. Frizzoni 2015: 132f.). All these aspects can be applied to the school shooter, as he is depicted in fictional and non-fictional media and as he represents and stages himself. However, Frizzoni's single argument against the school shooter as a popular figure lies in another criterion that must be met by popular figures in her definition: They can never violate the ethical core values of society, namely human rights (cf. ibid: 133). This notion is, of course, problematic, as the main premise of her argument – the core values of a society – are floating signifiers in the sense described by Claude Lévi-Strauss: They refer to everything and, at the same time, describe nothing; they are understood intuitively and are seldom questioned (cf. Gerster 2017: 34). With regard to school shootings, this means that, in its narrative of peacefulness (*sensu* Reemtsma), society relies on the common agreement that excessive acts of violence cannot be tolerated. Frizzoni rightfully points out that the school shooter is at times connected to popular figures with positive connotations, such as the avenger of the tormented – a title that various school shooters also claimed for themselves. However, Frizzoni does not acknowledge that, the fact that school shooters are in fact highly popular in certain social abysses, as the killers have a great appeal for a number of disturbed teenagers: As a number of studies have carefully analyzed, school shooters have not only admired figures of popular culture that were defined by their status as an outcast or criminal, or by their notoriety (most famously the protagonists of *Natural Born Killers* or the musician Marilyn Manson), but they have themselves acquired a horrifyingly enthusiastic fan base (cf. Böckler/Seeger 2010; Oksanen et al. 2014).[32]

Here, the connection to the fictional dimension of school shootings permeates the level of the shooter's identity formation: School shooters like Bastian Bosse from Emsdetten refer to Harris and Klebold as their idols and include the medially transported information about them in their own planning of the attack. However, as the (self-)representations of Harris and Klebold already contain fictional elements, those elements find their way into another shooter's identity formation. Fiction and the fictionally-influenced imagery of the school

---

[32] In an article about online fan communities of school shooters, Oksanen, Hawdon and Räsänen found out that school shooting fandom online – as seen on YouTube – exists internationally and is still mostly devoted to the Columbine shooters, while pre-Columbine cases are hardly ever mentioned (cf. Oksanen et al. 2014: 59f.).

shooter thus 'travel'; they serve as transmedial and transnational connections between different school shootings over time and space.

School shooters are well aware of the status they gain – most of the time *post mortem*, as their death has long become an integral part of the scrip they act upon. With regard to fame, this may seem contradictory at first, as they are not allowed to experience their new fame and harvest the fruits of their newly developed infamous identity. However, as the fictionally charged subject would most likely falter under media scrutiny, prison and public trial, it is no contradiction at all, but rather a logical conclusion: During the trial and in the uncontrollable media coverage, the notorious killer could re-transform into his old student persona and into 'normalcy'. Instead of taking this risk, school shooters choose to anticipate the fame that awaits them after their attack and do not insist on witnessing what really happens with their story: "Directors will be fighting over this story!" as Dylan Klebold famously said (qtd. in Rich 2012: 1310). And, while they did acquire the status of being a celebrity, parts of what they wanted to happen did not come true: "[T]hey would have hated the film version of the events at Columbine as represented in Gus Van Sant's *Elephant*" (Rich 2012: 1311). School shooters actively use the cultural script of school shootings – the recall value of their actions maximizes their impact:

> Today's youth terrorist can, through an (anti-)social media web, be 'producer, director, star' and, now, distributor as well. It is for this reason that Auvinen became known as the first 'YouTube' killer: He demonstrates a disturbing devolution of the mash-up ethos; his cyber-evidence bespeaks the dark potential of Web 2.0. If Cho's egomania – fertilized by the current climate of technology and celebrity – meant mailing a packaged narrative to NBC, Auvinen knew that he could land on countless screens without needing a broadcast network intermediary. His online presence was prolific; he wrote in English rather than Finnish to maximize his audience; and his home computer contained mash-ups (many of which made their way online) omnivorous in texture: pastiches of Auvinen himself, *Hitman* video game footage, a Discovery Channel docudrama on Columbine and, taking the viewer fully through the Baudrillardian looking-glass, a remix of *Natural Born Killers*. (Serazio 2009)

Unsurprisingly, these dynamics have found their way into the public understanding of school shootings and, as reports indicate, even into the direct perception of victims or immediate witnesses of school shootings; even while they are happening, school shootings perceived as mediatized violence. "It felt unreal", Franco Berardi quotes a witness of Auvinen's shooting as saying (Berardi 2015: 32),[33]

---

[33] Franco Berardi's recent book *Heroes* also claims to approach the complex issue of fame when it comes to perpetrators of excessive acts of violence, such as Auvinen or Cho. However, he follows an approach that favors monocausal patterns of explanation, and, most importantly,

and at other occasions, such as Anders Bering Breivik's mass shooting in Utøya (2011), witnesses have said they believed they were in a movie before they realized that the shooting was indeed real. While it is not uncommon in media cultures that unusual events that most people experience or know through medial representations feel 'unreal' when they are experienced or witnessed in 'real life', when it comes to school shootings, the blurring of fact and fiction and the feeling of 'being in a movie' is also rooted in the *modus operandi* of school shootings as a performative act.

School Shootings as Performative Acts

When the school shooter has successfully created his newly imagined, medially prefigured and fictionally enriched persona, he plans his school shooting according to this new image of himself and to the way he wants the outside world to see his actions – a process which *The Dirties* illustrates by showing how Matt plans his attack, from clothing, to blueprints of the school and a handwritten hit list. Fiction plays a crucial role here, as the performance follows preexisting cultural scripts that are realized and transported into the shooter's reality. He has created a narrative of his own, a justification that follows his own logic, using the narratives and cultural script available to him. While the school shooting can be understood as medially and fictionally prefigured, the school shooter refigures these fictions into his world of action. However, without the actual performance, the subject formation would remain incomplete and, thus, a mere fiction – it would take place in a different form, or, more likely, not at all. In the performance of the school shooting, school shooters finalize the process of their subject formation and, simultaneously, alter the social space in which the performance takes place (cf. Grzeszyk 2012: 129). "Performance", as Ute Berns writes "can take place in the real world (as in a wedding ceremony or a court trial) or it can depict fictional events (as in a theater performance). Verbal or visual scripts can prepare the performance in playtexts and stage directions, film scripts and choreographic sketches" (2014: 677). School shootings combine these aspects. In the shooter's medial self-representations, the observer views a performance, while the shooter follows scripts, incorporates various fictional elements and presents a version of himself that has not yet come into being.

---

at times implies just a little too much sympathy for "frail lives of a generation of loners who have grown up in the age of precariousness and telematics isolation" (2015: 72f.).

Simultaneously, however, the self-representations have a performative dimension. They take place in the real world, as they actively partake in the process of subject formation, and the actual school shooting transforms the social sphere of the school shooter. The space of the school and the suburban or small town community is affected and changed and irrevocably by the actions of the shooter. In a way, the school shooting is the corporeal presentation of an action (cf. Berns: 681ff.) that has been prefigured, prepared and rehearsed before. In various stages of the planning of the deed and in the process of subject formation that precedes the actual transformation into a school shooter, the performance as final realization of image and identity has been prepared. It is then brought into the world of action, including real victims and a dramatic modification of the social sphere.

School shootings as a performative act are the stage in the cyclical relationship of school shootings and fiction in which the fictional dimension and the extra-fictional reality meet and interact most clearly. While in the process of subject formation and planning of the attack, the school shooter draws upon the medially prefigured imagery and the available scripts, and configures them according to his own surroundings and individual needs. The performative act thus includes the active refiguration of the imaginary – he endows the prefigured and configured images and his newly formed subject identity with new meaning and transports them into his world of action.[34]

In his performance, the school shooter stages himself as someone else, someone he is not (cf. Iser 1989: 244), and, in doing so, brings the fictionally informed and refigured version of himself and of his actions into being. He thus finalizes his new identity and, in the most violent of ways, experiences the figure

---

[34] Here, I have consciously used the terminology used by Paul Ricœur in his concept of the threefold mimesis (cf. Ricœur 1984). On the level of the school shooting phenomenon, the three stages of Ricœur's mimesis can be applied to the school shooter as a recipient or 'reader' of the school shooting narrative. On the level of Mimesis1, prefiguration describes the school shooter's preunderstanding of the narrative that is possible through his own real-life experiences. The 'practical understanding' of the school shooter, it is important to note, must differ from the prevalent understanding of the school shooting narrative insofar as the school shooter does not struggle with the incomprehensibility of the actions of previous perpetrators. Their actions do not defy his practical understanding of real life. On the level of Mimesis2, the configuration, the school shooter partakes in the act of 'grasping together' the elements of the event and in the organization of the elements of narrative, creating a relation of the incidents and bringing them together. In the last stage, Mimesis3, the refiguration, the school shooter then takes the world of the narrative and applies it to his own life. The fictional world merges with the extra-fictional reality of the school shooter as it has been made intelligible by configuration (cf. Ricœur 1984: 54ff.).

he has assembled coming to fruition. This insight is not to be understood as a psycho-pathological analysis, but rather as an approach that takes into account the fictional elements at work in school shootings such as the ones committed by Harris and Klebold, Cho, Bosse, Steinhäuser, and Auvinen.[35]

Another aspect of the fictionally-informed staging of school shootings is the shooter's observation of the anticipated mediatization and fictionalization of their actions. In an article about intermedial performances, Philip Auslander states that "the televisual has become the intrinsic and determining element of our cultural formation" (Auslander 2001: 6), and that theater and other 'live forms', such as football games or concerts, are directly tied to their mediatization in television or elsewhere. While school shootings are by no means a performance in the sense of a theater play or a sports game, school shootings are a kind of mediatized violence (cf. Muschert/Sumiala 2012): Auslander points out how the televisual representation of live performances is essential to convey the impression of proximity and that the ubiquity of televisual representations may have the effect that only the mediatized is experienced as true proximity. This can only be "compensated for by making the perceptual experience of the live as much as possible like that of the mediatized" (Auslander 2001: 7). With regard to school shootings, the frequent references to films and the stylization of the shooter as a villain prior to and during the attack, as well as the discursive willingness to dwell on these references, cannot only be understood as the reproduction of pre-existing imagery and an effort to form a hypermasculine and notorious identity. These aspects are also the enhancing of the shooting as a live experience for both the perpetrator and the victims that he aims to threaten, scare, and kill by a grandiose staging of himself as if he were in a film. When, following Auslander, only mediatization is taken to indicate proximity, the school shooter's performances can be understood as creating the impression of 'being in a film' in those who witness the event in the media, and the immediacy and shock value of the attack are enhanced.

---

[35] It has to be noted, however, that other shootings, like those in Winnenden or Newtown, have not shown as much of a fictional dimension in the planning or staging of the attack and merit further analysis (cf. Braselmann/Ahrens 2017). In her analysis of school shooter's visual self-representations, Nathalie E. Paton observes that the shooters craft their identity in their videos by presenting themselves as masculine figures and underline the high degree of their premeditation by over-representing firearms and their use of them (cf. Paton 2012: 212), all the while constantly "re-producing textual, visual, and sound references" (ibid.: 213), rehearsing the standard narrative of justification for their planned attack (ibid.: 217), and engaging in threats directed at the perceived audience of their video (ibid.: 215). This last aspect already suggests that the shooters include the audience in the staging of their performance – first in the performance of their new identity of a school shooter, and later in the performance of their shooting.

Moreover, by using the aesthetics of movies and previous attacks and thereby directly activating the witness's image repertoire of school shootings, the perpetrator also contributes to and acts according to the aesthetic of school shootings discussed earlier. By staging the attack according to prefigured versions of himself and of his actions, he fulfills the (medial) expectations of what his actions have to look like. The school shooter uses this medially established look of school shootings and draws upon the floating imagery that is available to him. In doing so, he actively shapes the way his shooting is being experienced and – following contemporary media logic – the way in which it will be represented. School shooters since Columbine have known about the effect that their actions will have on the public, and it has been enhancing this effect has been framed as one of their perceived challenges (cf. Rich 2012). When Harris and Klebold imagined how directors would fight over their story, they were proven right. They aware that they would create new material for movies by doing everything in their creative power to commit a horrible mass murder, but they also presented a performance so drenched in the imagery of dread that they would ensure the mediatization and, indeed, fictionalization of their actions. In *The Dirties*, this dynamic is also mentioned; not only does Matt include the medially prefigured version of a school shooter in the formation of his new identity, he also shows that he knows what is expected of him and that he is aware that he can actively shape the image of himself that will circulate after he has gone through with his plan.

In the anticipation of the representation of the attack in media and fiction, the phenomenon and its representations merge inextricably: the shooter, who has included fictional artifacts of different kinds in both his identity formation and the staging of his attack, anticipates the fictional representation and remediation of his performance. These fictional representations in books, films and TV shows draw upon the imagery that the shooters have actively created and staged while preparing their *post mortem* representation. Considering that numerous studies have shown that school shooters act upon a script that is also partially informed by fictional representations of school shooting, they commit an act that consequently serves as a new contribution to the circulating imagery and that, in turn, can serve as source for the medial prefiguration of another school shooting.

3.2 Shifting Perspectives: New Understandings of Fictional Representations of School Shootings

It may be challenging to consider the relevance of fiction on the level of the school shooting and the school shooter's identity formation without presenting a reductive account of the dynamics at work. However, considering the complex interaction and reciprocal relationship between fictional representations and extreme violence is of great importance for understanding how fiction is an integral part of all levels of the school shooting discourse. Here, the phenomenon is understood not only as a mediatized form of violence, but as a phenomenon that is generated by its own discourse. Consequently, observing fictional representations of school shootings and their role and relevance for the school shooting discourse must include both the phenomenon itself and the public discourse from which it emerges. The cyclical structure of school shootings and fictional representations of school shootings can, moreover, also be observed on both of these levels.

The next pages will leave behind the observations of fictional influences on the level of the phenomenon and the perpetrator and focus on the fictional dimension that can be seen on the discourse level. These observations are necessary for understanding what informs and shapes the fictional dimension of the school shooting discourse.

As I have shown in Chapter 2, the school shooting phenomenon is strikingly similar to *amok* in its discursive dynamics. One of these similarities is that everything the public knows about school shootings is taken from (medial) accounts. And while the media has changed considerably in the time between the early *voyage narratives* and facebook, the usage of fictional elements in the creation of the narrative of this form of excessive violence can be observed in both forms of media. One cannot talk about school shootings or school shooting fiction without keeping in mind that fictional elements are in fact an integral part in the process of discourse formation.

As it has been established, the school shooting narrative is necessary for meaning-making and for establishing a sense of causality that society needs in order to cope with certain forms of violence and thus restore trust in society – which Reemtsma (2012) has pointed out is an integral part of a functioning civilization. However, the role fictional representation has in the creation of these necessary narratives of causality still has to be shown, as well as whether or not fictional representations can offer alternative approaches to the inexplicable violence.

I have established the fictional components of the school shooting discourse on the level of the phenomenon in the previous chapter and have shown how fiction is used in processes of identity formation and performance, therefore presenting the first two stages of the reciprocal relationship between school shootings and fiction. Chapter 3.2.1 will now focus on how the fictional dimension can be observed on the level of discourse formation and discuss how the first two stages are incorporated and used for the public perception and understanding of school shootings. After that, section 3.2.2 will serve as a transition to the subsequent case studies by evaluating how the functions of school shooting literature and film may be approached. Drawing upon findings from reception aesthetics and cultural memory studies, this last part will present the theoretical background for the further analysis of the narrative techniques and strategies employed in the fictional works that are central to the following chapters.

3.2.1 Outlining the Fictional Dimension of the School Shooting Discourse

As phenomena of excessive violence are inseparably linked with the way society understands itself, it may be tempting to reduce the analysis of the fictional dimension of the school shooting discourse to the observation that all narratives that cultures create and tell in order to find out 'who they are' and create meaning out of collective experiences mostly "turn out to be an imaginative (re)construction of the past in response to current needs" (Neumann 2010: 334). "Such conceptual and ideological fictions of memory", Birgit Neumann writes, "consist of predisposition, biases, and values, which provide agreed-upon codes for understanding the past and present" (ibid.). These agreed-upon codes for understanding have a fictional dimension that is rooted in the constructedness of memory. Memory and the "socially constituted forms, narratives, and relations" it is made from, as Mieke Bal states, remain "amendable to individual intervention" and therefore are "an instance of fiction rather than imprint" (Bal 1999: xiii).

This fictional nature of remembering, it has become clear over the last chapters, is an integral part of society's way of dealing with school shootings – and the predispositions, biases and values that form the reconstruction of the phenomenon have already found their expression in novelistic and filmic representations. But when the school shooting discourse is considered, the fictional dimension can also be observed on the level of the creation of narrative in earlier discourse formation, which, in turn, influences the phenomenon as such, as school shooting are understood as "a phenomenon of perception" (Ahrens 2015: 151).

The need for a coherent narrative becomes extremely relevant in the face of events that otherwise defy a sense of coherence and the onlooker's 'practical understanding' – the culturally prefigured approach to events and actions. Narrativization of events and experiences, as Hayden White has pointed out, means imposing the form of a story upon one's experience (cf. White 1980: 6). He distinguishes between "a historical discourse that narrates, on the one side, and a discourse that narrativizes, on the other; between a discourse that openly adopts a perspective that looks out on the world and reports it and a discourse that feigns to make the world speak itself and speak itself *as a story*" (White 1980: 6f). As he makes clear, "[n]arrative becomes a *problem* only when we wish to give to *real* events the *form* of story. It is because real events do not offer themselves as stories that their narrativization is so difficult" (ibid.: 8). White's observation that the cultural function of narrativizing discourse is "an intimation of the psychological impulse behind the apparently universal need not only to narrate but to give to events an aspect of narrativity" (ibid.) can help to understand the specifics of discourse formation in the aftermath of a school shooting – the point where the school shooting narrative is being applied, appropriated and, if necessary, modified. It is precisely at this stage of the reciprocal relationship and in this psychological impulse and cultural desire that fiction can enter the discourse. Here, the fictional representations that are already referenced in the school shooting as a performative act can begin to permeate the school shooting discourse in the media and thereby the public perception and understanding of the phenomenon as such.

Practices of Discourse Formation: The Construction of a Perpetrator

Niklas Luhmann's famous statement that "[w]hatever we know about our society, or indeed about the world in which we live, we know through the mass media" (Luhmann 2000: 1), I believe, can also be applied to fictional representations: Fictionalized versions of the shared reality of societies exert a vast influence on the way that people perceive, understand and interpret the world around them. The importance of these fictional representations in shaping the understanding of events or phenomena increases when that which is represented is known solely via its medial representation, as is often the case with acts of excessive violence. The fictional element of the school shooting discourse is relevant in this regard in two ways: First, school shootings are extremely rare and are only witnessed by few people; what exactly happens when a school shooting takes place is of part of the cultural imaginary, which incorporates elements from news footage as well as from fictional representations and popular culture.[36] Second, as pointed out in Chapter 2, school shootings can be understood in a discursive tradition of the ancient phenomenon of *amok*. The fictionally charged representations and accounts of *amok* can only be understood in terms of their sensational character and the practice of 'othering' (by creating a fictionalized image of the savage and, later, the mentally ill). This process is mirrored today in the school shooting discourse: Here, too, the act of violence is approached by 'othering' the perpetrator, either by pathologizing, or by drawing upon the concept of evil (cf. e.g. Eagleton 2010), or the fictionalized imagery of the 'monster'.

Fiction is integrated in the process of discourse formation through the performative act of the school shooting, which includes various fictional elements. Because of the extent of the shooter's planning, staging and self-representation, the perpetrator can only be perceived side-by-side with the fictional influences that he has himself incorporated. What the public knows and sees is a strictly mediatized version of the school shooter. This version has been carefully prepared by the school shooter, making the public into not only witnesses of the act, but an audience. Thus, the public itself becomes an integral part of the performative aspect of the school shooting. In the aftermath of school shootings, with the strong focus on the shooter's self-representations and explanatory attempts or stylizations, the fictional elements of his identity formation are then inevitably integrated in the discursive search for explanations and answers.

When Bastian Bosse, the shooter from Emsdetten (2006), uploaded videos of himself prior to the attack, he did not only carefully edit his self-representations, but also referenced and imitated scenes and images from *Fight Club* (Fincher, USA 1999) and *The Matrix* (Wachowski/Wachowski, USA, 1999). He included quotes, imitated postures and stances and even the angles of his amateur camera in order to recreate scenes from the movies (cf. Grzeszyk 2012: 119ff.). Similarly, Seung-Hui Cho included videos in his media package that were clearly reminiscent of the Korean film *Oldboy* (Chan-wook, South Korea, 2003). The most notable reference is to a scene in which Cho faces the camera in a medium shot, swinging a hammer with an enraged expression on his face. The use of the hammer in this scene is at first puzzling, but can be understood in light of Cho's identification with the character of an avenger. (cf. Grzeszyk 2012: 132, Schildkraut 2012: 244). To a varying degree, these fictionalized self-representa-

---

36 The notion of the cultural imaginary and the how fictional representations are included in this image repertoire will be discussed in the next subchapter.

tions were later integrated in the analysis of the perpetrator and the attempts to explain his actions.

Consequently, these partially fictional self-representations become part of the school shooting narrative. When Cho stylizes himself as an avenger, modelled after a fictional character from *Oldboy*, and Bastian Bosse as Neo from *The Matrix*, they draw upon the image repertoire of a certain cultural imaginary, hoping to make their audience understand them in the way they understand themselves: as cruel, yet righteous avengers who take action against all the people who have made them suffer. When Cho gave his video material to CNN, he wanted it all to be shown on television. Obviously, he was well aware that, in Luhmann's words, everything the public knows about phenomena of excessive violence they know from mass media. However, the news station chose to show only some parts of his self-explanations (cf. Muschert/Ragnedda 2011: 350). The medially transported version of the shooter's self-representation was therefore edited twice: Cho himself carefully edited his material, then composed a media package so that his perceived audience would 'understand' what he did and so that he could broadcast his newly created identity, which was so different from the one he performed in reality prior to the attack.

Bastian Bosse, before Cho, was more careful. He feared that his videos would not be made public at all, like the Columbine shooter's *Basement Tapes*, and so he uploaded them himself. Bosse's videos, too, are carefully edited; while they have the appearance of authentic, unedited, raw amateur-videos, Grzeszyk (2012: 70) has pointed out various signs of a very detailed and concept-based editing process (cf. Grzeszyk 2012: 70). The version of Bosse presented to the public is thus a performance and, ultimately, a fictional version of the shooter, with his self-representation at times dissolving into imitations of his fictional idols. Through the process of subject formation and the staging of the school shooting, the fictional components of the genesis and performance of the shooting are automatically included in the school shooting discourse and enter public perception. The performative act of the school shooting completes the medially prepared transportation of the fictional components into the social-material space, where the discourse formation begins.

The Fictional Dimension of 'Othering' the School Shooter

This leads to what has been identified as the third stage in the reciprocal relationship of fiction and school shootings, in which the medial discourse formation takes place and the public understanding of school shootings is shaped. In the process of discourse formation, the media plays a crucial role in the construction and the dissemination of the predominant school shooting narrative.

The quest for explanations, to answer the question "Why?", and for the construction of a clear chain of causality generally dominates the discourse; the approaches to the question and the emphasis put on central issues related to the deed, however, tend to differ over the course of the medial aftermath, as well as in the different school shootings (cf. e.g. Muschert 2002, Ahrens 2015).

One of the dominating discursive practices that is deeply engrained in the predominant school shooting narrative, and in most attempts to explain the inexplicable, is the 'othering' of the school shooter. Richard T. Evans, discusses this in terms of the imagery of masculinity, the homophobia and compulsory heterosexuality that permeates the school shooting discourse and asks how fictional representations of school shootings reinforce practices of 'othering':

> It is this immediate exclusion from normalcy that seems to haunt and warp the image of the school shooter in the collective minds of the audience that witnesses the tragedy either live or on television. The killer(s) must quickly be made 'other' somehow, be cast in the light of an encompassing abnormality that sits in stark opposition to the average 'middle-class white' boys who roam the hallways of countless American schools, from Bellingham to Boca Raton. Seemingly, the easiest and most comprehensive way to do so is to call into question and to deride the masculinity and heterosexuality of the shooter(s). (Evans 2016: 4)

In the creation of the school shooting-narrative, the perpetrators – who stylize themselves in the manner of their hypermasculine idols and stage a media spectacle that draws upon available imagery of violence and manhood (cf. Kellner 2008) – are immediately 'othered' and spoken of in terms of failed manhood by being labeled gay or denied the ability to act rationally because of supposed mental illnesses.

Both mechanisms, regardless of whether they hold water or not, serve to distinguish the perpetrator from the 'normal', white, middle-class boy. In the discursive dynamics that can be observed in the direct aftermath of a school shooting, a whole "range of mechanisms would be used to alienate the shooters and set them apart from their white youth peers in order to mitigate white male youth culpability" (Linder 2014: xv).[37] It is alarming that the categories of sexuality,

---

[37] In cases where the perpetrator was not a white, middle-class boy, the societal need to actively demarcate the normal from the abnormal is the most obvious: When Jeffrey Weise of the Ojibwe people killed seven people and wounded five more at his former school in Red Lake, Minnesota in 2005, after he had shot his grandfather and his grandfather's girlfriend on the Red Lake Indian Reservation in Minnesota (cf. Newman/Fox 2009), the aspect of race was overly emphasized in the aftermath of the school shooting. Framing the Red Lake shooting as a problem of the Native American community rather than a national one can be understood as an at-

gender and race are frequent discursive mechanisms of explaining and are used to form a narrative of causality that is meant to help find ways of preventing a similar attack.

The practice of 'othering' the school shooter is inherent to the discourse of excessive violence and is dependent on preexisting biases, values and notions of normality and abnormality. When the modes of prevention derived from the analysis of the perpetrators are based on the shooter's stylization and self-representation, they are also based on highly constructed and partially fictionally informed typologies and often on *post mortem* diagnoses.

The fictional dimension of the practice of 'othering' the perpetrator becomes even more obvious in the frequent labeling of school shooters as 'monsters'. The person who witnesses excessive violence, as Andreas Prokop has recently stressed, necessarily 'others' the perpetrator and situates him at the only place where such an individual can be tolerated – on the very outer rim of society (cf. Prokop 2015: 79f). Using the word 'monster' to describe somebody who has committed an otherwise unspeakable crime helps to make a phenomenon fathomable. By calling a school shooter a 'monster', the shocking and strange aspects of the crime committed acquire something of the familiar, at least in their description (cf. ibid.).

As pointed out earlier, the school shooting narrative serves as a way to construct a chain of causality and provide an explanation for the act – which, in Ricœur's understanding of narrative, would be the first and foremost task of any narrative: "A narrative that fails to explain is less than a narrative. A narrative that does explain is a pure, plain narrative" (Ricœur 1984: 148).

When scrutinizing the nature of these explanatory narratives, however, the historicity of school shootings and the school shooting narrative also has to be regarded. School shootings evolve in close interdependency with the conditions and the technological, medial and social backgrounds of the time in

---

tempt to make it forgettable (cf. Linder 2014: xv). Also, in the aftermath of the Virginia Tech shooting, Cho's racial 'otherness' was frequently mentioned.

When it comes to gender and masculinity, with 'othering' the male shooter as queer, the harmful effects of hegemonic masculinity are typically accepted socially rather than questioned or criticized. By including alleged queerness in the shooter's rationale, who might be seen as engaging in a process of re-masculinization, the fact that the perpetrators are in fact attempting to cultivate a hypermasculine version of themselves through excessive violence (cf. Kellner 2012: 301) is regarded as relevant. Yet, if the consequences drawn from this observation lead to a normalization of the hegemonic masculinity and to a depiction of the queer as a threat, this only serve to underline the real struggles of queer people at schools. The logic behind this is dangerous: "If the perpetrators of rampage violence are proven to be queer, then protecting youth from queer influences will guard against youth violence" (Linder 2014: 41).

which they take place; these events therefore have a high degree of historicity. As a phenomenon that is still emerging, that dynamically evolves and modifies its forms, the public and medial discourse is also constantly modified. The school shooting narrative, consequently, is retold, remediated and adjusted in order to fulfill its discursive task of explaining and of creating causality. It is on this level that the practice of 'othering' the shooter by ascribing a kind of monstrousness to him take place. When the emplotment (*sensu* Ricœur) – the ordering of events – relies on narrative strategies that are linked to the realm of fiction in terms of genre, the very narrative itself, consequently, inherits fictional elements. When real events are told in a manner that follows the narrative construction of a horror story in terms of emplotment and characterization, this is indeed a fictionalizing act, as horror is a fictional rather than a historical genre (cf. Ricœur 1988: 188). According to Ricœur's understanding, this fictionalization of real events has an ethical component: Narrative strategies of the horror genre can be employed to convey horror in the recipient of a historical narrative.

Labeling a school shooter a 'monster', therefore, is an act that is used as a societal and medial coping mechanism, and it cannot be understood without regarding the fictional dimension of this process: The label 'others' the perpetrator in the most extreme way possible, implying that the shooting is the inevitable outcome of an intrinsically evil perpetrator. It evokes a feeling of horror that fosters the repulsion that society needs in order to maintain stability in the face of acts of excessive violence.

Attempts to answer the question of why kids kill other kids are therefore highly fictionally charged. Even though the dynamics are different, the popular attempts for explanation as well as the explained in Chapter 2, as well as the 'othering' of the perpetrator have a coherence in their narrative structure that can only be understood in terms of fictionally prefigured and premediated understandings of threats to society. Where there are no causal explanations, where there is no coherence to speak of, fictional elements can help in establishing these missing elements in the discourse.

Premediation and the Fictional Dimension of School Shootings as Media Events

The most common strategy of prevention involves adopting the perpetrator's self-representation and previous medial and fictional representations and explanations. School shootings can only be understood as a media event; they are real events with real consequences, but it is only via their medial representation within mass media and other communicative practices that they become the *distinctive, recognizable* and *momentous* events that they are (cf. Erll 2007: 3). In the creation of this distinct event, it is not only the fictional elements inherent to the discourse or the fictions that have found their way into the discourse via the medial (self-)representations of the shooters that contribute the overarching fictional dimension. The fictional representations of school shootings also contribute to the medial communication of the event, becoming important parts of the discourse in the process. While remediation has already played a significant role in the creation of the 'look of school shootings' that influences the entire school shooting discourse with its prefigured imagery, here, the concept of premediation is of importance.

Premediation has been introduced by Richard Grusin as a kind of logical addition or "structural counterpart" (Grusin 2010: 13) to the double logic of remediation (cf. Bolter/Grusin 2000). It is very fruitful for understanding how the imagery of school shootings is established via media and fictions and for approaching the specific dynamics of the school shooting discourse. With premediation, Grusin (2010) has introduced a concept for describing the medial representation of things that could happen in the future, such as the medial anticipation of acts of terror after the collective trauma of 9/11, but also the fictional imagination of new media technologies and the cultural desire for an acceleration of their development. "Where remediation entailed the refashioning of prior media forms and technologies", Grusin writes, "premediation entails the remediation of future media forms and technologies [...]. In addition, premediation entails the desire to remediate the future before it happens, the desire that catastrophic events like 9/11 never catch us unaware" (2010: 13). Like the various images of planes crashing into skyscrapers in various fictional films before 9/11, school shootings also have their "uncanny cinematic predecessors" (ibid: 14).

As the "American understanding and representation of 9/11 was clearly premediated by disaster movies, the crusader narrative, and biblical stories" (Erll 2010: 393), the (international) understanding of school shootings, too, was premediated by movies that represent excessive violence, revenge narratives and previous school shootings. Not only have the perpetrators seen the films that they later refer to in their self-representations or in the staging of their attack, the people who are exposed to the shooting in the media may have watched films like *Natural Born Killers*, *The Basketball Diaries* or even *Elephant*. These prefigured images of kids killing other kids in schools certainly shapes the performance of the staged attack committed by the perpetrators, but also, in Grusin's sense, 'prepares' society for these forms of violence. That school shootings are premediated by previous medial and fictional representations is important for both the emergence of the phenomenon and the dynamics of its discourse. This premediation "can both prefigure the future event in the very medium within the event itself is experienced [...] and bring about a kind of affective response to media that helps to inure us to, or train us to endure, media events that produce frightening, shocking, fearful, or traumatic responses" (Grusin 2010: 17f.).

In her seminal study of medial representations of the Indian Mutiny, Astrid Erll (2007) offers a modification of Grusin's concept that can help to underline the role of premediation within the reciprocal relationship between fiction and school shootings: Rather than understanding premediation as a medial anticipation of the *future*, Erll uses the concept to focus on the perspective of *contemporary* medial representations. Premediation, in Erll's version of the concept, refers to the use of media schemata that have been constructed in the past and that are now being used to medially represent new and contemporary events (cf. Erll 2008: 29ff.).

As Erll's study shows, the use of media schemata is mostly not made explicit and most likely not intended; it is rather due to the broad cultural availability of the previous medial representations that they are being used for the (re-)presentation and interpretation of new and unknown situations. Consequently, premediation in the school shooting discourse helps to clarify how and why the discursive dynamics and the medial representations of school shootings follow clear patterns and have shown great similarities over the past two decades: In the representation of the shootings, the available media schemata for representation are always (re)incorporated. This notion is important on the level of discourse formation, of which medial representations are an integral part.

3.2.2 Functions of Literature and Film in the School Shooting Discourse

It has now been established how bound up fiction is with the school shooting discourse and to what extent fictional elements have permeated all levels of the discourse – from the perpetrator and the actual deed to its mediatization and the construction of the explanatory narrative in the aftermath of any school shooting. Fictional representations of school shootings in literature and especially in film, until now, have primarily used to underline this relationship or – like *The Dirties* – have served to illustrate this reciprocity.

The notion of the reciprocal relationship of fiction and reality that has now been established is the starting point for the analyses of the works of fiction being dealt with here. If fictional representations were not ascribed an ability to affect their recipient, the analysis of literature and films that depict and represent school shootings would have no direct connection to the real event and its discourse. In order to consider the functions of fictional texts for the discourse, the term *function* itself requires further elaboration.

As the debate about media violence has shown, the school shooting discourse – much like other discourses about violence and sexuality – ascribe immediate social functions and specific individual effects to fictional representation. But how the works of fiction being dealt with here is mostly left untheorized. In the scope of the present volume, the assumed effects and functions of fiction and the way in which they can influence the individual and, consequently, the cultural perception of school shootings, needs to be analyzed and further theorized. Without aiming to summarize at least four decades of increasing focus on the relevance, functions and effects of literature (and other media like film), I will outline some approaches to show that an analysis of how literature and film work and function within the complex school shooting discourse holds great promise. These approaches include reception aesthetics and literary anthropology, *Funktionsgeschichte* (the history of the changing functions of fiction) and cultural memory studies. Most of these approaches concentrate on literature but, from a cultural studies perspective, can also be applied to other media (like film) without neglecting the specificity of the various types of media. In order to do so, I will refer to literature first and elaborate on the intermedial relevance of the approaches later.

Ever since the 1960s, a shift towards the analysis of functions of literature, advanced by scholars such as Erwin Wolff, can be observed (cf. Nünning 1992: 199).[38] With Wolfgang Iser's reception aesthetics, feminist literary criticism, poststructuralism and New Historicism, the notion that literary texts are by no means mere mirrors of historical reality but rather exist as part of a dynamic reciprocal relationship became more prominent:[39] Over the last decade, this avenue of thinking has garnered new interest in studies by cognitive narratologists, who combine findings from psychology and neuropsychology with narrative theory and narratology to analyze how the reading and viewing of fiction can change the reader's mind and, consequently, impact their lives (cf. Nünning 2014).

---

38 For Wolff, who focused primarily on literature's function in mediatizing and multiplying knowledge and in the formation of collective identity, the relationship of literature and extratextual reality, however, was still considered to be one-sided: While literature was understood as clearly influenced by the changing social structures of society, its potential to influence this social, extratextual reality was not considered (cf. Stratmann 1984).
39 In the following pages, I will focus on Winfried Fluck's approach, which is based to a great extent on Wolfgang Iser's findings, and use it to analyze the potential functions of literature. However, other approaches based on systems theory (Reinfandt 1997) or cultural ecology (cf. Zapf 2005) also have contributed significantly to the ongoing theorizing of the functions of literature. On the difficulties of using Iser's theory in a US context, see Ben De Bruyn's Companion to Wolfgang Iser (2012: 97f.).

The study of functions of literature involves recognizing that literary texts are products of their context, because they represent, depict, interpret, comment and process cultural knowledge, ways of thinking and specific cultural problems (cf. Nünning 1992: 199). Furthermore, literary concepts, notions and (re-)presentations can influence societal ways of perceiving, interpreting and understanding the extratextual reality. Literature, consequently, does not only depict reality, but is a historical factor in and of itself.

This understanding is reflected in the fourth and fifth stage of the cyclical relationship between fiction and school shootings. Fictional representations of school shootings such as school shooting literature are part of the processes of discourse formation. However, before they can be (re-)intergrated in these processes, fictional representations draw upon the narrative and the imagery available in the discourse. Literary representations of school shootings are a product of their context insofar as they refer to and represent a very specific, contemporary phenomenon with the means the discourse provides. Because most cultural knowledge about the phenomenon as such can only be derived from previous medial representations, literary texts engage in remediation, representing one medium in another. School shooting literature is therefore a product of both its social-material and medial context. Stage four and five of the cyclical structure deals with how fictional representations are influenced by and, in return, influence the discourse. If fiction does have the ability to influence the public perception and understanding of school shootings, it is important to explain *how* it might accomplish this.

Aesthetic Experience and the Fictionalizing Act

The role of the reader is pivotal in approaching the ways in which literature is a historical factor *sui generis* and how it influences the extratextual world. Assuming that literary texts do indeed affect and possibly change the cultural perception and understanding of reality, this can only happen through the individual reader, the act of reading and the active reception of the text.

Wolfgang Iser, with his seminal reception theory, begins with the question of why humans are at all interested in reading literary texts, when they are well aware they are consuming fictions. This starting premise leads him to the observation that the function of a literary text must be derived from the process of reception rather than from the textual object alone. The meaning attributed to a text always differs from the text itself, and it can change from reader to reader, and even for the same reader over time. Iser, drawing upon the history of interpretation, writes:

> [T]he same text can be understood in many different ways over time, according to the prevailing codes that have been brought to bear on it. [...] Instead of seeking to pin down a single meaning, we may be better advised to recognize the multiplicity of possible interpretations as a sign of the multiplicitous availability of the imaginary. (Iser 1993: 19).

As the meaning assigned through the interpretation of the text is inseparably linked to the potential functions that a text can have, this notion is also relevant to the potential social functions of a fictional work: The potential functions of the text, i.e. the way it may change the reader's understanding of the world or herself, should be perceived as something dynamic rather than as a single or static category. The text and the meaning of the text for the reader, Iser points out, are non-identical. As Winfried Fluck, referring to Iser, states in an article about the role of the reader: "Any discussion of literature (and its 'relevance' as an object of study) that does not take into account this elementary fact of the non-identity of text and meaning must be considered inadequate" (Fluck 2002: 255).

This understanding of literary texts is highly dynamic, as even the text as an object – the book that the reader consumes – is not stable in its meaning.[40] This assumption of a "non-identity of text and meaning requires the reader to actualize the literary text by imagining objects that have an unreliable reference" (Fluck 2002: 258). The reader engages in an active communication; she has to provide links in order to fill the blanks of the text: "It is an intentional, often carefully crafted, suspension of relations in order to make us provide links for what is disconnected" (ibid.). Regarding this act of reading, Wolfgang Iser writes in *Prospecting*:

> Communication in literature, then, is a process set in motion and regulated not by a given code but by a mutually restrictive and magnifying interaction between the explicit and the implicit, between revelation and concealment. What is concealed spurs the reader into action, but this action is also controlled by what is revealed; the explicit in its turn is transformed when the implicit has been brought to light. Whenever the reader bridges the gaps,

---

[40] To understand Iser's reception aesthetics, it is important to note that Iser does not talk about a historical or empirical reader, but about the 'implied reader', whom he describes as a "transcendental model which makes it possible for the structural effects of literary texts to be described" (Iser 1980: 38), and who thus captures the textual as well as the "mental preconditions of the reading process" (De Bruyn 2012: 106). As Fluck summarizes, the term was created to "draw attention to the reading activity inscribed in the text" (2002: 257). Iser's theory should therefore be understood as a "theory of aesthetic experience, because it is the element of aesthetic experience that constitutes the literary text as an object with a distinctive function of its own" (ibid.). Instead of focusing on the text and its rhetoric alone (as Wayne Booth did), Iser promotes taking into consideration the expectations of the reader and the way the reader's mind deals with these expectations.

communication begins. The gaps function as a kind of pivot on which the whole text-reader-relationship revolves. (1989: 34)[41]

In *The Act of Reading* (1980), Iser uses the term 'negativity' to describe the unwritten base in a text that ushers in aesthetic experience. Negativity as an enabling structure generates the aesthetic experience of the reader by making her imagine what is absent. What is imagined by the reader, however, is not stable – it is created and modified during the process of reception. Thus, "[t]he literary text can thus be seen as a training ground for the ability to revise our interpretations of reality and to make us aware of their provisionality" (Fluck 2002: 260).

Here, the connection between the aesthetic experience that can be seen as the most basic reason for readers to consume literary texts and the functions of these texts becomes clear. In Iser's literary anthropology, he further stresses the relevance of literature and fiction. Iser proposes that the dichotomy between fact and fiction should be cast aside in favor of a triad of the real, the fictive, and the imaginary – a notion that is also helpful for approaching the blurred boundaries of the school shooting discourse. The literary text is "a mixture of reality and fictions, and as such it brings about an interaction between the given and the imagined" (Iser 1993: 1). Because it is "permeated with a vast range of identifiable items" (ibid.: 2), it is understandable to the reader, but "[w]henever realities are transposed into the text, they turn into signs for something else" (ibid.:3).

This transformation of the "determinate into the indeterminate" (1993: 1) is what Iser sees as the main quality of the *fictionalizing act*; it crosses boundaries and is linked directly to the imaginary, because it gives a form to the otherwise diffuse and unrepresentable imaginary. The fictionalizing act as a 'guided act' sets two processes into motion: "Reproduced reality is made to point to a 'reality' beyond itself, while the imaginary is lured into form" (ibid.).

School Shootings and the Cultural Imaginary

While there are a variety of approaches to the functions of literature, Iser's reception aesthetics and literary anthropology focuses on the reader's specific activity in 'generating' the functions by actualizing the text. These functions of the literary text, however, do not remain on the level of the individual. When the indi-

---

41 While in this passage, Iser still talks of gaps rather than blanks, Fluck points out that a "mere gap allows readers to indulge in their own projections, a blank compels them to set up relations between their own imaginary constructs and the text. Aesthetic experience is thus, in effect, defined as a state 'in-between'" (Fluck 2002: 258).

vidual's imaginary gains an intentional structure via the fictionalizing act, it becomes part of an ongoing process of cultural self-understanding, as Winfried Fluck states:

> For Wolfgang Iser, it is one of the major functions of fiction to serve as a medium for the articulation of this imaginary. In gaining this medium, the individual gains an ex-centric position towards itself. By providing a Gestalt to that which is otherwise unnamable, fiction enables an important act of articulation which helps to make the imaginary accessible to individual self-fashioning as well as to cultural self-definition. In this sense, the imaginary has an inherent potential of cultural dehierarchization, because it adds new elements to the ongoing conversation of a culture. (1996: 443)

In this process, the imaginary becomes the 'cultural imaginary', which is, in Fluck's sense, a place for imagined meaning that asks for articulation, as well as a stock of images, affects and desires that stimulate the individual's imaginary and challenge the perception of reality (cf. Fluck 1997: 21). The notion of the cultural imaginary is of great importance for the understanding of the fictional dimension of the school shooting discourse, as both the emergence of the phenomenon and the dynamics of the public and medial discourse exist within and emerge from the cultural imaginary.[42]

Fluck argues that Iser's focus on the experience of unknowability of the self does not suffice as a description and basis for the functions of literature, and has contributed substantially to the development of an approach called *Funktionsgeschichte*, which describes the changing functions of literature over the course of time. Whereas traditional approaches to *Funktionsgeschichte* in the 1970s reduce the functions of literary texts mostly to help the reader and scholar to gain insight into about the historical context in which they were written, more recent approaches aim to find out how (and why) certain literary texts have an impact on the reader over the course of decades and even centuries – even when the context in which the text is received is profoundly different from the one in which it has emerged (cf. Fluck 2005: 31). While the term function must always remain a heuristic category when applied to literary texts, as their impact on the reader can never be proven in a strict empirical sense, assuming that a literary text has a certain function is the basis of all interpretation (cf. Fluck 2002: 267).

---

[42] As has been shown earlier, school shootings and the public understanding of the phenomenon rely on the imagery and narrative available within the cultural imaginary. When it comes to the relevance of the fictional representations of the phenomenon, it is important to also consider their simultaneous contribution to the individual's imaginary and perception of reality.

'Function' in this sense, is therefore not to be confused with the empirical social function or the social effect of the text.[43]

The heuristic assumption about a text's functions, however, works like a "spotlight" that "is the pre-condition for identifying patterns of meaning and rhetorical strategies of effect in a literary text" (ibid.).[44] Fluck stresses the need to formulate *hypotheses* about potential functions and effects of literary texts in the extratextual reality, which "will become the basis for interpretive choices based on the hypothesis that certain textual features are designed to achieve certain effects" (Fluck 2002: 268). In this sense, the readers' ability to make hypotheses about the text's functions can be seen as essential for creating coherence and understanding a text and its structure.

Assuming that a literary text can have a number of – political, social, or individual – functions, the fictionality of the literary text plays a crucial role, as the social and political functions can only be realized via the aesthetic experience of the literary text:

> We search out fictional texts not primarily for information or documentation but for a special experience described here as aesthetic experience. In this view, the aesthetic function is the pre-condition of the realization of other functions, because the other functions can be realized only on the basis of the text's fictionality. (Fluck 2002: 268)[45]

While it is not possible to present some kind of form-to-function mapping that assigns certain textual elements or narrative techniques to specific functions, the forms and functions of literary texts exist in close interdependency; context, form, content, and narrative techniques and structures are therefore clearly interwoven.

In this regard, Iser's and Fluck's approaches are particularly relevant to the subject of this book: As it is assumed that works of fiction have an important role

---

43 The *potential* effect in Fluck's sense, moreover, should be distinguished from authorial intention or historical effect. As opposed to the potential effect and function, which remains theoretical and interpretive, the historical function of a text can be empirically proven and historiographically reconstructed; the *Werther effect* as explained in Chapter 2 is a prime example of the historical effect of a text.

44 When using the term 'function' in the study of literary texts, it is important to keep in mind the difference between internal and external functions. While internal functions concern the elements within a text in relation to one another, external functions involve the relationship of the text as a whole or textual elements within a text to the extratextual reality (cf. Gymnich/Nünning: 9). In this study, the term is used to describe the external functions of a text and its potential impact and effect on extratextual reality.

45 See also Fluck (1997: 10).

in the school shooting discourse and for the school shooting phenomenon as such, we must assume these representations have an extratextual function and effect. This effect is not based on their content or on the school shooting narrative that they present, but rather on the aesthetic experience that is linked to their form and the particular way these stories are told. By the realization of the fictional work in the reception process, these representations open up "possibilities of transfer" (2002: 268) in a discourse in which fictional artifacts play a crucial role in several discursive stages. While the aesthetic experience that is the result of this transfer and the realization of the text within the reader's imaginary appears to be highly subjective, it is its intersubjective level that is of interest in the study of the potential effect of a literary text on the extratextual world. Fluck points out that fictional texts link the "subjective and the social by means of a structural analogue" (2002: 270): "Because readers have to draw on their own mental images, feelings and bodily sensations in the transfer process, the actualization of the text establishes analogies between elements that may be wide apart historically but linked by structural resemblances" (ibid.). This is the 'articulation effect' of fictional texts, and it "contributes new elements to the ongoing conversation of culture and thus functions as a source for constant redescription, renewal and, potentially, cultural regeneration" (ibid.).

While Fluck and Iser both refer to literary texts, the potential functions of films can be approached using the same premises. While Iser argues in *The Act of Reading* (1980) that literary texts offer a higher potential for aesthetic experience than visual representations, Fluck points out the complex relationship between actor, character and the imaginary elements that the recipient contributes to the film via transfer. Even though the recipient may experience a film more directly than a literary text, the film still requires realization by the reader. It might even be that, because of the seemingly self-evident vividness of film, the imagination of the recipient is all the more activated and, simultaneously, coalesces with the image of the film (cf. Fluck 2005: 43f.). Therefore, like literary texts, films realize their potential functions via aesthetic experience.[46]

Naturally, when a study like the present one presents hypotheses about the potential effects and functions of a literary text or film, it is necessary to consider the context in which they have been produced. However, while Fluck's diachronic approach considers the functions of specific works over the course of decades

---

[46] Naturally, film and literature have different aesthetics and, consequently, different modes of reception. Without having to cast aside the qualities of film as *Gesamtkunstwerk* that includes several other forms of art (music, architecture, etc.), the focus on film narration and storytelling allows a fruitful analysis of potential functions and effects of the fictional representations in film, as it has been done by several scholars in cultural memory studies (cf. Erll 2007, 2010).

or even centuries, school shooting literature and film is decidedly contemporary. Because of their contemporary nature, the prerequisite for any functional hypotheses about the potential effects of these texts and films is that they are only assumed and formulated as theoretical possibilities; they are interpretative choices that can be made and are understood as potential effects inherent to the narrative techniques of the text. However, if fictional representations in literature and film are ascribed potential social and political functions, studying these possible functions and the semantic dimension of the form of the works is an important aspect of analyzing the school shooting discourse. Every culture has the potential for continuous change and the ongoing institutionalization and relevance of the cultural imaginary in the increasing presence and relevance of media, art, etc. increases this potential speed of change (cf. Fluck 1997: 347). Thus, in today's media cultures, the cultural imaginary finds a vast number of possibilities for articulation through an increasingly growing range of fictional texts, which means that society and society's various discourses are subject to constant and ongoing change. To understand the dynamics of school shooting discourse, it is fertile to ask how fictional representations shape it and public perception and how they engage in cultural processes of negotiating and processing the school shooting phenomenon.

Fiction and the Cultural Memory of School Shootings
Fictional texts in the past have disrupted and challenged, as well as underlined and reinforced, public discourse and opinions, power structures and perceptions of art and literary form. In tapping into the imaginary of the recipient in various ways, fictions have the remarkable ability to inspire changes in thought; the freedom of artistic representation has certainly been one of the reasons why there have always been politically progressive literary and other artistic forms alongside the ones that embrace existing power structures. In the school shooting discourse, I have highlighted a prevalent narrative of explanation and causality that functions to re-create social stability, but that has the negative effect of oversimplifying, of hardening existing structures of racial bias and hegemonic images of masculinity. Fictional representations of school shootings can either reinforce this narrative by re-telling it, using the imagery and narrative elements that have been constructed and established over the years, or they can challenge and disrupt this prevalent narrative.

In order to show the different potential functions that fictional works can have, the following chapters will focus on narrative strategies that employ challenging and disruptive narrative strategies and thus have the potential to challenge the prevalent school shooting narrative. By analyzing the possibilities of aesthetic experience that narrative strategies like multiperspectivity, multimodality and unreliable narration can have for the recipient, I will investigate if the fictional works can use the potential and refigure the reader's understanding of the discourse accordingly.[47]

Any representation of school shootings, however, can serve potential functions in the formation of cultural memory – the collective memory of the past that is shared by generations. Some works of fiction explicitly or implicitly create modes of remembering; they either thematize, reflect or represent collective and individual remembering, or they implicitly represent memory and acts of remembering in their narrative structure (cf. Neumann 2010: 333). Astrid Erll has articulated three main aspects that allow some works of fiction to become part of cultural memory cultural memory: intra-medial rhetoric intermedial dynamics, and pluri-medial contexts can contribute to a work's simultaneous building and observing of memory (cf. Erll 2010: 390f.). The intra-medial 'rhetoric of collective memory' describes the explicit reflection on the act of remembering and other choices of narrative strategy, form or media, and therefore focuses on the fictional work as (textual) object. Inter-medial dynamics are more closely connected to the dynamics of the school shooting discourse and the fictional representations of the phenomenon by means of re- and premediation, as defined by Astrid Erll. Both concepts are relevant for the stages of the fictional dimension of the school shooting discourse and the cyclical structure outlined above. Erll notes the existence of "a canon of medial reconstructions, [...] the narratives and images circulating in a media culture" (Erll 2010: 392).

Remembered phenomena, especially 'media spectacles' like school shootings (cf. Kellner 2008: 7ff.) are "transmedial phenomena" (Erll 2010: 392); as distinct events they are remembered in many different ways. They are re-told in various media in the process of remediation, and these medial representations shape the experience and understanding of future events through the dynamics of premediation. The pluri-medial contexts and networks, finally, approach the cultural and medial network in which a film or a novel that represents historical events is received. However, it should be kept in mind that

---

[47] Other studies, such as Kathryn E. Linder's study of rampage violence narratives (2014), have focused primarily on how fictional representations have contributed to the problematic understanding of motives behind school shootings and have reinforced narratives of causality that have proven to be harmful elements in the fictional dimension of the school shooting discourse, because the reinforce stereotypes or engage in processes of 'othering' marginalized groups. However, there are in fact other examples of the school shooting narrative that have the potential to exert the opposite effect.

> such strategies endow fictions only with a *potential* for memory-making. The potential has to be *realized* in the process of reception: novels and movies must be read and viewed by a community as media of cultural memory. Films that are not watched or books that are not read may provide the most intriguing images of the past, yet they will not have any effect in memory cultures. The specific form of reception which turns fictions into memory-making fictions is not an individual, but a collective phenomenon. What is needed is a certain kind of context, in which novels and films are prepared and received as memory-shaping media. (2010: 395)

This stresses the relevance of artifacts from popular culture that have previously often discarded as irrelevant due to a lack of quality or artistic 'value'. In contemporary media culture, film has become "the leading medium of popular cultural memory" (ibid.). Because it is consumed and thereby realized by an audience, it partakes in discourse and memory formation.

Movies that are concerned with recent history or contemporary events (which may include traumatic events such as 9/11 or wars, but also smaller yet culturally relevant phenomena like school shootings) are accompanied by contemporary cultural practices of reception. The seeds of reception are frequently sown by a number of public discussions in talk shows, by reviews in leading newspapers, academic controversies that sometimes find their way into medial discourse or even political speeches (cf. Erll 2010: 396). Another aspect that is of special relevance for the fictional representations of school shootings is their channeled reception in schools or in the training of teachers and other school staff (as it is the case with some Young Adult school shooting novels).

However, even novels and films that have not been surrounded by a context of reception that is channeled to this extent contribute to the (trans)medial archiving of a (trans)medial contemporary phenomenon. I would argue that even works that do not engage explicitly in the creation of a collective memory of the phenomenon they represent still serve as a repository of a contemporary phenomenon: Because of the close proximity of the production of the works analyzed here to the phenomenon they represent, these works serve as an archive for the imagery and the medial as well as social-material context of the work's as well as the phenomenon's emergence. Novels and films, no matter how they represent the phenomenon, can therefore be understood as an 'archive' of a decidedly contemporary phenomenon.

For this understanding, however, Aleida Assmann's idea that only canonic literature can be seen as important in the formation of cultural memory (cf. Assmann 2010: 100ff.) and as relevant in the sense of an archive[48] must be expanded

---

[48] Based on Foucault's concept, Aleida Assmann defines an archive as "the basis of what can

to incorporate popular culture in Erll's sense, who stresses that artifacts of popular culture, too, can turn into "powerful 'media of cultural memory'" (2010: 390):

> Fictions, both novelistic and filmic, possess the potential to generate and mold images of the past which will be retained by whole generations. Historical accuracy is not one of the concerns of such 'memory making' novels and movies; instead, they cater to the public with what is variously termed 'authenticity' or 'truthfulness'. They create images of the past which resonate with cultural memory. Usually, such fictions can neither be called 'valuable literature', nor do they enter the canon of artistic masterpieces [...]. And often, too, they will disappear as quickly as they appear on the scene. (Erll 2010: 389)

Even though some artifacts of popular culture may not be stand the test of time for their aesthetic value or their innovative storytelling, their analysis helps to understand the fictional dimension of the school shooting discourse. All novelistic and filmic representations of school shootings analyzed in the following chapters mirror the dynamics of the discourse *and* have the potential to influence it. School shootings are a phenomenon that is still evolving; as a form of mediatized violence, the school shooting reacts to emerging new forms of medial representations, draws upon the fictionally enriched cultural imaginary, and incorporates the discursive narratives of sense-making and identity formation. Furthermore, school shootings are intensely contemporary – as mediatized violence, they depend on the media and medially transported imagery available. Fictional representations, too, draw on the same imagery; none of the works analyzed in this book have to reconstruct the context of the phenomenon they represent, as they emerge from within the same context. Even works that were written or produced in the early 2000s and refer mostly or solely to the Columbine shooting cannot be reduced to a historiographical function, as they still play a crucial role as points of reference in today's discourse formation: As long as school shooters refer to previous school shootings, such as Columbine, and use the imagery provided by the media and fictional representations in the staging of their own attacks, these representations play an active part in the public understanding of the phenomenon. Instead of tracing a history of the effects and functions of the fictional works, approaching the potential functions of these works is

---

be said in the future about the present when it will have become the past" (Assmann 2010: 102), to which this study also holds.

much more fruitful for understanding the dynamics of the evolving and changing discourse and, as a result, the phenomenon as such.[49]

The theoretical approaches to potential functions of literature and film that I have just outlined serve as a background for the second part of this book. In the following analyses, I will at times refer back to the functions of literature and film as a repository of a contemporary phenomenon and as a potential medium for the formation of the cultural memory of school shootings. However, instead of reducing the textual functions to this more general observation, the focus will be on the specific potential that the works analyzed here and the narrative strategies they employ has within the school shooting discourse.

As it has now been established that fictional representations can indeed assume potential functions on several levels of the school shooting discourse and exert effects on all processes of discourse formation, the second part of this volume and the following analyses will approach specific narrative techniques and frame the ways in which they contribute to the social understanding of this form of excessive violence.

---

[49] This is especially important because of this book's interdisciplinary approach. Not only have reader response theories and reception aesthetics helped to establish an understanding of the importance of fictional narratives for extratextual realities, since the cognitive turn, narratology has focused on the nexus of stories and the perception, understanding, knowledge and remembering of the world. Cultural narratology, even as a rather indefinite and contested term for a broad field of approaches in narratology, has provided insights for the analysis of fictional texts with regard to the intersections of stories with the shared, extratextual reality. As in history and certain branches of contemporary sociology, studies in social as well as individual psychology has long acknowledged and stressed the effects of fictional narratives, e.g., fiction-based belief change as investigated by Green and Brock (2000). In my further analyses, I will also draw upon findings from cognitive narratology to underline the various ways in which narrative strategies can assume discursive functions.

Part II: **Discursive Functions of School Shooting Literature and Film**

ns of the School
4 Multimodal Representations of the School Shooting Narrative in *Give a Boy a Gun* (2000), *Shooter* (2004) and *Big Mouth & Ugly Girl* (2002)

As has been established, fictional representations of school shootings are an important element of the process of discourse formation and the fictional dimension of the school shooting discourse. They reinforce or disrupt culturally prevalent narratives of these acts of violence and shape the cultural imaginary of a rare phenomenon. As the role of the readers or audiences is of particular relevance for the specific functions of fictional artifacts, beginning the second part of this book with a focus on school shooting novels for young adults seems to be an obvious choice. Young Adult literature addresses the group of people who are affected the most by school shootings: readers aged 12 to 18, who attend high schools or comparable institutions for education (cf. Cart 2001: 96). They share the everyday reality from which this contemporary phenomenon has emerged. School shootings are inextricably connected to youth culture: they include elements of youth culture in their underlying cultural script and modus operandi, and most of both the victims and witnesses of a school shooting are peers of the perpetrator. Furthermore, young adults at American high schools are frequently exposed to the societal fear of school shootings, as metal detectors and emergency drills remind them of the possibility of a shooting at their school. Thus, like any other form of youth violence, school shootings can only be understood and approached by considering the lifeworld of teenagers.

Multimodal school shooting novels for young adults can be seen as attempts to consider and relate to the teenagers' reality, as they provide insight into adolescent ways of communicating, processing and coping with these events. YA literature always thematizes and represents processes of socialization and the individual struggles that result from these processes. School shooters refuse the socialization processes and step out of society in the most extreme way imaginable. In doing so, they leave a permanent reminder of their decision and of the possibility that socialization processes can fail. The YA school shooting novel thus presents narratives that illustrate and make tangible what the ultimate refusal of socialization processes means for adolescents. Here, the specific functions of multimodal literature are of particular relevance. Multimodal literature, this chapter will show, can be seen as the prime example for literary possibilities to react to the rapidly changing lifeworlds of the readership. Because they include various semiotic modes in the creation of their narratives, multimodal novels are uniquely suited to represent school shootings for young adults: they include a number of elements from the media and public discourse and thereby can communicate different aspects of the school shooting phenomenon, and their inclusion and imitation of contemporary communicative practices enhances their recognizability and experientiality to a high degree.

What further makes multimodal YA fiction an especially interesting element in the corpus of fictional representations of school shootings is their overt intended function. Young adult school shooting novels clearly serve an educational and didactic purpose, and having frequently focused on adolescent problems like drug abuse, poverty and violence at least since the 1970s (cf. Cart 2001: 96). The fact that an increasing number of YA novels over the last 15 years have thematized school shootings therefore comes as no surprise.[1]

Like the media discourse, which is dominated by adults trying to understand and grasp the lifeworld of their children,[2] YA fiction, too, is written by adults. The addressee, however, is different: while media, public and political discourse attempt to explain a phenomenon of youth violence to adults, YA fiction speaks and appeal to adolescents. By using modes of representation and narration and creating fictional storyworlds that adolescent readers can relate to, these novels want to include the way in which adolescents perceive the reality around them. In these efforts, a didactic element is inevitable.[3] As YA novels fictionalize youth violence with a strong focus on the youth culture from which it emerges, it directly addresses the young adult readers. In the act of reading, adolescents are effectively engaged in the school shooting discourse and, as I will show in this

---

[1] Obviously, the quality of these literary representations varies significantly. Even though it is considered to be bad practice, some novels – like Todd Strasser's *Give a Boy a Gun* (2000) or Jennifer Brown's *Hate List* (2009) – propose suggestive questions or present conclusive interpretations of the works in their paratext and are overtly didactic.

[2] The fact that adults fail to properly understand the lifeworlds of youths is by no means a new phenomenon – as mentioned in the previous chapters, already in 1972, Stanley Cohen analyzed societal reactions to youth culture and youth deviance (cf. Cohen 2002 [1972]: 200ff.) and developed his concept of "moral panics" and "folk devils". In the introduction to the third edition of his seminal study, he states that school shootings are a recent example for the dynamics of a moral panic (cf. ibid.: xii) and the discursive focus on causal explanations that are meant to find ways for prevention (cf. ibid: xiv). In the context of school shootings, Ferguson and Ivory (2012), as well as Kellner (2008: 61ff.), have investigated how the misunderstanding of youth culture is now focusing on the rapid development of media technologies, video games and the Internet.

[3] It needs to be said here that the way that some youth perceive youth violence such as school shootings may differ greatly from the way that adults do (for some aspects of adolescent Internet commentaries on school shootings, see Lindgren 2012).

chapter, actively partake in acts of meaning-making and the construction of the school shooting narrative.

For the adult reader, on the other hand, reading YA school shooting novels can also be beneficial: the aspects of high school lifeworlds that are represented in the novels can contribute significantly to the cultural imaginary of school shootings. In this respect, analyzing YA school shooting novels can be seen as a viable approach to understanding parts of contemporary youth culture. This, in turn, is necessary for the understanding of the phenomenon and its discourse, as it emerges from the rapidly changing reality that adolescents live in: "For youth today, change is the name of the game, and they are forced to adapt to a rapidly mutating and crisis-ridden world characterized by novel information, computer, and genetic technologies; a complex and fragile economy; and a frightening era or war and terrorism" (Kellner 2008: 61).

Because they live in a globalized and mediatized age, adolescents today are confronted with an increasing sense of instability, as they face a vast world of violent conflicts, threats and insecurities. On the other hand, they enjoy "access to exciting realms of cyberspace and the possibilities of technologies, identities, and entrepreneurial adventures unimagined by previous generations" (Kellner 2008: 61f.). These changes offer an abundance of opportunities and freedom. But the new technologies also require new literacies – as the school shooting discourse and its frequently helpless focus on media violence has illustrated. Adolescents today frequently realize that their parents and teachers do not know or understand their lifeworld, which consists not only of school and peers, but also of multiple activities in social media, gaming and emerging virtual realities.

Youths of "the new millennium are the first generation to live the themes of postmodern theory. Entropy, chaos, indeterminacy, contingency, simulation, and hyperreality are not just concepts they might encounter in a seminar, but forces that constitute the very texture of their experience" (ibid.: 62f.). As I showed in the previous chapter, this has shaped the contemporary phenomenon of school shootings, the public and media discourse around it, as well as the way in which the phenomenon is fictionalized.

YA school shooting novels are written explicitly for the people primarily affected by this form of violence and who are confronted with its effects and consequences in their everyday life, which makes the genre especially relevant for studying potential functions of school shooting fiction. However, to reduce the value of analyzing YA literature to a better understanding of contemporary youth's lifeworld would be selling the genre short. YA literature is rather understood as "viable destination literature" (Coats 2011: 317) that is a subject for analysis in and of itself and that assumes important functions in the school shooting discourse. From this vantage point, this chapter aims to analyze the functions of adolescent acts of reading and the resulting understanding of school shootings, but also the adolescent perspective on the phenomenon as it is conveyed by the novels.

In this chapter, I analyze three multimodal school shooting novels: Todd Strasser's *Give a Boy a Gun (2000)*, Walter Dean Myers' *Shooter* (2004) and, as a point of reference, Joyce Carol Oates' *Big Mouth & Ugly Girl (2003)*. In this chapter, I will concentrate on how the stories in the books are narrated, and ask how the novels reflect upon, depict and shape the adolescent school shooting discourse and the reader's understanding of the phenomenon. Strasser's *Give a Boy a Gun*, which has become one of the more widely received YA novels about school shootings in classrooms, focuses on the development of two school shooters and represents the shooting from various perspectives. In Myers' *Shooter*, the actual school shooting is presented as a highly chaotic incident that leaves two students dead, including the perpetrator, and is told mainly by the shooter' surviving friends. Oates' *Big Mouth & Ugly Girl* is only used as an occasional reference, as the school shooting was never planned or even intended and the story centers around the panicked reaction of a suburban community after a false alarm. Even though the novel does not represent the school shooting as such, I chose to include it because it provides a narrative reflection on the societal school shooting discourse and presents valuable insights for approaching YA literature's ways of dealing with and representing excessive violence to the teenage readers.

The subject of analysis, the subgenre of the 'multimodal YA school shooting novel', requires a thorough definition before the functions of these particular works of fictions can be considered. I therefore begin by outlining the existing approaches to multimodality, before illustrating them with the help of the novels. Besides providing information about the concept of multimodality, the first part of this chapter asks how multimodal literature reacts to the specifics of the adolescent act of reading. Here, the educational purpose and the didactic stance of YA novels is also addressed, as I ask how multimodal school shooting novels can be seen as 'tools for prevention'. In the second part of the chapter, I analyze the specific functions of the various semiotic modes that are used in the novels and ask in what way and to what end the fictional representations remediate and possibly reinforce the existing school shooting narrative.

4.1 High School Lifeworlds: Multimodality, Remediation and Authenticity in Young Adult School Shooting Novels

4.1.1 Multimodality in Young Adult Fiction

As humans always communicate through a number of semiotic modes at the same time, studying multimodality can be seen as a necessity: Multimodality is the "normal state of human communication" (Kress 2010: 1). In its most fundamental sense, the term 'multimodality' signifies "the coexistence of more than one semiotic mode within a given context. More generally, multimodality is an everyday reality. It is the experience of living; we experience everyday life in multimodal terms through sight, sound, movement" (Gibbons 2014: 2008).

Multimodal literature includes this everyday reality by employing more than just the semiotic mode of the written word. An increasing number of novels integrate other semiotic modes like images, graphics, (reproductions of) photographs and maps in the narrative discourse. However, "multimodal literature, that is literature that utilizes more than one semiotic mode in the expression of its narrative, is not a new literary form" (Gibbons 2008: 107). Indeed, the use of non-verbal or non-novelistic elements, such as paratextual images and complementary illustrations, is not at all uncommon.

Not all novels that include images are multimodal, however. For a text to be multimodal, the modes used must be at the narrator's disposal and be an "intrinsic part of the fictional world at different diegetic levels" (Hallet 2015: 638). Instead of being additional illustrations or information included by the author or the publishing house, the semiotic modes in a multimodal novel have to be "produced, used and located in the fictional world" (ibid.). The different modes therefore have to be integrated into the narrative discourse, rather than merely complementing it. Between a conventionally narrated novel that uses additional modes for illustration and a multimodal text, "it is the systematic and recurrent integration of non-verbal and non-narrative elements in novelistic narration that makes the difference" (Hallet 2009: 130). One of the key notions in the study of multimodality is the non-hierarchical, 'democratic' idea that all modes are equal. This understanding allows the questioning of language to be the dominant mode for communication (cf. Page 2010: 4). Herein lies the difference between novels that include images and multimodal novels:

> [A]lthough in the nineteenth century quite a few novels were published with additional (non-diegetic) illustrations to popularize the genre [...], reading has always been a primarily linear, page-turning act of decoding alphabetic signs, of word-based imagination and of making meaning of letters, words and sentences. (Hallet 2015: 637)

Conversely, in contemporary multimodal literature, even non-verbal semiotic modes are integral parts of the narrative, as non-hierarchical and democratic principles shape this form of literature. The multimodal novel can thus be regarded as an independent subgenre that requires an adequate approach in its analysis. It can be observed that "[m]ultimodality is an obvious and conspicuous feature [...], visible at a glance and represented in the layout of the book page that is totally different from the traditional printed page" (Hallet 2014: 150). And yet its specific potential to represent and imitate discourses and communicative practices are immense. A multimodal novel usually consists of a conventional narrative body; that is, verbal narrative discourse (Hallet 2009: 133). In addition to this conventional narrative text body, the multimodal novel employs non-narrative modes as a means to construct and communicate its narrative. The extent to which this is done differs – from a few integrated modes to a level of multimodality that might make it hard to recognize the book as a novel at all – as it will be seen in the analysis of *Shooter*. And yet, these non-narrative modes are not perceived as disturbing or disruptive (Hallet 2009: 131). Rather, "readers will perceive them as integral parts of the novel and will thus incorporate them in their cognitive construction of the narrated world and narrative meaning" (ibid.).

The Study of Multimodality

The study of multimodality can be characterized as an interdisciplinary endeavor originating from a variety of theoretical strands and disciplines: discourse analysis in linguistics, multimedia technology for interaction between human and machine and the social semiotic approach being the most important ones (cf. Hallet 2015: 641).[4] I draw primarily upon the social semiotic and the cognitive approaches to multimodality, as these have proven to be most fertile for the analysis of multimodality in literary texts with a special focus on multimodal meaning-making. Recent theoretical endeavors to approach multimodality have emerged out of necessity: on the one hand, they are a reaction to the realization that the monomodal analysis of any work of art (painting, literature, photography) leaves out the other modes involved in processes of meaning-making, while multimodality "represents the general insight that all cultural processes of signification and meaning-making comprise different modes and media" (Hallet 2009: 140). On the other hand, theorizing multimodality is a reaction to a broader

---

4 For a concise and informative overview of (further) approaches to multimodality, see Gibbons (2014: 11ff.).

cultural shift towards increasingly multimodal practices of communication in everyday life, which is mostly due to the rapid emergence of new media technologies. The study of multimodality recognizes and embraces this "increase in the visual and non-verbal orientation of culture at large" (Bateman 2008: 2) and explores methods and terms to approach and describe it.

It can be argued that new technologies for communication have prompted an increasing focus on the visual, which is increasingly used in everyday practices of (media) communication, meaning-making and identity formation. Multimodal literature reacts to this potential cultural shift towards the visual and actively challenges the "historically predominant role of language in literature and in literary studies and of the written word in printed form in particular" (Hallet 2014: 156). Simultaneously, multimodal literature benefits from the possibilities of 'multiplying' its ways of communicating stories:

> We are told (and shown) from all sides that our society today has become more 'visual'; this is no doubt true. It is also sometimes claimed that the old rule of the written word has been broken – the image has won out over the word. This is, in contrast, rather overstated: despite the increase in 'visuality', it is rarely the case that the written word disappears. What we instead find all around us is a far richer range of *combinations* of different ways of making meanings. Visual depictions commonly *include* words and so the visual and the verbal are evidently working together. When this is done well, what results is something *more than* either could achieve alone. (Bateman 2014: 11)

The historically predominant role of verbal language and text evolved over a long time, and was the result of a dense web of forces of distribution, production, and the constitution of the markets (cf. Hallet 2014: 152). In regard to this development, the social semiotic approach developed by Kress and van Leeuwen (2001) also takes into consideration the materiality of the multimodal artifact, its production and distribution (cf. Kress/van Leeuwen 2001: 4, Gibbons 2014: 15). Especially in an age of rapidly transforming means of production, distribution and marketing of cultural artifacts, considering these aspects in while analyzing these products is of particular relevance (cf. Gibbons 2008: 109).

When considering acts of meaning-making as one of the central aspects of narrative, the social semiotic approach is especially fruitful because it investigates "meaning in all its appearances, in all social occasions and in all cultural sites" (Kress 2010: 2). Human communication employs a variety of semiotic modes, all possessing a particular and "distinct potential for meaning" (Kress 2010: 1) that needs to be considered and regarded. Kress and van Leeuwen "see multimodal texts as making meaning in multiple articulations" (Kress/van Leeuwen: 4), in which the various semiotic modes interact and "semiotic principles operate in and across different modes" (ibid.: 2). They analyze cultural artifacts such as children's drawings, advertisements, street signs and kitchen implementations. Instead of focusing only on writing, color and image, they take into account each semiotic mode and consider the potentials of the individual modes and their interplay. Alison Gibbons provides another useful approach to multimodal literature by applying findings from cognitive poetics to the study of multimodal texts so as to shed new light on "the reading experience of literary multimodality, including insights into the interaction of word and image on the page and, crucially, the way in which cognitive structures underlie both verbal and visual modes of expression" (Gibbons 2008: 111).

As multimodality refers to the coexistence of several semiotic modes in the creation of a narrative, a multimodal text could include anything from (moving) images and graphics to sounds and smells. As this chapter is concerned with multimodal novels, however, the range of modes is limited, since the materiality of the novel restricts the possible modes to ones that can be located on the printed page. Moving images, music, sounds and smells are automatically excluded.[5] Furthermore, the semiotic modes have to contribute to the development, progression and communication of the fictional narrative. As a result, the separate, autonomous or extending use of material outside of the novel (e. g., the use of additional links and sources on the Internet or on DVDs and CDs) will not be considered.

The individual modes as well as their interaction on the page will be analyzed in a way which considers that, "while these modes have distinct means of communicating, they constantly interact in the production of narrative meaning. As such, one mode is not privileged, but rather narrative content, type-face, type-setting, graphic design, and images all have a role to play" (Gibbons 2014: 2). Especially in the representation of a disturbing, complex, and inexplicable phenomenon such as school shootings, the multimodal production of narrative meaning has a number of potential functions, as this chapter shows.

In the study of multimodality, modes are defined as semiotic resources (cf. Kress/van Leeuwen 2001) that have both theoretical and actual semiotic potential (cf. Hallet 2014: 152). This potential is drawn from the past as well as the potential use of the semiotic modes and can be recognized and uncovered by the readers. Frames and margins are thus as much understood as semiotic resources

---

5 Some of the exclusions are therefore simply due to the materiality of the printed book: "Generally speaking, on the one hand the medium of the printed book seems to set limits to the modes and media that can be integrated in novelistic narration. For instance, three-dimensional objects beyond a certain size cannot, for simple physical reasons, be included in a paperbound book. On the other hand, one could imagine all sorts of tangible objects, scents and material as inserts in the book and as supplements to the verbal narrative discourse" (Hallet 2009: 133).

as images, photographs or written language, and can be "drawn into processes of meaning making and communication" (Hallet 2014: 152). The most common modes in multimodal novels include maps, sketches and drawings, photographs, varying typography, works or art or physical objects, formal language and mathematic formulae. While some of the more common modes can be described in general terms (cf. Hallet 2009: 133–139), the number and design of modes is by no means limited and must be understood as dynamic and open to change in reaction to, for example, new modes of communication – as subgenres like the email- or cell phone novel already show (cf. Hjorth 2014; Rettberg 2014).

> Apart from visual images, reproductions or imitations of other kinds of texts and non-narrative genres can be integrated, like, e.g., handwritten letters, emails or other ephemera, but also formulaic languages like algorithms or mathematical calculations. There is, of course, no limited set of modes or media that can occur in the multimodal novel; the collage of written text, images, reproductions of documents and a large range of visual and distinct other textual elements (e.g., footnotes) make it difficult to identify a text as a novel in the traditional sense at all and to regard the novel as 'a text'. (Hallet 2015: 637f.)

No matter which modes are used to communicate a narrative, the semiotic modes in multimodal literature explore new ways of expanding the aesthetic experience for the contemporary reader. As these modes are frequently non-verbal, the reception process and the act of reading becomes hypertextual. The readers cannot focus on the written word, the most familiar mode of narration. Instead, they have to carefully detect, order, understand and assess the other semiotic modes. As readers must relate those other modes to and position them within the narrative discourse, reading multimodal novels requires more intense cognitive engagement and encourages a more active reading process.

Degrees of Multimodality in YA School Shooting Novels
Multimodal novels can employ different degrees of multimodality, any of which will affect the reading process. This, in turn, influences the potential functions of the text, as the three school shooting novels in this chapter can illustrate. Before analyzing the individual modes, I want to ask what effect the various degrees of multimodality can have on the reading process.

The novel with the lowest degree of multimodality – i.e., the lowest quantity and range of modes employed in the novel – is *Give a Boy a Gun*, written by Todd Strasser under his pseudonym, Morton Rhue. It was published in 2000 and clearly refers to the events at Columbine which occurred only one year prior to its publication. *Give a Boy a Gun* begins with three paratextual pages: first, a dedication "to ending youth violence", which communicates the authorial intention of the novel. This is followed by acknowledgements and an author's note which conveys the author's feelings about the fact that even he, an author of YA fiction, now "has to deal" with "murder, adultery, and various other immoral or criminal activities". On the next page, a quote in bold letters from *USA Today* (from May 21, 1999) states: "The hallways erupted in screaming, terror-stricken pandemonium as students realized that this was ... another, increasingly familiar scene: a student with a gun" (*Gun:* 6). As this quote precedes the actual beginning of the fictional events, it serves as a first connection between the fictional and the extratextual world. Moreover, it introduces the topic of the novel.

After a fragment from one of the fictional shooter's suicide notes, the readers find a longer text that is written by the fictional journalist Denise Shipley, who has returned back to her hometown "Middletown" – the name's resemblance to Littleton, the location of the Columbine shooting, is obvious. Shipley states that she has returned to Middletown after the death of Gary Searle, to tell the story of what happened there and "what is happening all around our country – in a world of schools and guns and violence that has forever changed the place that I call home" (*Gun:* 10). In Middletown, Gary Searle and his friend Brendan Lawlor plan a school shooting during prom night – while Gary has doubts and eventually kills himself before harming anyone else, Brendan goes through with the shooting, but is eventually overpowered and beaten into a coma. It is not until the very end of the novel that the readers learn that Shipley and Gary Searle were in fact related.

In this foreword, the narrator explains the different modes used in the novel and her motivation for collecting the information that the reader is presented with. Thus, she actively takes on the role of an archivist, who is motivated to find out and show what 'really happened'. Strasser employs footnotes, quotes, typography and the visual reproduction of online communication chatrooms to enhance the narrative text. The degree of multimodality is quite low, as the number and range of various semiotic modes in the novel is rather restricted. Different degrees of multimodality have varying effects on the reading process and therefore on the functions the text can assume. With a low degree of multimodality, readers are less required to engage in hypertextual and active reading in their construction of the narrative.

The main body of the text is constructed out of statements from various witnesses of the shooting. The different perspectives remain entirely uncommented upon and are ordered chronologically. The shooter's development, and other experiences from seventh grade until the day of the shooting, are recalled and presented from different perspectives. Transcripts of chatroom conversations, emails and parts of Gary Searle's and his friend and accomplice Brendan Lawlor's suicide notes are occasionally included. Variations in typography indicate the origins of the text, with chatroom transcripts appearing in bold and the suicide notes in a different font. The quotes used in the (non-numbered) footnotes are taken from magazines, newspapers and a documentary from the extratextual world and refer to extratextual events, such as the shootings at Columbine or Heath High School, school shootings in Jonesboro and Springfield, as well international school shootings.

However, while the *New York Times* and *Rolling Stone* are cited as the source of some of the quotes, most of the numbers, statistics and statements about guns and violence at schools in the United States remain unsourced. Denise Shipley's statement in the fictional preface to the collection of transcripts with additional statistics, numbers and quotes, shows that the different semiotic modes are in fact at the fictional character's disposal (cf. Fig. 1). Her choice to provide information in the footnotes or to include the suicide notes and chatroom conversations is thus meant to contribute to the further understanding of the fictional narrative.

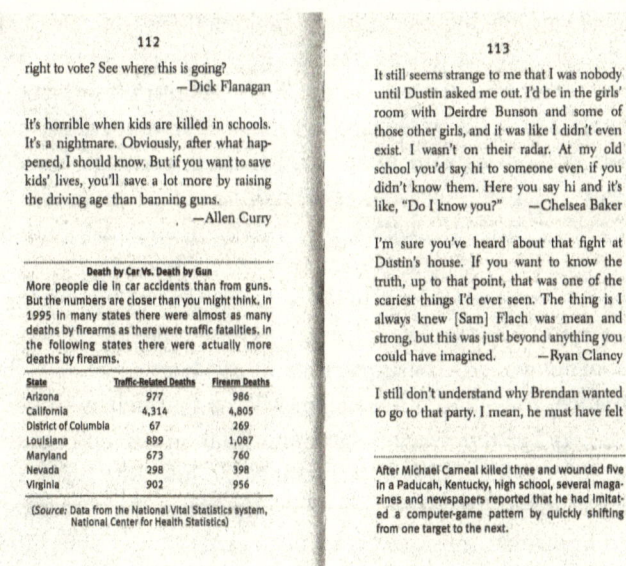

Fig. 1: Additional information and references to extratextual school shootings on the multimodal page in *Give a Boy a Gun*.

Big Mouth & Ugly Girl, written by Joyce Carol Oates and published in 2002, does not focus on a school shooting as such, but rather on the societal perception of and discourse around school shootings. *Big Mouth & Ugly Girl* tells the story of an alleged bombing at a suburban high school.[6] The consequences of the false alarm are told in a first-person narrative from the perspective of Ursula Riggs, who sometimes switches into third-person when she tells part of the story as perceived by her tough and untouchable persona 'Ugly Girl'. The story of Matt Donaghy, accused of planning the bombing by two of his classmates, is told by an omniscient third-person narrator. Additionally, a few third-person chapters present the dynamics of high school gossip, listing a number of statements made by mostly unnamed high school students to illustrate the school's reaction to the bomb scare. The conventional text body in verbal narrative form is frequently interrupted by emails, short notes in different typography and reproduced handwriting, as well as newspaper-clippings. These, unlike the quotations from newspapers in *Give a Boy a Gun*, are reproduced clippings that report the fictional incidents. They are collected by the character Matt Donaghy as an archive of the accusations made against him and his family. All of the modes used in *Big Mouth & Ugly Girl* clearly lead to a more comprehensive and better understanding of the characters and their fictional world – Matt's unsent emails offer particular insights into his feelings.

In *Shooter*, the novel with the highest degree of multimodality, there is hardly any conventional text body or narrative form left. Myers' novel, published in 2004, tells the story of a shooting at an American high school in a number of documents that resemble a case file or legal report rather than a novel. *Shooter* uses a variety of modes and can thus be understood as an example of "materialized multiperspectivity" (Hallet 2009: 147), as each of its modes represents "a different perspective and a different history of production and distribution" (ibid.). *Shooter* uses five different typefaces to signify the different fictional authors of the documents. Furthermore, it includes reproductions of handwriting and autographs, newspaper clippings, legal documents and terms, the shooter's diary and transcripts of interviews. The transcripts of the interviews with the shooter's two best friends and alleged accomplices form the main narrative. While the newspaper clippings and psychological and legal reports and assessments provide further information about the shooting, the interviews with the shooter's friends provide insights into the genesis of the event. These accounts are assessed by the professional interviewers in documents that include their commentary and interpretation of the interviews. The shooter's perspective, on the other hand, is provided in his diary, which is attached to the fictional report.

---

6 The plot of Oates' novels is reminiscent of the school shooting film *Bang Bang You're Dead* (Guy Ferland, USA 2004), which also centers around a false bomb threat.

Shooter begins with a cover page that indicates that the reader is reading a "Threat Analysis Report" by the fictional "Harrison County School Safety Committee". This appearance is underlined by a header on each page of the novel that includes the document number. An introduction of the officials involved in the submission of the report, a mission statement including the disclaimer that "the generated report will not carry a proma facie legal obligation but that it might be used in some legal capacity, and that all interviewees must be informed of their Miranda rights" (*Shooter:* 5) are also prefixed. The following 'report' consists of four parts: interviews, usually introduced by an explanatory note by the interviewers – two psychologists, an FBI agent and a sheriff –; a final report submitted by the superintendent and five appendices, consisting of newspaper clippings, the police report, Miranda Warnings; the diary of the shooter Leonard Gray; and the concluding medical examiner's report.

This novel's multimodality is particularly well connected to the very specific aesthetics and prevalent images and modes of the school shooting discourse. The resemblance of Myers' novel to the JCSO Columbine documents (see Chapter 3) is far too obvious to not be noticed. The extremely high degree of multimodality, which requires the reader to actively order and prioritize the different modes and elements of the novel, leads "to a multisemiotic, more comprehensive, at times also more authentic representation of the fictional world that tries to imitate or resembles the multifarious ways in which the non-fictional reality is perceived by the reader and in which knowledge and experiences are represented and communicated in the reader's lifeworld" (Hallet 2015: 638). A higher degree of multimodality consequently increases the effect of authenticity, as the semiotic modes refer to and imitate everyday practices of communication and perception. While each mode can have a specific function and a distinct potential for meaning (cf. Kress 2010: 1), the transmodal function contributes to this enhanced perception of authenticity and results in a more active, hypertextual reading process.

In multimodal novels, this specific reading process puts the readers in a position that closely resembles their position in real life. As the reading process requires the readers to organize different modes and symbols, the acts of meaning-making that they would perform in the aftermath of a real school shooting are imitated. In *Shooter*, the inclusion of elements that reference and imitate those from the school shooting discourse requires its readers to expand their repertoire of semiotic modes – by reading passages from legal discourse, for instance, or from a shooter's diary. Therefore, they can be challenged to take the perspectives of other individuals in the extratextual discourse, such as friends of the shooter, police investigators, or psychologists or parents who might find the diary. The reading process, as a consequence, has the potential to train readers to make meaning in the real world.

Young Adult School Shooting Novels as Failed School Stories
The particular recognizability and the perceived realism and authenticity of school shooting novels is also derived from the highly familiar setting of the story: the high school. School stories, of course, have always played a large role in children's and YA literature. In these stories, schools and school life traditionally serve as an allegory in a "narrative of a progress of the child through the 'little world' of the school towards the achievement of successful adulthood in the 'wide world' of modern life" (Reimer 2009: 210). Their basic plot focuses on the "initiation, conflicts and eventual successes of a new student" (ibid: 213) and the setting often functions as a metaphor and rhetorical structure: schools are here presented as complete systems, but at the same time these systems correspond to other world systems (cf. Reimer 2009: 213).

This correspondence was especially important when the subgenre of the school story emerged in the 19th century and depicted schools as places where future leaders were educated for their positions of power. The metaphor of the "school as a 'little world' preparing students for other, larger spheres of action" (ibid.: 212) originated here. The development of the school story and its connection to societal and national ideologies can be seen in the generic changes during the great wars of the 20th century. It was during this time that the first school stories "turned inside out" (Reimer 2009: 215) were published, such as William Golding's *Lord of the Flies* (1954), which depicts the unlearning of processes of civilization. While, at least since the late 20th century, school stories have recognized the importance of gender and sexual identity and have made the exploration of these topics one of their main tasks, school stories that criticize the structures of the institution and the values of schools as such are very unusual, and can still be regarded as highly provocative (cf. Reimer 2009: 223).

School shooting novels can thus be considered controversial, as they always inherently question the contemporary school system by representing an attack on it. This, as Reimer points out, is unusual in young adult and children's literature:

> Criticisms of schools as places of injustices, unhappiness and coercion have featured in narratives from the beginning of the genre, but such critiques have been a comparatively thin thread through the tradition. More typical is the story in which the new scholar learns first to understand, then to accept, and finally to excel at the ways of the strange world he or she is entering. (Reimer 2009: 224)

The notion of 'successful adulthood' is a very important one in school shooting literature and is directly connected to the school shooting phenomenon as such, since school shootings inherently question the failures and shortcomings of the school as an institution. When the school is understood as an allegory of the 'real life' in the 'modern world', attacks against it hold an even deeper meaning: school shootings transcend the boundaries of the high school because schools still function as a symbol and allegory for society as a whole. An attack against a school in real life is always understood as an attack against society and its values, norms and – as the school's purpose is to educate future citizens – societal hopes for the future. When the transformation of a schoolboy into a school shooter is told in a YA novel, the emphasis is put on the school's failure to turn the child into a responsible, 'functioning' adult.

YA school shooting novels highlight two major aspects of the school shooting discourse: first, the societal meaning and effect of schools is underlined, as the impact the school shooting has on the community is addressed. Second, the fact that schools are places of different kinds of victimization, violence and trauma – such as extreme bullying – is thematized by presenting what is commonly thought to be the most extreme reaction to these experiences of marginalization. The perpetrator's ultimate refusal to become a member of society is directly linked to his high school experiences.

In *Give a Boy a Gun*, institutional shortcomings in the face of bullying and the suffering of students is thematized in the main body of the text. Other explanations for the shooting, like exposure to violent media or the failure of larger societal structures, are located mainly in the footnotes. While Strasser also stresses the importance of being kind to one another and to end bullying in the novel's paratext, the aspects concerning high school culture and the immediate lifeworld of the adolescent reader are paratextually underlined in the 'final thoughts' to the book, where Strasser calls for a ban on semiautomatic hand-rifles and the restriction of handgun sales. He writes: "If these changes are going to occur, they will have to start with you, the young person reading this book. If this story has moved you, then it will be your job to keep those ideas alive, to examine your own life and your own school [...]" (*Gun:* 207).

The recognizable setting of the school and the experientiality of the realistic narrative serve as the connection between the fictional school shooting and well-known extratextual tragedies and helps the reader to transfer fictional content into their lifeworld. This openly declared educational aim of the novel may prompt young readers to change their extratextual behavior accordingly. Here, YA novels' desire to serve as measures of prevention is made explicit by openly addressing the adolescent readers. As established in the previous chapter, the potential functions of a text and the authorial intention are by no means identical. The didactic purpose of YA literature is, however, 'ensured' by this educational address. Even though this potential is also inherent in the main narrative of the text, the author reinforces his personal stance in the paratext.

The educational purpose of the novel, the direct communication of authorial intent and the appeal to the adolescent reader to think about his or her own life further establishes the readers' connection to the basic plot of the failed school story. The multimodal representation allows for an empathetic connection with the students by presenting their experiences of the school shooting in a very personal, authentic narrative form of the transcribed interview and in chatroom conversations and emails. The perpetrators in *Give a Boy a Gun* remain at the center of the narrative, as they are described repeatedly from various perspectives.

The focus on the perpetrators' status as victims rather than offenders and the insights into their emotional distress by inclusion of their suicide notes, can result in a sympathetic understanding of their actions. Readers who have experienced marginalization or bullying themselves may even respond to Gary Searle's suffering with empathy. As Searle does not harm anybody apart from himself, this empathetic connection does not appear improper. Instead, this ending stresses the severity of Gary's suffering and depression. Brendan, on the other hand, is presented as an unethical figure – only his brutal victimization at the end of the novel, when he is tackled by fellow students who beat him into a coma in an act of revenge, might prompt sympathy and pity. An empathetic connection with the perpetrator, however, remains impossible.

The majority of readers, it can be assumed, will identify with the silent bystanders to the bullying at their school – this underlines the novel's educational purpose, as it raises the question of whether intervening in bullying and noticing suffering can prevent school shootings. The culture of overlooking or ignoring processes of marginalization is presented as deeply rooted in the high school system, as the statement of the highly unlikeable principal underlines: "Boys fight. They always have and they always will" (Gun: 116). The teachers who voice their opinion about bullying know about the problem, but appear helpless and clueless.

In comparison to the extremely negative characterizations of the principal and the jocks, the perpetrators are defined by their emotional suffering, marginalization and development into school shooters. The causality between bullying and a school shooting is thus reinforced. The immoral revenge by the students who beat Brendan also raises the question of liability, which is repeatedly asked in the school shooting discourse. Since Gary and Brendan do not actually kill anybody, presenting them as tragic figures rather than monsters can be understood as an illustration of the general insecurity around how and where to assign blame in the face of school shootings:

> Clearly, the actions of school shooters are morally wrong, and one would be hard pressed to find a moral person who would defend the shooters' behavior. What evokes moral ambiguity about the school shooting cases is how to assign the blame for the actions. With regard to youthful offenders, it is not as simple as it seems to assign moral culpability [...]. (Muschert /Jannsen 2012: 186)

This insecurity becomes clear in Strasser's decision to represent an averted school shooting with no fatalities besides the shooters themselves. Only by this characterization and the clearly upheld dichotomic representations of the 'evil' jocks and their suffering victims, can the novel present its monocausal, consistent and clear causality between bullying and school shootings.

Multimodality, Empathy, and the Adolescent Act of Reading

Multimodality, as I have shown, comes in various forms and degrees, which affects the way in which the texts are received and understood by the readers. In the previous chapters, I have frequently pointed out the particular relevance of narrative in processes of meaning-making in the face of complex and challenging phenomena such as school shootings. The way in which different semiotic modes can influence these acts of meaning-making requires further consideration. Even though verbal language might still be considered to be the "native tongue" the "proper semiotic support" (cf. Ryan 2004: 11) or "the medium of choice" (ibid.:13) for narrative, it is increasingly important to note that "it is also possible to narrate and to make meaning of the world in non-linguistic forms" (Hallet 2009: 148) – or, as Marie-Laure Ryan writes: "There are, quite simply, meanings that are better expressed visually or musically than verbally, and these meanings should not be declared a priori irrelevant to the narrative experience" (Ryan 2004: 12). In the act of reading, the readers can experience and arguably practice active processes of meaning-making and can reflect upon the construction of narratives. Therefore, considering the act of reading, and the specifics of adolescent reading practices, is of particular relevance to the potential functions of YA school shooting novels.

In the context of school shooting literature, multimodal novels have a special significance on two levels: the levels of the readers and the level of the extratextual school shooting discourse. On the level of the readers, the multimodal novel is crafted in close proximity to the lifeworld of the adolescent reader. Representing this lifeworld by employing modes of communication drawn from it therefore seems highly logical. On the level of the extratextual discourse, multimodal novels represent a mediatized phenomenon in a way that takes into account the processes and modes of its mediatization. As I have shown, ever since the 1990s, school shootings have been planned, communicated and later debated in Internet chatrooms, emails, newspapers, in case files and threat assessment reports as well as in videos, films and music. Hence, the multimodal representation of this phenomenon, its genesis and its aftermath, draws upon the modes in which school shootings have been witnessed (cf. Linder 2014) or experienced by the readers of the novels. The fictional representations thereby enhance their connection to the extratextual discourse. By doing so, they become an element in the discourse formation and, due to their fictionality, an element of the fictional dimension of the discourse.

The three novels analyzed in this chapter dramatize and stage the school shooting narrative that has been established, communicated and perceived, albeit with different foci. The novels draw upon the modes in which the readers may have come across school shootings in their actual lifeworld and thereby activate and use the readers' knowledge and personal experiences. Thus, reproductions of newspaper clippings (and, additionally, recurring references to news coverage within the narrative) to report on the school shooting, interview transcripts in the investigation of the events, and emails or chatroom conversations closely resemble existing representations in the extratextual world.

Of course, most of the information that adolescents in the late 1990s or early 2000s had access to came from the news and live coverage on cable networks. Here, the historicity of the media representations becomes especially obvious. Considering the time in which all the novels were published, the multimodality of the texts can be understood as an attempt to include as much of the original modes of 'witnessing' into the fictional narrative as possible on a printed page.[7] As the readers are engaged in hypertextual reading processes and are confronted with a variety of semiotic modes that exist in the school shooting discourse, they are facing challenges that are similar to the processes of meaning-making in the extratextual school shooting discourse. Out of a vast number of accounts, perspectives, images and information, the readers have to construct a narrative that they can understand and make sense of. In the context of school shootings, the readers' knowledge that needs to be activated in order to make sense of the fictional events is inextricably connected to other media representations or even

---

[7] Interestingly (this will be analyzed further at a later point), *Shooter* attempts to convey the legal side of the school shooting phenomenon. Instead of remediating known material and modes within the construction of the storyworld and the fictional representation, it remediates material that may be unknown or at least unfamiliar to the adolescent reader – as, for example, its fictionalization of Columbine documents that were released but most likely not considered interesting by most adolescents at the time.

to other fictionalizations. Including various modes of mediatization enhances the possibility of 'transferring' (Fluck 2002: 263) the knowledge from the fictional world to the extratextual discourse. Therefore, instead of merely presenting a possibly more comprehensive understanding of textual world, the multimodal representation of a fictional school shooting can configure the reader's understanding of the extratextual events and her or his own lifeworld.

4.1.2 Aesthetic Experience and the Adolescent Act of Reading

Strictly monomodal, conventionally narrated texts may tell the same story of a school shooting as a multimodal text does; they may, however, fail to bring across a comprehensive and understandable representation of the specific dynamics of this complex topic. For readers who have internalized a multimodal way of perceiving the world around them, stimulating a more vivid fictional world by multimodal representation can encourage an active process of meaning-making in an hypertextual reading practice. It seems plausible that "transmodal reader-cognition should lead to meaningful narrative constructions, since this is the way in which individual make meaning in everyday-life discourses, too" (Hallet 2009: 140f.). By taking into account the multimodality of all cognitive processes and of all acts of meaning-making, multimodality helps the reader to construct the fictional world in the same way that she also constructs her extratextual, everyday experiences. Through the novel's imitation of these multiple modes of communication, the semiotic modes become part of the experientiality of the narrative (cf. Hallet 2014: 168; also: 2008: 238ff.).

YA school shooting novels can have the potential to inform adolescent reader about this inexplicable form of youth violence in a relatable way. The multimodal text enhances the possibility for a 'successful' transfer of fictional knowledge and meaning-making to the extratextual world by employing a more comprehensive mode of telling the story. While in a conventional and monomodal literary text, all modes and aspects of perception and experience are translated and mediated into verbal language (cf. Hallet 2008: 241), the multimodal novel draws upon various modes of experience and perception.[8] As a result, it can enable the actualization of the fictional text. The fictional narrative and images are integrated into the readers' and, consequently, the cultural imaginary.

---

[8] This by no means implies that the text is generally less 'literary', eloquent, challenging or artistic – on the contrary, crafting a narrative by challenging the reader with a hypertextual and multiliterate act of reading may require skillful storytelling.

However, like any other act of signification, the reader's response to the fictional text requires

> the cognitive ability to understand and interpret the real world, to process sensual data and perceptions into categories and experience-based knowledge, to apply social and cultural schemata, and to employ cognitive strategies to master the challenges provided by real life. These experiences and types of knowledge are required and activated in reading process when words on the page are turned into mental worlds. (Hallet 2008: 243)

For the creation of mental worlds and for reaching the state of the 'in-between' (*sensu* Iser), which is required for the aesthetic experience, the reader's knowledge and experience must be activated by the text.[9] The act of reading consists to a great extent of searching for consistent patterns and piecing together disparate elements of information (cf. Iser 1980). Furthermore, while reading a literary text, readers gradually create mental images based on the textual information. These mental images can have a variety of semantic connotations; arguably even more than actual visual images can have. To understand why the experience of reading is nevertheless frequently altered by including non-textual modes of narration in YA fiction, the specifics of the adolescent act of reading have to be considered.

The aesthetic experience of reading fiction can only happen through a physical and practical act of reading. Here, the difference between the fictional dimension of the school shooting discourse in general and the specific position that fictional works have as one element in that discourse can be pointed out: Due to the reader's awareness of the materiality of the fictional works and their knowledge of the artificiality, the fictional works take up their specific position as a discursive element which sets them apart from other, non-fictional elements. The readers of fictional representations realize knowledge, images, narratives and emotional responses in the act of reading, as they connect the fictional storyworld to their extratextual lifeworlds.

This connection is encouraged by multimodal novels that engage their readers in a hypertextual reading practice and, simultaneously, make them reflect

---

[9] Naturally, as the narratological category of experientiality shows and as I have argued before, this can be also achieved by monomodal textual representation and by the aesthetic experience that these textual representations evoke. Drawing upon the knowledge, cultural schemata and experiences available to them, readers can make sense of the textual world and are able to understand the literary characters and their interactions (cf. Hallet 2008: 244). Nevertheless, the multimodal novel has the potential to convey the communicative and semiotic practices used in the storyworld and experienced by the various modes in the novel. Readers can therefore relate those practices to their own lifeworlds more easily.

upon their act of reading. The inclusion of flipbooks in Jonathan Safran Foer's *Extremely Loud & Incredibly Close* (2012), or the partitioning of the text into separate sections, like in Myers' *Shooter*, are just two examples of techniques that demand a particularly active reading practice.

Adolescent reading practices can differ significantly from those of adults: adolescents engage in seemingly endless repetitions, re-reading the same book over and over again, or reading books that basically tell the same story with slight variations (cf. Coats 2011: 324; Heath/Wolf 2012: 151). Also, the way in which young adults partake in the process of ordering stories and approaching narratives differ significantly from those of adults. It can be argued that the 're-ordering potential' is one of the most important traits of young adult readers:

> Adolescents take charge of the order in which they will read their books. They want their books to be written so that they may replace the traditional story order of beginning, middle, and end with any one of several means of reordering how events turn out. In Young Adult literature reordering, young readers take control of aspects of both the sequencing and the scope of emergence – their own and those of the characters and actions in the books they read. (Heath/Wolf 2012: 148)

This active reordering can be achieved, for example, by reading the end first, or by skipping pages and entire chapters and revisiting them later or leaving them out completely. By reading this way, the adolescent engages in emplotment. In the act of reading and in the 'grasping together of events' in order to create an internal coherence, the adolescent reader thus experiences how a narrative and the understanding of stories and events are constructed by imaginative configuration.

YA novels can encourage this reordering habit in various ways. Some novels, like *The Catcher in the Rye*, use flashbacks or other temporal leaps. Other novels, such as *Shooter*, make the reordering potential an integral part of the novel's structure: *Shooter* invites the readers to skip through the pages, by making the novel appear like a lose collection of documents and by refusing to present any hierarchy. These strategies acknowledge the specific demands of adolescent reading and encourage an active engagement in reordering practices. This hypertextual and cognitively engaging reading practice allows for a different aesthetic experience than a conventionally ordered text does.

For school shooting novels, this more comprehensive actualization of the reader's knowledge of the fictional storyworld offers an abundance of possibilities in depicting a well-known phenomenon. Most YA school shooting novels use narrative conventions that create suspense and engage the readers in finding out 'what really happened'. In this structure, the media and public school shooting discourse is clearly mirrored. All school shooting novels, multi- or monomodal, at some point prompt the readers to ask the question 'Why?' They do so by choosing by focusing on the aspects that concern adolescents with a rather specific focus on the aspects that concern adolescents and their lifeworlds the most, as Chapter 4.2 will show. Moreover, some YA school shooting novels actively use adolescents' penchant for reordering and taking control over the plot by encouraging readers to bring together pieces of information, understand and order them as they see fit. This reading practice obviously resembles the practice of establishing causal school shooting narratives in real life.

By taking control of the order of the narrative, readers may also gain a sense of taking control over an otherwise inexplicable and uncontrollable event. Also, encouraging active reordering can help to establish causal links between loosely connected events or to recognize the difficulties of integrating various perspectives. Naturally, it must be kept in mind that YA literature is intended to serve an educational purpose:

> With few exceptions, as in all literature for children, Young Adult novels are written by adults, which means that they are in fact not about what it is to be an adolescent but are about what it might be or should be, since, perhaps unconsciously, adults want to instruct young people and guide them into adulthood. Here in fiction, representations of adolescence are images of what adults want teenagers to believe about themselves and their lives. Hence it is a very powerful ideological tool [...]. (Hilton/Nikolajeva 2012: 8)

Empathy and the YA School Shooting Novel as a 'Tool for Prevention'
This educational purpose needs to be kept in mind when another function of YA school shooting literature is considered: the issue of empathy in the face of an unspeakable crime. Empathy, as all of the following case studies will show, is one of the most difficult and most crucial aspects of fictional representations of school shootings. Even though evoking empathy at the 'right' time and for the 'right' persons is a challenge for all school shooting fiction, this has an even greater significance in YA school shooting novels due to the educational intent of the genre.

As school shootings take place in the immediate surroundings of the teenage reader and as the phenomenon is directly and inseparably connected to their lifeworld and their everyday experience, evoking empathy for the characters in a fictional storyworld is bound to have an effect on the teenager's perception of the people they encounter in the extratextual world. Establishing empathetic connections with fictional out-groups or victims can therefore be seen as an exercise in empathy and a way to reduce stereotypes in the extratextual world, as cognitive narratology has shown (cf. e.g., Nünning 2014: 234).[10] The way in which an adolescent reader connects to the characters in a school shooting novel, is further related to the teenager's perception of deviant adolescents in general and the images they have in mind when they think about school shooters.[11]

When approaching the topic of empathy, cognitive approaches provide helpful insights: as the study of empathy has received a new interest after the discovery of the so-called 'mirror neurons' by Leonardo Fogassi in 2003, which were found to stimulate the imitation of people's behavior and thus proved to be the first neuroscientific ground on which empathy could be studies. Over the last years, the interrelations of fiction and empathy have gained increasing scholarly attention among narratologists and has been investigated from various angles – frequently, as Vera Nünning has pointed out, in a close connection to decisively ethical readings of fictional works (Nünning 2014: 93). Within the broad range of definitions of empathy and the resulting variety of approaches, it is most accessible when defined as "feeling like someone else" (ibid.: 94) and can, as such, be summarized as "sharing the emotions of others" (ibid.: 99). Empathy, Suzanne Keen has pointed out, as

> a vicarious, spontaneous sharing of affect, can be provoked by witnessing another's emotional state, by hearing about another's condition, or even by reading. Mirroring what a person might be expected to feel in that condition or context, empathy is thought to be a precursor to its semantic close relative, sympathy. (Keen 2006: 208).

One difference between sympathy and empathy is that "[f]eelings such as sympathy usually do not involve sharing what the other is experiencing" (Nünning 2014: 99). Fiction cannot only foreground a character's emotions, it can also allow readers "to become aware of, observe and share nuances of emotions of narrators and characters" (ibid: 109). Readers "can also become aware of the simultaneity of different feelings within the same characters, which are frequently torn between discrepant and even contradictory feelings" (cf. ibid: 109ff.). In

---

10 How and by means of which narrative strategies empathy is evoked in the school shooting novels analyzed in this chapter will be examined further in section 4.2.
11 Neither the authorial intention nor an empirical attempt to prove or show the flesh-and-blood readers' responses is of interest here – keeping in mind Iser's notion of the implied reader that "incorporates both the prestructuring of the potential meaning by the text, and the reader's actualization of this potential through the act of reading" (cf. Iser 1974: xii), it is more interesting to investigate *whether* and *how* processes of evoking empathy with a fictional character are stimulated and where in the narrative strategies and semiotic modes this stimulation is located.

consuming fictions, readers are thus able to recognize feelings the characters themselves might not even be aware of.[12]

One aspect that emphasizes the special relevance of the interrelation of empathy and fiction in YA school shooting novels is that of experientiality. In order to evoke empathy and to share the emotional experience of the characters, readers must be able to draw upon their own knowledge, as any experiences, acts and feelings "are difficult to imagine if readers cannot draw on similar or comparable experiences in their own real world" (Hallet 2008: 235). This means that experiences and knowledge from the teenage reader's lifeworld need to be included. In the representation of extremely rare events such as school shootings, experientiality is enhanced by drawing upon more common and general knowledge and experiences – such as bullying, youth culture, and issues of friendship and disappointment. Alternatively, it can be achieved by referencing the ways in which adolescents may have been exposed to school shootings, such as newspaper clippings or quotes from witness statements. Here, multimodality can be understood as a strategy to enable empathetic understanding of the fictional characters and to stimulate behavioral or emotional reactions to this understanding.

School shooters are, of course, characters highly unlikely to evoke empathy in the reader. This is not only due to their unethical actions and behavior, but also because school shooters are not commonly associated with being capable of feeling empathy themselves. Rather, as in Eric Harris' case, they are represented as psychopaths incapable of any empathy, or as monsters, which makes it impossible for humans to feel *like* them. In an article about representations of emotions in YA literature, Bettina Kümmerling-Meibauer analyzes the ways that emotional connections between young adult readers and fictional characters that are clearly unable to feel empathy are established by literary techniques. She points out that foregrounding a character and the enhanced awareness of a character's emotions are relevant aspects (foregrounding in this sense refers to passages that are noticeably different from the main body of the text, for example that employ different semiotic modes, such as different typography or an unusual lexicon (cf. Kümmerling-Meibauer 2012: 131). These strategies of representation serve to

> present key emotional scenarios so that the reader will recognize the specific emotional situation on the one hand, and to stimulate certain emotional reactions on behalf of the reader

---

[12] Empathy and its relevance for YA school shooting fiction will also be thematized in Chapter 5, where I analyze multiperspectivically narrated novels and use the concept of perspective taking in order to approach those texts.

on the other hand. These literarily imagined emotions are created to activate stimuli that should elicit the reader's notional empathy with the figures presented in the text. (ibid.: 132).

The recognition of a character's simultaneous, different or even conflicting emotions is thereby made possible, as is a dynamic or changing attitude towards a character throughout the text. When it comes to representations of school shooters, this is highly complex issue, as the character is a mass murderer. This is of particular relevance because

> [a]lthough empathy is tightly connected with moral evaluation, both aspects might evoke different reactions. On the one hand, a person or character might be morally condemned because of her behavior and beliefs; on the other hand, one is nevertheless able to comprehend the same person's or character's feelings and thoughts. (Kümmerling-Meibauer 2012: 132).

Most YA school shooting novels avoid presenting the shooters as literary figures that enable an empathetic connection, for reasons that will also be thematized in Chapter 5.1. But as literary figures "affect the reader cognitively and emotionally" (Hallet 2008a: 198), an empathetic connection or identification with a morally deficient character is a slippery slope. This is even more the case when the educational purpose of YA literature is kept in mind. In the YA novels examined here, the unethical or morally deficient literary figures generally serve as counter-models to reinforce what is understood as 'normal' for the readers. As the school shooting narrative juxtaposes the abnormal perpetrator with the normal, peaceful narrative of society, YA school shooting novels depict the perpetrators as abnormal characters.

Give a Boy a Gun, however, is one of the very few novels that could allow for an empathetic connection to Gary Searle, as the shooter who is presented as much more 'humane' than his friend Brendan. However, as pointed out earlier, any empathy towards him is justified by his decision to not go through with his plan. Also, the reader's opinion about and connection to a literary figure can change over the course of the novel, so that the victimization at the end of *Give a Boy a Gun* and the fact that Gary Searle does not actually harm anyone but himself might make the reader rethink her or his position. The suicide notes and the transcripts of email- and chatroom conversations might make it possible for some readers to relate to Gary's feelings of depression and despair. Yet, the possibilities of empathizing with the (potential) mass murderer are still rather slim.

While both perpetrators in *Give a Boy a Gun* are clearly victimized, they invite sympathy or pity rather than empathy, because they are introduced from the very beginning as school shooters. As they remain "object of the descriptions and evaluations of narrators and focalizers" (Nünning 2014: 213) throughout the majority of the text, they are less likely to be understood and recognized, or to trigger empathic reactions in the readers than are characters "who are put in the privileged position of perceiving, interpreting and evaluating the events in the story world and the actions and intentions of others" (ibid.). This is clearly a fictionalization of the school shooting discourse, in which the perpetrator's versions of events are also 'heard' via statements they left behind before the event and, in most cases, before their deaths.

However, most school shooting novels invoke empathy with the people who are affected by school shooting – the victims and their friends and families. In this respect, the existing connections between the shooters and the 'regular' teenagers around them help the readers to reflect on similarities to their everyday experiences. The readers of the YA novels, however, are challenged to recognize the emotional struggles of both victims and perpetrators, albeit to different degrees. When the focus of the school shooting narrative on finding modes for prevention is considered, the texts' emphasis on bullying, verbal and physical violence at schools, marginalization and the pressure of high school societies and structures is a logical one. Naturally, representations of school shootings for adults also consider these issues – the story of the rather recently published *Luckiest Girl Alive* (Jessica Knoll, 2015), for example, centers around the ongoing struggle of a survivor and alleged accomplice of a school shooting to deal with her past of being assaulted, bullied and ostracized. However, the novels written for an adult readership frequently focus on other issues in which adolescent struggles are interrelated with adult responsibility – family life, estrangement from the adolescent child, the accusation of neglect at home, or grief and trauma – rather than detailed depictions of high school experiences and difficulties. Furthermore, it is interesting to note that school shooting novels for adults employ conventional textual narratives rather than multimodal or multiperspectivical modes of representation.

As multimodality has the potential to enhance readers' connection to the fictional characters and their actions, YA literature's educational purpose can be realized in part by empathizing with a fictional character – which can be easier in a novel than it is in real life situations (cf. Nünning 2014: 185). This experience of empathizing with a fictional character can help readers to practice and learn prosocial behavior by engaging with the character's emotions and practicing perspective taking (cf. Nünning 2014: 185), as I will further elaborate in Chapter 5.

YA school shooting novels draw upon the aspects of the school shooting narrative that present a clear causality between adolescent behavior and high school experiences and the genesis of a shooting. The texts evoke empathy with the people involved in and affected by school shootings. In the causal link between bullying and school shootings, which is well established within the narrative of school shootings, the educational purpose of YA school shooting literature not only creates awareness of school shootings, but also encourages a connection between the extreme events and the everyday experiences of adolescents. However, before further analyzing the importance of empathy when looking at depictions of perpetrators, victims and alleged accomplices in the multimodal novels in section 4.2, another specific potential of multimodal texts for young adult readers needs to be regarded. Multimodal YA school shooting novels also reinforce a causal school shooting narrative, which frequently present the events as avoidable.

4.2 Lessons from Columbine: Functions of Multimodal Fictionalizations of the School Shooting Narrative

4.2.1 Remediation and Modes of Remembering

The concept of remediation gains a particularly interesting dimension in the study of multimodal novels. Remediation, it has been established, is an important concept for analyzing and understanding the role and relevance of fictional representations of school shootings, as the phenomenon is mediatized to such an extent that the 'look' of a school shooting – the medially transported and commonly accepted notion of what a school shooting is and what it looks like – has been established by the constant remediation of existing media representations. By including and reproducing existing modes of representation of school shootings, multimodal literature actively engages in these processes of remediation in a more obvious and more direct manner than monomodal textual representations do.[13] Remediation in multimodal novels thus contributes to the establishment of the 'look' of school shootings. The re-telling of the Columbine narrative establishes a cultural remembering of this form of violence. The

---

[13] This is not meant to imply that monomodal, conventionally narrated texts cannot remediate existing representations, even when those were originally represented in a different mode. A literary text can create mental images that can be extremely powerful in their polyvalence and multifarious semiotic connotation, as Wolfgang Iser has shown in *The Act of Reading* (1980). Further, as Wolfgang Hallet stresses, the cognitive process of meaning-making and the construction of the textual world is necessarily multimodal. The readers create a "mental model that represents the textual world as a whole" (2008: 248) in a multimodal way, as they include various modes of perception. Therefore, even if other modes are "translated" into narrative representations, the experience is still related to the original mode. Thus, a narrative description of a video of a school shooting will most likely be experienced as a mental image of a video, embedded in the mental model of the fictional world, even though this is not its 'original' mode of representation.

implications that this can have for YA fiction will be approached on the following pages by asking what content is being mediated, as well as how the remembering of extratextual school shootings can be shaped by the multimodal representation of fictional shootings and/or the genesis and planning of the attacks.

Remediation and Multimodal Authentication

Multimodal school shooting novels represent both the school shooting narrative and the way school shootings are perceived and experienced. The remediation that occurs when existing media representations are used in the fictional representation serves as a means for authentication and is of great relevance for studying multimodal school shooting literature.

As explained in the previous chapter, remediation in film incorporates documentaries, photographs, or newspaper headlines either from the extratextual world or in fictionalized form, thereby authenticating the fictional storyworld (cf. e. g., Erll 2008). Literary multimodality accordingly remediates other semiotic modes to the same end: It authenticates the fictional world, depicts it in a more comprehensive and understandable way, and serves as "a semantic, cognitive, or epistemological surplus that multiplies aspects and dimension of the storyworld that are accessible to the reader" (Hallet 2014: 153). When fictional films integrate actual historical footage from extratextual films or imitate the aesthetics of the hand-held camera, as in war films or *The Dirties* (cf. Chapter 3), this serves as a means to generate immediacy and a sense of authenticity. Similarly, the reproduction of newspaper articles from the *New York Times* or the look of legal documents and diary entries give the impression of immediacy in multimodal school shooting novels. When YA school shooting novels remediate the school shooting narrative by using elements from the media discourse, they become elements of this extratextual discourse, as the boundary between fictional and extratextual world is deliberately blurred.

In *Give a Boy a Gun*, the school shooting narrative is remediated in language-based semiotic modes: brief statements by students, friends, parents and teachers present a chronological overview of the genesis of the school shooting, the atmosphere at the high school and the events that led up to the shooting. However, alongside this multiperspectival narrative, quotes from newspapers, magazines, films and websites are presented in the notes at the bottom of the text and expand the understanding of the phenomenon. As comments on the weapons industry, gun laws, statistics about violence and reference previous school shootings, the footnotes remediate form and content of the extratextual discourse on school shootings. Additionally, tables that show statistics about gun-related deaths in the U.S. citing official sources (cf. *Gun:* 112) or scientific studies introduce the adolescent readers to scientific and journalistic modes, even in cases where the sources are not identified (cf. *Gun:* 157).

Moreover, the plot of *Give a Boy a Gun* greatly resembles the events at Columbine High School and, as Strasser's novel was published not long after Columbine, this resemblance was clearly noticeable by readers at the time. Yet, the novel's connection to extratextual events and the 'tradition' of school shootings is made more obvious by the its multimodal remediation. Here, a close connection between the fictional genesis, planning and failed execution of a school shooting and the non-fictional events to which this story refers is reinforced. Considering both "the meaning that the single mode (textual entity) produces, and [...] the combination of various modes that result in one (transmodal) meaning of a multimodal text" (Hallet 2015: 642) is of great importance here, as the textual entity of the footnotes and the main body of narrative text each create different kinds of meaning – one focusing on the fictional violence and bullying at school, the other on the societal basis from which school shootings emerge.

As remediation in film both draws upon and simultaneously establishes a 'look' of school shootings, multimodal literature, too, uses parts of the visual aesthetics of the mediatized phenomenon and its media representations. Therefore, it reinforces the existing school shooting narrative, but connects this narrative to the familiar modes of its textual representation by means of multimodality. The multimodal novels thus

> enact(s) the material dimension of the depicted world beyond verbal manifestation, tapping generic riches unavailable to the novelistic narration that determines the textual world. In this process, what used to be the extratextual context has now to a great extent become integral to the narrative text itself. Culture is represented directly and extensively; above all, it is no longer re-mediated linguistically. As to the performative dimension of literature, multimodal novels *create the cultural archives that they claim to represent.* (Hallet 2009: 145f., my emphasis)

In the representation and simultaneous creation of this archive of the school shooting discourse, *Give a Boy a Gun*, *Big Mouth & Ugly Girl* and *Shooter* contribute to the cultural remembering of school shootings. They draw upon, re-tell and establish the school shooting narrative and discourse by using familiar approaches to explaining and engaging in the fictionalizing of a real school shooting like Columbine. Furthermore, they present and archive the modes of representation and communication used at the time of the extratextual school shootings they refer to. While each mode that can be found in the multimodal texts has its own distinct potential for meaning (cf. Kress 2010: 1), the next pages will outline those potential functions of the individual modes that appear to be most relevant to the school shooting discourse. This will show how the fictional representations create archives of the school shooting phenomenon and help the readers experience the dynamics of the school shooting discourse in the act or reading.

Archiving Communicative Practices

As established earlier, in the planning and staging of their attacks, school shooters in the late 1990s were dependent on available media images. However, they were also dependent on the contemporary media of communication. The fictional perpetrators, like the real school shooters, make avid use of the contemporary media in the planning of their attacks. The use of email and chatroom transcripts in *Shooter* and *Give a Boy a Gun* emphasize this (see e.g., *Gun:* 79). However, since the time of the novels' publication, communicative practices have changed rapidly. By now, the communication of any public event is shaped by the use of social media. As more recent acts of rampage violence have shown, live videos on Facebook, tweets by witnesses and the police, and footage uploaded to YouTube have enhanced the mediatization of violence in the public sphere. Moreover, the availability of social media platforms, instant messages and live videos has changed the perpetrators' communication of their plans and, as I have shown in Chapter 3, their identity formation as well.[14]

Naturally, these developments have had an impact on the increase of multimodality in YA literature. Representing various communicative practices in the novels can be seen as literature's way of staying in touch with the adolescent lifeworld.

> [P]ersonal technologies have changed the way adolescents interact and interface with their world. New rhetorics have developed around instant messaging and texting, and if we take poststructural claims about the significance of language in the creation of identity seriously, then changes in the way we use language and the way it uses us will alter who we imagine ourselves to be. If we expand the definition of language to include multiple semiotic systems, then we could say that today's youth generate their identities and subjectivities through an increasingly visual, iconic, and virtual web of images that has largely been stripped of traditional modes of authority [...]. (Coats: 323)

---

14 During a shooting by an adolescent at a mall in Munich in 2016, this close connection became clear once more. The shooter was an avid user of social media and in fact invited his witnesses – most of them his peers – to the mall, where he subsequently shot them. The event also made obvious how the posting of live videos on the Internet can affect the outcome of shooting. Videos posted online wrongly suggested the existence of more than one shooter, leading to greater panic in the entire city.

The outcome of *Give a Boy a Gun* and *Shooter* would have been different had they been written in the last five years: Students lying on the floor of the gym might have been able to text one another, and students and staff could have been ordered to hide via mass text messages, as they are in more recent school shooting novels (e. g., *Violent Ends* or *This is Where It Ends*, see Chapter 5). At the time of the novels' publication, the inclusion of the then-contemporary modes of communication gave the fictional world a verisimilitude that it would lack if the novels were published today. As Karen Coats stresses, this is of special importance in YA fiction, as adult writers have to "craft characters who are believably adolescent" (Coats 2011: 323). Contemporary representations of school shootings, even if they still draw upon the prototypical Columbine shooting, need to include semiotic modes and systems that teenagers can relate to, teens "have instant access to images, information, and communication than teens did 10 years ago" (ibid.).[15]

When these rapid changes in communication technologies and their impact on everyday life are considered, the historicity of the phenomenon is underlined. A multimodal novel that presents school shootings one decade later has to incorporate different forms of communication media, and has to refer to an even wider range of communication strategies than the novels from the early 2000s do. Most school shooters, as past events have shown, make use of many available modes of communication. Naturally, the way in which school shootings are mediatized and perceived changes accordingly: WhatsApp, text messages, Facebook, Snapchat and Twitter now dominate the way rampage violence is communicated and medially represented.

Multimodal novels that include contemporary modes of communication enhance the text's experientiality by endowing various aspects and elements of the narrative with a high degree of recognizability for the reader. Moreover, this functions as an archive both of what school shootings looked like and how they were perceived at the time, as well as of the media context in which they took place. The various modes of remembering correlate with the modes of perception and communication. In *Give a Boy a Gun and Shooter*, these representations of communication practices also transport important elements from the extratextual school shooting discourse into the fictional storyworld, as both novels directly refer to the JCSO Columbine documents.

Most young adult readers will not be familiar with the tens of thousands of pages of investigation reports, witness statements and photocopies of journals,

---

[15] Both *Violent Ends* (2015) and *This is Where It Ends* (2016), which will be analyzed in the next chapter, include these changes by showing how victims of a school shooting interact during the attack.

sketches and school essays by the Columbine shooters Eric Harris and Dylan Klebold. Nevertheless, both *Give a Boy a Gun* and *Shooter* quite obviously refer to the documents in their representation of the school shooting's planning and aftermath. In Strasser's novel, these resemblances are used mostly in terms of communication modes and media.[16] Here, the fictional shooters' chatroom conversations that are found on their friend Ryan Clancy's computer can be used as an example (cf. Fig. 2):

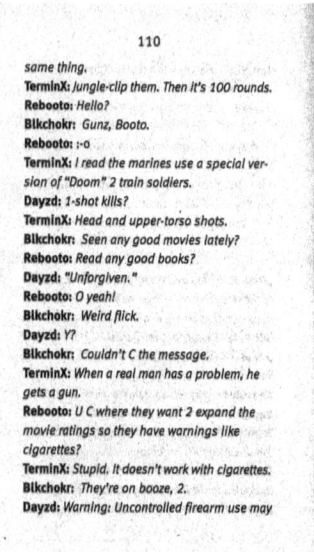 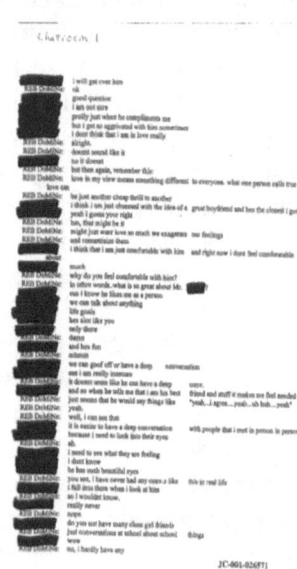

Fig. 2: Chatroom conversation in *Give a Boy a Gun*.

Fig. 3: Chatroom conversation, JCSO documents.

These conversations bear close resemblance to the communication between the Columbine shooters and their friends (cf. Fig. 3)[17]. The way in which these conversations are depicted and their references to guns and video games recall

---

16 It has to be pointed out that the JCSO documents had not been not fully released when Strasser's novel was written and published, and he has not publicly stated whether or not he had access to the documents. However, as many of the documents – especially those taken from the shooter's website – were posted online shortly after the shooting, and because the similarities are highly obvious, it seems to be very likely that Strasser used original documents for his novel.

17 All of the JCSO Columbine documents can be accessed and downloaded via https://www.acolumbinesite.com/report.php

the Columbine shooting as a mode for authentication. So as to frame the sudden change of mode, these conversations are explained Ryan Clancy in his interview with the fictional journalist Denise Shipley: "As soon as the cops found out, they got a warrant and came in here and took it all away, but my dad went to court and got some of it back after the cops made copies" (*Gun:* 66). The incorporation of another semiotic mode is indeed "indicative of practices of collecting and archiving, with actants and narrators as collectors and historians" (Hallet 2009: 136). Ryan is thus presented as a collector and archivist of the contemporary phenomenon.

Narrative elements thereby generate awareness of the cultural practices of creating archives and archives, as a regular conversation from a chatroom can serve as an important mode for documentation and remembering a historically relevant event:

> The multimodal novel thus represents the process of building up a personal and cultural archive of some sort that is then made accessible in the course of the narration and is part of the construct of memory within the story or novel concerned. In that sense, the multimodal novel also represents and makes accessible the multimodality of cultural archives, knowledge and memory. (Hallet 2009: 136f.)

Exploring School Shootings in Different Types of Interviews

While Strasser incorporates these modes only occasionally, Myers' *Shooter* is comprised entirely of representations that visually resemble the JCSO Columbine documents (see images) and, at times, the official Threat Assessment Report of the Columbine shooting as it was conducted by Vossekuil et al. (2002). These resemblances include the document number on the top of the novel's page design, the incorporation of signatures by officials and interviewees, as well as report headings. Furthermore, the generic attributions of the novel's various parts match the JCSO documents. Here, the most notable example is the "Investigator's Report" (*Shooter:* 159), which reconstructs the shooting committed by Leonard Gray. Gray, the readers learn, fired several shots from his school's window, injured several students and killed his former tormentor Brian, before finally shooting himself. In both the fictional "Investigator's Report" and the "Statements of Waiver of Privilege and Miranda Warnings" in the fictional 'appendices' to the novel, the signatures of the two friends and alleged accomplices of the shooter are included to personalize and authenticate the documents.

The transcripts of four different interviews, conducted and commented on by different interviewers, provide the main body of the narrative. It is noteworthy that for each interview, a different style of typography is used. This emphasizes temporal and spatial distance between the interviews and serves to "visualize textual 'difference' and identifiable textual elements, voices, ways, styles and modes of writing" (Hallet 2009: 138). Additionally, each style of typography used in *Shooter* matches the tone of the interviews and underlines the different perspectives from which the interviews were conducted, their different foci and the different reactions of the interviewees. The first interview, with Cameron Porter, conducted by psychologist Dr. Richard Ewings, is printed in fine typography and is held in a friendly tone. The second interview with Porter, conducted by FBI Agent Victoria Lash, is printed in bold Arial and is characterized by a harsh, straightforward and frequently even menacing tone. The third interview with Porter is printed in a typeface that reproduces the look of a typewriter (cf. Fig. 4) – here, the material side of the documents and the different technologies of writing are represented by means of typography (cf. Hallet 2009: 138). In the last interview, the suggested use of an outdated writing device underlines the setting and tone of the interview, conducted by a sheriff, who admits to not being very experienced. This interview presents an example for all the police officials and sheriff's offices in suburban or rural areas that are suddenly confronted with a high-profile case of mass murder.

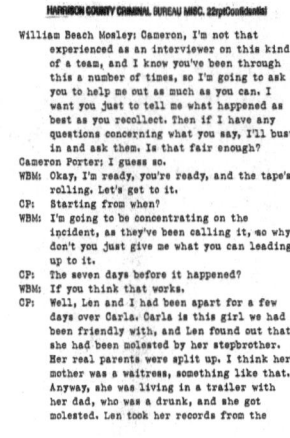

Fig. 4: Interview transcript in *Shooter*.

Fig. 5: Interview transcript, JCSO documents.

An important difference between the fictional interviews and those in the JCSO Columbine documents, however, is their narrative mode: While the witness reports and interviews in the official JCSO documents are presented as a narrative summary of the conducted interviews (cf. Fig. 5), *Shooter* presents full transcripts of the interviews.[18] This clearly has the function to invoke an empathetic connection to the characters, as they present their experiences, reactions and thoughts about the events. A sober summary of the interview, narrated in third person, could convey the same information, but would not invite active engagement by the readers. The form of the transcribed interviews thus encourages greater understanding of the different perspectives on the event.

Another function of these official documents, which distinguishes them from the journalistic interviews in *Give a Boy a Gun*, is that the readers gain insight into processes that accompany school shootings in the real world. By reading fictionalized interviews that are meant to glean information about the perpetrator and his motives and, at times, to find out whether or not he acted alone or with the help of his friends, the readers learn about the way school shootings are investigated in the real world. These fictional representations enhance the reader's imagination and understanding of the phenomenon. Through the connection to the extratextual school shooting discourse and the authentication of the fictional events, *Shooter* therefore contributes both to its readers' image repertoire and to the cultural archive of school shootings by remediating existing elements. The questions that the interviewers ask and the way the narrative explores the events that led up to the shooting corresponds with the questions that the readers ask in regard to both the fictional elements and real events. The form of the official interview is therefore another element in the cultural archive of school shootings.

Communicating Knowledge in Legal Documents
While the semiotic modes that represent ways of communication and perception draw a direct connection to the young adult reader's lifeworld, the remediation of legal modes assume a different function. *Shooter* ends with a "Medical Examiner's Report" – the autopsy report for Leonard Gray (cf. Fig. 6), stating "Cause of death was a gunshot wound with the point of entry being the hard palate. An exit wound was found in the left rear quadrant of the upper skull" (*Shooter*: 223). The report, however, also states that the body was found "beneath a sign, written in blood, that read 'Stop the Violence'" (*Shooter*: 223).[19]

---

[18] The one conducted by the FBI agent is annotated with a statement that Porter's pauses, which irritate the interviewer, are not to be noted by the transcriber (*Shooter*: 69, see images).
[19] The rather paradoxical plan of breaking "a hole in the wall of silence so big it couldn't be fixed" (*Shooter*: 65) by writing this demand on the wall in his own blood has been communicated by Leonard to his friends. He ultimately goes through with it, though without knowing that he also would decide to commit violence himself.

184 —— 4 Multimodal Representations of the School Shooting Narrative

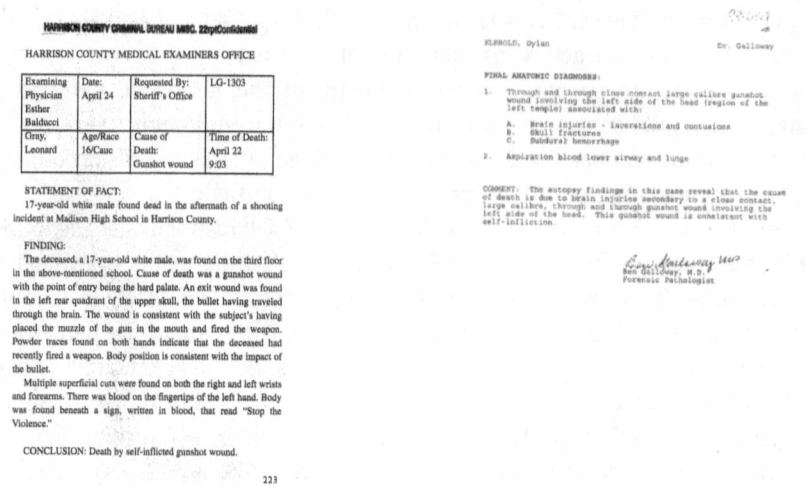

Fig. 6: Medical report in *Shooter*.   **Fig. 7:** Medical report, JCSO documents.

The most obvious function of the inclusion of fictionalized legal documents is the authentication of the fictional event and lifeworld, as the multimodal representation of legal documents endows the novel with the look of an officially investigated and, consequently, true story (cf. Fig. 7). The multimodal representation of the genesis of a school shooting is formally strictly realistic. The remediation of legal documents in the fictional narrative adds to the authenticity and therefore creates an impression of immediacy.

As the use of a "Miranda Warning" does not at first glance seem to contribute to the narrative, the act of reading has to be considered. What seems to be rather loose order of documents actively engages the young adult reader by drawing upon adolescent practices of reordering narratives. In the hypertextual reading practice, the proximity between the reader's lifeworld and the fictional storyworld is diminished even further, as she has to gather, weigh and prioritize the different pieces of information and the various perspectives in the novel.

Moreover, the delinearized presentation of information can "add to the richness of the reading experience by enabling readers to share in the making of meaning and encouraging them to situate themselves within the themes under consideration" (Coats 2011: 316).[20] For young adults, school shooting novels

---

[20] This also needs to be understood in a close interrelation with the content of the school shooting novel. In an article about realism in contemporary literature, Georgia Chistianidis writes that "extreme experiences [...] elicit affective responses that increase the likelihood of the experiences being perceived as authentic" (Christianidis 2013: 40). While neither *Shooter*, *Give a Boy a*

are not only about remembering past events, but also about understanding their own present. The structure of *Shooter* encourages this understanding by imitating different processes of meaning-making from the extratextual world – including the legal aspects of finding out what happened. As the interviews present the encounter or clash between the adult and the adolescent perspective on school shootings, the use of legal documents and legal language, which clearly references the adult world, can broaden the young adult reader's perspective. These documents provide her with insights into legal discourse on school shootings that she would most likely not be confronted with in real life. In *Shooter*, the reader has to take the legal documents into consideration in order to gain a comprehensive understanding of the fictional events. Her position of being a judge rather than a passive witness thus allows her to experience a new position within the discourse, as the reading practice resembles and communicates the practice of gathering, examining and prioritizing different pieces and parts of information in order to create a causal narrative.

Diaries and Insights into the *Amok*-Persona
Interestingly, it is not until the very end of *Shooter* that the reader is gains further insight into the shooter's mind by reading his diary. Diaries, like scrapbooks, are highly personal and very accessible forms of life-writing. Thus, the inclusion of diaries and the reproduction of handwriting creates recognizability, as the adolescent readers can relate to the mode of writing. In the case of the Leonard Gray, however, the inclusion of his diary takes on more gravity, due to its resemblance to the diaries of the Columbine shooters (cf. Fig. 8 and 9). And, indeed, the diary that can be found in the 'attachment' at the very end of *Shooter*, closely resembles the journal entries by Eric Harris and Dylan Klebold that were also released with the JCSO Columbine documents:

Printed in reproduced handwriting, the diary entries by Leonard Gray present the teenage reader with an adolescent who is clearly struggling with mental illness. There are various references to the Columbine shooter's diaries: Leonard, like Eric Harris, frequently uses language creatively ("it will be my die-ary", *Shooter:* 170), uses German words ("Ubermensch", *Shooter:* 171), writes in capital letters, underlines parts, repeats words and uses question- and exclamation marks.

Gun nor *Big Mouth & Ugly Girl* count as trauma narratives, they are concerned with the traumatic event of sudden, extreme violation of perceived societal safety and with the experience of excessive violence or the threat thereof.

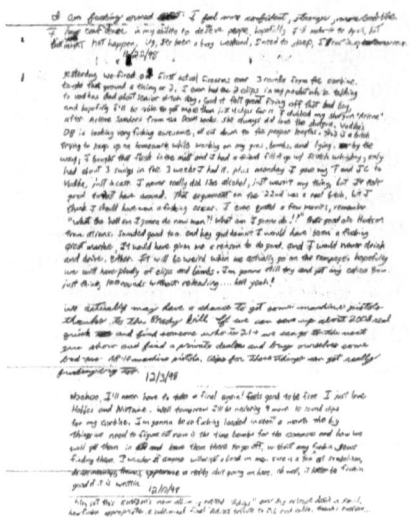

Fig. 8: Eric Harris' diary, JCSO documents.

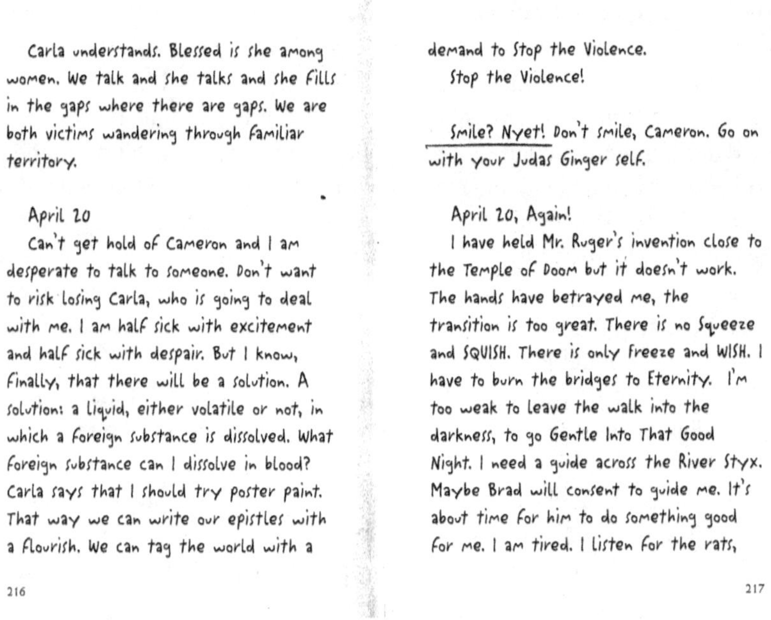

Carla understands. Blessed is she among women. We talk and she talks and she fills in the gaps where there are gaps. We are both victims wandering through familiar territory.

April 20
Can't get hold of Cameron and I am desperate to talk to someone. Don't want to risk losing Carla, who is going to deal with me. I am half sick with excitement and half sick with despair. But I know, finally, that there will be a solution. A solution: a liquid, either volatile or not, in which a foreign substance is dissolved. What foreign substance can I dissolve in blood? Carla says that I should try poster paint. That way we can write our epistles with a flourish. We can tag the world with a

demand to stop the Violence. Stop the Violence!

Smile? Nyet! Don't smile, Cameron. Go on with your Judas Ginger self.

April 20, Again!
I have held Mr. Ruger's invention close to the Temple of Doom but it doesn't work. The hands have betrayed me, the transition is too great. There is no Squeeze and SQUISH. There is only Freeze and WISH. I have to burn the bridges to Eternity. I'm too weak to leave the walk into the darkness, to go Gentle Into That Good Night. I need a guide across the River Styx. Maybe Brad will consent to guide me. It's about time for him to do something good for me. I am tired. I listen for the rats,

Fig. 9: Leonard Gray's diary in *Shooter*.

On the level of content, the resemblacnes are striking for those who have seen Harris's journal. The biggest difference from Harris's journal, however, is that, while Harris's writing might be difficult to follow, it remains lucid in the communication of his plans. Leonard's writing, in contrast, is increasingly frantic, and he admits to hearing voices. He also describes his abuse of prescription drugs. His writing becomes more and more incomprehensible as it is interspersed with made-up words and increasingly nonsensical passages:

> It doesn't feel like dying flying out of the hole but the K piece gets super busy muzzle muscling retri and bution all over de place and the nosie of it and the feeling of life jerking in your hands separates you from anything anybody can say except howdy retri and howdy bution. (*Shooter:* 193, spelling in original)

Even though the narrator's communication of his or her own perspective can invoke empathy in the reader (Nünning 2014: 213), the effect of the journal in *Shooter* may be the opposite. If readers are even willing to read through forty pages of increasingly incomprehensible utterances, they will learn that the perspectives of the shooter's friends did not do justice to how Leonard really felt – and, as the diary suggests, that they could not do so, because they did not understand Leonard's mind. "Nobody can read my thoughts", Leonard writes, "not even Cameron" (*Shooter:* 212), who is his closest friend and one of the protagonists of the novel. The notion of not being able to see what is really going on in the shooter's head directly relates to the reader as an important factor in the attempt to prevent school shootings for prevention. In the YA novels, this is closely connected to the aspect friendship and complicity, as the next section will show.

The most important function the shooter's diary assumes is to incorporate subjective practices of life-writing into the narrative. These practices, as I have shown in Chapter 3, are essential parts of the construction of the school shooting discourse, shaping and influencing the perception of the shooter and his motives. The diaries of Harris and Klebold, and the videos and writings of shooters like Bosse, Steinhäuser, Auvinen and Cho – even though their accounts of the genesis of their shootings were probably not at all reliable – have become integral discursive elements. These pieces of life-writing and the shooter's own construction of their personal narratives show the establishing and creation of the *amok persona* (see Chapter 3) in the act of writing. By reproducing the shooter's diary and referencing diaries from real shooters as important elements in the school shooting discourse, readers are presented with another, disturbing version of the genesis of a school shooting. They are also confronted with mental health issues as an important attempt at explanation. For the act of reading, on the other hand, the fictional diary assumes the function of creating an even more active reading process, as it requires prioritizing what or whom to believe.

The Transmodal Functions of Semiotic Modes

As discussed throughout this chapter, multimodal literature has a specific potential to communicate social and cultural phenomena to young adult readers by engaging them in a hypertextual reading practice. Via a variety of semiotic modes that each assume a specific intra- as well as extratextual function, the readers can get a broader and more comprehensive understanding of the fictional lifeworld. The authentication that is supported by the majority of available modes taken from everyday communicative practices also helps the reader to relate more closely to the fictional characters and events.

By challenging adolescent readers to actively order, prioritize and evaluate the various pieces of information, the fictional text engages them in an act of meaning-making. Especially in YA school shooting novels, the processes of creating causal narratives and making sense of the events that are portrayed by the different modes resemble and mirror the actual cultural practices of meaning-making in the aftermath of school shootings. Therefore, the multimodal novel participates in cultural practices of meaning-making and arguably helps the adolescent reader to learn these practices. Figuring out the transmodal meaning in text can be seen as one of the great challenges of hypertextual reading. In requiring this from the reader, the multimodal novel "can be expected to not only mirror such social and cultural practices in fictional form, but also to reflect and comment upon them critically and in a self-reflexive manner" (Hallet 2015: 644). As the novels draw upon familiar modes of communication and engage the readers in a stimulating process of ordering the narrative, adolescent readers can relate to the fictional storyworld and can establish a direct connection to their own experiences.

Based on this individual reading experience, adolescents' experience and understanding of the extratextual world can be refigured by the fictional text. Their understanding of their world of action is related to a larger cultural phenomenon. The act of reading connects their own experiences to the cultural remembering of broader processes and events, thus integrating the adolescent into the greater cultural discourse. As a result, multimodal novels have the potential to change the way that readers understand and perceive school shootings as well as how they engage in the discourse. The next section will explicate the different foci that the various novels put on specific aspects of the school shooting narrative and ask how they both represent and actively partake in the dynamics of the extratextaul school shooting discourse. A special focus will be put on the potential functions of the representation of processes of marginalization and the relevance of the recurring theme of friendship and complicity in YA fiction.

4.2.2 Processes of Marginalization in the School Shooting Narrative

The prevalent school shooting narrative is aimed at creating coherence and finding ways for approaching, understanding and preventing these inexplicable deeds. Especially in the efforts for prevention, young adults play a key role, as they have the closest connection to the circumstances from which school shootings emerge. Many adult attempts to explain youth violence result in a dynamic of 'moral panics', in which aspects of youth culture are constructed as 'folk devils'. [21] Young adults, on the other hand, can be understood as indispensable factors for the prevention of school shootings, as they understand and experience youth culture themselves.

The logic is compelling: When young adults understand the genesis of past school shootings and consequently learn how to recognize a school shooter, when they understand their own role within the system that causes something as horrible as a school shooting, they might be able to prevent the tragedy from happening again. Here, the assumption that fiction can have an effect on the readers and on (high school) society is the basis for the educational approach to school shootings in YA fiction. The recognizability, experientiality and perceived authenticity of the text, and the possibility of empathizing with the characters represented in the novels is crucial for the reader's ability to relate to the text. Only by this relationship the extended or transformed knowledge and understanding of the extratextual lifeworld can take place. Thus, multimodality can function as a means for using fictional representations of school shootings for the prevention of actual events by enhancing the immediacy of the text. To understand this dynamic, it is important to analyze how multimodality can shape the way the school shooting narrative is told and conveyed to the readers.

Shooter and *Give a Boy a Gun* both clearly re-tell the Columbine narrative, drawing upon common knowledge of the events in Littleton and the following public debate. Due to the short temporal distance between the publishing of the books and Columbine, the references to the shooting and the school shooting narrative as shaped by media and public discourse – including the stereotypical typologies of perpetrators, the public and media reactions of grief, despair and perplexitiy, and common attempts for explanation – were most likely understood by the readers at the time of the novels' publication. However, these possibilities

---

21 In the case of school shootings, the moral panic revolves around bullying and the notion of an increasingly violent youth culture. Computer games and Goth subculture are the 'folk devils' (cf. Cohen 2002 [1972], Ferguson/Ivory 2012).

for reflecting on acts of meaning-making and discursive dynamics are not always realized.

In their representations of the school shooting narrative, YA novels put a special emphasis on the aspect of friendship and the debate about complicity. They address some of most prevalent discursive questions: why did it happen, who knew and who could have known? In doing so, the aspects of bullying, and the possibilities for recognizing the factors that may lead to the planning of a school shooting are integrated into the narrative in a way that the adolescent reader can understand. However, the representation of adolescents who exist at the margins of their high school society can be rather challenging, as stereotypes can be reinforced instead of questioned. Therefore, how the novels represent the perpetrators and their friends, and which image of marginalized students and of processes of marginalization is conveyed, needs to be analyzed. As the reader becomes part of the school shooting discourse by the reception of a fictional representation of a school shooting narrative, it is also important to analyze the ways in which the narratives invite a transfer of the fictional knowledge to the understanding and assessment of the extratextual events. The novels become a part of the school shooting discourse as the active reading process engages readers in practices of discourse formation that can be transferred to and that reflect upon the extratextual discourse.

Processes of Marginalization

To invoke an empathetic connection with a character who differs greatly from the reader in behavior or perception of the world, as Suzanne Keen puts it, "might be used didactically, to develop a reader's moral sense" (Keen 2007: 71). Keen, who uses a number of interviews about empathy with readers from different groups to support her study on empathy and the novel, finds that "a character's negative affective states, such as those provoked by undergoing persecution, suffering, grieving, and experiencing painful obstacles, make a reader's empathizing more likely" (Keen 2007: 71).[22] As all school shooting novels thematize marginalized and ostracized people, this notion is of particular relevance. The first statement Keen uses to underline this finding refers directly to a YA school shooting novel: D.B.C. Pierre's controversial, but Booker Prize-winning *Vernon God Little*,

---

[22] Within the theoretical framework of this book, empirical studies that attempt to verify the effect of fictional works on their reader must be regarded critically. The claims of one individual reader therefore cannot be understood as a statement about the potential function inherent to the text, but only as one possibility of activated knowledge and transfer of the fictional knowledge to the extratextual life.

in which a young boy's life changes drastically after he is wrongly accused of the school shooting committed by his best friend. "Although I have never been in a situation in which I was charged with murder", the student quoted by Keen writes, "I have experienced empathy for Vernon, the 15–16 year-old boy in *Vernon God Little*. In my reading, I have been overcome with stress and frustration for him as he has been ignored by the 'grown-ups', wrongly accused, and tricked" (Keen 2007: 71). For this individual flesh-and-blood reader, empathy for the character Vernon is a result of a more general experience that can be easily shared by the reader: the sense of being ignored or misunderstood.

In *Give a Boy a Gun*, the adolescent readers are presented with several perspectives and modes to connect to and a number of characters to empathize with. As the setting remains mostly within the boundaries of high school as an almost closed system, the shooter's personal experiences and development are closely linked to the reader's possible school experiences. This can also be transferred to a general moral sense of injustice. The focus on bullying as the single cause for the school shooting and the representation of the shooting as an act of revenge is clearly oversimplifying the complexity of the phenomenon. However, for young adult readers, this may be the aspect that they can relate to the most. It has been shown that, while there is no empirically proven causality between bullying and school shootings, there is evidence that the perceived marginalization plays a crucial role in the creation of the perpetrator's *amok persona*. While the perpetrators "are not all loners and they are not all bullied, […] nearly all experience ostracism and social marginality" (Newman et al. 2005: 242).

Despite the fact that the focus on this attempt for explanation leaves out other important factors in the genesis of a school shooting, making marginalization the core theme in YA school shooting novels seems logical: All adolescent readers, it can be assumed, have found themselves to be either victim, bully, or witness of more or less severe acts of bullying in their own lifeworld. Of all three novels, *Give a Boy a Gun* refers most openly to the Columbine shooting, especially in its representation of the perpetrators' personalities. Like many YA novels, *Give a Boy a Gun* does not rely on subtle narrative strategies to foster a connection between the textual world and the lifeworld of the teenage reader. Instead, it underlines the obvious similarities between the shooters and the Columbine killers and reinforces the stereotypical notions: Brendan and Gary are loners and 'nerds' who hang out on the Internet and play *Doom*. Also, the modus operandi of the shooting – the two shooters are well armed, dressed up, and leave booby traps in the school – is reminiscent of the Columbine shooting. *Give a Boy a Gun* clearly is thus clearly a fictionalization of Columbine, with the openly communicated purpose to ensure that some lessons were learned from the event. Additionally, the frequent references to real school shooters and to the Columbine shooting in the quotes and footnotes authenticate the fictional shooting and thereby underline the topicality of the represented events. Strasser's novel fictionalizes and consequently reinforces the prevalent school shooting narrative and the assumptions about the genesis of these events.

Shooter, too, shows multiple similarities to the Columbine narrative. Its representation of various aspects taken from the school shooting discourse and the debate about the genesis of school shootings can be seen as much more differentiated and ambiguous. Marginalization remains at the center of the narrative, but *Shooter* illustrates the complexity of the processes of marginalization and the various effects it can have on adolescents, as all of the main characters in the novel experience marginalization. Of particular interest in this regard is the second interview with the shooter's friend, Cameron, who is presented as a complex character. A basketball player who comes from a rich family, he is described by his friend as "kind of gentle" and "built nice and cute in a young kind of way[,...] not like a rapper or anything like that" (*Shooter:* 111). Considering his family background and the fact that he does not seem like a stereotypical outcast, the interviewing FBI agent suggests at various times that Cameron cannot be considered to be a 'typically' marginalized student. Instead, in attempting to find out whether or not Cameron is an accomplice, she implies that he actively chose his position: "On the one hand", she says irritably in the interview, "I'm getting the idea that you and Len were being bullied and pushed away from the mainstream. On the other hand, I'm seeing you as a person who deliberately moves away from groups" (*Shooter* 93). The agent thus raises an interesting point for the adolescent reader – that some people might choose to be treated like outcasts and, consequently, might even deserve it. However, in the three interviews, Cameron's suffering is expressed as painful – he states that "deep inside, you know that whoever gets up in your face gets there because he knows you're nothing, and he knows that you know it too" (*Shooter:* 97). At a certain point, he mentions that their situation at school became so unbearable that Cameron and Leonard even went to the principal. The principal, however, tells them "that dealing with other teenagers was part of the growing-up process. It was something I had to learn how to do" (*Shooter:* 83). The principle therefore embodies and voices the prevalent belief in the successful overcoming of obstacles in order to become a successful adult. While Cameron seems to learn to deal with his situation, Leonard breaks. Here, the novel presents a direct criticism of the high school system and of the indifference of adults to teenage suffering and the normalization of bullying.[23]

In *Big Mouth & Ugly Girl*, the process of marginalization is treated in yet another way. The novel thematizes the potential danger of the school shooting panic and a high school's atmosphere of distrust. Matt, who is not portrayed as a stereotypical school shooter at all, is suddenly arrested, (wrongly) accused of having planned a bombing. With the tough, gender-role-defying Ursula as his new friend, the formerly popular Matt is gradually pushed to the margins of the high school society in which he was formerly firmly embedded. He resigns from his post as vice president of the junior class and does not attempt to stay in touch with his former friends who let him down. Matt is confronted with the new experience of being bullied and assaulted by the school's jocks. Moreover, he and his family experience institutionalized violence that begins with being ousted from a previously friendly community and later escalates into threats and acts of physical violence.

Matt is "victimized by the sweep of 'suburban hysteria' that demands youth violence be taken seriously" and, in presenting this form of violence and its result, "[t]he novel testifies to the power of gossip, innuendo, and modern-day vigilante violence" (Franzak/Noll 2006: 667). As he gradually retreats into himself, Matt slowly begins to have thoughts of revenge. Though previously represented as smart and kind, he begins to feel hatred for his parents (cf. *Big Mouth:* 105) and develops suicidal thoughts (cf. *Big Mouth:* 151f.). The readers witness how a once absurd claim begins to become more likely. At some point, Matt states that he is almost ready to "type out a message detailing his own hatred and how he'd like to, yes he'd like to bomb and shoot certain people, and a lot of them, he'd love to kill his enemies" (*Big Mouth:* 221). While he would still not go through with a school shooting, his feelings of hatred have become real. However, as *Big Mouth & Ugly Girl* is not concerned with an actual school shooting, it includes another interesting aspect of marginalization by focusing on the media dynamics of school shootings and the panic that false alarms cause.

This atmosphere of fear is illustrated by newspaper clippings that Matt comes across or that concerned neighbors send to Matt's parents – some including notes like, "Your neighbours are not safe we are not going to forget" (*Big Mouth:* 125, capitalization in original). The novel shows the increasing pressure on Matt and his family and the role that media coverage plays in the construction of a discourse of emergency or 'moral panic'. The semiotic modes taken from

---

[23] These same issues have been criticized by a number of scholars as well, cf. eg., Newman et al. (2005: 96f.).

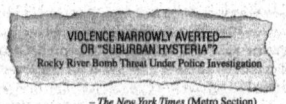

Fig. 10: Newspaper clippings in *Big Mouth & Ugly Girl*.

print media depict and exemplify the media's influence on the reaction of the community, but they also illustrate how the school shooting discourse is enacted in the media (cf. Fig. 10). One fictional newspaper clipping, for example, asks: "Violence narrowly averted or 'suburban hysteria'?" (*Big Mouth:* 78) and thus directly reflects on the school shooting discourse.[24]

While *Give a Boy a Gun* and *Shooter* focus mainly on the school as the system out of which a shooting emerges, *Big Mouth & Ugly Girl* goes beyond the school as the allegorical 'little world' and includes the media and public (over)reaction to the perceived threat. In this novel, not only the students at the high school, but the entire community partakes in processes of marginalization. As a result, the novel thematizes the way in which adults reinforce adolescent hierarchies. Adults, as Newman et al. have pointed out in their description of small town communities in which school shootings took place, "magnify the trials and tribulations of adolescence and reinforce the status metrics that govern it" (Newman et al. 2005: 137). Both Ursula's and Matt's parents are interested

---

24 It is interesting to note that the other clippings are taken from fictional newspapers like the *Rocky River Gazette*. However, as this particular article serves to underline the fact that the community is acting unreasonably, the authentication that the name of an existing newspaper (*New York Times*) offers supports the importance of this point.

in their family's status in the community, and struggle with the fact that their children refuse to participate in communal activities.[25] Matt's increasing withdrawal from his community, family and friends is framed as a direct result of the community's reaction to his damaged reputation. The novel therefore comments on the dynamics of the school shooting discourse, even without representing an actual shooting.[26]

Another interesting aspect of Oates' novel is the angle from which it thematizes the issue of 'leaking'. Katherine Newman et al., among others, have pointed out that in all the school shootings they investigated, the shooters issued threats and openly communicated their plans (Newman et al. 2005: 160, Newman/Fox 2009: 1298). These various forms of leaking have also found their way into fictionalized representations of school shootings and are represented in *The Dirties*, *Shooter* and *Give a Boy a Gun*. However, the researchers also state that "[m]aking outrageous claims to get attention is such a common habit among adolescents that the warnings issued by the shooters did not stand above the daily din" (Newman et al. 2005: 161). The fact that fictional representations of school shooting frequently thematize leaking and point out the failure of peers and authorities to understand how serious the threats were, assumes a didactic function, as it can potentially sensitize the readers and audiences to the possibility that even jokesters (like Matt in *The Dirties*, see Chapter 3) may go through with their threats. Oates, however, chose to comment on the downside of this growing sensitivity by focusing on the "suburban hysteria" that school shootings have caused. In the aspect of leaking the possibility for prevention and the discursive focus on the immediate surrounding and social interactions of perpetrators merge directly.

---

25 This aspect is briefly raised in *Give a Boy a Gun*, when Cameron's quitting of the basketball team is cast as a withdrawal from "normal" high school structures and activities.

26 However, it needs to be stressed that it is highly unlikely that a popular and well integrated kid like Matt would be accused of planning a bombing at his school, as false accusations most likely affect students who are already outcasts in their schools and who fit the stereotypical image of the school shooter. Especially in the case of false allegations, these stereotypes, as they are also communicated in both *Give a Boy a Gun* and *Shooter*, reveal their dangerous dimension. When wrongly accusing an innocent student of planning an act of violence has the effect of pushing a formerly popular kid to the margins of his school, what might happen when an already marginalized student is put in the same position?

4.2.3 Friendship, Complicity and the Position of the Adolescent Reader

It has been shown that both *Give a Boy a Gun* and *Shooter* rely heavily on their readers' knowledge of previous school shootings. *Give a Boy a Gun*, thanks to its multimodal references to extratextual events, can be seen as a part of the fictional dimension of the school shooting discourse. It fictionally represents past events, provides a simplistic and monocausal narrative that focuses on the possibilities for prevention situated in the readers' lifeworld, but still engages the readers in active practices of meaning-making. *Shooter*, too, remediates the Columbine narrative, but in a clearly more differentiated and challenging manner. While some of the references are rather stereotypical and constructed, the narrative structure and multimodal representation engages the reader more intensely than *Give a Boy a Gun* does. *Shooter*, with its high degree of multimodality, can thus be seen as a highly potent novel in terms of extratextual functions. One of the aspects from the school shooting discourse that is especially relevant for the young adult reader are the interpersonal dynamics and the "adolescent code" (Newman et al. 2005: 168). *Shooter* clearly focuses on these issues, and can therefore help to clarify why the question of 'who could have known?' is an especially difficult one in the attempt to explain and understand the genesis of a school shooting.

"Someone should have known!"
In *Shooter*, the readers gain most of their insight into the events that led up to Leonard's planning of the attack from the interviews with his two close friends. On the first pages of the first interview with Leonard's friend Cameron, the psychologist points out that he is "trying to get as full a picture of you as I can. To know you, or try to get to know you" (*Shooter:* 13). Instead of talking about clichéd ideas of school shooters and their friends, the readers learn, the psychologist wants to find out more about Cameron as a person and his relationship with his friend, and the readers thus become part of the investigation.

In the interviews, it is obvious that the novel was written in the aftermath of Columbine and that it expects its readers to recognize the frequently subtle references. When the psychologist asks the simple question of what music Cameron likes, for example, Cameron answers with a defensive rant:

> It changes. People think you listen to one kind of music – that's crazy. You turn the radio on or you play your own stuff and that's what you do. There was a big thing in the paper about Satyricon, but it was like other kids talking, not me. I listen to them, but I'm not a real freak

for them, and I'm not into any Fourth Reich number. That's why I agreed to talk with you, to get things straight. (*Shooter:* 13)

When the interviews for the "Threat Assessment Report" are conducted, some time has passed since the actual event of the shooting and Cameron has obviously become familiar with the media dynamics of the school shooting aftermath. At this point of the novel, the reader is not yet aware of the shooting or who committed it. In the quote mentioned above, she is confronted with the name of a fictional band and the notion of the "Fourth Reich" as if it were self-explanatory – it is up to the reader to fill in this gap and find out why Cameron's defensive stance might be necessary. Consequently, the readers' knowledge of the Columbine narrative is activated by a gap in the narrative.

Only gradually does the interviewer's interest shift towards Len (as the shooter Leonard is called), and it becomes increasingly clear that he is the subject of interest in the investigation. What is further revealed through the course of the first interview is the intensity of the friendship between Cameron and Len and their status at their high school. In representing the dynamics of a group of three ostracized and repeatedly victimized, *Shooter* raises one of the most common laments of the school shooting discourse. "Someone should have known!" has dominated the societal reactions in the immediate aftermath of school shootings ever since Columbine (cf. Muschert 2002: 144).

School Shootings and Subcultures

After Columbine, the media quickly singled out a group of Goths who were allegedly racist and hated athletes. The racist slurs found on Eric Harris' website, his and Klebold's their contradictory and incongruent statements about hating African Americans as well as Jews (despite the fact that Dylan Klebold came from a Jewish family) and their sympathy with Adolf Hitler and Nazism (cf. Larkin 2007: 124, 140f., 156ff.) quickly became the subject of media interest.

In the direct aftermath of the shooting, Harris and Klebold were associated with a group at their school that called itself the 'Trench Coat Mafia'. In his book *Columbine* (2009), Dave Cullen summarizes his observations of media coverage on April 20, 1999:

> One hour into the Columbine horror, news stations were informing the public that two or more gunmen were behind it. Two hours in, the Trench Coat Mafia were to blame. The TCM

were portrayed as a cult of homosexual Goths in makeup, orchestrating a bizarre death pact for the year 2000. (2009: 150)[27]

The prematurely established connection between the shooters and their alleged accomplices in the local Goth group has significantly contributed to the image of the stereotypical school shooter, which has affected subcultures at American high schools ever since. Here, the power and disproportionate influence of the school shooting discourse on American culture, along with fiction's role in reinforcing these notions, can be observed. By establishing a direct connection between school shootings and Goth culture, the image of the school shooter as Goth contributed to both the identity formation of later shooters as well as their public and media image.

However, the way in which Harris, Klebold and the shooters after them presented themselves during and before their attacks is more the result of a cultural script than of the shooter's affiliation with a subcultural music scene, as it has been explicated in Chapter 3. While references to some bands associated with the extremely broad and diverse Goth music scene – such as KMFDM and Nine Inch Nails – have become an element of the cultural script of school shootings after Columbine, the media and researchers of school shootings were all too eager to erroneously ascribe "everything that does not belong to the American mainstream youth culture to the Gothic label" (Kiilakoski/Oksanen 2011: 253). Marilyn Manson, for example, who is by far the most popular scapegoat for the Columbine shooting and many shootings afterwards, "represents the image of a Goth for everyone else except those who belong to Goth subculture" (ibid: 254).

But as the idea of a group of outcasts who plot an act of revenge against their tormentors offered an easy explanation, the notion of the Trenchcoat Mafia and their as accomplices in the shooting stuck in the popular and media school shooting discourse and has been fictionalized and remediated in different ways. In *Shooter*, for example, the "Trench Coat Mafia" and the media hype around it in the aftermath of the Columbine shooting has a direct counterpart in the "Ordo Saggitae" that was founded by Len, Carla and Cameron:

---

27 While Cullen claims that the group was known by almost no one at the beginning of the Columbine coverage (Cullen 2009: 150), Ralph W. Larkin states that "virtually every student at Columbine High School knew about the existence of the Trenchcoat Mafia, even though they may not have known any of the individual members" (Larkin 2007: 79). Reviewing research about the Columbine shooting suggests that, much like with the erroneous grouping of all subcultures under the Goth label, the majority of the student body may have used the Trenchcoat Mafia as an umbrella group for all outcast students.

There were only five of us in it. The papers played on it like they played on the idea that we all had super IQs and had all gone dark. That wasn't true. [...] Ordo Saggitae means 'Order of the Arrow', and it was cool. I liked it. There weren't any rules, or oaths or initiations, just five guys – actually four guys and Carla – who were going to do things together. We never actually did much [...]. (*Shooter:* 49)

Even though *Shooter* reflects on the media hype around the group, the connection between Goth culture and the group of friends is still reinforced in the novel's narrative: Carla is described as a Goth girl who wears black lipstick. Cameron, too, makes references to bands and music magazines that deal with harder guitar music. Even though it remains unclear whether or not he sees himself as a Goth, he clearly shows that he understands Goth culture and sympathizes, like Len, with 'going dark': "Wearing black is wearing black. Going dark is moving away from all those light things that seem to get some people through their day. Getting away from symbols and all that puffed-up way of living" (*Shooter:* 51). Embedding the shooter, a Goth who wears trench coats, in this subcultural group of friends serves as a reference to the extratextual discourse about the fictionally charged connection between Goth culture and school shootings. Furthermore, it provides an understanding of the novel's approach to friendship and complicity.

"Why Kids Don't Tell"
As established earlier, YA school shooting novels address school shootings in a way that the adolescent readers can relate to, so as to convey an understanding of the events that led up to the fictional shooting and, consequently, sensitize the readers to the issues related to their lifeworld. The "Ordo Saggitae" is directly linked to the issue of marginalization and it further thematizes and frames the problems of a friendship with somebody who has become a threat to himself or others. Thus, the reason why the "Threat Assessment Report" focuses on the group of friends is to find out whether or not 'somebody could have known', and thereby addresses an extremely prominent question in the school shooting discourse. The process of marginalization that connects the Ordo Saggitae and the Trenchcoat Mafia is highly reminiscent of events at Columbine High School, as their status as outsiders was constantly reinforced by attacks on their masculinity and accusations of homosexuality (cf. Larkin 2007, Linder 2014: xxi).[28] Nevertheless, the members felt a sense of belonging that is present-

---

[28] As Newman et al. (2005), Kellner (2008) and Larkin (2007) have shown, the labeling of school shooters as gay is one of the common strategies of marginalization by demasculinization

ed in a positive and unsuspicious way. *Shooter* provides insight into the lives of students who clearly exist at the outer rim of their school's society. No matter how close the friends were, the narrative slowly creates an image of the ambivalence that can characterize friendship between the outcasts – something that has frequently been thematized in regard to the Columbine shooters. For Cameron, being "in it together" (*Shooter:* 30) is the most important aspect of his friendship to Len and leads towards complicity in vandalizing a church and not telling anybody about Len's abuse of prescription drugs. The thin red line between friendship and complicity is shown by Cameron with the sense of belonging and feeling accepted: "That means a lot. You're in something with someone" (*Shooter:* 30).

As readers learn more about the shooter, it becomes clear that he was a volatile character and, in this, is reminiscent of Eric Harris. Like Harris as he is described in Cullen's *Columbine* or Larkin's *Comprehending Columbine*, Len, too, had an ambiguous relationship with his close friends. Both Cameron and Carla have to admit that they were repeatedly victimized by their friend. Eric Harris is said to have bullied his friends and even threatened to kill his 'friend' Brooks Brown, whom he would later warn about his plans by telling him not to come to school at the day of the shooting (cf. Larkin 2007: 127).

This behavior is mirrored in Len, who repeatedly mocks Cameron and even violates Carla's privacy by stealing her medical records about her sexual abuse from the hospital and makes them public to the entire school as an act of revenge after they have a falling out. These acts of violence against his friends show how volatile his character was. His ambiguous manner towards them is further reinforced in Len's statements about his friends in his diary at the end of the novel. However, *Shooter* powerfully represents the interpersonal dynamics of interdependency that can exist in a group of friends. It thus shows how these structures can keep people from recognizing the threat that Len started to become, as the next pages will show.

When the fictional event with the accounts of the genesis of extratextual shootings are compared, it becomes obvious that that even if Cameron and Carla may have had an idea about their friend's troubled thoughts, their experiences of being ostracized most likely prevented them from telling anyone about his actions. In their approach to the question of "why kids don't tell", Newman and colleagues call this behavior the "adolescent code". The goal of this code "is

---

(see also Chapter 2). This is especially the case when more than one shooter was involved and the nature of the perpetrators' relationship is thematized. In *Shooter,* Cameron reacts highly defensively when a homoerotic relationship to his friend Len is suggested (cf. Shooter: 31).

to beat the system, not to rat out one's compatriots. Being known as a tattletale might be an undesirable but acceptable social consequence, but losing a friendship is clearly not worth it" (2005: 168). This is of even greater importance for people who do not have a lot of friends and cannot risk losing one – as it is the case with Cameron. As the novel represents their lives on the margins of high school society, the readers can get an idea of how Cameron and Carla could have known about Len's path to violence, but not tell anyone about it. However, the text also sensitizes the readers to the fact that friendships have the potential to be ambiguous and destructive.

The 'Abject Hero' and the Reader as Accomplice
Len, who is a victim of abjection and bullying himself, perpetuates this behavior on to people who are weaker and more vulnerable than he is. Both Cameron and Carla accept this behavior: "Actually he kidded me a lot, but he had a way of almost putting you down but smiling as he did" (*Shooter:* 16), Cameron admits. Here, Myers' novel communicates another aspect that has been observed in extratextual school shootings, as a number of school shooters "seem to have given as good as they got" (Newman et al. 2005: 64). In fact, adolescents "who both bully and are bullied seem to be at the greatest risk; they are both victims and aggressors" (ibid.). Within the text, this ambivalence invalidates Len's claim that he merely wanted to "stop the violence" at his school. While the widely acknowledged belief is that school shooters are only victims of bullying, *Shooter*'s portrayal of Len as both victim and aggressor is closer to the more well-founded research findings. Since Len is himself a victimizer, his claim cannot offer a believable motivation – the simple causal connection between bullying and the school shooting is clearly disrupted by Len's ambivalent actions.

Len's violent thoughts, which are later underlined by his diary, and his behavior towards his friends illustrate the complexity of interpersonal relationships. In YA literature, the representation of interpersonal dynamics is of particular relevance, as young adults frequently struggle with finding their place among their peers and in society. These representations can assume the important function of reminding us "that part of that self-construction in community depends on abjecting others that we or our community revile while continuing to use them for our own purposes" (Coats 2011: 320). This reminder is presented by the "abject hero" character, who "forces the reader to confront his or her own complicity in the creation and maintenance of those oppressive cultural and psychic systems, not as victim, critic or mere spectator, but as someone who stands by and lets victimization occur at best, a victimizer herself at worst" (Coats 2011: 319).

Presenting a more complex and dialogic relationship between the perpetrator and his friends assumes the potential function of making readers question their own position in the face of victimization. Experiencing the genesis of a school shooting through the retrospective analysis of the people who are closest to the shooter puts the readers in the position of not only being a witness or a distant observer, but a friend and alleged accomplice. The feeling of empathy with the interviewees is crucial – only by feeling with Cameron and Carla can the readers think about what they would have done in their situation. *Shooter* reacts to the prominent discursive notion that the peers of the school shooter should have known about the plans by constructing a complex set of character traits and interpersonal dynamics.[29] The interviews put forward four varying accounts of the events and dynamics that led up the school shooting. However, all of the accounts in the interviews state that neither Cameron nor Carla were aware of Len's plans.[30]

The novel offers a number of meta-commentaries on the public discourse and the investigations that follow a school shooting. The psychologist who conducts the first interview, for example, stresses his intention to figure out what circumstances led to the things that Len and his friends did (cf. *Shooter:* 31), but also admits that "[o]ne of the dangers in these interviews is that the interviewer changes the importance of the answers. I try to be careful, but it's always a possibility that I might misinterpret something" *(Shooter:* 21). Here, the readers are sensitized for the fact that both the form of the interview and the information resulting from it are subject to many possible outcomes. This prompts them to question their own judgement about the events in the novel. In the first two interviews, Cameron addresses the problem of feeling pigeonholed by the investigators – a clear reflection of the *a posteriori* representations of school shooters and their friends. When Cameron is asked about the bullying that he and Len suffered, he replies defiantly: "You like that, right? You want me to say that it made feel really bad and that puts me into the right category. Kid felt really bad because of being bullied in school and reacted badly. That's what you want me to say?" *(Shooter:* 48f.). Carla, on the other hand, challenges her interviewer in

---

[29] The connection between multiple perspectives in a novel and empathetic connection with characters will be further analyzed in Chapter 5.
[30] The only interviewer who clearly aims at establishing the friend's involvement in the shooting is constructed as an unlikeable opponent to the adolescent through tone, typography and the mode of the interview. This impression is supported by the instruction to the transcriber not to include pauses in the transcription, as this supports the agent's authoritative and patronizing attitude towards the defensive Cameron.

a different way by repeatedly interrupting his questions or asking him about his intentions:

> FB: Did you ever have sex with Leonard or Cohen?
>
> CE: Are you investigating threats?
>
> FB: I'm analyzing the possibility of future threats.
>
> CE: So if I was having sex with Leonard, does that make me a threat?
>
> (*Shooter:* 111)

In this interview, Carla, who is portrayed as a rather callous girl who has obviously suffered through a very rough childhood, openly thematizes the arrogance of the adults as she states: "You know, when you talk like that, I don't know what you're talking about, so I'm not going to answer" (*Shooter:* 110). These extreme situations are highly relatable for the adolescent reader, as they underline the clash between adults and adolescents: Carla's demand to be talked to in a way that is appropriate for her age, to understand what the interviewer wants from her and to be understood, underlines the problem of intergenerational understanding: "Excuse me. Do you speak English? Do you understand what I'm saying [...]?" (*Shooter:* 113). This is also particularly relevant in the school shooting discourse, in which adults attempt to understand and explain a phenomenon of youth violence. In the novel, the officials do not understand the perpetrator, the events and experiences that led up to the school shooting, or the friendship that made Carla and Cameron direct witnesses of the attack. The readers, on the other hand, are connected to the characters by their shared lifeworld and knowledge. As in *Big Mouth & Ugly Girl*, some of the adults in *Shooter* actively partake in the societal dynamics that pushed the friends to the margins, instead of trying to understand what happened. Deliberately or not, the adults have become part of the process of marginalization that Leonard claimed to protest against.

While the voices of the adults in *Give a Boy a Gun* are the voices of passive bystanders who were incapable or unwilling to interfere with the processes of marginalization, the interviews in *Shooter* show that adults pigeonhole and falsely label adolescents by projecting their ideas of adolescent identity onto them. The adolescents in *Shooter* are constantly labeled, misunderstood and dismissed by adults, and the novel shows how these experiences can foster friendships that result in dangerous interpersonal dynamics. The fact that Len told Cameron that he was all right the way he was, that he "didn't have to do anything to be all right" (*Shooter:* 19f.), thus makes Cameron's acceptance of Len's abjection prior to the shooting rather understandable. In the face of marginalization, the friends stuck together, even though they were not necessarily good for one another.

In this dynamic of adult misunderstandings, the adolescent readers are themselves drawn into a position of complicity. Not only because of an empathetic connection to the adolescent characters, but also because they are not adults, readers are able to understand what was going on before the shooting, the narrative suggests. Also, the novel's critical take on the creation of clear explanations can be understood as a commentary on the way that the school shooting discourse constantly constructs clear categories in which to fit perpetrators, potential perpetrators and their friends. By being confronted with different perspectives and by engaging in a hypertextual, active reading process, the readers find trying to understand what happened. They are confronted with their own position and must recognize that they too are potentially the peers of school shooters.

Shooter questions these attempts at easy explanations and clear causalities not only by presenting characters as ambivalent and multi-layered, but also by 'attaching' Len's diary as one of the last documents, which stands out because of its very different typography. While it is mentioned in the interviews that Len was in psychiatric care and took antidepressants, the novel does not thematize mental illness to a greater extent. In Len's diary, however, his struggles appear greater than his friends imagined. Only Carla may have noticed that Len had mental health issues, and states that "[y]ou always got the impression that there was something spinning around in his head" (*Shooter:* 111). This notion is supported in his own writings, where his violent fantasies are mixed with visions that resemble psychotic episodes, which themselves are presented in a rather stereotypical and artificial way. In his diary, Len makes statements that fit the stereotypical school shooter: he talks about video games (cf. *Shooter:* 179), his hatred for his violent father and fellow students, and his abuse of his prescription drugs – the "magic pills" (*Shooter:* 180).

His friendship with Cameron and Carla, however, is presented as motivated by egocentrism: "Called Cameron just to talk, to hear the sound of my voice echo through my room. To hear how rational I sound when I am speaking to Other" (*Shooter:* 187). Len, it becomes clear, needs his friends to become his accomplices: "How can life work if you can't kill turtles? Turtles are a path. They are a path that leads you to forever outside" (*Shooter:* 203), he writes after he has a fight with his friends because he tricked them into shooting live turtles.[31] Len

---

[31] Amid the hateful entries about his plans, his thoughts of revenge and weapons, the few positive things Len writes about Cameron – whom he calls Pyramus, after the tragic Ovidian figure –

wants to teach his friends how to use violence, how to strike back, and he wants to share his new understanding about himself and the situation at their school: "What I see, what I should have seen all along, is that I have to create the real me. They have been creating me. [...] It is the Brads [one of the jocks at their school] that create us, beat us into existence, that make us their 'things'" (*Shooter:* 214f.). When he realizes that his friends are not willing to use violence, he tricks them into joining him on the day of the shooting and then threatens to shoot them when they realize what he is up to and refuse to participate. Here, the abusive dimension of their friendship is ultimately made clear.[32]

Functions of the School Shooting Narrative in Shooter
The similarities between Len's writings and the journal of Eric Harris – which are further underlined by Len's effort to hide his real thoughts from his friends and family – and the representation of Len as a stereotypical school shooter has a double potential function. First, it conveys an image of how a real school shooter might think by presenting a fictionalized account that overtly draws upon real documents and on popular notions of the school shooting discourse. In fictionalizing real school shootings by including various references to actual events, e.g., by presenting fictionalized versions of actual documents, the novel can make its readers transfer their position as a reader to the extratextual discourse. Thus, it can make them question their own position within the extratextual school shooting discourse and can make the reflect upon their own interpretation of what has led to the attack. Complicity is the main theme of *Shooter*, and it confronts the adolescent reader with processes of marginalization and their effect on the victims. By putting Cameron as the abject hero in the center of the narrative, *Shooter* forces its readers to confront their own role in processes of marginalization in their real life. The novel thus becomes an important 'tool for prevention', showing the readers their possible role in the genesis of a school shooting and attempting to sensitize them to the struggles of others. The reflec-

---

are hardly noticeable. However, after his falling out between with Carla, he states that he does not know what to do without his friends.

32 His actual plan is never clearly articulated in his diary, only hinted at by his growing interest in weapons, his obviously decreasing mental stability and fantasies of killing. The diary also includes a reference to the rampage movie *D.C. Sniper: 23 Days of Fear* (Tom McLoughlin, USA 2003), which tells the story of a series of rampage shootings in 2002. Len comments on how the shooter could have been more effective, which can be interpreted as an early hint of his plans and as a comment on his media use, as Len states that he has not seen the movie (cf. *Shooter:* 183).

tions on the public and media school shooting discourse also illustrate how the stereotypes and fears that have emerged from it can further marginalize people who already live on the outer rim of high school society. This may foster a better understanding of the school shooting discourse and the way it constructs the potentially harmful images of a stereotypical school shooter. It needs to be pointed out, however, that *Shooter* mainly draws upon and reinforces existing stereotypes in its portrayal of a perpetrator.

Second, the references to previous school shootings and perpetrators contribute to the dissemination of knowledge about actual school shootings and their genesis in a way that is relatable and understandable. As the multimodal novels remediate existing images of school shooters and their actions, the 'look' of school shootings and the cultural memory of these events in adolescent culture can be created (see Chapter 3). While *Give a Boy a Gun*'s references to extratextual shootings are more overt, *Shooter*'s remediation practices offer an insight into the way that school shootings are analyzed and approached by adults and officials. While *Shooter*, like *Give a Boy a Gun*, identifies bullying as the major factor in the genesis of a school shooting, it does so by refusing clear categories of 'good' vs. 'bad'. In *Give a Boy a Gun*, the representation of the shooter's victimization is meant to evoke sympathy for the perpetrators, even though they had cruel intentions themselves. In *Shooter*, the processes of marginalization are cemented on the level of the discourse itself, as they occur in media representation of potential school shooters.

By inviting the active reordering of the documents and the prioritization and assessment of the available information, readers can reach an understanding of the possibility of different approaches to school shootings. Encouraged to actively engage with the text by its multimodal structure, readers become active participants in choosing their approach to the discursive elements. Moreover, the different tones and styles of the interviews and the meta-commentaries by Cameron, Carla and the psychologist underline the subjectiveness of the accounts presented in the interviews. Misunderstandings, the interviews suggest, can occur in every act of communication, and are frequently the results of underlying prejudices and presuppositions. By commenting on these misunderstandings, the text can confront its readers with their own prejudices against the characters:

> As readers, we learn about the ways characters, indeed people, are constructed through their actions and the way society views those actions, through the impressions of others which are always more than half embedded in narcissistic self-impressions, and through more nebulous and abstract cultural expectations that help us fill in gaps in our experience with prefabricated subject positions. Unpacking these last is often the most disturbing for readers, as in doing so they unearth unconscious prejudices that filter our ways of perceiving the world. (Coats: 218)

The text's multimodality can thus help the reader to reflect on her own position towards outcasts as well as on her prefabricated ideas about school shootings. Therefore, while *Shooter* still presents a rather causal narrative and draws upon the prevalent school shooting narrative in most of its elements, its multimodality can potentially serve as a means for the readers to reflect their standpoint within the discourse. It can thereby encourage the young adult reader to develop a more comprehensive understanding of the complexity of the topic.

4.3 Conclusion: The Young Adult School Shooting Novel as a Tool for Prevention

In sum, the novels analyzed in this chapter fictionalize the existing school shooting narrative, borrowing from it their basic characters, setting and plot. However, there are notable differences in the foci of the narratives: *Big Mouth & Ugly Girl* presents a reflective approach to the public reaction to school shootings. It comments on the social construction of the school shooting discourse as a discourse of emergency, which can foster marginalization instead of providing explanations or strategies for prevention. The novel draws largely upon suburban reactions to events like these. For young adult readers, it can thus provide a valuable insight into the media dynamics following a school shooting threat, and reveals the overreactions that these give rise to. By casting an unconventional outsider, who blatantly questions gender stereotypes and is perfectly able to stand up for herself, *Big Mouth & Ugly Girl* presents a positive take on friendship in times of school shootings. Here, the multimodality of the novel decodes the media dynamics and establishes a more direct connection to adolescent forms of communication by partially telling the story in (sometimes unsent) emails.[33]

Give a Boy a Gun's multimodality, on the other hand, mainly serves as a form authentication of the story – by referencing extratextual events, existing laws and people, the novel underlines its educational purpose. In Strasser's novel, the perpetrators are clearly modeled after Dylan Klebold and Eric Harris. Their friends, who were not aware of what was going on, also resemble the friends of the Columbine shooters who were questioned in the aftermath of the shooting – therefore, it fictionalizes the Columbine story in an accessible way and en-

---

[33] Another female hero is found in the character of an outcast in *Give a Boy a Gun* – Allison, a friend of the two shooters, who prevents the actual shooting from happening and saves the life of a bully by providing first aid. Allison, too, is suspected of being an accomplice in Gary and Brendan's shooting – even when she stands up against them, some of the students have doubts about her involvement.

dows it with the possibility of a better ending. Also, the narrative focuses on establishing a causality – despite the different perspectives from which the story is told, the causal link between bullying and the shooting is never disrupted. The message of this novel is clear: if bullying stops, school shootings will not happen.

Shooter, on the other hand, asks its readers to find their own approach to the narrative. The functions and possibilities of multimodality become especially in this novel, as its structure invites a dynamic reading process and requires the integration of the different perspectives from interviews, newspaper clippings and official assessments and evaluations. However, even though the evaluations by the investigating psychologists and agent are included in the fictional "Threat Assessment Report", their authority is not presented as absolute. The reader is free to skip over and ignore them – even without them, she will still get a comprehensive account of the perpetrator, the planning of the attack and the relationship between the perpetrator and his friends. Cameron and Carla, left in the dark about Len's actual plans for the shooting, are presented as victims themselves – they are tricked into witnessing the shooting and, as a result of their unwillingness to participate in it, are threatened. Even though the adolescent characters are outcasts and express understanding for the perpetrator and his actions, they clearly invite an empathetic connection.

In both *Give a Boy a Gun* and *Shooter,* most of the prevalent explanations for school shootings are mentioned. Bullying, mental illness, family backgrounds, issues of gun control and media violence all play a role in the construction of the narrative and its characters. Thus, the novels clearly contribute to the adolescent's understanding of the school shooting discourse and engage the reader in practices of discourse formation. In *Give a Boy a Gun*, this is done by presenting a clear causal connection. Strasser's authorial intention and the extratextual functions of the text can be regarded as identical. Despite its multimodality and multiperspecitvity, the novel communicates a rather simple solution to the school shooting problem: if the adolescents are more kind and sympathetic and watch out for one another, and with the help of stricter gun laws, tragedies like these, the novel suggests, could be prevented altogether.

Shooter clearly points out the potential functions of multimodality in young adult novels, especially when these novels thematizes difficult topics. The shooting in Myers' novel is presented as being too complex to be fully comprehensible. In its narrative form, *Shooter* points out the complexity of characters. It illustrates processes of identity formation, interpersonal relationship and possibilities for conflict resolution. Further, the novel and enables empathetic connections with the friends of the shooter – but, for didactic purposes, not with the perpetrator himself. By presenting three interviews with the same person, the possibility that one person can present him- or herself in a completely different light, depending on the setting and the conversational partner, is represented.

Especially for young adult readers, who must constantly renegotiate their identity, *Shooter* shows the various possibilities for the process of identity formation to go wrong. The novel also represents marginalization as a complex and difficult issue, and asks the reader to reflect upon her own potential role in these processes. While in *Big Mouth & Ugly Girl*, the media is presented as an actant in the school shooting discourse and actively interferes with people's lives, *Shooter* portrays the media as perpetuating stereotypes that lead to further marginalization.

Young Adult fiction needs to be regarded as an important element of the school shooting discourse. It not only contributes to the cultural imaginary of school shootings, but also, thanks to its educational and didactic purpose, presents the highly complex topic in an approachable manner. However, by doing so, it relies on common knowledge about school shootings and references and fictionalizes previous events like Columbine in order to generate a more direct connection to the lifeworld of its teenaged readers. While this may result in a better understanding of the contributing factors in the genesis of school shootings and raise awareness of adolescent peers' struggles, the remediation of the school shooting narrative further reinforces the cultural script of school shootings. The 'look of school shootings' as well as the modus operandi in *Give a Boy a Gun* and the connection between the shooter, Goth subculture and mental illness in *Shooter,* can reinforce stereotypical images of school shooters. The novels' remediation therefore contributes to the collective memory of school shootings, and the novels thus become another fictional element in the school shooting discourse.

5 Experiencing the 'Rashomon-Effect': Functions of Multiperspectivity in *Violent Ends* (2015), *This is Where It Ends* (2016) and *Elephant* (2003)

In the years following Columbine, school shootings confronted both journalists and researchers with an increasingly difficult challenge: because of the rarity and disproportionate public attention that school shootings garnered, discord arose when it came to explanations or attempts at prevention. School shootings could not be understood separately from their public perception and representation in the media. The understanding of the phenomenon, consequently, has always been dependent on – and constituted by – a wide range of varying perspectives (cf. cf. Muschert 2007: 61). The attempts to explain school shootings are as multifarious as the events themselves are rare, and the various disciplines interested in the phenomenon each have different standpoints (see Chapter 2). These, as well as researchers' personal and scholarly perspectives and goals, determine the focus and the construction of their approach to school shootings. As a result, the divergent points of view of criminologists, psychologists, educational theorists and security specialists have resulted in a variety of approaches that have found their way back into the school shooting discourse and have shaped its attempts at explanation. As a multicausal and complex phenomenon, school shootings have not allowed for unified scholarly approaches or definitions.

In an attempt to describe this scholarly disjuncture, Muschert introduced the notion of the 'Rashomon-effect' (cf. Muschert 2007: 61, 2010: 245). Through this term, he connected the academic discourse to the realm of the fictional on yet another level by referring to the critically acclaimed film *Rashomon* (Japan, 1950) by Akira Kurosawa. In Kurosawa's *jigaideki* (period drama) film, the spectator sees four different accounts of the same event, as the murder of a Samurai warrior is investigated in court. Confronted with the contradictory accounts of what happened, the spectator eventually finds herself in the position of the judge (cf. Griem 2000: 317) who has to decide which of the 'truths' to believe. Instead of presenting the different accounts verbally, as the traditional detective film does, *Rashomon* depicts each of the accounts in a filmic episode – for the duration of each account, then, the film visually commits itself to this particular 'truth'. Over the course of the film, the spectator realizes that she is the one who must make sense of the different perspectives. Due to its innovative structure, *Rashomon* is considered a prime example of multiperspectival narration in film (cf. e.g., Hartner 2014, Griem 2000, Menhard 2009, Garry 2004) and has received scholarly attention in both film and literary studies. But *Rashomon* was adopted by anthropology in 1988, when Karl G. Heider used the term 'Rashomon-effect' to describe scholarly disagreement on ethnographic questions. The 'Rashomon-effect' has since been frequently used to emphasize the ramifications of differing perspectives on the same topic. Therefore, the research's perspectival limitation is both mirrored and illustrated by fictional multiperspectivity.

As a rather traditional narrative technique in literature and other media, multiperspectivity has proven to be particularly helpful in stressing the relevance of perspective for any human experience, knowledge or story (cf. ibid.: 3), as it clearly highlights the

> perceptually, epistemologically or ideologically restricted nature of individual perspectives and/or draw[s] attention to various kinds of differences and similarities between the points of view presented therein. In this way, multiperspectivity frequently serves to portray the relative character of personal viewpoints or perspectivity in general. (Hartner 2014: 353) [1]

While the multimodal novels analyzed in the previous chapter were also multiperspectival, I have not focused on the different perspectives until now. In this chapter, I show how multiperspectivity helps the readers and audience to experience and reflect upon the dynamics of the school shooting discourse. Multiperspectival narratives, I argue, can help to illustrate the polyphony of an international and transmedial discourse and can confront the audience with the relativity and idiosyncrasy of the different points of view – including their own – that are engaged in establishing a narrative of causality.

In the first part of this chapter, I analyze two very recent multiperspectival young adult school shooting novels: *Violent Ends* (2015) and *This is Where It Ends* (2016). Here, I draw upon and expand the analysis of YA school shooting novels from the previous chapter, and at times refer to those novels to support my findings. The discussion of multimodality provides a foundation for approaching multiperspectivity, a broader (and much older) narrative tradition.[2] Building upon this foundation, I now focus on the relevance of the fictional characters' perspectives to the recipients understanding of the fictional world and

---

[1] Of course, multiperspectivity can assume a variety of other potential intra- and extratextual functions (cf. Surkamp 2003, Bode 2011). Therefore, it neither can nor should be reduced to illustrating the relevance of perspectives and the relativism of human perception. In the fictional representations of school shootings, however, it can be observed that multiperspectival narration generally assumes this traditionally predominantly accepted function, as the following analyses show.

[2] Following Nünning and Nünning, multimodal texts are multiperspectival *per definitionem* (cf. Nünning/Nünning 2000: 18).

events and approach the potential functions of multiperspectival narratives in the school shooting discourse.

After presenting an overview of multiperspectivity, in section 5.1.1, I describe and analyze the perspective structure (cf. Nünning/Nünning 2000) of *Violent Ends* and *This is Where It Ends* based on models developed by Nünning and Nünning (2000a) and Carola Surkamp (2003). I want to ask which aspects of the school shooting narrative are foregrounded by the multiperspectival structures of the text and how the interaction of the various perspectives can broaden the readers' and audiences' understanding of the discursive dynamics and the phenomenon itself. Here, I show how the different perspectives contribute to the recipients' construction of the overall meaning of the works (cf. Hartner 2014: 315). In section 5.1.2, I analyze the potential functions of narrative multiperspectivity in YA school shooting novels, placing special emphasis on empathy and perspective taking. Different narrators and focalizers – and, in the case of *Violent Ends*, even different authors – present different aspects of the school shooting narrative and evoke different degrees of empathy. As the readers of multiperspectival works are prompted to take the perspective of the characters, the potential functions of these cognitive reactions to the texts is also considered (cf. Nünning 2014: 180ff.). The comparison between the texts further shows that multiperspectival texts have different effects on the readers, depending on the complexity of their perspective structures.

In the second part of this chapter, I analyze what is arguably the best known and certainly most researched school shooting film: Gus Van Sant's *Elephant*. In this aesthetically rich and highly valuable take on the school shooting phenomenon, Van Sant skillfully employs filmic multiperspectivity. In Chapter 5.2.1, I outline the specific functions and theoretical background of filmic multiperspectivity and the perspective structure in *Elephant*. While multiperspectivity in the novels discussed earlier is closely linked to notions of subjectivity and empathy, *Elephant*'s narrative structure highlights the partial and fragmentary nature of all perspectives, staging perceptual relativism and making the spectator question the notions of knowledge and reality (cf. Hartner 2014: 353). In order to understand the film's potential functions within the scope of the present volume, I then ask how the film's different perspectives, as well as its spatial and temporal dimension, result in a bleak image of American youth culture and youth violence. I further investigate how *Elephant* can be seen as an important fictional contribution to the school shooting discourse, as it remediates existing imagery and also actively contributes to the cultural imaginary of school shootings. By investigating how *Elephant*'s multiperspectivity approaches the genesis of the school shooting, section 5.2.2 focuses on the film's rather bold approach to the ultimate inexplicability of school shootings and asks how this can result in the spectator's experience of a denial of closure.

5.1 Taking Perspectives, Picking Sides: Multiperspectivity in Young Adult School Shooting Novels

Two very recent YA school shooting novels illustrate the ability of multiple perspectives to elucidate a multicausal and challenging phenomenon: *Violent Ends*, a novel written by 17 different YA authors, was edited by Shaun David Hutchinson and published in September 2015. *This is Where It Ends*, published in January 2016, is a best-selling debut novel by Marieke Nijkamp. These books represent a later generation of YA school shooting novels, as there is almost a decade between the three novels analyzed in Chapter 4 and these two texts. Hutchinson's book offers 17 different perspectives on the genesis and aftermath of the same event, with the various chapters, even though they work as a whole, employing different styles and modes of narration and varying in quality and persuasiveness. Nijkamp, a Dutch author, chose to write her debut in English about an American school shooting. In her native Netherlands, there has been only one school shooting to date (cf. Böckler et al. 2013: 11).

As is often the case in narratology, the definition of multiperspectivity is by no means universally agreed upon. Most scholars point out that a multiperspectival text must go beyond the mere presence of several points of view and should, instead, present the *same event* from different perspectives (cf. Nünning/Nünning 2000: 18). However, this definition has been criticized, as it might exclude the most intriguing cases of complex multiperspectivity, "those in which the reader quite properly wonders in what sense the 'same' event *is* actually being described, whether there is still any common ground at all between the different narratives" (cf. Bode 2011: 198f.). While a definition that includes all works that are told from a number of perspectives, even if they do not represent the same event, allows for a more far-reaching application of the concept, the novels that are analyzed in this chapter still fit the conventional, narrow definition of multiperspectivity: different narrators present their perspectives on the same event, i.e. a school shooting, which at times overlap temporally or spatially. In these narratives, the character's "points of view interact in salient and significant ways and thus create multiperspectivity" (Hartner 2014: 354),[3] as they

---

3 Nünning and Nünning (2000a: 42) point out that there are three different types of multiperspectival novels, as a novel can be narrated multiperspectivally, focalized multiperspectivally or

focus on the event of the school shooting and its genesis, as well as the effects of the crime on individuals or a community.

For reasons outlined in the previous chapter, studying YA fiction is a highly apt approach to multiperspectival school shooting fiction.[4] Written for the audience most directly affected by the phenomenon and communicating aspects of teenagers' own lifeworld from which this form of violence emerges, multiperspectival school shooting novels disseminate knowledge about the school shooting discourse more immediately than most novels for adults do. Furthermore, it is interesting to note that a great number of YA school shooting novels – including those analyzed previously – are multiperspectival. Most school shooting novels for adults, by contrast, are monoperspectival and narrated either by a homodiegetic first-person narrator[5] or by a conventional, omniscient third-person narrator. [6] While the intended audience of YA fiction will be kept in mind here, the potential functions of multiperspectivity – like those of multimodality – can serve to represent and reflect upon the dynamics of the school shooting discourse for both teenage and adult readers. In Chapter 5.1.1, I outline the basic concepts of character-perspectives and perspective structure, using the examples of *Violent Ends* and *This is Where It Ends*, and focus on the processes of reception and perspective taking fostered by the novels. Building upon these findings, section 5.1.2 then elaborates on the potential extratextual functions of these narrative strategies for the readers, as I ask how the multiperspectival narrative in these novels contributes to the school shooting discourse and the adolescent readers' understanding of the phenomenon.

---

can have a multiperspectival structure and organization (e.g., *Shooter* or other novels that tell the same event in different text forms).

4 Douglas Coupland's *Hey Nostradamus* (2003) is one of the few multiperspectival novel for adults.

5 Examples are: DBC Pierre's *Vernon God Little* (2003), Robert Harnum's *Exile in the Kingdom* (2001), Lionel Shriver's *We Need to Talk About Kevin* (2003) or Robert B. Parker's *School Days* (2005).

6 Examples are Jodi Picoult's *Nineteen Minutes* (2007) or Jessica Knoll's *Luckiest Girl Alive* (2015). As an empirical study has shown, this mirrors what can be described as a general tendency towards multiperspectivity in young adult fiction (cf. Koss 2009), which the author links to rather broad notions of changes in teen experiences and technologies, as well as changes in literary conventions and reading practices in an increasingly diverse society. Melanie Koss also ascribes an especially high educational value to multiperspectival narration, as perspective taking and the ability to evaluate and synthesize different perspectives can help students to use these abilities in the actual as well as the virtual world.

5.1.1 Perspective Structures and Perspective Taking in *This is Where It Ends* and *Violent Ends*

The term 'Rashomon-effect' links the dynamics of the school shooting discourse to a narrative structure in fictional works that acknowledges and emphasizes the relevance and restrictedness of the perspectives of individuals or groups of people. In multiperspectival novels, different characters gain a prominent role, as their perception of the narrated events is essential for the readers' understanding and construction of the narrative. The reception process is thus inextricably tied to the figures in the text. Analogously, the 'Rashomon-effect' in the school shooting discourse acknowledges the importance of the individuals who partake in its construction. With this analogy in mind, the analysis of literary multiperspectivity can serve as a commentary on the dynamics of the school shooting discourse.

If a single event is told from the perspective of different characters, these characters are not merely semantically empty elements of the narrative communication but, instead, integral to the textual content (cf. Surkamp 2003: 3). As soon as one character's version of the events is either reinforced or questioned by another character's perspective, a new understanding of the entire text arises. Thus, multiperspectivity prompts a new focus on the semantic meaning of fictional characters[7]; the characters in a multiperspectival narrative are crucial to the processes of meaning-making and narrative comprehension. In order to describe the individual character's role and position, the character's perception of the events and interrelations with the other characters needs to be examined. Only after the narrative structure that these perspectives create in their interrelation is described can the processes of reception, perspective taking and shifting empathic connection be integrated into the analysis of the school shooting novels' functions within the discourse.

Two crucial terms and concepts for the analysis of multiperspectival novels are character-perspective and perspective structure. Character-perspective can be

---

[7] Carola Surkamp summarizes a wide range of research on perspective in her description of character-perspective and further elaborates on and broadens Nünning's definition. Surkamp defines character-perspective as consisting of the entirety of the character's biographical data – e.g., age, ethnicity, sexual orientation, religion etc.; psychological and physiological dispositions; values and internalized norms; the entirety of the character's experiences and actions that can be found in or derived from his or her knowledge and competences; culturally shaped schemata of perception and interpretation, as well as other results of the figure's process of socialization; the amount of information the character has at his or her disposal; the character's motivations, needs, wishes and obligations during the narrated time and events; the spatial and temporal standpoint from which the character assesses the events in the story (cf. Surkamp 2003: 40)

defined as an individual's fictional system of preconditions or subjective worldview – the sum of all the models he or she has constructed of the world, or others, and of herself. A character-perspective is governed by the totality of an individual's knowledge and belief sets, intentions, psychological traits, attitudes, ideological stance, and system of values and norms that have been internalized. (Nünning 2001: 211)[8]

Nünning's definition stresses that "fictional mental states and motivations take up a position relative to the fictional world including the actions, psyches and intentions of other characters in all instances" (Hartner 2012: 85). Since the relation between one character-perspective and the entire fictional world is particularly important in multiperspectival texts, character-perspective is the most suitable term to describe the role and functions of the different narrative perspectives.

The narrative structure of a multiperspectival text is constructed from the interrelation and interplay between the individual character-perspectives in the act of reading. How and to what end the different character-perspectives in a multiperspectival text are interrelated can be described by the concept of 'perspective structure'. Originally used in drama theory, the term was introduced into the analysis of multiperspectival texts by Vera and Ansgar Nünning (2000) and has been adopted and extended in a number of narratological studies since then (cf. Surkamp 2003, Hartner 2008, 2012). It has proven fruitful in analyzing the potential extratextual functions of fictional works as they are realized in the reception process. The description of a literary perspective structure always includes the reading process, as the net of different perspectives is realized mentally during the act of reading (cf. Nünning 2001: 215).[9] The connection between the novel's perspective structure and the act of reading (and the reader's interpretation of the narrative) is therefore inextricable:

> The perspective structure of a novel reveals above all – as a model, something in process, not laid down or fixed – how the novel envisages its handling of divergent viewpoints, of different subjectivities. And since that is at the same time the way in which the novel itself

---

[8] This definition bears close resemblance to the notion of the 'fictional mind' (cf. Hartner 2012: 87), but character-perspective is more accurate, especially for the analysis of multiperspectival works. The fictional mind could be understood to be a self-contained entity, as it focuses on the character's mental state, viewpoints, knowledge, etc. Character-perspective, on the other hand, emphasizes that the literary mind of a character is always related to the fictional world and other fictional characters.

[9] The perspective structure of a multiperspectival text not only includes the different character-perspectives, but also the narrator-perspective, which is governed by the same elements as the character-perspective but is situated on the level of narrative mediation (cf. Nünning 2001, Surkamp 2003: 42f.), and the perspective of the fictional reader, if one is addressed directly (cf. Nünning/Nünning 2000a: 50; Surkamp 2003: 45).

is organized, it's only in this way that reader, too, can trace and reenact this kind of treatment of divergent viewpoint, divergent subjectivities: that is, in the spaces of possibility that the novel opens up or blocks off, via the connections that it has made available without prescribing them, or which it lays down so that only these may be followed. (Bode 2011: 203)

The correlations made by the reader, her understanding of the interconnections between the characters and their perspectives, therefore depend on the narrative modes of representation (cf. Surkamp 2003: 68f.). Consequently, both the formal and the semantic dimension of the multiperspectival narration must be considered in order to describe the perspective structure of a novel. Only if the different aspects are considered can the potential extratextual functions of the text be approached. Nünning and Nünning (2000a) have provided a helpful model for describing the formal dimension: they have identified different types of multiperspectivally narrated, focalized or structured texts (cf. Nünning/Nünning 2000a: 44ff.). With Nünning and Nünning's typology in mind, is helpful for analyzing Nijkamp's *This is Where It Ends* appears to be comparatively simple case to define, while *Violent Ends* proves to be a more complex case. In order to investigating the potential functions of multiperspectivity in school shooting novels, however, it is useful to compare the two novels.

The Perspective Structure of *This is Where It Ends*
In Nijkamp's novel, four first-person narrators present their account of a shooting that occurs at their high school in the idyllic, yet highly clichéd, suburban town of Opportunity. Reminiscent of the minute-by-minute accounts of school shootings well known from media coverage and academic publications, the novel's narrated time is no longer than one hour. The 26 chapters usually include all four perspectives, and sometimes cover no more than two to five minutes. After certain chapters, additional blog entries, text messages or tweets provide further information about some of the minor characters and how the public reacts to the news of the shooting. The quantity of semiotic modes used in the novel is rather low, and they serve as a way to include contemporary modes of adolescent communication, rather than as integral elements of the narrative. In Nünning and Nünning's terminology, the novel can thus be described as an 'intradiegetic polyperspectival narrated text' (cf. 2000a: 45), which is further multiperspectivally structured thanks to the inclusion of different text forms (cf. ibid.).

The minutely detailed accounts of the events in and outside of the school during the attack focus primarily on the student's fears, thoughts and memories. Most of the chapters are fraught with students' doubts about their role in the genesis of the shooting, or their heroic plans to stop the shooter. The brief epilogue focuses on the night after the shooting and presents an emotional ceremony in which the students and teachers remember the 39 dead and 25 injured victims of the school shooting, thus providing imagery for a culture of remembering school shootings.[10]

The novel begins with the perspective of Claire, the shooter's ex-girlfriend, who is not inside the school building at the time of the shooting. Almost all of the other students, as the readers learn in the next account by the shooter's sister, Autumn, are gathered in the auditorium and listening to a motivational speech by their principal. Her speech, reminiscent of the Columbine principal's speech as documented by Dave Cullen in *Columbine*, tells the students of Opportunity High School that "it's the choices you make now that will determine your future" (*Where It Ends:* 5) – a dark foreboding in this context. In the third account by Sylvia (called Sylv), Autumn's girlfriend, the readers learn that there is at least some reason to be afraid of Tyler, Autumn's brother. The day of the speech is the day when he was to return to school after he had dropped out, which causes great unease for Sylv, who was threatened and raped by Tyler, as the readers learn much later. In the next chapter, the last of the four narrators is introduced: Tomás, Sylv's brother, who broke into the principal's office with his friend Fareed to find compromising information in Tyler's files and assesses that Tyler is not only a "closet genius" but also "a harmless one" (*Where it Ends:* 12f.). Shortly after this is told, Sylv is the first to realize that they are locked inside the school's auditorium and Tyler's cruelly staged revenge shooting begins.

The perspective structure of Nijkamp's novel presents the events that occur during the school shooting in chronological order. In the various chapters, the spatial standpoint of the different narrators is important: the fact that some characters are outside of the auditorium and thereby spatially detached from what is going on inside determines their actions and thoughts, as they try to figure out ways to help their peers. The shots they hear provide additional temporal orientation to connect the perspectives. Autumn and Sylv are not only closer to the school shooter and his attack in terms of spatial proximity, they are also at the center of the narrative's attempt to explain what led to the school shooting. Here, the hierarchy of different perspectives is of particular relevance: despite its

---

10 So as to justify the many events that happened in the extremely short time span of one hour, Nijkamp not only chooses to present a school shooting with more fatalities and injuries than any real (and, most likely, even fictional) school shooting ever caused, but also stages it as a performance by the school shooter who, after the successful attempt by two students to rescue those who are locked in the school's auditorium, goes through the school's hallways seeking out those who ruined his plan.

use of different character-perspectives, *This is Where It Ends* does not present highly discrepant versions of the school shooting. Instead, comparable to Todd Strasser's *Give a Boy a Gun*, it uses alternating perspectives that provide a chronology and contribute to a more comprehensive version of the shooter's background and personality. Both Strasser's and Nijkamp's novel use multiperspectivity to make the reader experience the number of people affected by the school shooting and represents the variety of experiences that predate and potentially even contribute to the genesis of a school shooting.

In Nijkamp's novel, the character-perspective of Autumn helps the reader to frame the narrative, as it contributes to a coherent connection of events (cf. Wolf 2000). Autumn connects all the other perspectives and is ultimately presented as the motivation for most of the actions within the story: she triggers both the shooting[11] and her friends' heroic attempts to save her.

Autumn's prominent role is further relevant as she synthesizes different characterizations of the shooter for the readers: in Claire's perspective, Tyler is friendly, caring and somebody with a great desire for stability. Sylv, by contrast, has experienced Tyler's 'dark side' – flashbacks of sexual assault, through which he wanted to 'cure her' of her homosexuality, clearly show his potential for cruelty. His sister describes two versions of her brother, the caring and loving one and the cold and detached one, in whom she no longer recognizes her brother.

Tomás, the school's most troublesome student, bullies Tyler and voices his contempt for him on different occasions. While bullying is usually given as an explanation for school shootings, the different perspectives in *This is Where It Ends*, however, relativize the shooter's experiences: here, the worst acts of bullying are presented as Tomás' attempts to protect his sister from Tyler's threats. As Tomás is presented as a hero rather than a villain, his bullying is justified rather than condemned.

The Perspective Structure of *Violent Ends*

In *Violent Ends*, the perspective structure provides a richer and more complicated net of interrelations that the readers have to understand, untangle and correlate. Twelve of the 17 chapters in the book are narrated by an intradiegetic, first-person narrator. The remaining five are narrated by an extradiegetic, omniscient third-person narrator. All 17 chapters are interrelated at least by some reference

---

11 Much in line with findings from school shooting research, Nijkamp presents Tyler's fear of losing the one person he cares about to her girlfriend as his final motivation for going through with his school shooting (cf. Böckler/Seeger 2010).

to the shooter, and at times also by other interpersonal relationships and references.

The book starts with the nine-year-old Susanna Byrd, who is bullied on her birthday and cruelly takes her frustration out on a boy from her neighborhood, who just wanted to help. The young boy is introduced as the twelve-year-old Kirby Matheson. As the readers learn shortly afterwards, years later, at the age of 17, Kirby kills seven and wounds five people at his high school before shooting himself. The first chapter introduces the main character of the book and provides background information about the shooter's history of being bullied. Together with the last chapter, which refers to the incidents described in the first one, this structure provides a thematic framework for the narrative: the last perspective in the novel is by one of the boys who bullied Kirby throughout his childhood and adolescence.

The second chapter provides basic information about Kirby's school shooting and explains the major event of the narrative, to which all of the following chapters refer from various perspectives. Over the course of the novel, the readers learn about the shooter, the shooting and its aftermath from the perspectives of a good friend of Kirby's, his acquaintances from school and summer camp, a former neighbor, the shooter's former girlfriend, a girl who rejected him, his sister, a waitress who used to live in the shooter's family's house, a bullying jock, and – in the most experimental chapter – even the gun that Kirby uses during the shooting.

The relevance of the interrelation of the different perspectives becomes clear in the chapter about Reba Landrieu, who survives the shooting because emergency drills had been preparing her for the event ever since elementary school. Reba, the readers learn, has just moved to Middleborough, and she is a Southern girl from a conservative family of gun enthusiasts. The experience of the school shooting thus makes her reflect on issues of gun control – because she did not know him personally, she only gets her information about the shooting and about Kirby Matheson from the media.[12]

---

[12] There are three other characters who did really not know Kirby Matheson, but are forced to position themselves in relation to him: Ruben, who is thought to be an accomplice due to his violent writings – a clear reference to the debate about Seung-Hui Cho in the aftermath of the Virginia Tech shooting – but who only shared a passion for certain films with Kirby, whom he did not know personally; Allie, a girl from the high school's stoner gang, who had a secret crush on one of the jocks that Kirby shot; and Laura, from the high school paper in a neighboring town, who was Kirby's neighbor and is thus expected to analyze him in a feature about the school shooting in the penultimate chapter of the novel.

Even though Reba's account is not a personal one and she does not present any insight into the shooter's mind, her perspective plays an important role in the perspective structure, as it introduces the readers to a broader societal debate about possible reasons for school shootings. In her attempt to come to terms with what she experienced, she reacts to the aspect of the school shooting debate that she can relate to the most, the issue of gun control. The girl who knows how to hunt and skin a deer clearly sees guns as a necessary means for self-defense (cf. *Violent Ends:* 193).[13] Here, even though Reba struggles with what to believe, *Violent Ends* clearly provides a pro-gun perspective presented by a likeable, all-American Southern girl.

This perspective, however, unfolds its controversial potential not only because of the school shooting – the fact that the gun control debate is quickly co-opted by the political right after each new school shooting is well known – but also because the previous chapter was narrated by the gun with which Kirby shot his schoolmates. Interestingly, the gun itself, purchased illegally from a criminal, 'struggles' with its new owner and with the realization that he is an "angry, frightened boy" (*Violent Ends:* 175). "In him", the anthropomorphized gun states, "I feel deeper emotions than I ever knew existed" (*Violent Ends:* 175). The gun also refers back to the second chapter of the novel, in which Kirby offered his gun to his friend Zachary for self-defense against her abusive father, but she refuses to take it.[14] In her hands, as the outcome of the story suggests, the weapon would have been better placed – violence committed by the victimized Zachary would have been justifiable, whereas the school shooting is not. Even though the readers are presented with two completely different takes on weapons, the combination of both perspectives creates a consistent narrative: guns are for self-defense, as the perspectives of Zachary, the gun and Reba Landrieu suggest. Only in the hands of the wrong people can they do great harm.

What guides the reader through each chapter and can be seen as the navigating principle through the perspectives – rather than temporal or spatial markers, as in *This is Where It Ends* – is the focus on Kirby's motives or any possible rationale for his actions. In many of the chapters, physical, emotional or structural violence are thematized to a disturbingly high degree. The only adult per-

---

[13] Even though her statement at the end of the chapter – "It's her job to protect me. It's my job to be in control" (*Violent Ends:* 198) – is made about her dog, the analogy between her dog and her previous observations and questions about the gun control debate in the media is more than obvious.
[14] The fact that Zachary is a girl with a boy's name is used in the novel to underline her difficult situation at home.

spective is that of the teacher Ms. Leeland, who experiences abuse at home and stalks her students as a coping mechanism.

As in *This is Where It Ends*, the perpetrator does not speak for himself, and therefore the readers do not get to know his perspective. Naturally, as the next subchapter will show, this is closely related to the question of empathy and the ethical implication that the focus on a character's perspective has. But the refusal to present the shooter's perspective also enhances the novel's potential to serve as a mirror and fictional equivalent to the dynamics and processes of meaning-making in the school shooting discourse. In the actual world, the shooter's perspective can hardly ever be heard after the school shooting. The readers of *Violent Ends* are thus put in the position of having to reconstruct the events that led up to the school shooting from the perspectives available to them. The narrative structure therefore creates a direct connection between the reading process and the process of meaning-making in the aftermath of actual school shootings.

In this regard, the perspectives that are presented and their interrelation and hierarchization assume a particular function for the readers' processes of meaning-making of the fictional events – and, consequently, of school shootings as such. Here, the framing function of certain perspectives and its consequences for the hierarchy in the perspective structure of a text is of particular relevance (cf. Wolf 2000): the characters and the events of the first chapter, "Miss Susie", and the last chapter, with the meaningful title "History Lessons", are more closely connected than any of the others chapters, which provides the readers with an impression of coherence and orientation. Because everybody knows that he bullied Kirby and his best friend was killed in the school shooting, Nate feels that he is being blamed for what happened. In this light, his statement that "[e]veryone wants to know why but I've always known the answer. Kirby Matheson has always had a gun in his hands" (*Violent Ends*: 334) appears like the meek attempt to assuage his own conscience rather than a hint at Kirby's 'monstrous' character.

Clearly, the two chapters not only frame the novel in terms of structure, but also serve as framing perspectives for explaining the otherwise contrasting and, at times, relativizing perspectives on the shooter and the events. In this process, the effects of frictions and correlations of different literary perspectives become clear: Kirby Matheson's life, no matter from which perspective it is told, has not been easy. Especially in the various representations of the shooter's experiences of marginalization, the semantic dimension of the perspective structure and of the individual characters is underlined, as the various character-perspectives clearly emphasize the subjectiveness of all experience – even the experience of suffering. However, the perspective structure of *Violent Ends* also suggests that Kirby's history of being bullied and marginalized has to be relativized – the suffering of the transgender girl Billie Palermo, or the abuse that Zachary and the teacher Ms. Leeland experience at home, for example, appear to be much worse than anything Kirby has ever experienced.

By presenting various forms and degrees of adolescent and adult struggles in life, *Violent Ends* thus shows that experiences of violence, suffering and marginalization cannot sufficiently explain the school shooting. The perspective structure of the novel does, however, highlight the subjectiveness of all perception, as it enables the readers to see that the degree of suffering that a person can endure varies from one individual to the other. Therefore, even though the novel suggests a causality between bullying and the school shooting, this explanation is not total. When the reader takes all perspectives into account, the question of 'why?', even though it is asked by each character, remains unanswered, and the question 'who could have known?' is foregrounded.

Perspective Taking and the Young Adult Reader
In *Violent Ends*, the narrative situation of each chapter adds to the readers' understanding of the novel's perspective structure. In contrast to *This is Where It Ends*, where the structure of the novel clearly highlights the perspective of the shooter's sister, the readers of *Violent Ends* are challenged to construct the narrative of the genesis of Kirby's school shooting. While both novels clearly address the question asked in the novels analyzed in the previous chapter – namely, *who could have known?* – and thus center the experience of a school shooter's peers in the wake of a shooting, *Violent Ends* presents a much wider range of perspectives. Despite the fact that Nijkamp has chosen to include perspectives that foreground diversity of ethnicity, religion and sexuality, and attempts to present her characters' perspectives as multi-faceted, all the characters eventually rise above their troubles and fears in the face of unspeakable violence and thus appear almost superhuman in their heroic efforts to save their friends before themselves.[15]

In *Violent Ends*, the struggles of the adolescent victims and witnesses are much more believable. Their reactions to the shocking event range from a perplexed helplessness (*Violent Ends*: 36ff.; 299f.) and despair (*Violent Ends*: 25f.), to traumatized stupor (*Violent Ends*: 237) and anger (*Violent Ends*: 284f.) – de-

---

15 The town of Opportunity (even though some of the characters have always wanted to leave it) is presented as home, even as family, in which the school shooting fosters a new sense of belonging and unity. This draws upon the narrative and social myth that emerged after the Columbine shooting (cf. Cullen 2010); nevertheless, it is remarkable that in the novel, these notions are already voiced while the school shooting is still going on (e.g. *Where it Ends*: 235f.).

pending on how close the characters were to the shooter, how much they can identify with Kirby or feel empathy for him, and whether or not they lost anyone during the shooting. The teenagers in *Violent Ends* who are only loosely connected to the shooting and may have only witnessed the events through the media also contribute important perspectives to the novel, as they illustrate how adolescents at American high schools are affected by school shootings, even if they were not direct witnesses or victims themselves. Here, the novel clearly communicates cultural knowledge, offering a wide variety of young adult readers a perspective to relate to.

The importance of perspective taking for the reader's realization of a novel's perspective structure and the process of meaning-making has been pointed out by Vera Nünning (2014). The term 'perspective taking' describes a range of cognitive activities in the reading process:

> First, it can designate the act of trying to gauge the other's dispositions, attitudes, beliefs, traits and preferences, i.e. to understand his or her perspective. Second, it can refer to adopting character's local position, seeing or visualising a scene from their spatial point of view. And third, perspective taking can entail mind-reading and simulating what the other feels, thinks, and intends to do at a given moment. (Nünning 2014: 194)

Perspective taking, in this regard, can be understood as "the royal avenue to understanding others" (2014: 178f.). Consuming fiction and practicing taking several and even shifting perspectives can therefore contribute to the reader's ability to connect empathically with people in the actual world. Within the safety of the fictional realm, and with the benefit of hindsight or privileged insight into a character's perspective, the readers can practice and refine their abilities, which they can then employ in the actual world. Reading multiperspectival narratives can be understood as the readers' 'playground' on which they can practice to understand others in a sensitive way (cf. Nünning 2014: 194). Complex perspective structures prompt the reader

> to combine and coordinate different beliefs, desires and wishes of a wide array of actors and perspectives in order to understand the character's behaviour in any given situation. Moreover, they are obliged to create chronological sequences and make out reasons for understanding attitudes, desires, beliefs and intention (Nünning 2014: 193)

Novels that challenge their readers to take on different perspectives and engage in constant evaluation and re-evaluation can be seen as especially valuable to the YA genre, as perspective taking in fictional texts always has an educational or didactic dimension.

The obligation to understand different attitudes or beliefs is especially dominant when the readers are confronted with fictional narratives told by omniscient or homodiegetic narrators with hindsight (e.g., *Violent Ends*). Here, narrators can explain, analyze emotions and provide further knowledge about the events in the fictional world that needs to be ordered and weighed by the reader. Furthermore, in these narrative situations, the internal perspective of the character dominates. This, as Nünning points out, is one of the valuable aspects of fiction:

> In addition to providing insights into the intricacies of a single character's emotions, fictional stories frequently stage the interconnections between the respective emotions of several characters. They show not only how a character feels, but in how far this is related to the (re-)actions of and interrelations with other characters and to events which happened in the past or are expected to take place in the future. Fiction can thus present forms of successful and unsuccessful communications between the characters; it can show which forms of dealing with and regulating one's own emotions are likely to succeed or fail in given situations. (Nünning 2014: 110)

Perspective taking is inextricably connected to empathic sharing and, consequently, always has an ethical implication. Whether or not a certain perspective, such as the school shooter's, is made available to the reader, or which position this perspective has in the structure of the narrative, has an effect on the reader's ability to take the perspective of the character.[16]

One of the most valuable and powerful aspects of fiction lies in the reader's "access to the minds, thoughts, and reflections of literary figures so that the reader can gain insight into a figure's motives, ways of thinking, values and judgements" (Hallet 2008a: 198). If a multiperspectival novel, however, does not provide the perspective of the school shooter as a clearly ethically derailed subject, but represents the perspectival limitations of the real world where the "mental dimension of behavior and the way of thinking that leads to certain actions remains oblique" (Hallet 2008a: 198), this obviously has a great impact on the novel's potential functions, as the next subchapter shows.

---

16 The fact that most school shooting novels do not include the school shooter's perspective is connected to the discursive dynamics and the societal approaches to perpetrators of excessive violence. School shooters have to be 'othered' and dehumanized in order to re-integrate their actions into the societal narrative of peacefulness, since perspective taking and empathy would imply that the readers could connect to the feelings, thoughts and decisions of the shooter. The ethical implications of this are dealt with in the following subchapter.

5.1.2 Functions of Literary Multiperspectivity for the School Shooting Discourse

Multiperspectival narration in the novels analyzed here has three major potential functions in the school shooting discourse: first, as has already been established, the perspective taking of and empathic connection to various characters can help the adolescent reader to practice sensitive understanding and can question stereotypes (cf. Nünning 2014: 234). Especially if the role of YA school shooting novels as 'tools for prevention' (see Chapter 4) is considered, encouraging empathy fulfills an educational purpose, as the novels prompt their readers to reflect upon their part in the genesis of a school shooting. How this is realized in the act of reading will be analyzed by drawing upon the findings from Chapter 4.

Second, multiperspectival narration can make the reader experience the multicausality of the school shooting phenomenon and can thus prompt her to acknowledge complexity and polyvalence (cf. Nünning 2014: 290). In analyzing how this is achieved on the level of perspective structure and narrative, I will focus on the way the narratives present the discursive dynamics and depict or incorporate different attempts at explanation. Furthermore, I will ask how the understanding of these explanatory attempts is connected to the perspective in which they are presented to the readers.

The third potential function that I ascribe to multiperspectival school shooting novels is directly linked to the dynamics of the school shooting discourse and the inexplicability of these acts of violence. Generally, multiperspectivity has the possibility to deny its readers the closure that they seek in the act of reading. I ask whether the two novels in this chapter realize this particular potential and actually confront their readers with the inexplicability of a shooting, or whether their perspective structure and character-perspectives provide causal explanations.

Shifting Perspectives and the 'Fundamental Attribution Error'
When considering the individual perspectives and their position within the perspective structure of the text, the connection between the structural, pragmatic and functional dimensions of a text's perspective structure becomes obvious (cf. Nünning/Nünning 2000: 22). Whether a perspective serves, for example, as a framing narrative has a significant effect on the reading process.[17] An attempt

---

[17] A perspective can exist on a higher level in a text's perspective structure when it is clearly marked as a framing narrative, when, for example, the character from whose perspective the

to explicate extratextual functions of a multiperspectival text therefore always has to consider the entire perspective structure and the way it is realized by the act of reading:

> In general, it's certainly fair to say that the multiplication of narrative perspectives increases the demand on the reader and on the activity of reading – *provided that* the individual perspectives are sufficiently dissonant or discrepant and *provided that* an integrative conclusion from a higher perspective remains withheld, or no discernible hierachization or privileging emerges from such a perspective. (Bode 2011: 200)

Comparable to multimodal novels, where the degree to which readers are engaged in an active and hypertextual reading process depends on the degree of multimodality, the degree to which multiperspectival novels engage their reader depends on the discrepancy of the perspectives and on the transparency of existing framings or hierarchies.

Devices such as the journalist in *Give a Boy a Gun*, who collects and orders the different perspectives and adds additional information in the footnotes to the text, provide a clear framework for the narrative. As framing narratives, they are most easily understood as 'prioritized' narrative levels that provide a certain guideline for the reader. Thanks to the framing devices, readers are not required to engage as actively as they are in, for example, Walter Dean Myers' *Shooter*. In *Shooter*, the readers are mostly left alone to determine whose perspective they want to believe and how the different accounts correlate. Whereas *Give a Boy a Gun*'s perspective structure provides the reader with a fairly obvious integrative conclusion, *Shooter* clearly refuses to do so. However, a perspective's position as a framing narrative is not necessarily immediately recognizable as such, and yet can still serve as a covert guideline for the reader's reception of the text and her realization of the perspective structure with all its implications. Even if hierarchical position is less easy to identify, it can still have significant impact on the perspective structure and, consequently, on the extratextual functions of the text.

Arguably, a less overt hierarchy of perspectives, which requires more active engagement by the reader, such as a character-perspective's position within the textual structure, can highlight a certain perspective. The fact that *Violent Ends* begins and ends with an account focused on Kirby's history of being bullied, for example, influences the reader's perception of why he did what he did – even though other perspectives provided a multitude of additional factors and possi-

---

event is narrated invites a strong empathetic connection, or the certain character-perspective is revisited more often than others throughout the novel. Also, other characters in a text can refer to a certain character-perspective in a way that emphasizes its relevance.

bilities for explanation. The readers have not been told explicitly that Kirby's experience of bullying caused the shooting, but the narrative structure clearly suggests the connection. Here, it becomes clear once more that the perspective structure is dependent on a number of textual and structural elements and that the totality of the interrelations is responsible for the text's extratextual function (cf. Nünning/Nünning 2000: 20).

Even multiperspectival texts that do not present highly discrepant perspectives, such as *This is Where It Ends*, can engage young adult readers with complex issues (like school shootings) and can engage them in interpretative activities that the young adult reader can then transfer to the extratextual discourse:

> The understanding of multiperspectival texts therefore requires not only simulation, but creativity from readers. The unmediated juxtaposition of different perspectives generally creates a broad scope for interpretation in the reception process, stimulating readers to make considerable efforts in order to reach synthesis. In order to make sense of the events, readers have to critically evaluate the characters' views and to decide whether to adopt the interpretation given by one of them or to arrive at a completely different interpretation by themselves, on the basis of their superior state of information and their own beliefs and emotions. (Nünning 2014: 275)

Teenage readers are challenged by the fictional text as they are by the aftermath of a real school shooting. However, when reading, instead of learning about the genesis of the event from only one perspective, they have to synthesize different ones. In texts that present various perspectives, as Wolfgang Iser writes,

> the task of coordination is handed over to the reader, for he alone has all the information at his disposal. The one-sidedness of these viewpoints gives a sharp outline to the world that is described, whereas their blending results in its modification. It is this interrelation that forms lively images in the mind of the reader and enables him to be transported into the individual character and his experiences of reality. (Iser 1974: 75)

In the act of reading, readers are confronted with shifting perspectives that they have to adopt in order to make sense of the text. While one perspective presents a very clear explanation of what happened – e.g., the perpetrator was bullied or rejected by a girl (as in *Violent Ends*) – the next perspective forces the reader to re-think and modify what was presented before.

Here, blending is an important concept: when reading multiperspectival texts, readers blend the input they get from the different perspectives and then modify their model of the fictional world and events by "backward projection" (Hartner 2012: 102), based on the different pieces of information and knowledge they gain from the different perspectives. This shows that the reading process of a multiperspectival text is much more active than, for example, that of a homodiegetic first-person narrative. As the analysis of multimodal novels in the last chapter has shown, readers' active engagement results in immediacy more immediate connection to the fictional world and an enhances the successful connection of the fictional events to the extratextual world.

This active reading practice is fostered by encouraging the reader to engage with various character-perspectives and subjective accounts of the same event. Readers have to dynamically follow the shifts in perspective while keeping track of the spatial, temporal and interperspectival differences and relations between them. By shifting perspectives and prompting readers to "adopt the perspectives of different characters, novels can arguably reduce readers' tendency to fall into the trap of the fundamental attribution error" (Nünning 2014: 270). The 'fundamental attribution error', which is "inherent in the differences between the perspectives of actor and observer" (ibid.: 268), refers to the observation that people in Western cultures tend to look for dispositional causes and explanations for the actions of others. That is, they usually look for a psychological, rather than a circumstantial or social, explanation for a boy's transformation into a school shooter. In describing or explaining their own actions and behavior, however, people are more prone to explain it by referring to outer circumstances or specific situations which required a certain action, rather than relating their behavior to their own character or personal preferences (cf. ibid.: 268).

A multiperspectival texts allow its readers to adopt the perspectives of both characters and narrators, actors and observers. The novels use a narrative convention that induces readers to consider the thoughts and feelings of a character by taking his or her perspective. Thus, the readers are more likely to understand the circumstances that lead to the events in the fictional story and to resist dispositional explanations. They have more information about the events from different perspectives, which gives them the opportunity to come to balanced and more comprehensive conclusions about the events and characters. They may further be prompted to consider the same scene from contradictory perspectives – at times, these perspectives even vary between observer and actor – and to recognize the different perspectives and the subjectiveness of all perception. Moreover, especially in novels that include perspectives from both observers and actors, "readers practice a mode of cognition that counteracts the fundamental attribution error" (Nünning 2014: 271). Due to this effect, multiperspectival novels "allow readers to arrive at less tendentious judgements than they would in real life" (ibid.). Therefore, the novels that approach a topic through multiperspectival narration are much less likely to present their readers with one-sided or oversimplifying and dispositional explanations.

Encouraging young adults to reach a differentiated and more balanced view on the various and multiple causes and events that may lead up to a school shooting can be seen as desirable educational aim. As the novels' narratives are clearly shaped by the prevalent and well known school shooting narrative, the readers can transfer their experience of polyvalence and subjectivity in the fictional world to their evaluation of the extratextual discourse.

(Un-)Ethical Literary Figures and Emotional Responses to School Shootings
School shooters as adolescent mass murderers are rather prototypical 'unethical figures'. This poses many challenges to media, educators and the legal system in the actual world, but to the fictional representations of school shooters – especially if their intended audiences are young adults who share the lifeworld, many of the experiences and similar generational or age-related struggles with the character. Although almost no YA school shooting novel encourages taking the school shooter's perspective, unethical literary figures still have the potential to serve as ethical models, as they provide the counter-image to the readers' perception of normality.

This is especially interesting when the 'unethical' figures are teenagers, since readers are likely to relate the characters to their own concept of adolescence and their own experiences as teenagers. Adolescent readers can easily identify with their fictional peers in the novels; the events in the fictional story world have a high degree of recognizability. For this reason, the shooter's perspective in most school shooting novels for young adults is either unheard or very clearly 'othered'– for example, by characterizing it as mentally ill, as in *Shooter*.[18]

The reaction of adult readers to adolescent characters, on the other hand, depends on their projections of ideas about teenagers rather than on processes of identification:

> We will always have at least a faint idea of what sort of person or personality we would like a teenager to be. These may be very general visions and concepts of non-violence, honesty, open-mindedness and the like, and we will even develop vague concepts of their future lives conceiving of them as individuals can look after themselves, live in peace and good health and be decent men and women who are aware of and responsible for what they are doing, who are autonomous to a good degree, and who are dependent on other people's good or bad will, and so forth. (Hallet 2008a: 200)

---

18 While most of the novels for adults also abstain from presenting the shooter's perspective, Robert Harnum's *Exile in the Kingdom*, in which the school shooter is the homodiegetic first-person narrator of the events, is the exception to the rule. In Harnum's novel, the shooter – who is an athlete and by no means a stereotypical school shooter – appears baffled and confused by his actions and cannot really tell what motivated him.

Adult readers of YA novels connect the teenage characters to general ideas about teenagers as the future of society. A school shooter, however, clearly contradicts all these positive and hopeful notions of adolescence.

The perpetrator's ethics stand in stark contradiction to those of society. This friction between societal expectations and the teenagers' ultimate rejection of them and the refusal to become a 'successful adult' is inherent to the school shooting discourse and, consequently, its representations. School shooting novels communicate this basic dynamic on the level of the characters and character-perspectives.

All school shooting novels contribute to the cultural imaginary of the phenomenon by referencing and fictionalizing actual school shootings and referring to prevalent societal reactions and modes for explanation. However, the novels not only communicate general knowledge of the phenomenon, but also specific knowledge about the emotions that are culturally accepted or viewed as adequate in regard to the events represented. Thus, literature can become an important element in the socialization of the teenage readers, and in this regard, the various perspectives in multiperspectival YA school shooting novels assume an educational discursive function. Very few readers will ever experience a school shooting in their real lives, yet the disproportionate presence of school shootings in the lives of teenagers – due to security measures, emergency drills and so forth – means that they at least theoretically know how to react to and how to understand and categorize these events. Fictional works can disseminate 'feeling rules', "which provide a rough guide to what people should fear or enjoy and which degree of emotion is adequate in a given situation" (Nünning 2014: 115), by illustrating appropriate and inappropriate emotional responses.

Most school shooting novels assume this function by focusing on the aftermath of the shooting and by the presenting reactions of the shooter's family and peers. The degree of outrage, insecurity, helplessness and fear that a community experiences after the shooting – as described and experienced by the characters in both *Violent Ends* and *This is Where It Ends* – clearly corresponds with the predominant societal reactions to school shootings in the real world. Moreover, the societal reactions to the shooter, the questions about his motivation, along with processes of 'othering' the perpetrator as monstrous or mentally ill, are all thematized or represented in the novels. These discursive dynamics and prevalent narratives can be either reinforced or challenged by the fictional narratives, depending on the way in which the multiperspectival narrative represents them, as the novels' analyses show.

This is Where It Ends is an obvious case of reinforcing discursive notions, since, despite the novel's multiperspectival narrative, its characters' reactions to the school shooting hardly differ from one another. The first-person narrators all respond with shock, fear and helplessness, but eventually overcome their immediate responses to discover heroism and a sense of unity and belonging in their high school and town. The perspectives on Tyler, the shooter, differ significantly and could therefore theoretically present him as multidimensional and complex character. However, even though Claire and Autumn, for example, think positively about Tyler, their recollections of his friendly and caring behavior prior to the shooting mainly underline that he successfully hid his true nature. His violent behavior towards Sylv, on the other hand, is presented as the occasion on which his 'true self' was revealed. Even though Tyler may have been or at least acted like a 'nice guy' at times, this perception cannot be shared by the readers with the hindsight that the characters gain after the shooting.

In *Violent Ends*, the different perspectives reveal more discrepant reactions to the school shooting – depending, as I have shown earlier, on the character's proximity to the event and/or the perpetrator.[19] The reader therefore has to actively organize and weigh the different perspectives, and is prompted to reflect upon the subjectiveness of the emotional responses to both the shooting and the perpetrator. Here, the "spaces of possibilities that the novel opens" (Bode 2011: 203) are rather wide. From the combination, assessment and tracing of the different perspectives, readers can also piece together a more complex image of Kirby. Just as the characters in the novel have very different experiences with the shooter and different opinions about him, so too can the readers choose to either believe one of the accounts or, more likely, blend them into a more comprehensive view on the character. What is of relevance here is that, as opposed to *This is Where It Ends*, not all perspectives are tainted by the knowledge of the perpetrator's later actions, because the novel presents various perspectives from before, during and after the shooting. For example, through the perspective of the cheerleader, whose suicide Kirby prevents and who he ensures is at home on the day of the shooting, Kirby is presented as a 'regular' person with a personal history and both positive and negative character traits.

When the dissemination of adequate emotional responses to a school shooting is considered, the perspective structure of the text is crucial. In a multiperspectival structure, the novel indirectly communicates cultural knowledge about different possibilities for responding and about which perspectives one should or should not take (i.e., with whom readers should or should not empathize). As unethical figures, school shooters might still invite sympathy, especial-

---

19 A common theme in the various emotional responses to the school shootings in both novels, however, is the struggle with the feeling of guilt. In both novels, almost every character at some point asks whether or not they could have known or prevented the shooting.

ly when their suffering as victims of bullying is highlighted (as in *Give a Boy a Gun* or *Violent Ends*). However, if their perspectives were to be heard in the novels, and if readers were invited to take their perspectives – which would include the norms and values of the unethical subject – this would make it harder for the adolescent reader to fully condemn the shooter's actions, as has been shown in the previous chapter.

In a multiperspectival narrative, readers have to "adopt the perspectives of fictional characters and narrators in order to make sense of the story" (Nünning 2014: 185). If the shooter's perspective were to be included, readers would be prompted to take the perspective of the school shooter into account. The perspective structures in both *Violent Ends* and *This is Where It Ends* avoid putting the reader in the position of adopting the unethical perspective of the shooter, further underlining the educational and didactic aspect of YA school shooting novels. Instead of an empathic connection with the shooter, readers are offered various perspectives on his character, which might help them to feel sympathy and realize the complexity of any human personality. In *Violent Ends*, the perspective structure relativizes these experiences, as it includes the perspectives of other characters who have suffered. *This is Where It Ends* does not present any specific accounts of Tyler's history of being bullied, and further justifies the few experiences of bullying that are mentioned, so that this explanation is, in fact, invalidated. While loneliness and bullying are thematized in both novels – as in the other YA school shooting novels – these texts do not explain why the shooters fail to deal with these experiences in a healthier way.

Experiences of Closure in YA School Shooting Novels

In sum, literary multiperspectivity can be regarded as an apt narrative strategy for underlining the complexity of school shootings and for mirroring the dynamics of the school shooting discourse. Multiperspectival novels can communicate knowledge about school shootings and, at the same time, prompt the readers to reflect upon their own position within the extratextual discourse. Due to the active reading process they require, the texts force their readers to fill in gaps, order and weigh different pieces of information. Multiperspectival novels thereby foster a connection between the fictional storyworld and the readers' lifeworld. As in the multimodal novels, this serves a didactic purpose: even though most YA school shooting novels take various explanatory approaches – via the mental health issues raised in the shooter's diary in *Shooter* or the comments on gun policies in the footnotes to *Give a Boy a Gun* – they focus on the issues that affect teenage readers in their everyday reality, most notably bullying. Through the different perspectives offered by the novels, readers are prompted to reflect upon and question their own stance on issues connected to the genesis of school shootings.

While the multiperspectival novels, especially *Violent Ends* and *Shooter*, may present the complexity of the shooter's personality and history and stress the constructedness of causal narratives, none of the YA school shooting novels deny their readers the experience of some sort of closure – even though *Violent End* does not present an ultimate or definitive explanation for the shooting. Closure, a term frequently employed when it comes to traumatic incidents, is something that humans and societies strive for. The ability to move on and make sense of past experiences is essential for the individual, the community, and society (see Chapter 2.3). As I have shown earlier, the school shooting narrative, with its focus on explanations, is a perfect example of a narrative that allows for a sense of closure. Even though the school shooting narrative of cause(s) and effect(s) is always constructed multiperspectivally – as it includes the points of view of peers, parents, officials, journalists and experts – these perspectives are generally 'grasped together' (in Ricœur's words) by the public in the effort to create a 'meaningful whole'. In this meaningful whole, closure can be found, and the essentially inexplicable act of school shootings can be re-integrated into societal narratives:

> To follow a story is to move forward in the midst of contingencies and peripeteia under the guidance of an expectation that finds its fulfillment in the 'conclusion' of the story. This conclusion is not logically implied by some previous premises. It gives the story an 'end point', which, in turn, furnishes the point of view from which the story can be perceived as forming a whole. (Ricœur 1984: 66)

Fiction, to its great benefit, is expected to be polyvalent, and readers thus accept a higher level of ambivalence and complexity in it than they do in real life (cf. Nünning 2014: 287). Narrative techniques such as multiperspectivity take this potential further by making it difficult for the readers to come to definitive conclusion. Due to their aesthetic constructedness, fictional representations of school shootings have the possibility to withhold the creation of a meaningful whole – for example, when the different perspectives cannot be reconciled into one overarching explanation or account of events.

The more obvious the gaps between the different perspectives are, the more the readers have to enlist their knowledge about the extratextual world to fill them in. However, as this extratextual discursive knowledge – such as the connection between bullying and school shootings – has to be used, the fictional incidents become even more connected to readers' extratextual reality. As a result, during the act of reading, the connection between the school shooting in the fictional world and their lifeworld is established. If the narrative then, for instance by means of its perspective structure, leaves the reader without an integrative and congruent 'end point' or definitive conclusion, the reader is necessarily prompted to reflect upon her reading experience and inability to reach this conclusion. It is at this point of the reading process that the fictional text's possibility to make the readers reflect upon the constructedness of any narrative and discourse becomes clear. Thus, the readers can realize and, ultimately, accept polyvalence and complexity:

> Novels featuring narrative conventions which heighten the degree of ambivalence and indeterminacy make it necessary for readers to acknowledge complexity and openness, and to practice cognitive flexibility. In some novels crucial pieces of information are lacking, and existing descriptions of events invite contradictory interpretations. Sometimes it is impossible to arrive at a mental model of what occurred on the level of the plot. When different interpretations are both possible and irreconcilable, readers have to deal with complexity and ambivalence, and accept a denial for closure. (Nünning 2014: 290)

While *This is Where It Ends* (similar to *Give a Boy a Gun*) presents a congruent narrative, as the various perspectives are not too discrepant and easily allow for a causal understanding of the story, *Violent Ends* confronts its readers with a more complex and ambivalent narrative. Denial of closure is often a result of "open questions, which cannot be solved with reference to the information provided in the narrative" (Nünning 2014: 186). In school shooting novels, the leading open question is the one that dominates the extratextual school shooting discourse: 'Why?'

In *Violent Ends*, this question remains unanswered, but the readers are still provided with possibilities for constructing their own 'end point' and finding closure within the narrative. The readers learn about various aspects of Kirby's life and character, but these – apart from his suffering from constant bullying and perceived marginalization – cannot fully explain why he resorts to such violence. Since the novel presents a number of perspectives on the shooter and the genesis of the shooting, so that the readers at times "have to reject their interpretive hypotheses, since new information makes it necessary to revise and adjust the mental models of the characters" (Nünning 2014: 286), it provides a complex and ambivalent image of the perpetrator and his actions. Like in *Shooter*, bullying is presented in a causal connection to the school shootings (both novels thus serve as 'tools for prevention', as they highlight one of the underlying problems, thematized in the discourse, that directly affects the young adult readers), but as the readers create a mental image of the shooter, they are confronted with the realization that there are indeed no easy explanations, since these experiences are relativized by other character's experiences (*Violent Ends*) or by the shooter's status as an ambivalent figure (*Shooter*).

Multiperspectival narration is employed more frequently in school shooting novels for adolescents than in those for adults. The discrepancy between the perspectives in the novels differs, as does the complexity of the perspective structure and, consequently, the challenge that the construction of the narrative presents to the reader. While in some novels, the different perspectives actually highlight one of the discursive elements (e. g. bullying) by having many perspectives confirm it (as in *This is Where It Ends* and *Give a Boy a Gun*), *Violent Ends* or, most notably, *Shooter*, challenge the reader to integrate various pieces of information and come to their own answer to the question 'why?' However, all of the YA school shooting novels provide at least a certain degree of orientation, foregrounding those aspects of the school shooting discourse that readers can relate to. While this may not lead to a comprehensive feeling of closure, it still highlights the impression that the reader has the power to intervene and actively partake in the prevention of these events in his or her everyday life. One work that denies closure and fosters an aesthetic experience that forces the audience to accept the inexplicability, complexity and ambivalence of the school shooting phenomenon is Gus Van Sant's *Elephant*, addressed in the next subchapter.

5.2 A Labyrinth of Explanations: Multiperspectivity in Gus Van Sant's *Elephant*

The literary analyses in this book have shown that school shooting literature for young adults always serves an underlying didactic and educational purpose, even when it employs challenging narrative strategies that help to underline the complexity and ambivalence of the events. Even the more complex novels, such as *Shooter* or *Violent Ends*, highlight aspects from the school shooting discourse that the young adult reader can relate to and can easily transfer to his or her extratextual lifeworld. Nevertheless, consuming multiperspectival or multimodal YA school shooting novels can be highly beneficial for the adult reader as well, as these representations provide valuable information for the adult's imagination of contemporary high school lifeworlds, and can foster reflection upon the adult's expectation of successful adolescence.

Multiperspectival narration in fictional works intended for an adult audience can use the strategy's potential to underline polyvalence, ambivalence and complexity to a much higher extent: without the educational stance of YA fiction, representations for adults have the aesthetic freedom to refuse satisfactory conclusions or to question the possibility of re-integration of the events. *Elephant*, a multiperspectival film not intended for an adolescent audience, is the most remarkable representation of school shootings to this day. Not only is the critically

5.2 A Labyrinth of Explanations: Multiperspectivity in Gus Van Sant's *Elephant* — 237

acclaimed film aesthetically rich and highly innovative in its approach to the phenomenon, it is also a prime example of the possibilities of multiperspectival narration. In three major parts, it represents day-to-day life at an American high school by following a number of students during their daily routine. This normality is interrupted by scenes showing the meticulous planning of a school shooting by two perpetrators at their suburban home. The film ends with shooting itself, which clearly remediates images from Columbine. Instead of covering scenes from various angles and editing them in conventional manner, *Elephant* is composed mainly of long, single-take shots that "depict dialogue interactions but also activity – such as walking from one part of the school to another – that would normally be edited out of a film" (Garry 2004). Due to its aesthetic and formal complexity and unconventional approach to the phenomenon, Van Sant's film has been extensively analyzed. Academic and critical attention has, by and large, put a strong focus on the potential extratextual functions and the effect that the film's idiosyncratic approach to the phenomenon has on the audience. This does not only allow me to draw upon a number of works that have already identified the specifics of Van Sant's film, but the attention that the film has garnered also underlines my assumption about the relevance of fictional works in the school shooting discourse.

The following subchapter therefore focuses on two main aspects: first, the film's multiperspectival representation is described. I describe the film's narrative structure and its filmic realization: I show that, while Van Sant's film is filmed multiperspectivally, this does not automatically foster an impression of subjectivity or allow for an empathic connection between the spectator and the characters. Here, the major difference between the literary works and *Elephant* can be located. In section 5.2.2, I then point out how this filmic multiperspectivity and *Elephant*'s aesthetics result in a process of reflection on the school shooting discourse by forcing the spectators to acknowledge complexity and the partiality of all knowledge. Further, it confronts the recipient with experiencing a denial of closure that resembles the extratextual experience made in the aftermath of a school shooting. I investigate how *Elephant*'s approach to school shootings has given it such a prominent position in the discourse and examine which aspects of the school shooting discourse are highlighted in the film. I argue that *Elephant*'s remediation of the Columbine narrative, its contribution to the cultural imaginary of adolescent lifeworlds and the genesis of school shootings has made the film an integral part of the fictional dimension of the school shooting discourse.

5.2.1 Describing Multiperspectival Representation in *Elephant*

As discussed in the previous chapters, the Columbine High School shooting is collectively understood as a 'problem-defining event' (cf. Muschert 2007b), and has rather quickly become the prototype of this form of violence, establishing the cultural script of school shootings to which other school shooters now refer (cf. Newman et al. 2005, Kiilakoski/Oksanen 2011, and Chapter 2). Literary and film studies, too, refer to Columbine as a caesura: YA school shooting novels have now developed their own genre conventions in order to approach a mediatized phenomenon that defies existing assumptions about cause and effect, as I have established in Chapter 4 and 5.1.[20]

Film scholars have also observed changes in filmic representations of juvenile delinquency and violent youths since Columbine. As Timothy Shary (2005) points out, depicting male juvenile delinquency is a long-standing tradition in Hollywood cinema. This tradition ranged from early post-war tropes of the struggling adolescent who wants to be a part of society but chooses questionable ways to achieve his goal to full-blown *ephebiphobia* (the fear of teenagers), fed by depictions of increasingly cold-blooded, hedonistic and cruel adolescents in the 1980s. However, while the 1980s seemed to revel in new ways of depicting delinquent boys, Shary argues that "everything about depictions of 'bad boys' would change by the end of the 1990s, after a series of high-profile school killings [...] would make any fictional depictions of delinquents not only precarious but also less harrowing than the truth" (2005: 23).

In this account of the filmic history of male juvenile delinquency, the inextricable connection between the school shooting phenomenon and its fictional representations becomes clear once more. As it has been explicated in the previous chapters, due to its own *fictional dimension*, its various references to fictional representations of violent crimes, Columbine reinforced the notion of the copycat crime to a degree that made any filmic representation a suspect for fostering copycat-crimes.

The film industry reacted swiftly to Columbine, as the suppression of the release of Tim Blake Nelson's film *O* (USA 2001) reveals. *O*, a 1990s version of Shakespeare's *Othello* for adolescents that ends in a shooting at a high school, was in post-production in April 1999 and due to be released later that year. But after Columbine, the distributor did not want to go through with the release date, and so *O* was not released until Lion's Gate bought the rights from Miramax in 2001 (cf. Colón-Semenza 2005: 100). By the suppression of *O*, Shary argues,

---

20 See also Coats (2011: 317).

5.2 A Labyrinth of Explanations: Multiperspectivity in Gus Van Sant's *Elephant*

"Hollywood made it clear that it no longer knew how to handle or how to hype juvenile delinquency. Now it seemed that Hollywood and the rest of America would rather avoid the topic of boys' badness altogether than take the chance of being responsible for changing it" (2005: 37).[21] Whether or not one wants to subscribe to this rather generalizing remark, Gus Van Sant, too, encountered the film industry's new hesitance towards teen violence: until HBO eventually decided to produce it, nobody wanted or dared to release a movie about a school shooting (cf. Van Sant 2003), especially not one that clearly references Columbine without claiming an educational purpose.[22]

The unconventional aesthetics of *Elephant* may have an unsettling effect, as I show in Chapter 5.2.2., but are clearly embedded in the director's oeuvre. After Van Sant had commercial success with two studio films – *Good Will Hunting* (USA 1997) and *Finding Forrester* (USA 2000) – the so-called *Trilogy of Death* marked his return to his roots in independent cinema (cf. Weber 2015: 262). *Gerry* (USA 2002), *Elephant* (USA 2003) and *Last Days* (USA 2004) are connected by a number of aesthetic, formal and thematic features. With camera movements that visualize and construct the character's 'searching movement', all three works are form- and event-driven films, in that they represent the singular event of death rather than presenting a causal narrative (cf. Weber 2015: 267). The *Trilogy of Death* does not present a linear narrative and thus refuses to provide the spectator with clear causes and effects. This break with narrative conventions, as *Elephant* shows, can have a disturbing effect on the spectator.

Not unexpectedly, Van Sant's choice to withhold this causality in a fictional narrative led to harsh criticism (cf. Van Sant 2003). *Elephant* depicts a contemporary and, especially at the time of its release, highly topical phenomenon without attempting to 'come to terms' with it or to explain it. As the school shooting discourse is shaped by its constant attempt to explain why school shootings happen, the film therefore disturbingly breaks with and, simultaneously, reflects upon established practices of discourse formation.

---

[21] And, indeed, it can be observed that filmic representations of school shootings in the early 2000s, like Guy Ferland's *Bang, Bang, You're Dead* (USA 2002), sometimes chose to provide the school shooting story with a happy ending – in Ferland's film, reminiscent of *Give a Boy a Gun* or even *Big Mouth & Ugly Girl*, the shooting is not only averted, but the previous shooter even turns into a hero who changes his mind and keeps his accomplices from going through with the killing.

[22] Van Sant himself states that a number of scenes were taken directly from Columbine footage, made widely known by Michael Moore's *Bowling for Columbine* in 2002 (cf. Van Sant 2003). In fact, *Elephant* was originally intended to be a mainstream TV program about Columbine, to be released shortly after the shooting.

Naturally, this critical reaction to the film was based in the portrayal of the school shooters as well as on the depiction of the school shooting. The unexpectedly calm approach to the otherwise highly sensationally mediated phenomenon, that also stems from the film's multiperspectivity, apparently had a highly disruptive effect for the critics. The multiperspectival and fragmentary representation of the events in the film refuse the aesthetics of the spectacle and the sensational that are predominant in the school shooting discourse (cf. Rich 2012: 1326).

Multiperspectivity in film has a long-standing tradition; *Rashomon* is the most famous example of the challenges it poses for the audience. Describing multiperspectivity, however, is linked to a number of theoretical challenges, as the narrative structure is always dependent on the narrator. The existence of a narrator – in a literary sense – in film, however, is by no means uncontested. The narrativity of the medium as such has also been debated. But while film is a "narrative medium, or, at least, a medium of many narrative capacities" (Kuhn/Schmidt 2014: 384), and "the main features of narrative strategies in literature can also be found in film, although the characteristics of these strategies differ significantly" (ibid.: 385), it has to be analyzed with regard to its medium-specific possibilities.

Filmic 'narration' is at times understood as reduced to the words spoken in a film, or refers to "the spoken words of a person who relates information in a film directly rather than through dialogue" (Beaver 1994: 252), i.e. to the words of a character or person in a film who tells the audience what is happening in the film, or to voice-over narration. Since the early 2000s, however, the "narrative power of language, image, sound, movement, face-to-face interaction, and the various combinations of these features" (Ryan 2014: 30) has been widely acknowledged in the various semiotic approaches in inter- and transmedial narratology. When analyzing multiperspectivity in film, therefore, these different modes and their role within the narrative structure of the work have to be considered.[23] Especially in films like *Elephant* that appear unmediated, that do not

---

[23] One of the main issues of film narratology, which is closely linked to the notions of focalization and point of view, is the question of the film narrator. While some have pointed out the filmic narrator is distinct from the actual filmmaker and that narration in film is ubiquitous, others have focused on the spectator of direct perception analysis as developed by Bordwell (1985), in which the film is understood as being presented unmediated and the film understood as an "anonymous trigger for the viewer's construction of the story" (Grodal 2008: 169).[### error - illegal character ###] Indeed, in most films, the spectators regard their visual access to film as direct, because the existence of the camera as a mediating device is not usually made obvious (cf. Keating 2008: 441; Ryan 2004: 18).

5.2 A Labyrinth of Explanations: Multiperspectivity in Gus Van Sant's *Elephant*

have an overt narrator and include minimal dialogue, considering media-specific narration is of paramount importance for understanding the film's narrative structure. Only by including auditive, visual and verbal elements can the potential functions of a film be described, as they contribute to the narrative structure and to the spectator's aesthetic experience.[24]

When watching films, the spectator makes sense of the narrative based on the information that she or he is provided with in the film.[25] Even without any overt narration or dialogue, films possess narrativity. Whether "one follows the notion of film narrator or not, and whether or not one emphasizes the role of the spectator in the process of making meaning, the act of audiovisual narration is to be described as in interplay of different visual, auditive and language-based sign systems or codes" (Kuhn/Schmidt 2014: 393). This is especially relevant in a film like *Elephant*, in which there is hardly any meaningful verbal narrative. Instead, the film's story and its effect on the spectator are dependent on the visual and aural means of representation.

Multiperspectivity in film can be realized in different ways. The multiperspectival representation in *Elephant*, for example, differs significantly from that in *Rashomon*. Even though the perspectives in Van Sant's film are not as restricted to the characters' subjective account as in *Rashomon*, the multiperspectivity is still the result of the presence of different focalizers. Focalization, a term coined by Gérard Genette, "denotes the perspectival restriction and orientation of narrative information relative to somebody's (usually, a character's) perception, imagination, knowledge, or point of view" (Jahn 2008: 173). In film, focalization is closely tied to the notion of the film narrator and the role of the camera[26] – in *Elephant*, the camera follows individual characters and, by focusing on

---

[24] While employing narratological concepts and terms in regard to other media, such as film, it is important not to "ignore the film apparatus that mediates the events, thus regarding film as a mimetic narrative medium or as a medium without a mediating agent" (Kuhn 2009: 260).

[25] The realization of the film's potential functions by the spectator, the aesthetic experience of the film in Wolfgang Iser's sense, is therefore based on the events depicted in the film as well as on the way they are depicted. Keeping this in mind is especially important when the director is understood as and sees himself as an *auteur* – as is the case with Gus Van Sant (cf. Weber 2015: 14ff.), who constantly engages in the discourse on his films and discusses his authorial intentions. Here, it must be stressed that the authorial intention and the potential function of a fictional work are not the same – they can be congruent, as in many YA school shooting novels, but the various structures in the text can also generate potential functions that may differ from the intended effect of the author and that are subject to change.

[26] However controversial the debate may be, "in almost every narratological model of focalization and narrative perspective, the camera perspective (in a technical sense) is not understood as the only factor for determining focalization and/or narrative perspective (focalization/ narrative

only one character at a time, makes that character the focus of narrative perception.[27]

Spectators do not need to be granted insight into a character's consciousness in order to see that character as a focalizer– here, a major difference between Nünning's definition of the character-perspective, as used in Chapter 5.1, and the focalization in *Elephant* can be detected. While the character-perspective normally includes the character as a whole, with her or his particular understanding of life, knowledge, experiences and consciousness, *Elephant* does not provide the spectator with information about the character's interiority. Nevertheless, as the perspectives in *Elephant* underline the perception and the importance of a particular character in a sequence, the spectator is cinematically connected to that character's perception of events, even though he or she neither sees what the character sees at any given moment in the film, nor is presented with insight into the character's emotions.

Multiperspectivity in *Elephant*

Multiperspectivity is the most essential structural and formal aspect of *Elephant*, as the film's title already suggests. Van Sant named *Elephant* after the 1989 short film by Alan Clarke, which thematizes the troubles and problems in Northern Ireland as the proverbial 'elephant in the room' that everybody sees but nobody talks about. However, Van Sant states that when he decided to name his film after Clarke's, he thought that "the title referred to the Buddhist parable about a group of blind men who each touch a different part of an elephant, each concluding it's something different since none sees the whole. It was an apt meta-

---

perspective ≠ camera perspective). To analyze focalization, one has at least to take into account the complex interplay between camera parameters, montage and auditive elements" (Kuhn/Schmidt 2014: 397). In an effort to create terminological clarity and to separate the term focalization from questions about the perception of the characters, Schlickers (2009) and Kuhn (2009) operate with the terms 'ocularization' (for seeing) and 'auricularization' (for hearing). While Schlickers herself admits that "these are awkward categories" (Schlickers 2009: 246), in distinction to these terms, focalization can now be used to refer to the "relation of knowledge between the narrative instance and the character" (Kuhn 2009: 263). The "audiovisual narrative instance", in Kuhn's model (2009: 261f.), is employed by the implied director on the extradiegetic level to achieve filmic narration. By separating focalization from the notion of visual perception and thus freeing it from the dominating idea of the subjective camera and the first-person shot, it is possible to understand focalization as dependent as much on editing and montage as on the camera perspective.

27 For a comprehensive description and critique of Genette's frequently vague and ambiguous understanding of the concept of focalization, see Bode (2011: 170ff.)

5.2 A Labyrinth of Explanations: Multiperspectivity in Gus Van Sant's *Elephant* — 243

phor for the way our society tends to look for a single answer to a problem" (Van Sant 2006). Here, on one of the many occasions that the director-as-*auteur* engaged in the emerging discourse about his film, he stresses the relevance of multiperspectivity in his film. It is, indeed, so central that even the title already hints at the intended functions of the narrative structure.

Elephant consists of three major parts. In the first, the spectator observes the day-to-day life at an American high school as the camera follows (groups of) students through its labyrinthine hallways. The second part is set mostly outside of the school and shows the planning of the school shooting by two students who have already been briefly shown entering the school in full army gear. Here, a clear formal break that underlines the spatial and temporal change can be noted. The third part shows the school shooting, during which all the students whom the spectator followed through the school earlier are encountered once more. While this last part is cinematically clearly connected to the first part, as the camera now follows the shooters and some of their victims through the school's hallways as it followed the other students before, the transformation of a recognizable, ordinary setting into a surreal and violent one clearly distinguishes this part from the first.

Throughout the film, black screens with the names of the characters mark the beginning of new 'episodes' or introduce new characters.[28] The episodes in the film and the different perspectives from which they show the events are clearly distinguished from one another, and the fact that they only ever present one part or aspect of the events is underlined in the few moment where the paths of the students cross and the same scenes are shown from a different perspective. As the students move through the hallways, the camera frequently films them from behind, employing over-shoulder shots and a shallow depth of field, thereby firmly focusing on the sequence's main character. Sometimes, this focus is further intensified when the camera circles the character, always keeping him or her in the center of the frame in close-up shots, or by filming everybody around him or her in soft focus. This first part of the film is at times reminiscent of a documentary film – even though it is obviously staged and highly stylized. This effect is created by the on-location shooting and Van Sant's decisions to encourage the exclusively nonprofessional actors to improvise parts of

---

28 However, the camera does not always begin with, or continue to follow, the particular individual or group introduced by the black screen. For example, the episode with Acadia (Alicia Miles) focuses on the meeting of the Gay-Straight Alliance that she attends after briefly meeting with a visibly distressed John (John Robinson).

the dialogue and to not cut out unexpected or coincidental parts, which creates an air of authenticity (cf. Van Sant 2006).[29]

In this first part, the spectator observes a number of students going about their everyday lives: Elias (Elias McConnell) is walking into the school on his way to develop pictures he just took. Nathan (Nathan Tyson) and his girlfriend Carrie (Carrie Finklea) meet to leave school for an appointment – presumably to get an abortion. John (John Robinson) is walking through the school, trying to organize his brother's pick up of their drunk father. On his way, he meets Elias, Acadia (Alicia Miles) and the two shooters, Alex (Alex Frost) and Eric (Eric Deulen). In another episode, Alex is shown being bullied by Nathan and another boy in class. Michelle (Kristen Hicks), who was already seen in the film's gloomy opening sequence, is also shown being bullied on her way from the sports field to the library. Three anorexic girls, who were flirting with Nathan earlier, are followed to the cafeteria and into the bathroom, where they throw up their food. These episodes are mostly filmed in long sequences and single-take shots.[30]

In the second part, a formal break from the long takes in the hallways and the rather documental style can be observed, as the film now focuses on the perpetrators and on remediating a number of discursive elements that connect the events in *Elephant* to the Columbine shooting. Alex, who is presented as the mastermind behind the shooting – he is the one who maps the school and lays out the plans for his accomplice, Eric – is the primary focalizer. He also introduces the spectator to a new interior space, as the camera films him at his parents' house after school. This change of setting and location already signals another

---

29 In this respect, Christian Weber stresses the obvious influence of Hungarian filmmaker Béla Tarr – Tarr, like Van Sant in the Trilogy of Death does years later, used documentary techniques, worked with laymen and shot on location with frequently improvised dialogue. Furthermore, Tarr employs multiperspectival narration and confuses the spectator by combining natural and artificial sounds in the soundtrack of his films, while the camera frequently follows the actors from behind, like in *Elephant* (cf. Weber 2015: 264ff.)

30 In his analysis of *Elephant*, John P. Garry III points out that "Van Sant is practicing the mise-en-scene, depth of field, sequence shot or long take aesthetic favored by French film critic/theorist Andre Bazin (1918–1958) and practiced by filmmakers such as Robert Flaherty, Jean Renoir, Max Ophuls, Orson Welles, Jacques Tati, Andrei Tarkovsky, Miklos Jansco, Andrei Sokurov, Rob Tregenza, and Béla Tarr. This style emphasizes the continuous shot and the orchestration of multiple characters and objects within the frame. The long take contrasts with montage—the creation of meaning through the editing of dissimilar shots, whose seminal practitioner and theorist was Sergei Eisenstein. It also differs from the continuity style—the dominant mode in Hollywood filmmaking—in which the mise-en-scene of different shots is coordinated to create unobtrusive or "invisible" edits and create a fictional space by linking numerous, often static shots rather than exploring space in a continuous moving shot" (Garry 2004).

5.2 A Labyrinth of Explanations: Multiperspectivity in Gus Van Sant's *Elephant*

part in the film. The lengthy sequences shot in Alex's painfully sterile suburban home, where he lives in the basement, contribute to the imaginary of a school shooter's life before the shooting – clearly influenced by accounts of the Columbine shooters.

The multiperspectival representation of the high school scenes in the first part contribute to the spectator's imaginary of the teenagers' lifeworld. The shots focus on events that are usually left unaddressed in the school shooting discourse and media coverage: the everyday routines and smaller problems and pleasures of adolescents. The second part of the film, on the other hand, remediates a strikingly large number of discursive elements in a comparatively short amount of time. While some of the shots are quite lengthy – for example, when the camera rests on the back of Eric's head while he plays Beethoven's *Für Elise* and parts of the *Moonlight Sonata* – a quick montage disrupts the aesthetics of the film that have, until now, been dominated by the strikingly long takes. The boys are shown studying the school's blueprint, and the montage illustrates what Alex is explaining. Here, Van Sant employs a comparatively conventional editing technique, well known from heist films like *Ocean's Eleven* (Soderbergh, USA 2001). The disruptive effect of this reference is further intensified when Alex says "most importantly, have fun", and thus quotes the shockingly cynical diary entry by Eric Harris quote "Have fun!" – taken from the Columbine shooters' "To Do List" they made prior to the attack.

After this obvious formal break, the cinematography in the third part resumes the multiperspectival mode, resembling the cinematography of the first part, as the camera follows the students through the now-apocalyptic hallways. Sometimes Eric is filmed frontally or from the back; sometimes the victims are filmed in their attempts to flee the scene. While the formal break in the second part of the film clearly signaled a spatial and temporal difference to the first part, the cinematographic resemblance between the first and last parts provides spatial and temporal orientation and create an unsettling effect. On yet another black screen, Benny (Bennie Dixon) is introduced: just like John's yellow shirt that has served as a point of orientation in the labyrinthine hallways, Benny is wearing a bright shirt, which make him stand out. Further, his poised stride through the hallways and his assistance to the panicked Acadia, whom he helps to escape, suggests that he might be the hero who interrupts the school shooting and restores normalcy. However, he is shot dead by Eric after only a little more than two minutes, before he even has the chance to talk to the shooters.

Empathy and Orientation

The introduction and subsequent death of Benny can be seen as paradigmatic for the possibilities of perspective taking and empathy that *Elephant* offers to the spectators. Perspective taking, as was shown in Chapter 5.1, is closely connected to establishing an empathic connection with the character whose perspective is presented in the narrative. In order to make sense of the narrative, the readers of multiperspectival novels have to engage with different characters and weigh, order and evaluate the information provided in their accounts.

In a multiperspectively narrated film, the spectator is also engaged in an active process of watching the film. In *Elephant*, the spectator has to make sense of the different episodes and the various characters to orient her- or himself in the fictional world. To beat the constant feeling of temporal and spatial dislocation, the spectator has to connect the different episodes, endow the different sequences and moments with meaning, and create a mental image of the social nexus. Thus, even though the camera ties him or her to the character who meanders the hallways and thus makes the spectator feel like a passive witness to the events, the act of watching the film is still extremely active. The process of orientation is constantly disrupted in the film. The episodic narration, the sequences that enable temporal and spatial orientation – such as John playing with a dog outside the school as the shooters enter it, or Michelle running past John and Elias in the hallways – are sometimes rather subtle and can easily be overlooked. Furthermore, spatial orientation is made difficult as the film refuses conventional practices of continuity editing, and does not provide any conventional techniques for orientation, such as wide-angle shots of the school building or a full view of a room (cf. Rich 2012: 1319, Garry 2004). Instead, most shots of the buildings, rooms, hallways or outside areas enhance the spectator's impression of only being provided with partial impressions and information. In the multiperspectival novels such as *Violent Ends*, the various perspectives provided the reader with an amount of information that could – after being blended, weighed and ordered in the act of reading – result in a fairly comprehensive account of the events and could further serve as training in perspective taking and empathy. The multiperspectivity in *Elephant*, by contrast, evokes the impression of never being able to get the full picture.

Even though the camera in *Elephant* is "anthropomorphic" (Weber 2015: 301), as it seems to 'decide' when to follow whom for how long, and as it appears, at times, to hesitate – for example, when the camera waits outside instead of following Elias into the school – the perspectives it presents to the spectator are not autonomous. Instead, most of the sequences suggest a high degree of subjectiveness, as the focalizing character remains in the center of the shot. A shallow depth of field, which makes other people appear in soft focus, for example, clearly highlights that the spectator is now tied to this particular character's experiences (cf. Beaver 1994: 105) – even if it is only for a limited amount of time, and even if the perspective can shift at any moment. Especially in the first part of the film, the spectator only sees those events and parts of the school that the character sees. Therefore, the spectator is tied to the anthropomorphic camera, which appears to freely determine the focal character of the scene, as well as when to follow, when to stop and when to interrupt. As a result, the spectator does not passively witness, but actively experiences the events in the film, as she or he tries to 'keep track' of what is going on. Consequently, the perspective is not omniscient, and the spectator is not a passive witness to a presented reality. Instead, the spectator interacts with the film, taking the position of a character but not gaining insight into his or her psychology, and experiencing close proximity to, but not identifying with, the character (cf. Weber 2015: 271).

The spectator experiences the lifeworld of the teenagers from their perspective, simply by tagging along and focusing on a 'normal' teenager at a 'normal' school; the restrictedness of the perspectives connects him or her to the characters. However, *Elephant*'s multiperspectivity does not encourage perspective taking, nor allow for a lasting empathic connection with any of the characters.[31] Making a lasting empathic connection impossible is, in fact, "an integral part of the dialectic of association and de-association that Van Sant promotes throughout the film" (Rich 2012: 1318): whenever the spectator begins to associate with a character, the film's structure immediately counters this experience with an instance of de-association. This is achieved by interrupting any interaction between the students, not paying attention to dialogue and thereby devaluing language-based narration. For example, when the three friends Brittany (Brittany Mountain), Jordan (Jordan Taylor) and Nicole (Nicole George) are followed on their way to lunch in the cafeteria, the camera abruptly 'decides' to go into the cafeteria's kitchen and later focuses on girl sitting at a different table, while the three friends walk and talk in the background. Another scene that stresses this aesthetic of interruption is the meeting of the Gay-Straight Alliance, which is filmed in a long circular pan – however, the students interrupt each other in a lively discussion and the faces that the camera focuses on hardly

---

[31] Christian Weber argues that the 'modified point-of-view' that is created by the camera's constant focus on one character, whom it sometimes shoots from behind before moving to a frontal shot, or filming the character in a close-up or medium shot with low depth of field, does not create a connection or signal any form of subjectivity, but rather cinematographically illustrates a feeling of being trapped, observed, and isolated (cf. Weber 2015: 301ff.). The school's hallways, in this understanding, are a place of repression and isolation from which the shooting can emerge.

ever correspond to the person who is talking at that moment. Therefore, the spectator has almost no possibility to match the verbal utterances to a character's face.

This de-association is further fostered by temporal or spatial dislocation that makes the spectator lose "the linearity of the tracked character's narrative" (Rich 2012: 1319). The combination of these techniques with the "long-tracking shot and single-shot structure of the film prevent[s] the experience of interiority" (ibid.: 1319). While the spectator is mostly tied to the experiences and impressions of the focal characters, the cinematography only rarely establishes a lasting empathic connection. Any moment in which the spectator may experience empathy is either structurally interrupted, or hindered by the lack of insight into the interiority of the character – as, for example, when Alex appears to be highly distressed by his surroundings in the cafeteria, which is signaled by an increasingly loud ambient noise and his putting his hand to his temple.[32] As this scene shows, *Elephant* does not avoid to make the school shooters focal characters and thus does not distinguish between 'normal' adolescents and school shooters. Whereas most novels avoid presenting the perspective of the school shooters, *Elephant*'s dialectic of association and de-association and its refusal to provide identification with the characters allows it to include the shooters' perspective. In fact, it is in the shooting scene that the only conventional point-of-view shot is used – in a shot reminiscent of a first-person shooter game, the spectator sees the school's hallways through Alex's eyes. Traditionally, this cinematography stands for radical subjectivity. The effect, however, is hardly one of identification, but rather of shock and disgust.

Within the perspective structure of the film, two character-perspectives stand out. John and Michelle fulfill important functions within the film's narrative structure and, to a certain degree, even allow for a more lasting empathic connection. In Michelle's case, this function is one of providing both temporal and spatial orientation. Her status as an outcast in high school society – which is highlighted by her being the first victim of the shooting – evokes sym-

---

[32] André Grzeszyk observes that this scene remediates a scene from the TV series *Buffy the Vampire Slayer* (B. Kimble, USA 1999) that depicts a school shooting and, like *Elephant*, was not released for quite some time after Columbine (cf. 2012: 247f.). Grzeszyk writes that the medially prefigured images of school shootings and the references to the actual events at Columbine coexist in *Elephant* without any form of noticeable hierarchy: Van Sant refers to images from other medial representations of school shooting or rampage violence as well as to images from news media and surveillance cameras.

pathy with her.[33] Van Sant introduces her in the opening sequence, where she stares in awe at the sky that the spectator, too, observes at the beginning of the film. Here, the spectator and Michelle share an experience that goes unnoticed by the other people on the sports field. When Michelle is later shown in the locker room – a fully dressed, awkward body between naked bodies – and the camera zoom in on her face while the mean utterance around her become more and more audible, the spectator experiences her perception of a hostile surrounding that is closing in on her. The first victim, therefore, is the one that the spectator was prompted to empathize with to a comparatively high degree.

John has the most emphasized position in *Elephant*'s perspective structure. On the one hand, John is the only student who connects the interior space of the school with the outside world, and the teenagers' lifeworld with the world of the adults, as he dynamically enters and leaves the school throughout the film. While this later saves him from becoming a victim of the school shooting, it is punished in the beginning – a paradox that is stressed by the death of Mr. Luce, who is encountered first while punishing John for being late to school, even though this was his father's fault, not his. Also, the portrayal of John's personal troubles provides an insight into his interior that is further stressed by showing him crying in a classroom later, an emotional image that is not provided for any other character.[34] Moreover, John fulfills an important structural function for spatial and temporal orientation: with his yellow shirt and his blond hair, he serves as an easily recognizable and clearly highlighted element in and outside of the school. As a result, when he leaves the school, the spectator not only knows why he does so, but also learns that this is the moment that signifies the beginning of the school shooting. When John is seen playing with the dog Boomer for the first time, Alex and Eric are walking towards the school, partly obscured by John in the foreground. When John greets them, Alex tells him to leave as "some heavy shit is about to go down". This clear remediation of Eric Harris' famous warning to his friend Brooks Brown signals that John cannot possibly prevent the shooting from happening: Brooks Brown could not save his fellow students either. John later tries to keep other students from going into the building, but his warnings remain unheeded and his helplessness in the face of the school shooting is only highlighted further. Like Benny's death, John's in-

---

[33] Even though Alex and Michelle are cinematically connected, she is not spared during the shooting. This highlights the lack of solidarity among the victims of bullying and heightens the impression of social isolation that the teenagers experience.

[34] The dialogue in this scene is self-reflexive: when Acadia asks him why he is crying and if something bad has happened, John answers that he does not know. Here, the detachment is also seen on the level of the characters.

ability to interfere with the plans of his schoolmates stresses the inexorability of the events.[35]

5.2.2 Functions of *Elephant*'s Aesthetics

As the description of the multiperspectivity in *Elephant* has shown, the film puts its spectators in an ambivalent situation of reception. On the one hand, they are drawn into the events as they find themselves tied to an anthropomorphic camera that makes them follow parts of the events, while it remains opaque why the camera follows a certain person or why it moves on to another situation. Here, the spectator's position is rather passive – an impression that is further highlighted by the elements of association and de-association and by the continuous spatial and temporal disorientation, all of which leave the spectator confused. On the other hand, this seemingly voyeuristic, passive position is contrasted by the active engagement required of the spectator. As the perspectives shift, the spectator is challenged to 'keep up' with the characters and the events. Just as the camera keeps up with the characters in the hallways, the spectator now finds herself trying to deduce causality and biographical information so as to complete the character-perspective she has just been introduced to. This active engagement is also fostered by the need for spatial and temporal re-ordering of the different episodes. Here, the spectator is not left entirely to her own devices. Instead, a number of sequences, characters – like John and Michelle – and narrative elements provide possibilities for the successful ordering and weighing of the events before and during the school shooting.

The role of the spectator and the fact that the she or he needs to recognize the narrative gaps and actualize them with knowledge from the extratextual world. This activity is the basis for the three major functions that *Elephant* assumes. First, the film contributes to the fictional dimension of the school shooting discourse by effectively remediating, illustrating and fictionalizing existing discursive elements. Without resorting to any kind of hierarchy, it both draws upon and extends the cultural imaginary of school shootings. The second function, which is closely connected to this remediation of discursive elements, is also the most widely acknowledged one: nearly all the YA school shooting novels ultimately provide at least some possibility for the re-integration of the events

---

[35] This is also a paradigmatic sequence for the film's multiperspectivity, as it stresses that what is a crucial moment in John's life is only a side note for the three girlfriends, who comment on his leaving the school as they look out the window of the cafeteria.

into the readers' lifeworld, guiding the readers towards an engaged position in the discourse and the genesis of the events by an active (and, in the case of multimodal literature, hypertextual) reading practice. The multiperspectival narrative in *Elephant*, moreover, not only highlights the ambiguity and complexity of the discourse, but also denies the spectator the experience of closure, even prompting her to reflect upon the effect of this denial. The third and last potential function of the film's narrative structure is its reflexive stance towards the school shooting discourse and its own position within this discourse. Aesthetically, Van Sant's film powerfully illustrates the juxtaposition of the societal narrative of peace and normalcy with the abnormality of the school shooting and the sudden violation of this apparent peacefulness. *Elephant* simultaneously makes the spectator reflect upon these notions by aesthetically underlining the fragility of this societal normalcy. In the representation of the school shooting, the film provides images for the violation of a peaceful zone (*sensu* Reemtsma).

This reflection upon the discourse, as established earlier in regard to multiperspectival novels, is fostered by the reader's or spectators' active engagement with different perspectives. The processes of ordering and weighing different pieces of information makes it easier for readers and spectators to connect with the fictional events and to transfer them to their extratextual reality. In its obvious refusal to tell a causal or linear story, *Elephant*'s narrative and multiperspectival structure lay open the processes of emplotment and of meaning-making, as the spectator has to make an effort to create an internal logic and causality, and to establish a meaningful temporal dimension of the story.

As a result of these three potential functions, I want to show, *Elephant* provides a representation of complexity and ambivalence that engages the spectator in a critical reflection on the school shooting discourse and on her or his own role within this discourse.

A Multitude of Explanations: Remediating Columbine
Fictional representations of school shootings – especially in the early 2000s – were always understood and discussed in immediate relation to the real-world phenomenon they referred to. Due to its multiperspectival structure and its open depiction of the school shooting, *Elephant* proved challenging to some and shocking to others. One of the most famous reviews by Todd McCarthy in *Variety* describes *Elephant* as a "failed attempt to find a fresh method to deal dramatically with a traumatic topic" that is "gross and exploitative". "To make a film about something like the Columbine student shootings incident", McCarthy argues, "and provide no insight or enlightenment would seem to be pointless at

best and irresponsible at worst, and that is what Gus Van Sant has done" (McCarthy 2003). In his book about school shootings, journalist Joseph Lieberman criticizes *Elephant* for not making a clear statement about the causes of the events:

> While *Elephant* won both the Golden Palm and a Best Director award at Cannes, audiences there and nearly everywhere else were divided regarding its value as a deterrent. By contrasting the cold-blooded, casual planning of the shooters with the routines of daily school life seen from the view of ordinary students, *Elephant* builds into a quiet kind of horror. But by ending abruptly while the lead shooter is still on a euphoric high, and by including so much footage shot from the emotionless perspective of both killers, no moral statement is made at all. (Lieberman 2008: 217)

In the school shooting discourse, fictional representations are expected to make some sort of 'moral statement' or 'provide insight'. This understanding underlines the close connection between the fictional representations and the actual events and stresses the 'responsibility' of fictional works. Apparently, the narrative structure in *Elephant* successfully produces the effect that Van Sant intended, as it avoids presenting any form of causality or explanation of the shooting (cf. Van Sant 2003).

What *Elephant* does, however, is to provide a comprehensive overview of societal reactions to school shootings. It includes imagery of the perpetrators that clearly references the Columbine shooters: the basement where Alex lives, for example, illustrates the cultural imaginary of the infamous *Basement Tapes* recorded at Eric Harris' home, which are not available to the public. This illustration, by now, has become a part of the cultural imaginary of a school shooter's home, as *The Dirties* shows: Matt Johnson's film references *Elephant* not only by having Johnson wear the same shirt as John does, but also by having him live in the basement of his parents' house, where his friend Owen visits and where Johnson looks at his school's blueprint while planning the shooting. *Elephant* thus illustrates the fictional dimension of the school shooting discourse, as it exemplifies the dynamics of circulating imagery. It has left its mark on the school shooting discourse, having been referenced by school shooters like Jeffrey Weise (cf. Newman/Fox 2009: 1290) and by later fictional representations of school shootings (*The Dirties*). As much as *Elephant* draws upon the school shooting narrative and its imagery, it also establishes and produces new elements and thus is a prime example of the prominent role of fiction in the school shooting discourse.

Furthermore, *Elephant* remediates images known from the surveillance cameras at Columbine High School – as in the shot where Alex sits down in the school's cafeteria during shooting and drinks from a cup of soda at one of the deserted tables. While these surveillance images can be seen on YouTube, they

5.2 A Labyrinth of Explanations: Multiperspectivity in Gus Van Sant's *Elephant*

are known to most people from documentaries like Michael Moore's *Bowling for Columbine*, or from fictionalized remediations like *Zero Hour*. *Elephant* references these images, but does so without employing the aesthetics of surveillance cameras, and thus changes the spectator's position by enhancing her awareness of mediation. But in Van Sant's film, they unfold an even more shocking effect, as the director does not grant these images the power of explanation – as opposed to *Bowling for Columbine* or many documentaries. Instead of serving as elements in an argument of cause and effect, the scene of Alex drinking his victims' soda is followed by scenes that further emphasize the arbitrariness and inexplicability of the shooting. First, Alex shoots his accomplice in the middle of Eric's speech about how many people he's shot. Then, he finds Nathan and Carrie in the cold room of the cafeteria and tortures them by playing "eenie, meenie, miny, mo". Before he 'decides' whom he will shoot first, the scene ends and the spectator finds herself not understanding what has just happened. Here, the illustrated arbitrariness forces the spectator to reflect upon her own desire for sensation and the spectacular, which the film refuses to provide.

In the second part of the film, which shows the meticulous planning of the school shooting in Alex's basement, the change of the setting raises the hope that more information about their family background, interests, psychological dispositions and emotional interiority will be presented. The spectator has previously seen Alex at school, where he was bullied and clearly overwhelmed while 'mapping' the school's cafeteria ("What are you doing?" a girl asks when she sees him. "You'll see", he answers cynically). These hints at Alex's experience of high school as a hostile, repressive and overwhelming space, however, do not suffice to explain his actions.

In its approach to the problem of bullying, *Elephant*, like *Violent Ends*, includes another victim of bullying as a focalizer and even cinematically connects Michelle's and Alex's experiences at several points (cf. Garry 2004). Therefore, "bullying, a common explanation for the schoolyard shootings of the last decade, is obviously a motivation for Alex but not for Michelle. She doesn't turn against her fellow students. In fact, she works in the school library, serving the very community that pressures and ridicules her" (Garry 2004).

Van Sant presents numerous elements of the school shooting discourse and opens up several possibilities for interpretation. In the basement, a long shot shows Alex playing Beethoven at the piano – this has sometimes been interpreted as a sign of his 'soft side' or 'queerness' (cf. Bond-Stockton 2009: 179), or as a hint of a shooter's complex and ambiguous personality (cf. Rich 2012: 1235, Scott 2005). When Alex stops playing and gets up from the piano, he begins looking for guns on the internet. The possibility that the shooters are homosexual, raised by them kissing in the shower on the morning of the shooting, can either be seen as another reference to Columbine, mirroring the speculations about Eric Harris and Dylan Klebold's sexuality (cf. Evans 2016: 18), or as yet another red herring (cf. Rich 2012: 1326), an empty signifier that only forces the spectator to reflect upon her own search for possible explanations.

As the camera moves around in a circular pan, the spectator automatically takes in the room, scanning it for possible clues to the shooters' motivations. But neither the personal belongings nor the drawings on the wall provide any hints. The circular pan, interestingly, echoes the sequence at the Gay-Straight Alliance, where the spectator could not match the verbal dialogue to the faces. In the meeting, the students even talked about recognizing signs of homosexuality, though they did not reach a conclusion about whether or not homosexuality can be 'seen'. As the cinematography links both scenes, the students' debate can now be connected to the school shooting discourse: whether or not a school shooter can be recognized remains unclear.

Van Sant also references the well-known discussion about Harris' and Klebold's presumed Nazism. When the shooters watch a Nazi documentary on TV – the camera focuses on the television and forces the spectator to watch, too – the reference to the Columbine shooters is established. Here, however, the film directly comments on the school shooting discourse: as much as Harris and Klebold's fascism was just one of the many elements in their violent *amokpersonae*, Alex and Eric are indifferent to what happens in the documentary and do not even recognize Hitler at first. When Alex asks whether one can still purchase Nazi paraphernalia and Eric answers, "Sure, if you're an idiot", any ideological connection is rendered absurd. Nazism could not explain Columbine, and it cannot explain Alex and Eric's actions.

The scene in the basement in which Eric plays a first-person shooter game that references Van Sant's film *Gerry* has been commented on rather frequently. In this scene, the connection between the dynamics of the school shooting discourse and the fictional representations of school shootings becomes obvious once more: since the public and media quest for explanation so frequently focuses on violent media and computer games, it does not come as a surprise that Van Sant uses this element in his film and that the discussion of the film, too, would focus on it. Especially because the first-person shooter perspective of the game Eric plays is mirrored in the shooting scene, when the spectator briefly sees through Alex's eyes and the hallways are aesthetically transformed to resemble the setting of a computer game, the reference to computer games has been seen as an "explanatory emphasis" (Garry 2004).

But, in fact, none of the discursive attempts at explanation is satisfactory. In no respect are the shooters 'unusual'; the film presents other people associated with guns (John and his father talk about hunting) and other people being bullied. Alex's home seems intact. Even though the discursive rhetoric of the 'superficially intact' family home could be deployed here, it could apply equally well to John's obviously troubled family background.

Experiencing the Denial of Closure
All of these explanatory elements – the bullying (maybe even as a possible repercussion of the shooters' homosexuality), the video games, Hitler references, etc. – are a commentary on the school shooting discourse rather than a narrative element for the creation of causality. The aspects raised here are too numerous, too stereotypical, and too incongruent. All the possible explanation that *Elephant* considers, or at least touches upon at some point, are as unsatisfactory in the film as they are in the real school shooting discourse.

As the film still does not provide insight into the shooters – enabling no connection to the 'suspiciously unsuspicious' perpetrators (cf. Ahrens 2017: 17ff.) who could be perfectly normal adolescents until they dress up in army gear and enter their school with loaded guns and home-made bombs – the spectator cannot make sense of all these possible factors. Instead, as Jennifer Rich writes, "Van Sant is force-feeding us the same cornucopia of misinformation that we consumed in interpreting the real Columbine massacre. All of these incongruities – red herrings, if you will – pointedly direct us away from the popular interpretations of the motives behind the shootings" (Rich 2012: 1326). In its many references to Columbine and the societal attempt to create a narrative of cause and effect, *Elephant* raises these issues only to discard them – and, by doing so, mirrors the dynamics of the frantic media activity in the aftermath of Columbine.

> Van Sant omits the (now-discredited) Goth/Trench Coat Mafia angle as well as the killers' expectation of celebrity status. It's clear that jocks will be a favored target, and Alex is a victim of jock bullying, but it isn't severe or prolonged enough to provoke murder. When planning the attack Alex says, "Most importantly, have fun, man" (a quote from the Columbine killers). How their sense of fun got so warped is not clear. None of these explanations – either individually or together – satisfactorily explain how the boys made the leap to murder. (Garry 2004)

The multiperspectivity of *Elephant* forces the spectator to engage in the film and to make sense of the events and create temporal and spatial orientation. Thus, it prompts the spectator to reflect upon the complexity and ambivalence of the school shooting discourse. It does not, however, present incongruent versions of the same event, as *Rashomon* does. Instead, the action within each version of the events and each perspective is the same, but limitations of perspectives and the gaps in information become clear. The multiperspectivity in *Elephant* highlights not subjectiveness, but rather incompleteness and the perspective-dependency of the reconstruction of a school shooting.

In a way, *Elephant* illustrates the perspective-dependency of the 'Rashomon-effect' as the spectator's experience of having to create a comprehensive narrative and to come to an understanding of what happened, by taking into account a variety of perspectives. But it does so to a rather pessimistic end, as it suggests the impossibility of ever seeing the full picture. Moreover, the multiperspectivity stresses the constructedness and perspective-dependency of the entire school shooting discourse, as it makes the spectator experience how restricted any perspective on the event must be. Finding herself unable to integrate the different pieces of information into a comprehensive whole, the spectator is put in a position that mirrors her position after a real school shooting. While after a real school shooting, people are confronted with a vast number of explanatory attempts, none of which can possibly suffice. This disproportionality between cause and effect and the resulting inexplicability, is characteristic of the school shooting phenomenon. The prevalent school shooting narrative, however, attempts to re-integrate the violence, either by emphasizing an explanatory element (such as violent media, family problems, bullying) and endowing it with more meaning than it actually has, or by dehumanizing the perpetrator and making him monstrous, as I have shown in this book. In the portrayal of the perpetrators, *Elephant* comments on the first narrative practice rather than engaging in the creation of the narrative of causality.

The depiction of the perpetrators illustrates just how little is known about school shooters, about their lives, their interiority, as well as how a set of clichés and standardized attempts at explanations can be applied without actually providing any illumination, possibility for prevention or relief. The multiperspectival structure in which the high school lifeworld is represented also serves as a commentary on the school shooting discourse, as Weber points out: if it is already difficult to construct a meaningful, causal narrative out of the different perspectives and pieces of information about teenagers' experiences on what appears to be a normal day at a regular high school, the construction of a meaningful narrative about something as complex as a school shootings appears to be almost impossible (cf. Weber 2015: 292).

Forced to realize that she or he cannot get 'the full picture' – quite literally, in some scenes, as parts of the events occur outside of the frame[36] – the specta-

---

[36] This effect is further emphasized in the school shooting scenes: only the first murder is filmed in the conventional shot/reverse-shot style that Van Sant avoids throughout the film. After that, the spectator can see only the action of the perpetrator or the effect that these actions

tor, in the safety of the realm of the fictional, experiences a denial of closure. In the school shooting discourse, closure and the successful establishment of causal explanation is the ultimate goal, as this equates to a chance for prevention and re-integration of the events into societal self-perception. In fictional representations, this closure is not needed; instead, the spectator can be prompted to "practice cognitive flexibility and to acknowledge ambivalences" (Nünning 2014: 303).

Loci of Terror: Spatial Illustrations of Discursive Dynamics
Elephant's contribution to the cultural imaginary of school shootings and its denial of closure to the spectator make it a very interesting fictional representation of school shootings, but these two possible effects also contribute to the third remarkable possibility of the film. As a fictional element of the discourse, *Elephant* illustrates the discourse that it is a part of and provides impressive imagery for the otherwise rather weak juxtaposition of the societal narrative of peacefulness with the experience of instability and threat.

This illustration is closely connected to the dimension of space and to the setting of the film. As the multiperspectival narrative structure produces a general sense of disorientation and fragmentary perception, and the lack of interiority leaves the spectator unable to construct congruent psychological motivation, the film's representation of space illustrates the discursive dynamics very vividly.

On the one hand, the first part of the film contributes to the spectator's imaginary of the lifeworld from which the school shooting phenomenon emerges. That the film, like YA school shooting novels, presents the setting of the school shooting from the teenagers' perspective and prompts the spectator to engage in an active reception process – i.e., to actively imagine and partake in the lifeworld that is presented – provides information that is usually left out in the news coverage of school shootings. Here, *Elephant* partly resembles *Violent Ends*, as it presents the 'normality' of various characters, including their sorrows and struggles (even the entirely 'normal', friendly and popular Elias hints at problems with his parents). But while the teenagers' problems in *Violent Ends* provided insight into the individual character's interior, the struggles in *Elephant* are not as extreme and remain superficial. They appear to be placeholders and symbols for adolescent life rather than elements of individual characterization and invitations to empathize. Whereas the spectator may be able to relate to the normality

---

have, but is hardly ever presented with a direct connection between the two. Here, *Elephant* cinematographically undermines the most basic notion of cause and effect (cf. Weber 2015: 299).

of the teenagers' lifeworld, he or she is not able to fully identify or empathize with either the victims or the perpetrators.

By following the teenagers through the hallways, the spectator is drawn into the characters' high school lifeworld. The sensation of being 'trapped' in the school is evoked by the film's aesthetic. The camera 'hesitates' to follow Elias and Nathan into the school at first, but once it is inside, the spectator is forced to follow the students through the endless hallways. The characters appear trapped and isolated – and, when the shooting begins, the school corridors actually become death traps. The low depth of field, the camera's focus on one character, as well as the film's unusually narrow 1.33:1 format augment this isolation (cf. Garry 2004; Weber 2015: 300ff.). The camera's movement around the characters, which appears to examine them closely from all sides, Weber argues, also generates a feeling of surveillance and repression – the school appears like a 'massive control apparatus' that is meant to ensure the successful process of growing up and the transformation from an adolescent into a socially conforming, functioning adult (cf. Weber 2015: 302f.).[37]

The sensation of feeling trapped inside the school and the defamiliarizing soundtrack can also function as a filmic representation of the school shooting discourse and its construction of normality and abnormality. The spectator, who is trapped in the school with the characters, experiences the transformation of a space of normality into a space of violence. John's helpless warning, as he tries to keep other students from entering the school during the shooting, can be understood as general warning: the school, it becomes clear, can become a trap.

The school shooting is not the first instance of violence that the spectator comes across, however. But the violence seen in the first part of the film is normalized – just like in the real world, structural and emotional violence are understood as an unavoidable part of growing up. Here, *Elephant* can be related to the genre traditions of YA fiction and the school story, as explicated in the previous chapters: the student's movements through the school represents a searching movement, as they try to find their way through the building as much as through life. This search can be difficult, problematic and, at times, painful.

---

[37] Weber understands this particular aesthetic feature of the film as a possible explanation for the school shooting and supports his argument with an analysis of the shooting scenes. In these scenes, he argues, the feeling of being isolated and trapped is further underlined by the film's sound design. When Alex appears overwhelmed by the increasing noise in the cafeteria, or when his walk through the hallways during the shooting formally resembles the representation of the other characters in the first part of the film, but is accompanied by the sounds of a jungle, this highlights his experience of existing in a strange and hostile surrounding (cf. Weber 2015: 304ff.).

5.2 A Labyrinth of Explanations: Multiperspectivity in Gus Van Sant's *Elephant*

But in the end, as the conventional school story suggests, these experiences will help the adolescents later in life. In school shooting fiction, however, this search is then brutally interrupted, just as school shootings interrupt the development of teenagers: the victims never get the chance to become successful adults, because the shooters have decided to refuse to undertake this development.

Van Sant takes this notion of adolescence even further than the other fictional works do. *Elephant* not only represents the radical and ultimate refusal to become a functioning part of society, but its approach appears even less optimistic about the general possibility of growing up in a constructive way. Instead, the film questions the very notion of 'successful adulthood' from the first sequence on: John's father, who cannot even take care of himself, is the first adult introduced in the film. Mr. Luce, the second adult, is hostile and unable to show any kind of compassion – emphasized by Eric's rather stereotypical revenge speech, in which he tells the principal to listen more carefully to students' problems in the future. However, this 'educational' stance ends in a very bleak moment: after pretending to spare him and teaching him a lesson, Eric shoots him. The principal never gets the chance to change his behavior.[38]

Again, the (adult) spectators are confronted with their own position in the school shooting discourse. Like the interviews in Walter Dean Myers' *Shooter*, Van Sant's film suggests "that adults and teenagers live in the same space but occupy different worlds" (Garry 2004). The adults in the film mostly appear outside of the frame, are only partly shown or remain entirely unidentified. For a while, the adult spectators are offered an experience that connects them to the teenagers in the film, as they can see the high school lifeworld and experience a certain kind of normality, only to see its violent transformation.

The second part of the film also serves as formal connection between the normality of the high school on the morning of the shooting and the brutality that this normality can trigger. In the quick montage in the second part, the school shooters' plan and the partly successful realization of this plan – as in Columbine, the bombs do not explode as intended – connect the reality of the shooters' life in the basement to the reality inside the school. This montage illustrates the sudden invasion of violence into the high school lifeworld, which is otherwise constructed and perceived as an allegedly non-violent zone.

The shock value of the excessive violence and the way that its suddenness changes social space is enhanced by a radical transformation of the familiar

---

[38] In the case of John and his father, Van Sant even reverses an image that is inextricably linked to school shootings. Instead of fleeing the building into his worried father's arms, John runs outside to find his confused and speechless father, whom he then has to comfort in front of the burning school.

hallways of the high school into a strange new setting. After the shooters have entered the building, the formerly realistic setting is defamiliarized by extradiegetic sounds and an aesthetic of destruction, as the camera follows Alex's now predatory movement through the school and only allows occasional glimpses of fleeing students. In the brief scene where the point-of-view shot resembles a video game, the school shooting sequence ultimately breaks with the realism of the earlier parts.

By aesthetically transforming a formerly familiar space into a place of terror and destruction, *Elephant* illustrates the societal perception of school shootings and their effects. This transformation in fact provokes an experience of terror comparable to that of watching of a horror film. While *Elephant* does not dehumanize the school shooters as monstrous, the shooting is still presented as entirely abnormal: "The familiar is rendered unfamiliar and, as such, prevents the audience from feeling safe within what should be a familiar environment. We are terrorized because the loci of safety – our home, a motel room, a vacation spot – become loci of terror" (Rich 2012: 1313).

Only by having established this sense of normalcy and this connection to the setting does the instability of the school as a peaceful zone (*sensu* Reemtsma) become clear. The societal reaction to school shootings is rooted in the fact that they occur in places defined as peaceful (even though they are not, as the representations of emotional and structural violence in the first part of the film shows) and are directed against an institution that stands for a functioning society. In the first part, Van Sant establishes the setting of the school shooting as a 'normal' and peaceful place in order to mirror the effect that this perceived normalcy has for the spectators. In the abnormality of the school shooting, signaled by the aesthetic transformation of the space, the constructedness of the normalcy introduced in the first part of the film is revealed. The school shooting appears to show that what happens within this space is, in the end, contingent. The school as a non-violent zone is a social construction that is volatile and, as *Elephant* shows, can be redefined by just two boys who decide to use it as the stage for a killing spree.

Van Sant's film refuses to answer the question 'why?' Quite the contrary: it does not even raise it. Instead, it mirrors the societal perception from which the discursive dynamics of school shootings emerge on three levels of the film. First, its multiperspectivity illustrates the impossibility of a comprehensive understanding of the school shooting phenomenon – all information is perspective-dependent, partial and fragmentary. Second, it thematizes a multitude of possible explanations that are taken from and, simultaneously, refer to the discussion and public discourse on school shootings. However, because none of these explanations suffices as an explanation, and because the film frequently reflects upon its own refusal of causality on both the narrative and the formal level, the spectator has to acknowledge complexity and ambivalence while being denied a feeling of closure. Third, by the formal and aesthetic transformation of the normal high school lifeworld into a realm of sudden and inexplicable violence, *Elephant* represents the societal narrative of peacefulness and the attempt to re-integrate the abnormality of school shootings by restoring it. The school shooting in *Elephant* obviously emerges from and is directed against the familiar. As school shootings as an 'abnormal' and disruptive form of violence resist any explanation. *Elephant* powerfully represents the discursive attempts to create causal narratives and re-integrate this form of violence in its self-understanding.

5.3 Conclusion: The Aesthetic Experience of Polyvalence, Complexity and the Denial of Closure

Multiperspectivity, as this chapter has shown, is a narrative technique that has traditionally focused on highlighting polyvalence and complexity. It reveals the constructedness of any reality and the perspective-dependency of all perception. It engages the reader or spectator in an active reception process and thus fosters an aesthetic experience that can be connected to the their actual lifeworlds. Readers and spectators must use their knowledge and cognitive abilities to connect the various perspectives and blend different, and sometimes even diverging, pieces of information. If the different perspectives provide contradictory evidence, they have to re-evaluate and re-assess information they received earlier. Thus, multiperspectival fiction fosters a more active and more life-like reception process, and, arguably, results in a more comprehensive understanding of the events presented in the fictional work. Additionally, the complex processes of perspectiv taking generate an impression of subjectivity – readers and spectators who are given a chance to take on someone else's perspective may find their capacity for empathy to be enhanced in the real world as well (cf. Nünning 2014).

School shooting research has, for some years now, acknowledged that school shootings are a multicausal and multifaceted phenomenon. As the Rashomon-effect in school shooting research shows, all approaches to the phenomenon are dependent on the researcher's own disciplinary background and on the question that she or he wants to answer. As a result, everything that is known about school shootings is necessarily perspective-dependent, and no perspective is comprehensive. While this is the case with every phenomenon and all acts of perception, in the school shooting discourse this realization is especially relevant: almost no other discourse is as determined to create causality as the school shooting discourse. This, as it has been established in previous chapters, is due to the nature of the violence, its suddenness and its apparent lack of any causal or logical explanation. Those people who are meant to become functioning parts of society commit a horrible crime against the normalcy that they are meant to uphold. In a considerable societal effort, the school shooting discourse attempts to use the abnormality of the crime to reinforce the prevalent narrative of peacefulness and non-violence.

In school shooting fiction, multiperspectivity therefore has the potential to illustrate the fragmentary nature of all perception, to mirror the processes of discourse formation in the school shooting discourse and to make readers or spectators reflect upon their position and activity within the discourse. The gaps that a fictional representation leaves open are usually the ones that the prevailing school shooting narrative attempts to close. What can be seen as a societal necessity for re-establishing order and reinforcing the narrative of peacefulness can be reflected upon in the safety of the fictional realm. Here, the aesthetic experience can leave the readers or spectators confused and in a position to acknowledge that some acts may be inexplicable.

In this chapter, it has become clear that multiperspectival school shooting fiction can, but does not have to, realize this potential of the narrative technique. Marieke Nijkamp's multiperspectival novel surely is an example of that. But, in line with Christopher Bode

> I don't see why one should wish – without becoming normative or prescriptive – to deny multiperspectivity in a novel with two or more narrators only on the ground that it does not satisfyingly develop the different perspectives (i.e., that it claims rather than really provides them), or because these versions don't diverge from each other in their essentials. Event poorly realized multiperspectivity is still multiperspectivity – an instance of regrettable failure, true, but these things happen. (Bode 2011: 199)

Even though it is poorly realized, Nijkamp's novel provides insights for this chapter, as it shows that multiperspectivity can but does not necessarily have to make the readers experience multicausality, complexity or ambivalence. Instead, in this YA school shooting novel, various perspectives are used to highlight the possibility of a positive resolution to a horrible event. While all characters whose perspectives the readers were prompted to take raised the question of whether or not they could have known or prevented the shooting, the focus remains on the way they deal with the situation they are facing. In an entirely unrealistic representation, Nijkamp presents the possibility of heroism in the face of violence, of selflessness and the power to overcome a tragedy like a school shooting by unity. The perpetrator and his actions, however, cannot be explained by the text – here, again, the difference between the authorial intention and the potential function of a text can be seen, as it appears that Nijkamp wanted to present at least some explanation for the shooter's actions by stressing his family problems and loneliness.

Violent Ends, by contrast, presents a number of perspectives that differ significantly. While they all refer to the same event and raise the unavoidable question 'why?', the perspectives presented in the novel are too diverse to be simply merged. Instead, *Violent Ends* makes its young adult readers experience the 'Rashomon-effect'. By referencing actual school shootings, it also allows for an immediate connection between the fictional incidents and comparable extratextual events. The various perspectives show how different people are affected by a school shooting, but they also underline the complexity of the school shooter's personality. Kirby is only partly a stereotypical school shooter; first and foremost, he is a human being with many different sides to him. *Violent Ends* raises a number of issues thematized in the school shooting discourse and well known to the young adult reader, particularly the connection between the school shooting and the shooter's experience of being bullied. However, *Violent Ends* presents no definite explanation. Instead, it relativizes the shooter's experience by juxtaposing it with experiences of other characters that, objectively, appear to be much worse. Here, the novel highlights the subjectiveness of all perspectives and stresses the characters' different coping mechanisms and capabilities by allowing comprehensive insights into their interiority. While Nijkamp's novel exaggerates its didactic purpose, *Violent Ends* provides an exercise in empathy and makes the readers experience the complexity of the phenomenon and the inability to understand what led to the shooting.

In regard to the character-perspectives, *Elephant*'s multiperspectivity results in a different effect. Due to the dialectic of association and de-association throughout the entire film, no lasting empathic connection between the spectator and any single character can be established. While the shifting perspectives and with the invitation to empathize with a number of different characters challenge the spectator to acknowledge subjectivity and the experiences and perceptions of different people, *Elephant* only presents stereotypical figures, blank canvases rather than actual characters. Nevertheless, the multiperspectivity fulfills an important function, as it highlights the partiality of all perspectives. No matter how hard the spectator tries, she or he is never fully able to beat the feeling of temporal and spatial dislocation. The identificatory potential of the film is tied closely to the setting: while the first part of the film establishes a sense of normalcy and ties the spectator to the characters, the third part traps them within the school's labyrinthine hallways as the abnormality of the shooting unfolds its full effect. But no matter how shocking the school shooting is, the effect of the earlier multiperspectivity still emphasizes the fragmentary understanding of the fictional events. And, as *Elephant* clearly remediates images from the Columbine shooting, the aesthetic experience of watching it closely resembles and mirrors the spectator's extratextual realization of the inexplicability of school shootings – the fictional experience of a denial of closure can thus be transferred to the spectator's experience and position in real life and can help to acknowledge and come to terms the contingencies of excessive violence.

6 Unsettling Narratives: The Inexplicability of School Shootings in *We Need to Talk About Kevin* (2003) and its Film Adaptation (2011)

The previous chapters have established that fact and fiction have become inseparable in the school shooting discourse. Neither the event as such nor the public perception or understanding of the phenomenon is unmediated. And it is not only the media representations of the events, but also the perpetrators themselves and even the academic discourse, that contribute to a school shooting narrative emphasizing of cause and effect. In the creation of this narrative of an 'abnormal' form of violence, the various fictional representations of school shootings have contributed to the fictional dimension of the school shooting discourse. Societal attempts to create a narrative of causality so as to make sense of the inexplicable are not only highly constructed and reliant on fictional elements, but they are, in fact, frequently unreliable.

In the face of excessive violence, as Jan-Philipp Reemtsma (2012) has powerfully argued, trust in society's peacefulness is crucial for social stability and, consequently, civilization as such. Especially at a time in which 'fake news' serve as both a tool for deception and denunciation, the extent to which trust and reliability go hand in hand becomes all the more obvious (cf. Nünning 2014b: 3). As a consequence, the school shooting narrative, if it is perceived as unreliable, undermines the attempts it makes to reassure society of its peacefulness. Although the forms unreliability takes in literary and extra-literary contexts differ significantly (cf. Dernbach 2015: 315), being confronted with an unreliable narrative of explanation in a literary text prompts the reader question the reliability of the school shooting narrative as such. Because the school shooting discourse and its fictional representations are closely interwoven, the extratextual functions of literary and filmic unreliability may thus reveal the unreliability of the school shooting narrative.

To approach the functions of unreliability in literature and film and the technique's extratextual functions, I will compare Lionel Shriver's *We Need to Talk About Kevin* (2003) with its film adaptation by Lynne Ramsay (USA 2011). The comparison of the two works exhibits a number of functions that are significant for the school shooting discourse. Especially the novel presents its readers with a very dense representation of the public debate about motives, reasons and explanations and creates an archive of the contemporary phenomenon. Moreover, both works, especially when examined alongside one another, serve as examples

https://doi.org/10.1515/9783110649017-007

of the effects of unreliability and its functions in a discourse that is so closely intertwined with fictional representations.

Reading an unreliable text about school shootings can, by means of aesthetic experience, make the readers experience the unreliable factors that the school shooting narrative includes. The unreliable narrative presents its readers with the choice to either comply with or to refuse the narrative of explanation; this is a challenge that contemporary readers are familiar with from the extratextual confrontation with school shootings, in which they are confronted with the narrative of causality presented by the media and public discourse and the inexplicability of the act itself. Unreliability in school shooting fiction thus illustrates the effect that school shootings have on society: the school shooting as an inexplicable phenomenon of excessive violence calls into question any sense of security or understanding of itself espoused by modern society, this insecurity and the unsettling effect of the realization of societal instability is represented and fictionalized by unreliable fictional narratives. In the next pages, I want to investigate how unreliable narration communicates this discursive insecurity and which effects this can have on the reception process of the work.

Shriver's novel, I will argue, does not provide any answers to the questions raised in the school shooting discourse, but rather echoes a number of questions and uncertainties surrounding the genesis of a school shooting by depicting the personal history and background of a school shooter from the traumatized and grief-ridden mother's perspective. The novel actively raises questions about responsibility and guilt and offers alternative views on the public perception of these profound problems. This approach, however, cannot be fully understood without addressing the narrative techniques of the work and their potential functions – specifically undermining the reliability of the narrative. One of the most relevant points in this regard is that the work confronts the reader directly with what has been established as the greatest societal challenge in dealing with school shootings: the sheer inexplicability of these acts of violence and the inability of society to grasp these events. In *We Need to Talk About Kevin*, the unsettling effect of this confrontation is based on three textual aspects: the genre of the epistolary novel, the perspective of the mother, and, most importantly, the narrative technique of unreliable narration. These aspects, which undermine much of the distance that can exist between text and reader, the novel enables the reader to rethink his or her presuppositions not only about fictional, but potentially also about real school shootings.

The distressing and unsettling effect of the unreliable narration is further intensified by the novel's focus on two highly controversial aspects from the public discourse about school shootings: maternal regret and the question of whether a child can be innately evil. These aspects embed the novel within the broader debate about the responsibility and accountability of juvenile offenders and their parents, as will be discussed in section 6.1.2. By taking the effects of unreliability into consideration, the novel's contribution to the public debate about the personality of school shooters as well as the responsibility of parents (with special regard paid to the image of 'successful' motherhood and gender-related issues) can be approached. Especially with regard to these complicated topics, the question will be raised as to whether the novel aims to assign blame to the mother or if it stands as another example of 'othering' the school shooter by portraying him as monstrous. These questions are inextricably connected to the narrative technique of unreliable narration.

In the second part of this chapter, I focus on Lynne Ramsay's 2011 adaptation of Shriver's novel and will investigate how the aspects of the novel mentioned above are represented (or left out) and interpreted in the film. As the concept of remediation implies, the representation of one medium in another is neither a new nor a rare occurrence. Neither is the concept of adaptation, i.e. the transfer of an entire story from medium into another (cf. Hutcheon 2004: 108). Adaptations of literary texts provide particularly fertile ground for study in this case because the school shooting discourse has been strongly tied to visual representation from the beginning. The school shooting narrative, I have shown, is constantly represented and remediated in all kinds of textual, audio-visual and new media. As a media event, school shootings are a transmedial phenomenon (cf. Erll 2010: 392) that is reflected in the transmedial representations of the events.

As mediatized violence, school shootings are also highly dependent on the available media and imagery of their time – a fact that can be illustrated by analyzing the process of adaptation and the way in which fictional elements are interpreted and reused. Another important reason why a comparison of Ramsay's adaptation and Shriver's novel is fruitful for this book is that the representations fulfill potentially different cultural and discursive functions. This can best be understood when not only the singular artifacts, but also the process of adaptation is considered: While the novel plays with the reader's need to 'take sides' in the imagined dialogue between Franklin and Eva and leaves them struggling with their understanding of Eva's account, the film adaptation – despite its emphasis on the subjectiveness of Eva's memory – presents the audience with a possible interpretation of the events described in the novel and, in doing so, reduces the ambiguity of the original text.

6.1 Inexplicability, Insolvability and Social Taboos: Lionel Shriver's *We Need to Talk About Kevin*

We Need to Talk About Kevin is an 'unsettling narrative', making the reader question the narrator's reliability with regard to the mother's role in the genesis of a school shooting. The novel is composed of letters from a school shooter's mother, Eva Katchadourian, to her absent husband, Franklin. In her letters, she writes about her life and her thoughts about her role in her son's developments. She reflects on her past, her decision to have children, and on her difficulties with her son Kevin during his childhood and since his incarceration after committing a school shooting in a suburban town. The letters relate how, despite her reservations about motherhood and children, Eva, a businesswoman in her late thirties, decides to become pregnant. After an emotionally difficult pregnancy and birth, and growing doubts about her decision, the relationship between Kevin and his mother turns out to be extremely difficult from the day of his birth. The antagonism between mother and son starts to disrupt Eva's happy marriage, which even the birth of their daughter Celia cannot change. Shortly after Franklin tells Eva that he wants a divorce, Kevin kills his father and sister at home, then goes to his school and shoots nine people. This story is also told in Ramsay's adaptation, which translates the narrative structure of Eva's letters by telling the story of Kevin's childhood in flashbacks that disrupt Eva's present life as the mother of a shooter.

Much like Gus Van Sant with his film *Elephant* or Tim Blake Nelson with *O* (USA 2001), Shriver initially faced major difficulties in publishing the novel, with her agent objecting "that this novel could inspire copy-cat crimes [...] for which the author and her poor unwitting agent would be implicitly responsible" (Shriver 2005).[1] Despite these reservations – which foregrounds the close connection between fictional artifacts and the debate about media violence in the school shooting discourse – the novel was published in 2003 and was a critical as well as commercial success in both Britain and the United States (cf. Jeremiah 2010: 172). It sold over a million copies, was debated heatedly (yet mostly favorably) in the media, won the Orange Prize for Women's Fiction in 2005[2] and gained a reputation as a reading group and book club favorite.

Curiously, most of the debate surrounding the novel was not about its representation of a school shooting, but its underlying themes of 'nature vs. nur-

---

[1] For the debate about copycat crimes, see Chapter 2.
[2] Now the Bailey's Prize for Women's Fiction.

ture' and maternity.³ Because of its harsh depiction of a mother's resentment of her violent son, it was frequently criticized for its negative depiction of parenthood, while others praised it for breaking societal taboos about maternity and maternal regrets. Because it addresses these questions in the face of an act of excessive violence from a mother's perspective, *We Need to Talk About Kevin* has also gained attention among scholars in gender studies, with some embracing the novel as "a valuable, if reluctant contribution to feminist thinking about motherhood" (Jeremiah 2010: 169), and even as queering "dominant ideas about gender" (ibid.: 169, see also Evans 2016). In its deconstruction of motherhood and modern family life, the novel does indeed offer an interesting perspective on maternity, parenthood and women's roles in modern society. However, rather than understanding the school shooting solely as a starting point for gender-related issues, these topics will here be analyzed with regard to their contribution to the understanding and discussion of school shootings.

6.1.1 Epistolarity, Subjectivity and Unreliable Narration

We Need to Talk About Kevin, as the title already suggests, is a novel about talking, and more specifically the need and the inability to talk in the face of an 'unspeakable' crime. The novel begins with the narrator, Eva Katchadourian, reflecting on her 'need to talk': "[S]ince we've been separated", she writes to her husband Franklin, "I may most miss coming home to deliver the narrative curiosities of my day, the way a cat might lay mice at your feet" (*Kevin:* 1). The narrator begins her story about her murderous child with a characterization of herself as a woman who goes hunting for stories and sees them as bait that needs to be presented triumphantly. Eva's existence is dependent on having stories to tell, and, simultaneously, on the man at her side as her audience. Eva's obsession with story, it becomes clear during the course of the novel, is part of her character, and her life is driven by a need for fresh subjects to talk about. Before Eva met Franklin, she used to be "an efficient little unit" (*Kevin:* 34), travelling the world, driven by the desire to not become her agoraphobic, home-bound Armenian mother.⁴ As a couple, the readers learn, Eva and Franklin were happily mar-

---

3 As I will elaborate on further later in this chapter, I understand this effect to be highly symptomatic of the discourse, highlighting the tendency of scholars and the media to focus on the sociopsychological dynamics surrounding school shootings instead of the phenomenon as such.
4 Even though her relationship to her own mother is highly problematic, Eva insists that Kevin is called Katchadourian, because she clearly wants to distance herself from America – a fact that Kevin harshly criticizes. However, Eva's Armenian heritage clearly gains more gravitas in the

ried and content in their comfortable life as young professionals, and, despite her constant travelling, Eva herself developed "a horror of being left" (*Kevin:* 37). In her letters, she carefully (re-)constructs the narrative of her life and her marriage and admits that her greatest fear is running out of things to talk about with her husband (cf. *Kevin:* 27f.). It is out of her desire to create a new story and to "have something else to talk about" (*Kevin:* 27) that she proposes and ultimately decides to become pregnant – even though she is scared of having a child and afraid of ending up "trapped in someone else's story" (*Kevin:* 37). Her decision and motives to become a mother are ruthlessly scrutinized throughout the novel, as her initial reservations are ultimately confirmed in the worst possible way: Kevin's school shooting effectively robs the narrator of all sovereignty over her own life story and instead reduces her to becoming the tragic protagonist of another person's story

Instead of providing a stimulating new talking point, Kevin destroys Eva's marriage and eventually takes Eva's conversation partner from her. Franklin, the letters suggest, is no longer available for the talks and discussions that are so vividly imagined by Eva, and she painfully realizes:

> Oh, but it never entered my head what, once I was finally provided with my fresh subject matter, I would have to say. Much less could I foresee the aching O. Henry irony that in lighting upon my consuming new topic of conversation, I would lose the man that I most wanted to talk to. (*Kevin:* 28)

The story of Eva's parenthood turned out drastically different from the one she originally wanted to tell. Unable to talk and converse, her detailed and elaborate letters are attempts to reclaim her narrative and to find solace. At the very end of the novel, she even achieves some semblance of peace of mind, insofar as this is possible for the mother of a school shooter. Before reaching this point, however, she meticulously dissects her past and present emotional state by recapitulating her life before the birth of her son and her life with him. She searches for clues and justifications for Kevin's actions and tries to deal with her own feelings of guilt and responsibility for the deaths of seven schoolmates, a cafeteria worker and a teacher. With 'story' as one of the dominant motifs in *We Need to Talk About Kevin*, the narrative structure of the novel quickly becomes the focus of attention, and with it how the novel conveys this subject and represents the inabil-

---

face of Kevin's arguably genuinely American crime, and when she tells her mother about the shooting, she reacts calmly. In the face of the horrors that the Armenians had suffered throughout history, Kevin's rampage fits into a cruel tradition, as Eva observes somberly at one point.

ity to sufficiently speak about and, consequently, to make sense of school shootings.

Functions of Epistolarity in *We Need to Talk About Kevin*
The epistolary form seems at first glance like an odd choice for a highly contemporary novel, especially since writing elaborate letters has become a somewhat dated way of communication and modern successors of the genre, such as e-mail novels, would seem a more logical choice.

Even before letter writing had gone out of style, the epistolary novel was frequently criticized for its unrealistic elements, for its "clumsiness, redundancy and occasional absurdity" (Beebee 1998: 386). Especially when considering novels by Samuel Richardson, the question arises as to how someone who writes so much could still have time to *actually* experience anything to write about. In Eva's case, however, this characteristic of the epistolary novel seems to underline the fact Eva does not have a life at all and that her writing is meant to compensate for the lack of actual experience and personal contact. Tellingly, her choice to start writing to her dead husband begins with a painful confrontation with the mother of one of Kevin's victims in the supermarket, as Eva has not left town after the shooting. This comparatively trivial, yet revealing, incident forces her to realize the extent of her weariness and loneliness, which she then chooses writing combat by writing.

Consequently, the epistolary novel does not only reflect the narrator's desolate situation; it also ironically reverses the classic epistolary novel, in which more things are happening than the letter writer could possibly process in writing. Eva's letters, on the contrary, create the impression that her life has already happened, in all the positive and negative ways that one could imagine, and that her only option left is to retreat into herself and to find a way to cope with her past. The genre thus stresses the protagonist's isolation and suffering and, in doing so, already conjures up an atmosphere of the aftermath of excessive violence. With its epistolary form, the novel embeds itself within a tradition that broadens the functional scope of the popular text.

The epistolary novel was a popular genre during the early modern period, which can be understood as related to the general preoccupation with creating order out of an increasingly large and chaotic world at this time (cf. Beebe 1998: 385). These doubts and questions were "best conveyed in pluralistic, fragmented textual forms, such as encyclopedias, dialogues and letters" (Beebee 1998: 385). As it has been established, the school shooting discourse, too, has been shaped considerably by the desire to assign meaning to seeming chaos: In the face of an inexplicable crime, Shriver's retreat to the epistolary genre thus not only echoes but also contributes to the discursive attempts at meaning-making via narrative.

Lionel Shriver, however, claims that the choice of genre was random, insisting that the letters in her novel are nothing more than "thinly disguised bog-standard chapters" (Shriver 2005) and that turning the chapters from her first draft (which were written in the second person) into letters did not take much effort. She claims only to have framed her chapters with 'Dear Franklin' and 'Love, Eva' in reproduced handwriting after having finished the novel. While this may well be the case, the epistolary form opens up a completely different functional potential of the novel. The epistolarity of Shriver's novel, is at times hard to distinguish from the very similar form of the diary novel, with which the epistolary novel shares "a focus on subjectivity and self-expression through language, and a concern with placing narrative within a concrete social context" (Beebee 1998: 385). Indeed, Eva's meticulous dissection of her past, the way she searches for explanations for her present situation in the smallest events and words and the sole focus on Eva's perspective lend the text certain qualities of a diary. While the "diary often functions as the last residuum of a self that's in danger of breaking apart under the pressure of the outside world – as the last bastion of self-communion, the place where identity and individuality find their final refuge [...]" (Bode 2011: 123), Eva's letters to Franklin seem to fulfill the same purpose. And, as Monica Latham has pointed out in her article about voices and silence in *We Need to Talk About Kevin*, even though the exterior structure of the novel is monologic, "the semantic and stylist structure is essentially dialogic" (Latham 2009: 133).[5] Despite focusing exclusively on Eva's perspective, the novel employs a strategy of the epistolary novel in representing additional or conflicting perspectives within the account.[6] As Latham argues, this mostly results from the narrator's ability to re-create the absent addressees presence by constantly taking into account the potential responses of her husband, frequently anticipating or trying to avert her husband's antagonistic reactions to her statements.[7] This antagonism between husband and wife, which evolves around their son's actions

---

[5] The understanding of the dialogic structure of Shiver's novel is based on Mikhail Bakhtin and his notion of *dialogic consciousness* (cf. Bakhtin 1983).

[6] This is, however, not a necessity for an epistolary novel since many representative works of the form only present letters from one writer (cf. Beebee 1998: 386).

[7] "You're rolling your eyes", Eva assumes, and later asks: "Are you chuckling yet?" (*Kevin:* 35, 41). Or she notes: "You're astonished. You shouldn't be", when she tells her husband about her frequent visits to jail (cf. *Kevin:* 46). When she makes a negative statement about Kevin's arguably devious nature, she anticipates Franklin's aversion to her saying this "[b]efore you get your back up..." (*Kevin:* 103).

6.1 Inexplicability, Insolvability and Social Taboos — 273

and character and which slowly drives them apart over the course of the novel, governs the entire narrative; Eva knowingly anticipates Franklin's reactions at all times (*Kevin:* 103). In the process, she does not only keep up a dialogic form in a Bakhtinian sense, but also emphasizes the intimacy that still exists between herself and the addressee. In the introduction to her feminist study of epistolary novels, Linda Kauffman states:

> Dialogism also signifies the speaking voice, a crucial aspect of the letter, which is written because the writer cannot speak to the addressee. THe traditional *je crois te parler* motif informs all epistolary production: writing nurtures the illusion of speaking with one whose absence is intolerable. (Kauffman 1992: xix)

Eva's letters help her cope with the clearly intolerable absence of Franklin, but they also verge at times on a 'talking cure', or a conversational therapy session (cf. Beebee 1998: 386; Latham 2009: 136). In this, they are reminiscent of Gabriel-Joseph de Lavergne Guilleagues' 1669 epistolary novel *Letters of a Portugese Nun*, in which a heartbroken nun writes five passionate letters to her former lover, needing to voice feelings that pour into her letters; Eva, too, lets her feelings 'pour out on paper'. These feelings, however, are not exclusively concerned with love and heartbreak, but with existential questions of guilt, hate, isolation and broken relationships. In this respect, Eva's letters are a therapeutic form of writing, a dissection of her past and present in dialogic form and an attempt to cope with her life as the mother of a killer. The letters thus not only serve as a substitute for an actual conversation partner, but as an active search for redemption for her son's actions, for her role in them and, ultimately, for her role in the disappearance of her addressee. Each of the twenty-eight letters more or less openly thematizes the question of guilt. The narrator's relentless examination of her own role in her son's wrongdoing can only emerge from the friction between Eva and Franklin. And it is this friction that effectively turns the imagined dialog into an argument, which can be understood a necessary tool for the letter writer to establish her coping mechanisms and to reach some kind of closure. Even though the original purpose of the letters is never explicitly stated as therapy, it becomes apparent as the novel describes the evolving relationship between Eva and Kevin, who "[fight] one another with [...] unrelenting ferocity" (*Kevin:* 467) and yet end up with a sort of mutual acceptance, respect and affection for one another.

During this process, Franklin's perspective, as it is represented and interpreted by Eva, serves as a challenge of her own devising as she questions how she perceives herself and her role in Kevin's development. To achieve this, she verbally reconstructs Franklin's position in the debate. While Eva and Kevin seem to resent one another from the day of Kevin's birth, Franklin insists that Kevin is simply a child and blames Eva for her hostile behavior towards their son. This is the marital dispute that gradually leads to their estrangement, and by recounting it Eva not only offers an account of a marriage falling apart, but also a representation of her own doubts and presents the reader with another perspective and narrative of her son's development. After voicing these conflicting views within letters and recollected or imagined dialogs with her husband, the narrator finally reaches a point where the constant pondering of questions does not take her any further:

> [S]ince then – and throughout writing these letters to you – I have come full circle [...]. In asking petulantly whether *Thursday* was my fault, I have had to go backward, to deconstruct. [...] The truth is, if I decided I was innocent, or I decided I was guilty, what difference would it make? If I arrived at the right answer, would you come home? (*Kevin*: 467)[8]

However, Franklin will not come home. It is not until the very end of the novel that the readers learn about his death at the hand of his son. This paralipsis is one tool offered by the epistolary novel: The fact that Eva discloses less than she is able to serves as a means of fostering suspense and curiosity. Moreover, as will be discussed later, this paralipsis is a crucial factor in the assessment of Eva's reliability. The dialogic structure of the narrator's letters also highlights the therapeutic purpose of her writing emphasizes the relevance for coming to terms with this inexplicable phenomenon by creating narratives of causality. In the beginning of Shriver's novel, Eva is unable to admit to herself that her husband and daughter are dead. Working through the events helps her to finally come to terms with her own guilt and the motivation behind the crime and, consequently, to adjust to her new situation.

But Shriver's choice of the epistolary form is not only logical on the diegetic level. The genre situates the novel within the greater discourse of feminist literature, as this subgenre has repeatedly provoked debates about authorship and male and female voices in the past (cf. e.g. Kauffman 1988), and can further be understood as a means of giving a voice to marginalized women. *We Need to Talk About Kevin* touches upon rather sensitive gender-related issues, which will be explored in greater detail in the next subchapter. Curiously, however, the choice of the genre has not yet been mentioned as one of the reasons why

---

[8] *Thursday* is Eva's way of referring to Kevin's school shooting. This conscious choice of a synonym represents the difficulties that describing school shootings pose for society. "The *atrocity* sounds torn from a newspaper", says Eva, "*the incident* is minimizing to the point of obscenity and *the day our son committed mass murder* is too long, isn't it?" (*Kevin*: 14).

Shriver's text has often been discussed in terms of its contribution to discussions of gender in writing.

The epistolary form, especially in women's writing, is sometimes understood as restricted to love letters or to the "ideology of romantic love" (Kauffman 1992: xviii). Even though Eva thematizes loss, anger and hate, she also writes love letters to her deceased husband. Despite her express efforts to remain a 'tough' woman and her struggle with classic gender roles, she openly ascribes to the 'ideology of romantic love' as a goal in her life. These notions of sentimental love, however, can also be used to "expose the snares and delusions of this myth" (Kauffman 1992: xviii). This is also the case in *We Need to Talk About Kevin* when the disintegration of this romantic ideal – which can be found on the earlier pages of the novel – is depicted as inevitable and inexorable. No matter how inclined to cling to the ideal, pre-Kevin marriage, the narrator is eventually left with the imagined dialog with her husband. Franklin, for his part, is reduced to being an archivist–of the stories that he is told, but also of the romantic ideal that is dissected *a posteriori* (cf. Altman 1982: 53). Eva only imagines Franklin's answers and statements, and thus the male account of the story is essentially confined to the female imagination. Eva's imagined perspective makes Franklin a silent auditor of her account of their marriage and a witness to her regaining of strength and independence. This is a conscientious and defiant choice on her part: "[...] I intend to take ruthless advantage of the fact that this is my account, to whose perspective you have no choice but to submit. I don't pretend to know the whole story, because I don't think that's a story that you or I will ever know" (*Kevin:* 270). Her husband's prerogative to interpret is now revealed as a trap that did not allow her to talk about Kevin in her own words or express her feelings about him and her role as a mother without being judged (cf. *Kevin:* 14). The letters she writes after the fact help the narrator to express her subjective version of the story, to reclaim *her* story, and thereby gradually reclaim sovereignty of her life.

The (Un-)Reliability of a School Shooter's Mother

By choosing the epistolary form, Lionel Shriver has found a way to represent two conflicting perspectives within one person and to simultaneously represent the terrible effects of a school shooting. In taking up the perspective of a school shooter's mother to approach this highly complex subject, the novel challenges its readers, as Eva's highly realistic account of her everyday life and her 'regular' experiences before her son's shooting convey a high degree of experientiality. This experientiality enhances the empathic connection to the protagonist (cf. Nünning 2014: 231), which is of particular interest when the narrative presents the version of the story told by someone who is usually blamed for the school shooter's actions in the school shooting discourse. The perspective of the shooter's mother has frequently been discussed in the school shooting discourse; when a mother choses to talk about her experiences, as Sue Klebold (2009, 2016) did, this is accompanied by massive media attention and controversy. However, a mother's choice to remain silent about her son's deeds is also discussed heatedly, as was the case with Eric Harris's mother, among others. Shriver presents her readers with an intimate account by a mother, and presents a protagonist who is neither a classic victim who longs for her reader's sympathy nor a classic villain who easily accepts blame. She is presented as an essentially ambivalent character that undermines societal presuppositions about motherhood and gender stereotypes, which makes her perspective even more multi-layered.[9] The novel also employs several strategies that invite the reader to form an empathetic connection with Eva. The familiar epistolary form, for example, requires that the reader identify with the narrator in some way in order to follow the course of events. Also, the high degree of subjectivity within the novel because it is restricted to Eva's perspective and the high degree of realism enables the readers to not only feel *for* the narrator, but feel *with* her.[10] This, as I will show, is vital to developing a differentiated understanding of the genesis of a school shooting and the dynamics of the discourse in its aftermath.

In the narrative representation of the internal debate about guilt and responsibility, Eva pledges that her letters serve to voice everything that she could never tell anybody before and thus suggest radical honesty. "It may have been disingenuous of me to imply at the start of my last letter that when we confided at the end of the day, I told all", Eva writes in one of her first letters. "To the contrary, one of the things that impels me to write is that my mind is huge with all

---

9 As Christopher Bode points out, epistolary novels often portray victim-aggressor or victim-exploiter relationships. In Shriver's novel, however, the question about who is the victim and who is the aggressor remains unanswered. The character-narrator is therefore an ambivalent one, since the reader has to 'come to terms' with the different sides of herself she presents throughout the novel (cf. Bode 2011: 125).
10 In Eva's quest for answers regarding guilt and responsibility, textual features such as italics, gaps, boldface, hyphens and the unusually frequent representation of spoken dialog create an intimacy between narrator and reader. Eva writes down her dialogs with Franklin as she remembers them, and recollects the painfully taciturn dialogs with the imprisoned Kevin. The inclusion of these elements suggests she is presenting a rather comprehensive account of her life and, consequently, of a school shooter's background. By representing the mother's perspective in this way, *We Need to Talk About Kevin* acquires a potential extratextual function; in many accounts, the mother's version of the story frequently remains unheard and her position as a victim is subordinated to her position as a parental authority.

the little things I never told you" (*Kevin:* 13). Eva implies that her loneliness and her present situation enable her to finally share all her secrets and her most private thoughts. Here, the therapeutic mode of the novel acquires the air of a confession: When she admits to not liking her son, the reader is inevitably drawn to her side, even if they might find Eva's attitude towards her child ethically and morally appalling, because the narrator makes the reader her confidant, promising that they will be privy to the secret thoughts and emotions of a mass murderer's mother. This perspective reflects on the public's interest in school shooters' parents, which is manifest in many newspaper articles, documentaries and in the civil lawsuits against the parents after some of the crimes. In Eva's account, the reader is presented with a desperate woman who is eager to tell the whole truth – and it is the whole truth that the various participants of the school shooting discourse are eager to deliver. The whole truth, however, cannot be delivered by the homodiegetic character-narrator, no matter how often she pledges her honesty. And while Eva tells the story of a monstrous and callous child, the readers have cause to gradually begin to doubt her reliability. While the novel starts with a narrator who is a suffering but strong and emancipated woman, Eva's desolate state, social isolation and mental instability become obvious as her letters reveal the story of her past. With the revelation of Franklin's death towards the end of the novel, the reader receives a glimpse of the scope of her suffering: Realizing the degree of the trauma she has suffered, and knowing that she has withheld crucial information, the reader is prompted to question her reliability. However, how precisely this narrative unreliability can be described and detected must still be described, as this narrative strategy is inextricably linked to the reader's understanding and the potential extratextual functions of the text.

Forms of Unreliability and Their Functions
Unreliability has been debated rather heatedly over the last decades, and many scholars have gone to great lengths to describe exactly where unreliability is situated, i.e., within the text or within the reader-text-interaction, and how the reader can detect or assess it.[11] In the case of *We Need to Talk About Kevin*, Eva's reliability is closely linked to the fact that she is a homodiegetic narrator. As Nünning states, "the link between unreliable and homodiegetic narration makes [...], since the narrator has to be recognizable as a personality who unwit-

---

[11] For a comprehensive summary of the debate and the various models that have emerged from it, see Hansen (2007) or, more recently, Vera Nünning's introduction to *Unreliable Narration and Trustworthiness* (Nünning 2015) and Sternberg/Yacobi (2015).

tingly lays bare his or her faults, be it their psychological dysfunction or obsession, their lack of knowledge, interpretive faculties or morals" (2015a: 90). The reader is privy only to Eva's limited account of her experiences and to her interpretation of their life-world, and can only ultimately read her subjective account of her son's actions. "As inhabitants of their textual worlds", as Greta Olson points out, "these narrators cannot have metatextual, omniscient knowledge. [...] Homodiegetic narrators are subject to the epistemological uncertainty of lived experience" (2003: 101). However, homodiegetic narrators are by no means always unreliable (ibid.), and more indicators are needed for the reader to doubt a narrator's reliability.

Eva's unreliability can only really be understood in close connection to her internal dialogue with Franklin, which does not only serve the purpose of helping her to work through her feelings of guilt, but also depicts her inability to rethink and renegotiate her version of the events; instead of seeking an actual dialogue with a therapist or a live confidant, she withdraws even further into herself. Engaging solely in imagined dialogue, however, cannot help her to get past her own account of Kevin's development, nor does it change her point of view about her role in it. Eva actively rejects outside perspectives and alternative interpretations of events; the reader is thus entirely restricted to her version of the story. However, the unreliability of Eva's story only becomes obvious when the extent of her trauma and her way of dealing with it is revealed. With regard to her unreliability, the fact that Eva withholds information about Franklin's death can be seen as the most obvious indication of unreliable narration in the novel. But neither the text's subjectivity nor this paralipsis as single indicators would make Eva's narrative unreliable – instead, as with most texts, it is a conglomerate of indicators that make the reader doubt the narrator's account.

A homodiegetic narrator can omit information for various reasons and does not automatically constitute unreliability, as it can also derive from the lack of knowledge at the time of the narration that is followed by later disclosure once the knowledge has been acquired (cf. Olson 2003: 101).[12] Eva's omission

---

[12] Also, regarding the narrative structure of a text, the narrative strategy of building up towards the climax of the story can come at the expense of the "full coherence between the character-narrator's dual roles" (Phelan/Martin 1999: 93). In *We Need to Talk About Kevin*, the late information about Franklin's death certainly serves the purpose of creating suspense, because the readers are aware of the fact that they do not know the addressee's whereabouts and the circumstances of the couple's separation. Since the fact that Kevin is the school shooter is revealed at the very beginning of the novel, the anticipation of this information makes the reading process more suspenseful. In this sense, Eva's unreliability with regard to Franklin's death is, in Tamar

of the fact that Franklin is dead can be classified as *underreporting* in Phelan's and Martin's (1999) terms, because Eva does not tell the reader everything she knows. Moreover, she even lays a false trail by suggesting that she and Franklin are only separated, which could also classify as *misreporting* according to Phelan (2005: 52).[13]

However, as Vera Nünning points out with regard to unreliable homodiegetic narrators who provide stories that seem to be reliable for the major portion of the text (in Eva's case, until she reveals Franklin's death), "it is possible to search for motives and potential faults of the narrator and ask why he or she gave a wrong account of the facts in the first place" (Nünning 2015a: 91). While the paralipsis in *We Need to Talk About Kevin* indicates that Eva may not have kept her promise to be entirely honest in her account, the reader does not perceive her as intentionally deceptive. Instead, leaving out the crucial information about her husband is a necessity for her development and is presented as a valid coping mechanism of Eva as a character-narrator – only by doing so can she uphold the pretense of conversation with Franklin until she finds closure at the end of the novel.[14] Both the narrator's unreliability and the explanation for it can be found on the diegetic level and thus closely link the narrative technique to the dynamics of the school shooting discourse: Eva's account of the events leading up to Kevin's attack are likely tainted by the obvious trauma that the loss of her husband and daughter at the hand of her own mass-murdering son must have caused. On the textual level, this trauma can be seen in the pace of 'talking' that can be observed in the letters, where her "words spew out like vomit" (Latham 2009: 136). With this character-narrator's situation in mind, leaving out the details about Franklin's death makes perfect sense on the level of story, which, as Bode stresses, is a necessity for detecting unreliable narration:

Yacobi's terms, strictly functional, as it serves aesthetic or creative ends (cf. Steinberg/Yacobi 2015: 407f.).

13 In the very first letter, for example, Eva writes, "Anyway, even with the two of us *estranged*, I knew you would worry about whether I was eating. You always did" (*Kevin:* 8, my emphasis), thereby suggesting that they are merely divorced or separated. Later she writes: "I worry that throughout that handwritten passage you've been skimming, reading ahead" (*Kevin:* 46), which gives the impression that Franklin actually receives and reads her letters.

14 Eva is in desperate need of a conversation partner, someone who will listen to her subjective account of her life and the way that Kevin changed it. As elaborated earlier, she needs her husband as her confidant to explain her ambivalent thoughts about her own and his guilt (cf. *Kevin:* 385), and to openly discuss topics that are social taboos and thus restricted from public discourse. By questioning her love for her son, Eva, as the center and scapegoat in the aftermath of a terrible school shooting, invites more blame, which is why she keeps these thought to herself.

> Alongside reasons for doubt, the reader must have a second prompt – a prompt to make a new *configuration:* there must be a *diegetic motivation* for unreliability, *internal to the text,* as a core, so to speak, in which the assumption crystallizes that we're dealing with an unreliable narrator here. The narrative itself must suggest a reason for its own faultlines. (Bode 2011: 213)

Here, this diegetic motivation is Eva's psychological state, to which the reader's attention is then directed. The narrator's way of dealing with the past and the atrocious deed committed by her son remain at the center of attention. Because of her desolate state of mind, Eva could therefore be classified as a 'fallible narrator', who, according to Olson's definition does not "report on narrative events because [she is] mistaken about [her] judgments or perceptions or [is] biased" (Olson 2003: 101). Even though she tries to be honest about her own problems and shortcomings, her honesty can only go as far as her high degree of emotional involvement and bias towards her husband or son allow. She even admits that her letters, written one and a half years after the actual events, may lack accuracy: [15]

> I'm no longer sure whether I rued our first child before he was even born. It's hard for me to reconstruct that period without contaminating the memories with the outsized regret of later years, a regret that bursts the constraints of time and gushes into the period when Kevin wasn't there yet to wish away. (*Kevin:* 84)

She thus admits to the possibility that her memories, just like anyone else's, may be tainted by later events and that she herself is not entirely sure that her subjective account and her memories are reliable. Eva's ambivalence regarding concepts of truth is frequently voiced throughout the novel, but while the truth about herself and her perception of her role in Kevin's development is questioned and revised, her narrative about her son's actions essentially remains the same.

Fallible narrators, Olson points out, are much more easily 'forgiven' by their readers than their intentionally unreliable counterpart, untrustworthy narrators; Eva's fallibility can be understood as another strategy to gain the reader's empathy.[16] While the textual and diegetic indicators might prompt the reader to dis-

---

[15] Personal involvement can be understood as one indicator of unreliable narration (cf. Rimmon-Keenan 2002 [1983]).
[16] One of the effects of the narrator's unreliability is estrangement (cf. Phelan 2007): Once the reader realizes that the narrator's account is not correct, the gap between reader and narrator grows wider. Nevertheless, I would argue that, in Eva's case, unreliability also has a kind of

trust Eva's account, the verdict about her reliability remains up to the reader. On the one hand, Eva's account is constantly questioned through the recollected dialogs with Franklin. On the other hand, Eva presents 'proof' for some of her previously suspect stories at a later point.[17] Following Ansgar Nünning's integrative cognitive-rhetorical approach, the textual inconsistencies help the reader "to recognize an unreliable narrator when he or she sees one" (Nünning 2005: 101). The reader's interpretation of the narrative situation, however, is dependent on the frameworks they rely upon and/or their historical and cultural background (cf. Zerweck 2001: 152, Nünning 2015: 14) which can foster divergent readings of the text.

We Need to Talk About Kevin, as I have pointed out, suggests that Eva is a fallible narrator who is incapable of always telling the whole truth because of her own inability to cope. Her account is suspect on various levels: Textual inconsistencies, underreporting and an openly subjective narrative by a traumatized narrator that serves the clear purpose of emotional healing further ground this suspicion. Consequently, Eva is at least partially unreliable, because she admits to the shortcomings in her account and because the textual signals as well as the diegetic level suggest her fallibility. And yet, the final 'verdict' about her reliability must be made by the reader and thus depends on his or her recognition of the signs of Eva's unreliability and willingness to accept the implications that the narrator's (un-)reliability have for the text's explanation of a school shooting. Inherent to the decision about Eva's reliability is the ethical and moral question of whether the reader believes that a child can be born as a killer or not. The reader's decision about the narrator's reliability thus acquires a decisively extratextual function, as it forces the reader to position themselves with regard to one of the most black-or-white questions in the school shooting discourse.

It is in this ambivalence of the narrative and the narrator that the novel becomes especially relevant for the school shooting discourse. As a text that is centered on the need and simultaneous inability to talk, and which is narrated by an ambivalent and unreliable narrator, it can confront the reader with their inability to fully grasp the dynamics of these crimes.

Scholars have suggested that unreliability serves to mediate "between the real – i.e. the extratextual elements a literary text can select form the empirical

---

bonding effect, since it reveals her traumatized state of mind and help the readers sympathize with her otherwise rather coldly narrated situation.

17 For example, when Kevin presents her with Celia's eyeball towards the end of the novel, which could be understood as a rehabilitation of Eva's reliability and as confirmation that her version of Kevin is the right one (cf. Kevin: 460ff.).

world – and the imaginary" (Zerweck 2001: 168), and that this narrative technique has the ability to represent and allow thoughts, feelings, phantasies and experiences that cannot occupy a place outside of the realm of the fictional (cf. Fluck 1997: 15; 20). By representing cultural blind spots – such as the inexplicable cruelty of a school shooting and the suffering that precedes and follow it or the inability of a mother to love her son – unreliable narration can be one possibility to help articulate the unspeakable. In this sense, unreliable narration can help to reintegrate the unspeakable into the cultural imaginary, as it allows for a transfer of the fictional into the reader's own life-world (cf. Fluck 1997: 12). In the case of *We Need to Talk about Kevin*, Eva's unreliability undermines the need for explanation and understanding and instead confronts us with an unsolvable narrative.[18] At the same time, the narrative suggests that any single version of a school shooting can be viewed from a number of perspectives and, in the end, often requires revision and should be viewed critically. Unreliable narration within Shriver's novel enables its most relevant and powerful potential functions.

6.1.2 Representations of Motherhood, Responsibility and Accountability

Even though *We Need to Talk About Kevin* addresses a topical, sensitive and controversial topic, the representation of Kevin's brutal school shooting only seems to be the starting point for a broader debate about family and motherhood. Indeed, the novel thematizes how schools shootings question the functional of the cultural construct of family – and, arguably, with it the entire Western value system. As a result, the families of school shooters are frequently subject to shunning and shaming in the media and by their communities and the public, as everyone suspects that if "the family is truly admirable [...] this could not come to pass. The community must have been mistaken, fooled, or just blind to the defects on the inside of families such as the Goldens or Carneals" (Newman et al. 2005: 196). Like Eva, many parents have had to face public accusations of well-hidden dysfunctionality, neglect or abuse, as society struggles for coherent explanations. The way in which the role of the family is debated in the school shooting narrative, consequently, is central to societal processes of meaning-making and renegotiation. Shriver's novel represents the downfall of a nuclear

---

[18] For further analysis of the potential functions of unreliable narration, see Bläss (2005). A concise overview of the emotional functions of unreliable narration can be found in Hillebrandt (2011).

middle-class family and thus questions this stronghold of societal values, only making the novel's depiction of discursive dynamics more explosive. The strong focus on motherhood and family is therefore understood as characteristic of the school shooting discourse, where sociodynamic and psychological modes of explanation predominate. Analyzing the text with regard to its potential to challenge this existing narrative with unreliability allows for great insight into the dynamics of the debate about responsibility in the school shooting discourse.

Maternal Love, Maternal Ambivalence and Mother's Guilt
As Emily Jeremiah puts it in her article about mothering and masculinity in *We Need to Talk about Kevin*, the novel "in its very 'harshness', even perversity [...] triggers questions that a sentimental, glossed-over treatment of motherhood could not do", and that it "constitutes progress, enriching existing debates about parenthood and opening up new lines of inquiry" (Jeremiah 2010: 181). Ruth Robbins argues that the depiction of motherhood in the novel "offers a corrective vision that modifies cultural ideals", furthermore "drastically call[ing] into question the liberal ideals of family in the west" (Robbins 2009: 95). Indeed, motherhood, as presented in Shriver's novel, is neither easy nor fulfilling, and it does not come naturally to Eva. For her, the decision to have a child was something much more difficult and something that she considers to have been a mistake.

Long before Kevin's school shooting, Eva used to be a beautiful, successful, happily married and independent woman, who in hindsight sees her existence as destroyed by her son and her decision to become pregnant. Recapitulating her life before Kevin, Eva asks: "*What possessed us?* We were so happy! Why, then, did we take the stake of all we had and place it all on this outrageous gamble of having a child?" (*Kevin*: 14). What 'possessed' them were in fact social conventions of family life and womanhood: "When I hadn't gone into maternal heat by my mid-thirties, I worried that there was something wrong with me, something missing", says Eva (*Kevin*: 31). In addition to this feeling of biological deviation or even failure, combined with Franklin's growing dissatisfaction with Eva's frequent travelling, her self-sufficient lifestyle started to strike her as boring: Travelling seemed repetitive and her happiness dull (cf. *Kevin*: 20f.), whereas motherhood would be a foreign country still worth exploring (cf. *Kevin*: 22). The crucial factor for her decision, however, is Eva's dependency on Franklin and her deep, irrational fear of losing him: "No offspring could replace you", Eva says about the night when she worried that Franklin had an accident and, as a consequence, decides to have a child. "But if I ever had to miss you, miss you forever, I wanted to have someone to miss you alongside, who would know you if only as a chasm in his life, as you were a chasm in mine" (*Kevin:* 58).

Eva is an emancipated, modern woman who is proud of her independence,[19] fiercely argues for women's rights, insists that her son has her last name and is in charge of contraception. Nevertheless, Eva is highly emotionally dependent on Franklin. Her decision to become pregnant – a decision she makes on her own by conveniently 'forgetting' her diaphragm[20] – is not only based on her need for something new to talk about, but stems from her fear of being alone and her urge to "arrange a backup, for you and for us" (*Kevin:* 59). It may have been induced by boredom, and by societal and cultural norms (cf. Jeremiah 2010: 174), but ultimately it was an entirely irrational decision. As a result, it cannot be questioned and understood on rational grounds, as Eva's incapability of coming to terms with her past shows.

Therefore, when she decides to become pregnant, driven by a feeling of urgency that is not motivated by any biology, she has to violently cast aside all her previous reservations, self-doubts and anxieties[21] that have been formed based on cultural images of motherhood (Jeremiah 2010: 174). The fact that family "is a concept about which [she] had always been uneasy" (*Kevin:* 54) and that she was not, as expected, "drowned by the hormonal imperative" to bear a child (*Kevin:* 31) does not keep her from going through with her plan. As a result, she finds herself in an ambivalent position from the very beginning, as she later confesses:

> Franklin, I was *absolutely terrified of having a child*. Before I got pregnant, my visions of child-rearing – reading stories about cabooses with smiley faces at bedtime, feeding glob into slack mouths – all seemed like pictures of someone else. I dreaded confrontation with what could prove a closed, stony nature, my own selfishness and lack of generosity, the thick, tarry powers of my own resentment. However intrigued by a 'turn of the page', I was mortified by the prospect of becoming hopelessly trapped in someone else's story. (Kevin: 37)

---

19 E.g., she is appalled when Franklin talks about her quitting her job and, before her pregnancy, she insists on not being picked up from the airport after her trips abroad.
20 Ruth Robbins, who wrote an otherwise interesting article about maternal ideals and monstrous children in *We Need to Talk About Kevin*, starts her argument with the misconception that Eva forgot her diaphragm and that Kevin was not planned. This, however, is not the case: Eva deliberately did not put it in (cf. Robbins 2009: 100).
21 "Indeed, the ideologies of motherhood and femininity are closely intertwined, even interdependent. To disrupt one – to suggest, for example, that women might not be naturally caring and selfless – is to disrupt the other, in, one hopes, productive and interesting ways. This is what Shriver's novel does" (Jeremiah 2010: 170).

Already during her attempts to get pregnant, Eva feels used and neglected as an individual, as if "swallowed by a big biological project that [she] didn't initiate or choose" (*Kevin:* 61).[22] Later, pregnancy makes her uncomfortable and she resents her new status and the way that a pregnant woman is viewed by society – no longer as an individual, but as social property. Her own desires and needs, she feels, are of no importance and she is constantly forced to act against her will, because it is expected of her. "The right to boss pregnant women around", she cynically states, "was surely on its way into the constitution" (*Kevin:* 62).

In Eva's accounts about pregnancy, childbirth and parenting, she voices strong criticism about the social construct of motherhood. Shriver, as Emily Jeremiah so rightly points out, "understands (maternal) experience as constructed, or performed" (Jeremiah 2010: 175). Eva indeed performs her pregnancy as well as her maternity and tries to be a "normal pregnant woman" (*Kevin:* 77) and a good mother, although it is not second nature to her. And she is profoundly disappointed by her new role: Directly after Kevin's birth, she cannot seem to feel the strong emotions that she expected and that people had been telling her about (*Kevin:* 95f.). However, she cannot and will not talk about this ambivalence, about the fact that childbirth left her unmoved – least of all to her husband, who is the embodiment of the stereotypically enthusiastic, modern American middle-class father. This, as Emily Jeremiah puts it, is "an interesting detail, suggesting that motherhood in contrast to sex, is still surrounded by taboo" (Jeremiah 2010: 180), or as Shriver herself states: "While we may have taken the lid off sex, it is still out of bounds to say that you do not like your own kids [...] or that, perish the thought, you wish you never had them" (Shriver 2005).

Eva's performance of motherhood is bound to go wrong. Disappointed about her son and herself, she abuses him verbally and physically, feeling a "gush of savage joy" (*Kevin:* 177) while doing so, yet always blaming him for having provoked her actions. Instead of seeing him as a child, she sees a mean individual whose sole purpose in life is to make his mother's life miserable – an entirely egocentric point of view that make a positive relationship between mother and son impossible.

This hostility only comes to an end when the necessity to 'perform' her relationship stops after Kevin's school shooting. Honesty, the reader learns, makes

---

[22] When Franklin forbids her to dance to a *Talking Heads* song and drink a glass of wine, she angrily mocks the overprotectiveness of her husband for their unborn child, saying: "Maybe by listening to 'Psycho Killer' we're feeding him bad thoughts. Better look it up" (Kevin: 76). This detail, left uncommented by the narrator, reveals a whole new meaning in the face of the school shooting, and sheds new light on Eva's behavior during pregnancy by suggesting that the prenatal experiences of the child could in fact have influenced Kevin's character.

communication between mother and son possible. Her frequent visits to Kevin's prison begin as an attempt to prove to herself that she is in fact a 'good' mother (cf. *Kevin:* 46), but the reader witnesses a gradual resolution of the mother-son antagonism that had previously dominated their relationship. This take on motherhood as presented in Shriver's novel can be understood with Judith Butler's concept of gender performativity. Judith Butler states that "there is no gender identity behind the expressions of gender; that identity is performatively constituted by the very 'expressions' that are said to be its results" (Butler 2006: 34). This notion has already been extended to the performance of the maternal (cf. Hill 2011) and can be easily applied here. Eva's notion of how she has to behave as a mother is highly constructed and manipulated by patriarchal society. And while she defiantly tries to fend off this expected role during pregnancy, she almost desperately wants to live up to it after Kevin is born. However, her performance of the 'good mother' is disturbed by Kevin, who seems to be able to look through her. Presented as an experienced performer of the 'good son' in his relationship with his father, he is depicted as personally provoked by performances of other people and, the novel suggests, this may have even been the reason why he killed his father.

Shriver's novel undeniably touches upon very sensitive and even shocking subjects by thematizing a mother's resentment of her own child and her failure to love and accept him because of her own emotional state. Her anxiety and ambivalence, however, would be conceived of as much more trivial and – owing to more differentiated guidebooks for parents that also discuss postpartum depression and parental anxiety – less of a taboo if her rejected child had not become a mass murderer. Because of this development, the question of responsibility gains new urgency alongside that of the mother's culpability. Here, Shriver's novel does not only represent and ask questions that the readers are familiar with from the school shooting discourse, it also actively engages the reader in the process of finding possible answers to that question. By confronting the reader with the highly subjective and realistic (cf. Nünning 2015a: 95) account of the mother and provoking doubts about her reliability that are closely linked to her perception of motherhood and the trauma that she suffered as a mother, the reader is allowed to experience these highly topical issues as they engage with and try to evaluate Eva's perspective and reliability.

Responsibility and Accountability in the Face of School Shootings

By indirectly asking whether his mother's ambivalence, rejection and resentment turned Kevin into a school shooter or if he in fact might be innately evil, the novel leaves itself upon to a number of interpretations. Taking Eva's representation of her son to be the true one provides an explanation of school shootings that is deliberately provocative. Because the narrative technique employed in the novel allows for the possibility that Kevin might have been malevolent, the text broadens the scope of the discussion of school shootings, yet leaves the final verdict to the reader.

The notion of the innately evil child is both obsolete and socially unacceptable, but the school shooter is frequently portrayed as a monstrous figure within the discourse (see Chapter 4). Naturally, this idea derives from the very 'monstrosity' of the crime: As elaborated in the second chapter here, school shootings defy rationality – *causa aequat effectum* does not apply to *amok* or school shootings (cf. Vogl 2003: 217). When confronted with these acts of excessive violence, the public often resorts to strategies that reduce the complexity of the act, relying on determinist understandings of human nature that are geared towards 'othering' and ultimately dehumanizing the school shooter as a monstrous creature. These reactions can be understood as utterances of helplessness, as a result of the incapability to cope with the suddenness and inexplicability of the attacks and as an attempt to explain how a child can be a mass murderer.[23]

The school shooter as monster is reliant on an essential understanding of childhood as a state of innocence, with which 'abnormal', especially 'abnormally cruel' behavior conflicts (cf. Eagleton 2010, Gerster 2016). Eva, too, seems to resort to the complexity reducing strategy of attributing to her child a certain abnormality at birth – a reaction that calls to mind Doris Lessing's novel *The Fifth Child*. In Shriver's novel, the reader is clearly confronted with two contesting understandings of childhood; while Franklin's view of Kevin represents the socially acknowledged, positive understanding of children as innocent, Eva's account challenges the reader to engage with her deeply pessimistic view of human nature. Eva's perspective is all the more challenging because she is an unreliable narrator. Whether or not the reader chooses to believe her version of the story can therefore have extensive ethical implications.

The common understanding of a child as innocent might be traced to Jean-Jacques Rousseau. "God", he famously wrote, "makes all things good; man meddles with them and they become evil."[24] While the monster rhetoric in the school

---

[23] Here, the problematic fact that juvenile school shooters are publicly sometimes understood as children – which is manifest in the legal prosecution of the offenders and their parents – is significant. See Chapter 2.1.1.
[24] What exactly is responsible for the emergence of evil in a society that consists exclusively of originally innocent individuals remains unclear throughout Rousseau's work. While he tries to find explanations in various areas of life – e.g. possessions, amour-propre, etc. – he ultimately fails to present a satisfying solution (cf. Jostock 1999: 21).

shooting discourse seems to call into question the validity of this notion, Shriver's novel revisits the nature vs. nurture debate in a very radical fashion. These two understandings of childhood are debated openly within Eva's account of Kevin's development, but they are also represented on the character level. On the one hand, the reader is presented with Eva's perspective. She sees her son as "a singular, unusually cunning individual who had arrived to stay with us and just happened to be very small" (*Kevin:* 103) and, from the very moment of his birth, imputes willpower and agency to him. She is convinced that Kevin did not only reject her breast but his mother as a person in a deliberate act of meanness. As a result, she cannot see him as a 'normal baby' and, in her eyes (like Ben in *The Fifth Child*) he does not act like one, either. From the very moment of his birth she observes a lack of enthusiasm and purpose, and his "unlit eyes" and "unfocused disaffection" (*Kevin:* 132) do not seem childlike at all. Instead, Eva attributes to her son a will to destroy and hate everyone who possesses the enthusiasm he seems to lack. His constant screaming is used as a weapon against his mother and is not caused by pain or appetite, but fueled by outrage (cf. *Kevin:* 106). In his face, she sees the "I'm gonna get you expression of a convict who's already started digging a tunnel with a nail file" (*Kevin:* 59), and later, when Kevin refuses to speak to Eva, this is interpreted as a plot against her. Everything that Kevin does has a purpose and is motivated my malevolent intentions against his mother.[25] Franklin, on the contrary, sees him as a child, a blank slate (cf. Jeremiah 2010: 180), and is first startled, then appalled, by Eva's attitude towards their child. Eva, however, is convinced that she saw through Kevin from the very start, which she sees as confirmed by the school shooting he carries out.

In these conflicting perspectives that later lead to the estrangement between husband and wife, Shriver's novel illustrates how a school shooting reveals the instability and vulnerability of the nuclear family. In such close proximity with the narrator, who finds herself at the center of her model middle-class family's dissolution, the readers experience and are empathically involved in the search for causality and meaning-making that is the result of the realization of the system's brokenness. In the face of excessive violence, the nuclear family as the stronghold of Western values is questioned. Eva's scrutiny of her role in the tragic downfall of her happy family can be seen as a micro-version of society's reactions to school shootings. As it has been shown in Chapter 2, societal notions of normalcy presume that a n intact, 'normal' family should not produce a school shooter. In approaching the societal problem posed by school shootings, *We*

---

25 For textual references to Kevin as a monstrous child, see Robbins (2009) and Latham (2010).

Need to Talk About Kevin remediates the media narrative of the 'superficially intact' family of the school shooter (cf. e.g. Cullen 2009) by suggesting that something was truly going wrong behind the façade of the shooter's family or, more specifically, in the mother-son relationship.

This contrast between an alleged familial idyll and the genesis of a school shooter is emphasized by the birth of Celia, which unfolds as a classic narrative of maternal bliss. While Kevin was seen as a small adult with bad intentions, Celia is a baby who needs love and protection. Eva's idea of childhood thus does not apply to Celia, whom she sees in the way that Franklin saw Kevin. As a result of this juxtaposition, Eva's understanding of Kevin is portrayed as rooted within him as an individual. By introducing Celia, the full extent of the mother-son antagonism becomes obvious.[26] From his mother's perspective, Kevin is capable of nearly everything. While all the things he allegedly did – torturing and killing of animals, destroying a teacher's career, deliberately hurting his sister – always remain speculations, they are very deliberate deeds in Eva's mind. However, her ambivalence becomes obvious in the aftermath of the school shooting. When a journalist asks her the leading question "Who could have known?", she responds: "I saw it coming for nearly sixteen years [...] A fat lot of good that did" (*Kevin:* 114), offering an unequivocal understanding of Kevin that makes all other attempts at explanation seem invalid and trivial. However, elsewhere Eva admits that she did not at all expect her son to have been the killer when she first heard that there was a school shooting at her son's school, but was as worried about him like any other parent would be – another indicator that her account of her emotional relationship towards her son is tainted in hindsight by his actions.

---

[26] However, when Kevin is sick as a child, Eva's and Franklin's positions are directly contrasted and Eva's understanding of Kevin as an innately evil child is undermined. Weak as he is, he only wants to be with his mother and suddenly shows interest in toys and stories and needs to be tended to. For Eva, this is only proof that the way he acts normally – with open resentment of his mother and allegedly insincere cheerfulness with his father – is as much of a performance as Eva's maternal role: "He wasn't mad. He was sad", she realizes (*Kevin:* 280). This understanding of Kevin's character, however, fosters a feeling of complicity in Eva, and she and Kevin begin to openly thematize their aversion and therefore seem to be forming an antagonistic but honest relationship that slowly leads to cautious attachment, as their conversations toward the end of the novel suggest. Both dwell on their antagonism, and keep 'souvenirs' so as to remind themselves of their mutual disdain: Kevin keeps a scar from the time that Eva broke his arm, and Eva keeps maps of her travels that Kevin destroyed when he was a child: "'I needed something you'd done to me, to reach out and touch it. To prove that your malice wasn't all in my head.' 'Yeah', he said, tickling the scar on his arm again. 'I know exactly what you mean'" (*Kevin:* 205).

All of this ambivalence surrounding the unreliable narrator suggests that Eva, instead of presenting the reader with her actual thoughts about Kevin, uses her interpretation of his developments and actions as a strategy to deal with her guilt. Consequently, while Eva constantly reflects on the question of her responsibility, her ability to do so is called into question by her unreliability. Additionally, several intratextual contradictions point to her inability to accept responsibility, even though she fiercely claims otherwise:

> I'm determined to accept due responsibility for every wayward thought, every petulance, every selfish moment, not in order to gather all the blame but to admit *this* is my fault but *there, there*, precisely there is where I draw a line and on the other side, *that, that*, Franklin, *that* is *not*. (*Kevin:* 84)

Even though Eva seems to consciously relate Kevin's development to her failures as a mother, she ultimately does not accept that her resentment and treatment of Kevin as a boy may have turned him into a school shooter. She understands his school shooting as personal revenge (*Kevin:* 460), which is supported by the fact that he keeps her alive and refers to her as the "audience" for his shooting (ibid.). *We Need to Talk About Kevin* ultimately suggests that Eva not only laid the groundwork for the school shooting, but that she is in fact both the motive and the triggering cause for the school shooting and that "Kevin's gesture was meant to test the limits of the mother-son antagonism in an extreme way" (Latham 2009: 140). At the end of the day, Eva's account suggests, she was at the very center of the events, a notion that is as arguably motivated by self-aggrandizement as much as guilt. The mother of another convict in prison states:

> It's always the mother's fault, ain't it? [...] And nobody ever say they some kids just damned mean. Don't you believe that old guff. Don't you let them saddle you with all that killing. [...] It hard to be a momma, nobody ever pass a law say 'fore you get pregnant you gotta be perfect. I'm sure you try the best you could. You here, in this dump, on a nice Saturday afternoon? You still trying. (*Kevin:* 195)

As one of the very few passages in the novel in which dialect is used and thereby direct proximity is created (cf. Heyd 2006: 238f.), the sentence "some kids just damned mean" underlines what Eva has been suggesting all the while: She may have had her faults, but in the end Kevin's nature is the only true explanation.

The questions the novel raises about responsibility and guilt are rather nuanced and at times paradoxical. The civil law suit that Eva has to face and that thematizes those questions as well, therefore functions as common thread that connects the novel's various explorations of motives, reasons and explanations. In doing so, Eva's struggle with the law suits also connects it to a number of extratextual school shootings, such as Pearl, West Paducah, Jonesboro and Columbine.[27] Eva's story fictionalizes the lives of mothers like Susan Klebold, who recalls in an essay how she experienced the aftermath of her son's killings:

> [W]hile I perceived myself to be a victim of the tragedy, I didn't have the comfort of being perceived that way by most of the community. I was widely viewed as a perpetrator or at least an accomplice since I was the person who had raised a 'monster'. In one newspaper survey, 83 percent of respondents said that the parents' failure to teach Dylan and Eric proper values played a major part in the Columbine killings. If I turned on the radio, I heard angry voices condemning us for Dylan's actions. Our elected officials stated publicly that bad parenting was the cause of the massacre. (Klebold 2009)[28]

Unreliability in Shriver's novel exerts much of its functional potential because it is bound up with the themes of motherhood and maternal guilt and regret. Within the school shooting discourse, the deeply unsettling effect of thematizing mother's guilt and responsibility can be seen as very fruitful; the question of whether a mother can be held responsible for her child's actions at all is raised as the reader is forced to decide whether they can or want to trust Eva's ambivalent account.

The novel's focus on family, maternity, and motherhood in connection with the inexplicable and gruesome crime committed by an adolescent reveals an aspect that makes school shootings and their aftermath especially disturbing: School shootings violently undermine the narrative of the functioning middle-class family and thereby confront society with the erosion of yet another assumption of safety and security. The myth that the 'apple does not fall far from the tree' is unmasked as such, because, even though a number of school shooters in the past have experienced various degrees of discord in their homes (cf. Newman et al. 2005: 244f.), neglect and even dysfunctionality cannot suffice as an explanation for the severity of the deed.[29] The rhetoric of the 'superficially intact' family that is frequently employed, which points at deeper faults behind a seemingly normal, can only be seen as a discursive reaction to the insecurity generated by the realization that a regular family could possibly give rise

---

27 For the functions of references to real school shootings and commentary in the novel on circulating assumptions about motives and explanations, see Chapter 6.1.3.
28 For Sue Klebold's account on the aftermath of the Columbine shooting, see also Klebold (2015).
29 Andrew Solomon has authored a book titled *Far from the Tree* (2013) in which he portrays families with children that are very different from their parents. Among the portrayals are Sue and Tom Klebold, Dylan Klebold's parents.

to a mass murderer. The societal and media reflex of "trashing the family" (Newman et al. 2005: 196), as is also depicted in Shriver's novel, has by now become an integral part of the school shooting discourse, and the question of the family's responsibility is one of the main elements of the school shooting narrative (see Chapter 2). However, the novel does not only raise these questions in a relatable way, but Eva's unreliability also illustrates the fragility of the familiar narratives of explanation. Not even the societal narrative of motherhood and maternal love are stable and viable in Eva's account. In this unreliability, *We Need to Talk About Kevin* makes the inexplicability of school shootings tangible, comments on the tropes within the school shooting discourse and conveys to the readers the various aspects that make the phenomenon so disturbing and complex.

6.1.3 Remembering, Forgetting and the Cultural Memory of School Shootings

And yet, *We Need to Talk About Kevin* is not only a novel about a school shooting or about the issues of responsibility and motherhood in this particular discourse; with its narrative structure, it also addresses and represents acts of remembering and forgetting in the face of an unspeakable crime and individual trauma and suffering. By representing Eva Katchadourian's retreat into the realm of her own interpretation and understanding of her son's school shooting, it inevitably refers to the greater discourse of school shootings as a medially refigured and remediated act of violence. Next to the gender and motherhood-related issues discussed above, the novel's focus on memory and remembering simultaneously fictionally represents and contributes to the dynamics of discourse formation.

As I have suggested in the first parts of this chapter, Eva's unreliability is essentially caused by her inability to remember correctly; her memory is tainted by the traumatic experience of having lost her husband and daughter at the hands of her own son. She is all too aware of this fact, even though she constantly presents herself as struggling to find the 'correct' version of events and 'real' motive for her son's actions. Her letters to Franklin are not merely a testimonial to her loneliness and inability to communicate with the people around her. Moreover, as a chronologically ordered series of written documents, they represent an act of remembering and capture the struggle to recollect the traumatic events. Eva, as she puts it, is constantly "rooting around in [her] mental attic" (*Kevin:* 30), as she tries to remember her initial reservations about motherhood, her reservations towards Kevin as a child and her relationship with her husband before Kevin was born.

6.1 Inexplicability, Insolvability and Social Taboos — 293

The attic is an appropriate metaphor for the approach to memory in Shriver's novel. In Eva's letters, the readers are presented with an extensive store of her memories, from which she tries to create meaning by arranging them into a coherent narrative of a mother whose antagonistic relationship with her son culminates in a school shooting. In order to arrange this narrative, Eva has to work through various, at times contradictory, memories in her attempt to re-integrate later events into a "meaningful whole", to use Riceour's words (1984: 67). For this reason, some episodes and stories about her life as a mother and about Kevin's childhood and adolescence initially seem irrelevant, but can be interpreted as ill omens in retrospect.

While Eva is frank about the inaccuracy of some parts of her memory, she recollects other stories and conversations in great detail and suggests her ability to remember every spoken word, every gesture and every look on either Kevin's or Franklin's face. These descriptions are especially detailed when she remembers disputes about the interpretation of her son's behavior during his childhood and adolescence (e. g. *Kevin*: 244ff.). Her memories of the past are both nostalgic, when she remembers life before the birth of her firstborn, and incongruent, when she tries to make sense of what led him to commit mass murder. Eva has forgotten events that would have made her story even more incomprehensible to her. Moreover, she wants to reclaim her own life-story by writing it down without a live addressee. In this process, she rearranges her own past in order to comprehend Kevin's development. Here, the parallels to the school shooting discourse become obvious, as Eva herself states that the "testimony of witnesses to an event is notoriously shambolic, especially on its immediate heels. On-scene, misinformation rules. Only after the fact is order imposed on chaos" (*Kevin*: 431). With this remark about the media and public strategies of dealing with a catastrophe like a school shooting, she also comments on her own process of 'imposing order on chaos'.

Her attempt to structure and rearrange the chaotic narrative of Kevin's inexplicable actions points, at the same time, towards the greater dynamics of the school shooting discourse and the societal efforts to make sense of the events. By reading Eva's letters, the reader is able to experience the creation of a meaningful narrative; they can see how the arrangement of events that the novel presents is geared toward making Kevin's actions foreseeable and framing them as a logical consequence of his nature. The revelation of Eva's unreliability, however, reveals how narratives of cause and effect are both constructed and unstable – an insight that is easily transferable to the school shooting discourse.

As has been established, Eva's unreliability mostly stems from the fact that her memory is tainted by trauma and grief, which, as Aleida Assman points out, is only natural:

> When thinking about memory we must start with forgetting. [...] In order to remember some things, others must be forgotten. Our memory is highly selective. Memory capacity is limited by neural and cultural constraints such as focus and bias. It is also limited by psychological pressures, with the effect that painful or incongruent memories are hidden, displaced, overwritten, and possibly effaced. (Assmann 2010: 97)

When Eva's individual and fallible memory of the events that led to Kevin's shooting to the societal dynamics of remembering in the school shooting is transferred to the school shooting discourse, it can be seen that the novel has the potential to critically reflects on the dynamics of cultural memory. Simultaneously, the novel conveys knowledge about these events by presenting a fictional but highly realistic school shooting and by referring to well-known extratextual shootings. Of course, this is not a unique trait of Shriver's novel, because, as Astrid Erll and Ansgar Nünning stress, "[l]iterary texts are characterized by their references to other version of the past and concepts of memory of other symbol systems [...] and by their ability to illustrate cultural knowledge with specific literary means [...]" (2006: 23).[30] The particular relevance of novels for cultural memory and, therefore, for the school shooting discourse has also been stressed by Birgit Neumann, who states that

> on the textual level, novels create new models of memory. They configure memory representations because they select and edit elements of culturally given discourse: They combine the real and the imaginary, the remembered and the forgotten, and, by means of narrative devices, imaginatively explore the workings of memory, thus offering new perspectives on the past. Such imaginative explorations can influence readers' understanding of the past and thus refigure culturally prevailing versions of memory. Literature is therefore never a simple reflection of pre-existing cultural discourses; it proactively contributes to the negotiation of cultural memory. (Neumann 2010: 334f.)

When understood as a proactive cultural force, novels such as *We Need to Talk about Kevin* can well be regarded as actively shaping and molding 'memory-in-

---

30 Contrary to Aleida Assmann's notion of 'cultural texts' that refer to canonized texts that are ascribed with a somewhat universal cultural meaning (such as the Holy Bible, cf. Assmann 1995), I agree with the notion that popular literature, too (if not *especially*), contributes to cultural memory by transmitting and distributing cultural knowledge, an understanding of history as well as values and culturally accepted norms (cf. Erll/Nünning 2006: 24) and actively models and configure cultural understandings and negotiations. As explicated in Chapter 3, it can be argued that, besides canonization, best-seller lists, frequent reviews in newspapers and the Internet and forms of institutionalization such as frequent use in syllabi or the use of quotes in everyday language can be strong indicators of the cultural relevance of a novel or film (cf. Erll 2002: 247f.).

6.1 Inexplicability, Insolvability and Social Taboos — 295

the-making' by rearranging preexisting and prevalent narratives. In Shriver's novel, especially, the frequent reference to extratextual school shootings can serve an important extratextual function: novels historize and distribute knowledge in ways that also allow them to comment on culturally prevalent strategies of meaning-making, thus enabling them to become active and productive elements of the school shooting discourse.

The predominance of extratextual discourse within the novel is underlined by the particular timeframe in which the story takes place: Eva's letters are written between November 2000 and April 2001, ending almost two years after the Columbine shooting, and also cover Kevin's youth in the 1990's. The novel is, therefore, set precisely during the period in which the "miniepidemic"" (Newman/Fox 2009: 1286) of school shootings shocked the United States. Consequently, school shootings run like a terrifying common thread throughout Eva's account of her life and help to organize her narrative, while other major political events are only mentioned in passing. Events such as Bill Clinton's affair with Monica Lewinsky, the political situation in the Baltics and the recount in Florida during the election of George W. Bush only serve to underline how motherhood and life in a nuclear family make the narrator *feel* isolated at first, and how Kevin's school shooting later actively isolates her from the rest of the world. Major political events merely serve to provide context and historicize the school shootings that are referred to in the novel and, consequently, Kevin's own contemporary act of violence. This strategy makes yet another aspect of school shootings tangible, as it forces the reader to experience how traumatic experience causes events to be weighed differently. Whereas political debates are no longer of any greater interest to Eva, other shootings at high schools throughout America have gained a new relevance and manage to actually arouse her interest in the world around her. While reading, the readers of the novel only gradually realize how the narrative makes them skip over other historical and contextual information, while they read extensively about the chronology of school shootings in America: "My God, there's been another one", Eva writes in her letter on March 8, 2001, three days after fifteen-year-old Charles Williams "a scrawny, unassuming-looking white kid", as she describes him, shot two students and injured thirteen (*Kevin:* 335). She comments: "I should have known on Monday afternoon when all my coworkers suddenly started to avoid me" (*Kevin:* 335). When she refers to school shootings that happen in the present of the novel Eva is shocked – not primarily because "it" happens again, but for the egocentric reason that the shooting reminds her of her own fate. As a reaction, she almost obsessively memorizes all the victim's names (cf. *Kevin:* 336) and harshly comments on the public's focus on the perpetrators and the desire for easy explanations to what happened. In contrast to her comments about school shootings before Kevin's deed, her hostility towards other school shooters is presented as a coping mechanism. Before Kevin's shooting, she recalls, the topic of school shootings made her angry about the young shooter's alleged reasons and motives:[31]

> I did feel a concentrated dislike for those boys, who couldn't submit to the odd faithless girlfriend, needling classmate, or dose of working-single-parent distraction – who couldn't serve their miserable time in their miserable public school the way the rest of us did – without carving their dime-a-dozen problems ineluctably into the lives of other families. (*Kevin:* 305)

Her recollections of her reactions to the school shootings in the late 1990's are narrated in a bitter and extremely cynical tone: "That nearsighted Woodham creature", as she refers to the murderer of two students and his own mother, was "staging a tantrum with his father's deer rifle" (*Kevin:* 305). Michael Carneal, who murdered three and injured five members of a prayer group at his school in Heath, was "overweight, teased [and] wallowing in his tiny suffering like trying to take a bath in a puddle" (*Kevin:* 305). Eva's angry disdain for the school shooters contributes to her characterization as a rather cold person and highlights the difference between her and her husband and, in hindsight, their differing approaches to their son. In their heated debate about school shootings following the school shooting of "two unpleasant little boys" (*Kevin:* 364), namely eleven-year-old Andrew Golden and thirteen-year-old Mitchell Johnson, who killed five people and injured ten more in Jonesboro, Franklin reacts to Eva's outburst with a plea for empathy (cf. *Kevin:* 370). Where Franklin firmly believes in the good nature of the school shooters – like he believes in Kevin's good nature – Eva assumes the worst.

This debate between husband and wife is a highly condensed version of the public debate about school shootings, made all the more explosive because one participant in the discussion turns out to be a school shooter himself. Because the reader only has access to Eva's recollection of the debate and therefore has the 'benefit' of hindsight, more interpretative authority is easily attributed to her stance than to Franklin's. Kevin's actions, the novel suggests, prove Eva right. But she does not only claim to be the expert on Kevin's personality, she also presents herself as an expert on school shootings in general. Eva's letters offer the reader a history of the most infamous school shootings in America, reflecting, at the same time, on the motives and discursive dynamics at play. When she refers to extratextual school shootings, Eva closely adheres to the classic

---

31 When she thinks about her naïve, misinformed and judgmental rants, Eva even recalls having blamed Luke Woodham's mother for his school shooting in Pearl (cf. *Kevin:* 304).

narrative of school shootings, presenting the reader with thorough lists of dates, names, casualty figures, and first assumptions or publically and medially accepted versions of the shooter's motives.

By positioning itself in a tradition of extratextual school shooting narratives, *We Need to Talk About Kevin* potentially exerts three important extratextual functions: It reflects on the dynamics of public discourse and the reader's role within this discourse, it embeds the fictional events in extratextual discourse and it transmits knowledge about school shootings. That the extensive commentary on extratextual school shootings functions as an archive of the contemporary phenomenon and its public perception is rather obvious. The reflection and commentary on the discursive dynamics, as well as engaging the reader in the debate by the means of unreliable narration, however, can be understood as the most important potential function of the novel. In the remembering and rearrangement of the narrative of school shootings, the novel illustrates individual and societal attempts to reintegrate school shootings into the social narrative of trust and stability. In this regard, Eva's struggle to reintegrate Kevin's actions into her own life-story and position in with regard to societal dynamics can be seen as a reflection on public and media attempts to represent school shootings as comprehensible and logical events.

Eva's retrospective analysis of the genesis of a school shooting can thus be seen as a micro-version of the societal process of meaning-making, of 'grasping together' elements (Ricœur 1984:54) and understanding all events prior to the school shooting as inevitably contributing to its end. The reader can thus experience the discursive dynamics of creating causality and attempting to re-integrate the crime into social normalcy during the act of reading. Eva's unreliability, however, can gradually prompt the reader to realize the constructedness of the school shooting narrative and confronts them with an individual decision about 'what to believe': Either the child must have been monstrous, or the home must have been broken, *We Need to Talk About Kevin* suggests. The reader has to decide about Eva's reliability and, consequently, her culpability. By being forced to make this decision, the reader can therefore feel confronted with her or his position in the extratextual school shooting discourse. In the aftermath of actual school shootings, too, she or he has to decide whose side or version of the school shooting narrative to believe.

Different versions of this narrative exist, and the shooter's own perspective is seldom voiced. The readers are thus left to their own devices to understand and position themselves between Eva's account and her representation of Franklin's understanding – two contrasting positions that represent opposing sides of the school shooting debate. Another function of the extensive commentary on other school shootings is the transmission of knowledge: No matter how biased the narrator's comments about and rendering of the extratextual events may be, they can be understood as an archive of this contemporary phenomenon and its public perception. The last important function, discussed in the following pages, is the critical, aesthetically constructed reflection on the act of remembering and the dynamics of the public perception of school shootings, which manifests itself most strongly in the debate about motives.

"I wreck, therefore I am" – Explanations, Reasons and Motives in *We Need to Talk About Kevin*

As with most school shooting novels, *We Need to Talk About Kevin* raises the question of why Kevin did what he did and what circumstances may have contributed to the final act. As I have argued in the previous subchapter, the question of the parent's responsibility is explored most extensively in this novel. However, Shriver's novel also thematizes a multitude of other possible reasons, consisting of prevalent types of explanations for school shootings in general and for Kevin's actions specifically. As observed earlier, the way that these motives are represented changes throughout the novel, while the narrator's perspective on school shootings that happened before *Thursday* is presented in a cynical and spiteful tone that makes the readers cringe. After Kevin's shooting, however, Eva's perspective changes completely: Instead of analyzing the shooter's possible motives, she observes the reactions following school shootings. In this way, the reader witnesses and, due to the close proximity of narrator and reader, experiences a change in perspective. In terms of the novel's function as knowledge distributer and archive, the perspective and unreliability of the narrator are of great importance when analyzing how *We Need to Talk About Kevin* reflects upon prevalent modes of explanation – no matter if this explanation originates with Eva herself, draws upon Kevin's own statement before or after the sheeting or is offered up by the media or legal commentators. Especially with regard to the discourse-defining quest for answers, the narrative situation and narrative techniques reveal the functional potential of Shriver's novel to challenge predominant discursive dynamics.

As the mother of a school shooter, Eva has experienced the chaos and confusion after such an act of unrestrained violence. She has been subject to blame and guilt and had to answer question from the judge and the public about Kevin's motives. This, of course, provides new fodder for her own search for redemption and struggle with guilt and responsibility; accepting motives for what Kevin did that are outside of herself would cast doubt on her position as an interpretative authority about Kevin's life and character. It is vital for Eva that she has understood Kevin, that she has seen the real and true version of her son, as opposed to Franklin's perspective, which is presented as distorted by misplaced fatherly emotions. Eva thus needs remain the authority on her son's actions and dismisses all questions by lawyers or journalists as trivial or misplaced. Even Kevin's own attempts at explanation on television are rejected by his mother. Only when he claims that he simply "jumped into the screen", transforming from "watch*er* to watch*ee*" (*Kevin*: 417), does Eva, despite dismissing it as a carefully constructed motive to impress the media, admit to some more general truth behind it. While the novel debates and eventually dismisses almost all motives and explanations – bullying (Kevin was the bully rather than having been bullied), jealousy and heartaches ("Hump'em and dump'em", Kevin casually comments when topic is raised; *Kevin*: 365), severe depression (taking Prozac was a scam, if one chooses to believe Eva), gun control issues (Kevin chose a crossbow), insufficient prevention (all common prevention methods had been installed at Kevin's high school) and parental abuse – Kevin's meta-comment about media consumption is used to reflect on the very dynamics of the discourse. Eva argues alongside Kevin that the attention that the "wayward 1 percent" (*Kevin*: 417) gain from scholars, the media, filmmakers and the government seems out of proportion. In this way, the novel reflects on the sensationalism, modes of reciprocity and particularities of the discourse as described in the third chapter of the present volume.

> 'They're also imitative boys. Think they didn't hear about Bethel, Pearl, and Paducah? Kids pick up things on TV, they listen to their parents talking. Mark my words, every well-armed temper-tantrum that goes down only increases the likelihood of more. This whole country's lost, everybody copies everybody else, and everybody wants to be famous. In the long term, the only hope is that these shootings get so ordinary that they're not news anymore. (*Kevin*: 370)

This comment, however, does not provide the readers with any definitive idea about Kevin's motives, because the only possible reason, the reader is led to believe, could have been his nature or his mother. Even though Eva, by pointing out Kevin's allegedly devious nature, tries to reject the blame, her analysis of his actions seems to put her in the center of Kevin's past and present life. This notion is emphasized by Kevin himself when he comments on why he left his mother alive, stating callously, "When you're putting on a show, you don't shoot the audience" (*Kevin*: 460).

Eva's claim to interpretative authority regarding Kevin's actions and her dismissal of most of the prevalent explanations and more widely discussed motives foregrounds the ethical and discursive implications of the unreliable narration in the novel. When it comes to the explanations for Kevin's actions, the reader is not only made to decide whether they think the narrator is reliable or not; they also must confront whether the motives for school shootings are believably psychosocial and sociodynamic in origin and can thus be explained sufficiently, or not.

In this respect, the guilt-ridden mother is an interesting change of perspective for the reader to explore a rather common problem that occurs after school shootings: None of the explanations actually fit the course of the events, and no motives seem to check out. Most common modes of explanations and possible motives (see Chapter 2) are at least mentioned in the novel's description of Eva's struggle to understand her son's actions. But the references to extratextual school shootings also serve a potential function besides providing context for Kevin's school shooting: As Kevin's deed is compared and understood as related to previous school shootings and Eva's interpretation of the events is clearly influenced by observations made after following shootings, the motives and explanations mentioned with regard to his shooting automatically refer to school shootings in the reference world.

That *We Need to Talk About Kevin* does not present the reader with answers to the question of why he did what he did can be understood as one of the novel's most valuable qualities. Instead, the desire to understand his actions is embedded in the rather futile, but ever-present attempt to explain school shootings. All are bound to fail because of Kevin's opaque nature and because the narrative structure of the novel does not allow further insight into the events that led up to the shooting. Naturally, Eva's assessment of Kevin's personality does not work in his favor, and so she ascribes to him an essentially nihilistic attitude that helps her to reintegrate his actions into his personality: "I wreck, therefore I am. [...] And there's an ownership to destruction, an intimacy; an appropriation. [...] Destruction may be motivated by nothing more complicated than acquisitiveness, a kind of ham-handed, misguided greed" (Kevin: 293).

For readers who have detected issues with and made judgments about the narrator's reliability, these evaluations will remain unrewarding and leave them with the feeling that, despite the meticulous dissection of Kevin's personality and uncanny characteristics, they have not understood why he did what he did. Instead, the readers have born witness to the childhood and adolescence of a boy who may have been neglected by his callous mother, but who had a loving father and sister and relatively stable surroundings, and nevertheless became a mass murderer. What motivated him to do so, as with most of the school shooters in the extratextual world, remains hazy – as the novel suggests, even to Kevin himself. Instead of providing answers, the novel's ambiguous characters and unreliable narrative raises more questions. Lionel Shriver's novel reflects on the school shooting discourse and tackles the nature vs. nurture discussion in a way that almost violently confronts questions of culpability and the lack of explicability surrounding school shootings. Lynne Ramsay's adaptation, as the next pages will show, presents a bold and controversial interpretation of the ambiguity cultivated in the novel's unreliability.

6.2 Modes of Interpretation in Lynne Ramsay's Adaptation of *We Need to Talk About Kevin*

When Scottish director Lynne Ramsay decided to make a film adaptation of Shriver's novel roughly six years after it had become a best-seller, school shootings had not lost any of their topicality. With Shriver's novel being such a success, a film version clearly had commercial appeal. However, adapting a novel with narrative particularities such unreliable narration and a high degree of subjectivity, and which thematizes the polarizing subject of school shootings in combination with the nature vs. nurture motif, can be regarded as a challenge for filmic adaptation. As most bestselling novels are adapted in into films sooner or later, it is not surprising that Ramsay chose to make a film out of the book, despite its unreliable epistolary form. Looking at the specific functions of an adaptation of a school shooting novel will serve here to broaden the understanding of the importance of narrative techniques in fictional representations of school shootings.

Adaptation is by no means a new phenomenon and can be observed across all media: Novels are adapted into feature films, operas into plays, poems into music lyrics, films into videogames or videogames into films, and films into TV series. The adapters behind these works "relate stories in their different ways. They use the same tools that storytellers have always used: they actualize or concretize ideas; they make simplifying selections, but also amplify and extrapolate; they make analogies; they criticize or show their respect and so on" (Hutcheon 2006: 3). When analyzing Ramsay's adaptation of Shriver's novel, it is therefore important to point out that adaptations are "aesthetic objects in their own right" (Hutcheon 2006: 6) and that they should be treated as such rather than only evaluated and analyzed with respect to their fidelity to the original text. But adaptations are also "inherently 'palimpsestuous' works, haunted at all times by their adapted texts", which constantly shadow their reception (Hutcheon 2006: 6), and they are always interpretations of the original text. Even though I will not judge the film only in relation to the original text, analyzing the filmic interpretation in relation to Shriver's novel is a way of exploring the work's specific functions in the school shooting discourse, as will be shown in the next two subchapters.

6.2.1 Adaptation as Product and Interpretation

In the first scene, there is the image of a white curtain blowing in the wind in front of an open door, transporting white light into a dark room, accompanied by the rhythmic sound of a garden sprinkler as the camera slowly moves towards the curtain, fading into white. While the sound becomes indistinct screams, the audience is confronted with the aesthetic leitmotifs of Ramsay's film: the color red, with all its obvious associations with blood and violence, which is used excessively in the film. In the first red scene, it comes in the form of a slimy mass that covers a crowd of half-naked, ecstatically heaving bodies. As the camera slowly descends towards the crowd from a bird's eyes angle in a long shot, the previously confusing, indistinct image becomes clearer: The people are not panicking but enjoying themselves, splashing around and rubbing themselves in squashed tomatoes at the annual *La Tomatina* festival in Spain. Amongst these half-naked characters is Eva (played by Tilda Swinton), who is crowd surfing; another bird's eye shot focuses on her ecstatic face, covered in red. This is the first of a series of recurring images: Eva's face will be covered in red again when another shade of red is thrown at her tiny duplex house in the form of crimson paint. What was once connected to joy and freedom now stands for the protagonist's fight against this predominant color. Again and again, the impossible ordeal of scrubbing the paint off the walls and windows of her house, her car, her hands and her face is shown in great detail. The overtly symbolic process of scrubbing the color of blood out of her life serves as a chronologically structuring element throughout Eva's present, while the past is shown in flashbacks that are dominated by much lighter and cooler colors.

To understand Ramsay's adaptation as a product in Hutcheon's sense, as the translation or 'transcoding' of the novel's aesthetic and thematic code into a cinematic, aural and visual code, media-specific techniques such as lighting, colors, editing montages and sound are all important. The overarching question here is how the highly subjective homodiegetic narration of Eva is transposed from the telling to the showing mode: What exactly has been adapted? Eva, as it already becomes clear in the opening scene at the *La Tomatina* festival, is at the center of the narrative. No matter how desolate and cadaverous Eva is depicted after the school shooting, she is in control of what is said and what is left out. As the adaptation of homodiegetic narration is one of greater challenges to cinema (cf. Griem/Voigts-Virchow 2002: 171ff.), it is interesting to consider the way in which the subjectiveness of Eva's account is transmitted by cinematic means.³² The adaptation, in Hutcheon's words, is always "haunted by the original text" (2006:6). The protagonist's intense subjectiveness is one of the novel's most noteworthy narrative features and is also connected to the unreliability of the narrative; a filmic adaptation would not really be an adaptation without it. If filmic adaptations approach subjectivity in a way that is substantially different than the novels on which they are based, this has consequences for the process of reception and the extratextual functions of the work

Eva is the focalizer in Ramsay's film, and as such is neither a mere object nor the narrator of the story, but rather serves as the source of the experiences featured in the film (cf. Griem/Voigts-Virchow 2002: 169). Even though the focalizer's feelings, experiences and thoughts are what is depicted or transmitted in the film, they can be presented with various degrees of subjectivity. Of course, films have a whole range of ways to represent subjectivity, and "superimposition, titles, slow motion, spinning images, intercuts, lighting, or color" are only the most common techniques (Thon 2014: 90). Thon delineates different degrees of subjectivity, which vary with regard to their intersubjective validity: While a classic spatial point of view sequence can be regarded to be intersubjectively valid and has the lowest degree of subjectivity, the so called "(quasi-) perceptual point of view-sequence", which is created mostly with postproduction effects, such as filters or soft focus, represents "subjective aspects of his or her perception and/or consciousness, resulting in a representation that can often not be considered intersubjectively valid anymore" (Thon 2014: 73).³³ Both categories can be found in *We Need to Talk About Kevin*. The spatial point of view sequences, for example, are frequently used and underline the feeling of subjectiveness in the sequences in which Eva and Kevin engage in direct verbal or non-verbal communication. The sequences in which the audience sees Kevin and perceives his actions 'through Eva's eyes' are of particular relevance here.

Only about 15 minutes into the film, Eva visits Kevin in prison. At that point, the audience has already gathered that something terrible must have happened, because they have seen various incidents in which Eva was abused verbally and

---

32 As an example, the authors choose Robert Montgomery's 1946 adaptation of Chandler's novel *The Lady in the Lake*. The film is widely considered a failure in the attempt to depict homodiegetic narration, since the camera takes the point of view of Robert Marlowe, the protagonist, and makes the audience see the whole story – brawls and kissing included – from his exact perspective. This cinematic attempt seems to have taken the visual metaphor for point of view too literally, and can therefore be understood as having failed in the process of transcoding from one sign system to another in Hutcheon's sense (cf. Griem/Voigts-Virchow, 171).
33 Thon develops two more categories that involve techniques of overlay and representations of internal worlds, which constitute the highest degrees of subjectivity (cf. 2014: 75).

physically – she has already been confronted with the paint-attack on her house and has been slapped in the face by a woman on the street – but it is not yet clear what exactly. While the novel discloses Kevin's crime at the very beginning, Ramsay's adaptation does not reveal the school shooting until the end of the film. The director uses temporal rearrangements in the form of flashbacks. Eva's present is depicted chronologically, with a clear movement forward that is clearly organized by the scenes in which Eva scrubs off the paint from her house. The flashbacks, however, are arranged more erratically and only slowly reveal a course of events by means of repetition and other temporal markers, and take on approximately the same temporal order seen in Shriver's novel. Eva's clearly desolate mental state, Kevin's imprisonment and the use of indistinct screams in several scenes convey the sense of a fatal and tragic outcome. The exact outcome, however, is only revealed gradually in Eva's flashbacks.[34]

The first scene in which Kevin appears directly introduces the mise-en-scène. Eva, who is most frequently presented in frontal mid-shots and close-ups throughout the film, sits in the visiting room in a prison, staring. The door behind her is opened and a boy, who is yet unknown to the audience, walks in and passes Eva, who remains in the focus of the image. Then, Eva's stare turns into a disgusted look; an extreme close-up of Kevin's mouth (here played by Ezra Miller) is the next shot, showing him biting his nails and meticulously spitting out his fingernails, which he then positions on the table in front of Eva. The recipient has not seen much of Kevin yet – their encounter ends without another shot of him – but has already seen him from Eva's perspective. As she is in the center of the image and her facial expression is 'explained' by the following shot, the audience has already formed an opinion about Kevin through Eva's eyes, and she gains (at least some of) the audience's empathy. Two other remarkable spatial point of view sequences that serve the same purpose can be seen when Eva tries to play ball with Kevin (here: Rock Duer), who just glares at her and refuses to roll the ball back to his tense mother even once, stopping again as soon as he sees the happiness about his reaction in her face. Later, Eva walks in on a pubescent Kevin while he is masturbating and, instead of stopping, he stares at her and, consequently, at the recipient. The effect is disturbing, and makes the audience feel for the mother these actions are perceived through.

---

[34] An effect that resembles the flash-forwards to the fatal outcome of the story, which is used in some kinds of tragic melodrama, as Grodal points out: "Some types of tragic melodrama will use flash-forward at the beginning of the film to prepare viewers for the tragic outcome, to direct their curiosity to how- (as opposed to why-) questions and to recreate the sense of an inevitable and fatal undertow." (Grodal 2008: 171).

While the extremely high degree of subjectivity of Shriver's epistolary form is not achieved in these sequences, they serve to create empathy for this strange, suffering woman. While Eva clearly is the protagonist of the film, it gradually becomes obvious that her life and life-story revolve around Kevin. He has become the center of her attention, even if it is in the form of suspicion and contempt. Eva's perception of Kevin as dubious and uncanny is further stressed by (quasi-)perceptual point of view shots. In this respect, one of the most noteworthy sequences is set on the streets in front of her house on Halloween: The trick-or-treaters are presented as monstrous creatures that dance manically and wander through nightmarishly surreal streets covered in red light. Their joyous demeanor seems threatening, their laughter turns into screams and their harmless scares seem like vicious attacks. All the while, Buddy Holly's *Everyday* is playing, creating a rather eerie discrepancy between the sounds and the look of terror on Eva's face. In this sequence, the color, the lighting and the focus make Eva's subjectiveness and altered perception of the world around her tangible. However, as scenes like these do not appear often in the film, the markers of subjectivity remain rather subtle. As with Eva's reliability in the novel, whether the film presents a subjective account or is a matter of fact representation of the genesis and aftermath of a school shooting ultimately remains up to the viewer (cf. Griems/Voigts-Virchow 2001: 170). This decision is crucial, however, to film's potential extratextual function and its contribution the school shooting discourse. If the audience believes the film's representation to be true and trustworthy, the film suggests that the school shooter is indeed a monster and thus actively engages in the discursive practices of 'othering' and dehumanizing the perpetrator.

As adaptation, Ramsay's film transcodes various aspects of the original text into the sign system of films: The temporal rearrangement as well as the subjectivity and the empathy cultivated by the novel for its disturbingly desolate yet ambivalent and difficult protagonist are present in the film as well. The unreliable narration of the protagonist, however, is much more complicated to transcode into film.[35] While unreliability in the novel is marked rather clearly by the extremely subjective and limited viewpoint of the main protagonist, film often gives the impression of objectivity, because it predominantly focalizes externally;

---

[35] "Though there are filmic devices to give a scene the appearance of unreliability or deception, the 'visual narrator' in film cannot tell a downright lie that is visualized at the very same moment unless the veracity of the photographic image is put into question [...]", Kuhn and Schmidt write (2014: 395). However, a film can use various strategies of misreporting and underreporting or use a number of forms of "irritating, ambivalent or misleading editing" (ibid.: 396) or complex flashback structures that create tension between verbal and visual narration. For a concise overview of unreliable film narration, see Koch (2011).

more subjective cues are easily overlooked by viewers (cf. Deleyto 1996: 224f.). With flashbacks often presented as collages that are mostly connected to Eva lying in bed or to a close-up of her face that signals her state of recollection, Ramsay's film takes a clearly subjective approach to representation. Nevertheless, the film presents an interpretation of the original text that is directly connected to the film's position and role in the school shooting discourse. This position, as with the original text, cannot be separated from the question of whether Eva's account is reliable or not. Shriver's novel, as established earlier, draws much of its discursive relevance from the unreliable narration and the reader being forced to confront the reason for the school shooting, culminating in the question of whether Eva was a bad mother or whether Kevin was a monstrous son.

The depiction of Kevin as an evil child with demonic traits might be seen as a false trail laid for the viewer, borrowed from the genre of horror film, and as a signal that Eva's subjective perception of her son is being shown rather than an objective portrait of the boy. I would argue, however, that the monstrous or demonic character traits and features are actually the predominant mode of depiction and that they are not signaled by techniques of subjectivization like other memories of Eva are. This interpretation, as evident in the adaptation's focus on the two main character's psychological development and growing antagonism, clearly leans towards a biologism that harks back to the genre of horror film more than simply a melodramatic representation of the decay of a happy family. A sense of predetermined fate is conveyed from the very beginning of the film – for example in the passionate love scene in which Eva conceives Kevin. This follows a night out of ecstatic dancing in the rainy streets of New York, a scene emblematic of free and joyous life, and Franklin's barely audible "I wish you'll never go away again". Then, after a close-up of Eva's rather unhappy face, a time lapse of in vitro conception follows.

Ramsay does not leave out the struggle with pregnancy, childbirth and the adjustment to life as a mother. Eva's memories of her pregnancy in particular are clearly marked as subjective, for example when an extreme close-up shot of her eyes while she is standing at the copying machine at her miserable new workplace is followed by the memory of her decision to have a child. Her unhappiness during pregnancy is later depicted in a scene in which she seems lost, fully clothed in a dressing room full of half-naked women happily showing off their pregnant bellies. During childbirth, a sequence that revealingly blends in with Eva's first visit to prison, the recipient only hears her screams and see her pain-struck face through a distorted camera shot, while Eva is told to "stop resisting". After this scene, she looks exhausted and lost, while her baby screams constantly. Even though these scenes might be well known to many mothers, her distanced and frequently abusive behavior towards her son, whom she positions next to a jack hammer so as to not listen to him scream, do not only signal her difficulties but also emphasize the abnormality of her situation. While scenes clearly suggest that Eva must have been extremely callous towards her child from the day of his conception, the abnormality is further stressed by Kevin's representation as a cunning, mean and sometimes even demonic boy. All three actors that play Kevin through childhood and adolescence master a piercing stare and an evil-looking smile that is frequently used when the film suggests that Kevin does something only to torment his mother – for example when he still refuses to be potty-trained at the age of seven.

The filmic interpretation of Eva's unreliability is also highlighted by Franklin's character in the film (played by John C. Reilly). Franklin, the good-hearted, loving father, who is continually pushed away by his wife's hostile behavior, is presented as clueless and naïve. His frequent absence further makes him an outsider in the story of Eva and Kevin, which further emphasizes the deep, yet antagonistic bond between mother and son – an effect the film achieves visually by having Eva and Kevin sometimes melt into one person with blending techniques, for example when Eva washes her face. In this respect, the film is quite faithful to the novel; Shriver's novel also highlights a bond between mother and son that leads the reader to develop greater sympathy for Eva's account, not matter how unbelievable her version of the supposedly evil child sounds. But while the readers of the novel are torn between the unspeakable notion of a monstrous child and the idea that a mother is solely responsibility for her child's actions, the film is much more suggestive, representing Kevin as uncanny and cold. Whereas at the end of the novel Eva's unreliability simply confronts the readers with their own inability to fully understand what led to the school shooting and thus has the potential to divert the readers' attention to the inexplicability of schools shootings in general, Ramsay's adaptation focuses on the protagonist's psychological development: Eva's symbolical process of scrubbing paint off her house and getting her life back in order, her coming to terms with the past and Kevin's development. Thus, the viewer of the film is less engaged in the process of making meaning out of the inexplicable and is confronted much less with the cruelty of condemning a child from early childhood on. In this regard, while the film may be unsettling in its depiction of a 'monstrous' school shooter, as the next pages will show, the adaptation as process and interpretation (cf. Hutcheon 2006) presents the audience with a much clearer resolution of the inexplicability of school shootings by 'othering' the school shooter in the most extreme way, offering a causal narrative that leaves little room for ambiguity or the audience's own interpretation.

6.2.2 Representations of the 'Bad Mother' and the 'Monstrous Child'

As the film at least partially ascribes to conventions of the horror genre in its depiction of Kevin, the possibility of him being intrinsically evil is raised rather bluntly. His monstrosity is suggested not only by his behavior towards his mother, but by his empty stares and smug smiles whenever something terrible happens to somebody.

The image that the film creates of Kevin as a monstrous child is underlined by close-up shots of Kevin's mouth while he is eating – in these scenes, the detailed depiction of devouring make the boy appear alarmingly disgusting. For example, in a scene in which Kevin slowly eats a Lychee while Celia's eye prosthesis, which is being discussed by his parents, is depicted at great lengths, a link between Kevin and the monster that devours other humans is openly suggested. As in the scene in the novel, the "emphasis is on the mouth, a central element which is in keeping with the image of the monster in general: the monster devours, ingests, regurgitates and mutilates" (Latham 2009: 145). Kevin as a monster appears like a character from a horror film, an association that is further underlined by the reliance on a filmic tradition described by Sara Arnold in *Maternal Horror Film*. In the book, Arnold uses the categories of the 'Good Mother' and her opposite, the 'Bad Mother', as introduced by E. Ann Kaplan, "indicators of how maternal representation functions within Western patriarchal culture" (Arnold 2013: 182). Arnold frequently identifies an antagonistic mother-son relationship at the center of horror films but also points out that the genres of horror and melodrama frequently appear to intersect in the representation of the mother (ibid.: 4): While the 'Good Mother' is a figure that belongs to the genre of the melodrama, the 'Bad Mother' is a figure of the genre traditions of the horror film. Analyzing *We Need to Talk About Kevin* with the genres of melodrama and horror in mind is especially fruitful for understanding adaptation as a process of interpretation and the effects that choices of genre can have on the process of reception.

Even though Eva's struggle with her life as a mother is not depicted as exhaustively as it is in the novel, the film clearly shows what she had to give up for her son. When Eva lies in bed, she hears Franklin say "When are you coming home? I miss you", followed by images of her at *La Tomatina* in Spain, tomatoes in her hair and face, looking confused as she seems to react to Franklin's voice. This scene is followed by the montage of her and Franklin dancing in the streets and later the conception of Kevin, clearly drawing a connection between her reaction to her husband's wishes and the decision to have a child; here, too, Eva's dependency on Franklin is underlined. *We Need to Talk About Kevin* overly exaggerates the trope of maternal self-sacrifice, as it can be found in various films that thematize mother-child-problematic (cf. Arnold 2013: 22). In the film, Eva's individual development is constrained by the relation to, or, more accurately, the distinction from her son. In one of the first scenes of the film, in which Eva and Kevin are visually blended into one person, the film suggests that she is no longer an individual, that she can only exist in relation to her murderous son and, consequently, to a son whose actions overshadow and ultimately rule her life.

This blending of Eva's and Kevin's characters is highly symbolic of the self-sacrifice that lies at the core of many maternal narratives. And, as in the genres of the maternal melodrama and horror films, this self-sacrifice lays the groundwork for the collision of the two most common key roles of women in fictional narratives, which can be boiled down to the good mother/bad mother binary. On the one hand, the good mother is presented as nurturing and self-abnegating and dissolves in her role as a mother; as a consequence, she usually only plays a marginal role in the narrative. On the other hand, there is the bad mother, who is mean and hurtful and actively refuses the role of the good mother out of egocentric motivation. The bad mother often dominates the narrative with her behavior, but eventually "is punished for her violation of the desired patriarchal ideal, the Good Mother" (Arnold 2013: 23).

Eva Katchadourian's role in both novel and film is clearly that of the bad mother. Even though she does in fact give up her own career for her son, she does so begrudgingly. When she decorates her study in the shockingly empty and impersonal space of the new suburban family home, this symbolizes her longing for her past life as a globetrotting, independent woman. When Kevin sprays paint on the carefully arranged maps on the walls, smiling vindictively, it can either be seen as a symbol of the blame that Eva assigns to her son for changing her life or as emblematic of his deliberate destruction of it.

"Often in film", Arnold points out "the good and bad mother binaries are collapsed on to the one figure; the selfish mother may 'correct' her behavior and ultimately give up her own desire for the child, or the mother may struggle between both positions" (Arnold 2013: 23). And "mothers tend to resist the role of motherhood only to compensate for this resistance through extreme acts of sacrifice and denial of independent desire" (ibid.), and ultimately give up this resistance. While Eva's relationship to her son during his childhood is dominated by her mean and hurtful behavior and her openly displayed anger about her decision to have a child, her relationship with Kevin changes when she actively centers her life around him by visiting him in prison, staying in the town where the shooting happened and enduring the open aggression towards her, and allowing the removal of the crimson paint from the walls of her home to culminate in the refurbishment of a room for Kevin. Consequently, both of Arnold's maternal archetypes apply to Eva, and this has far-reaching implications for the process of interpretation and reception.

First and foremost, Eva is represented as an ambivalent mother. Not only does her demeanor towards Kevin change throughout the film, it encompasses both the stereotypical figures of the good and bad mother in her contrasting behavior towards her two children. As is depicted in the original work, the film shows how Kevin is treated with contempt and hostility, while Celia is admired by her mother. In the film, the relationship between Kevil and Celia constitutes a central aspect. While the book only later reveals that he actually has a sister, one of the very first scenes in the film, set on the morning of the school shooting, shows Kevin interacting with his little sister. By making the children's interactions and differences more central to the narrative, the film suggests that Eva, who is capable of being a good mother, is not at fault. This interpretation is further stressed by Franklin's overstated ignorance towards the struggle that the mother is facing, making viewers more likely to believe Eva's account as presented in her memories. Moreover, her extreme acts of sacrifice are depicted in the novel through her life in the aftermath of the school shooting. Her cadaverous, tired appearance, her living conditions in a run-down house full of empty bottles of wine and pills and her self-flagellating endurance of abuse from the people in her town, hint at a final decision to be a good and selfless mother to her murderous son.

We Need to Talk About Kevin is a melodramatic film that uses the example of an extreme case of violent behavior to depict how the protagonist slowly finds her way out of the misery that her life has turned into without help from anyone. However, while this would present the audience with a melodramatic representation of a school shooter's mother Ramsay's adaptation also uses genre conventions of the (maternal) horror film; the effect is that Kevin's gruesome deed acquires the air of the inevitable, with which Eva is left to cope. Because of this mixing of genre conventions, the adaptation has a different effect on the audience than the novel and consequently assumes a different extratextual function in the school shooting discourse: While the novel leaves the reader confused and forces him or her to make sense of the events, reflecting the unsettling inability to find an explanation in the aftermath of real school shootings, the film's gloomy and horrifying portrayal of Kevin suggests a rather simplistic understanding of what happened. Even though Eva's characterization presents her as ambivalent, the aesthetics of the film clearly contribute to 'othering' Kevin as the monstrous, inhuman school shooter.

In making sense of the film, the usage of sound is of great importance because sound "is one of the most versatile signifiers, since it contributes to field, tenor, and mode as a powerful creator of meaning, mood and textuality"

(Fulton 2005: 108). The usage of extradiegetic sounds in the adaptation shapes the reception and interpretation of the diegetic events by creating moods that are distressing and, at times, highly threatening – for example, when indistinct screams are heard in the background at several points. Another horrifying effect is created by adding the sound of cheerleading to the scenes depicting Kevin's school shooting. Here, the sounds illustrate the inevitable psychological diagnosis of Kevin, suggesting delusions of grandeur and stressing the relevance of fame (see Chapter 3). Additionally, the film's stance on the phenomenon of school shootings becomes especially clear in this combination of image and sound, as it also underlines the performative character of the school shooting as a thoroughly staged offense and represents Kevin as a shooter who craves this attention. This interpretation is further supported by his deep, theatrical bow at the end of the shooting.[36]

In sum, it can be stated that, throughout the film, Kevin is represented as a disturbed and terrifying boy, whose callous and disdainful behavior is inexplicable. Instead, his demeanor is so unnatural that – despite the difficult relationship with his mother – the possibility of his monstrosity is indeed presented as a viable interpretation and is even suggested in the depiction of his character and by certain cinematic conventions of the horror genre. In this respect, the film's stance is clear. Shriver's novel uses narrative techniques that, at the end of the novel, leave the reader none the wiser about the course of events and possible motives, and can thus be understood as a commentary on the discursive dynamics of the school shooting discourse. In stark contrast, Ramsay's adaptation merely hints at the possibility of Eva's unreliability and instead stresses an explanation that the novel undoubtedly offers, but does not present as valid. The ethical dilemma of the novel, the reader's decision about Eva's reliability and the

---

[36] The strategy of contrasting sound and images is in fact employed throughout the entire movie, which has a deeply unsettling effect. Here, especially, the soundtrack in Ramsay's adaptation is noteworthy. When Eva drives to visit Kevin in prison, the flashbacks of her son's shooting are drowned out by Lonnie Donegan's folk-country song *Ham 'n' Eggs*. Even more obvious is a scene in which Washington Philipp's *Mother's Last Words to Her Son* (with which the line "You are leaving, my darling boy, you always have been your mother's joy") plays as the young Kevin shoots a plastic arrow at his mother. Lonnie Donegan's country ballad *Nobody's Child* (with the lyrics "No mother's arms to hold me or soothe me when I cry. Sometimes it gets so lonely here I wish that I could die") contrasts with Eva's last efforts to decorate Kevin's room in her new house, which she is preparing for when he is let out of prison. The contrasting effects of song and image are clearly unsettling and add to the eerie atmosphere of the film, but they might also be seen as a marker of subjectivity and unreliability. I would, however, argue that the portrayal of Kevin as monstrous and devious outweighs these rather subtle signals of unreliability and that the audience is consequently primed to believe Eva's subjective account.

implication that this has for the explanation of the school shooting, is clearly resolved in the film.

The portrayal of Kevin in the film is likely to provoke disgust and horror. The audience is more likely to identify and empathize with Eva, the focal character with stoic endurance that suffers endlessly; her version of events, even though it is presented as subjective, is most likely understood to be true. These effects echo negative dynamics of the school shooting discourse, as the audience is most likely to engage in the usual practices of 'othering' and dehumanizing a school shooter. However, this empathy for the school shooter's mother does more to subvert a discourse in which school shooter's mothers are often blamed and hardly ever heard. As the focalizer, Eva makes it possible for her audience "to become an immersed experiencer, who shares the focalizer's mental processes" (Nünning 2014: 196). As the filmic representation of Eva's life also includes glimpses of her inner life (evident in the acting, but also cinematic techniques of lighting, sound and montage), it invites the viewer to assume the perspective of the shooter's mother (cf. ibid.). Through Eva's suffering and her desperate attempt to rid herself of guilt, as represented by the scrubbing of paint from her house, the empathetic relationship with the protagonist is further encouraged. Kevin, on the other hand, remains enigmatic and taciturn. This is not quite changed by the last scene, where Kevin displays feelings of fear and pain for the first time on the second anniversary of his offense. This, however, might only arouse a moment of sympathy for him. It is not until this scene at the very end of the film that the question of why he did it is raised. After a long stare, Kevin answers his mother's questions simply by saying: "I used to think I knew – now I'm not so sure". The relief in Eva's eyes and the despair in Kevin's face indicate a change in their relationship, which is then emphasized by a long and intense hug between them. Even though Ramsay's adaptation does not go so far as to present the audience with a definitive answer to question to *why* the school shooting happened, the last scene seems to prove that Eva's perception of her monstrous son was accurate.

6.3 Conclusion: Unreliability in the School Shooting Narrative

The brief analysis of the novel's adaptation has been presented here not in order to comment on the limits of the interpretation as presented by Lynne Ramsay – even though these limits have been made clear – but rather to stress the potential function of the original text and the position of the reader in the process of reception. Ramsay's adaptation, in this sense, presents the audience with one possible interpretation of the original text. The novel, as I have pointed out, becomes particularly relevant to the discourse through its bold rejection of the societal taboo of the unloving mother and by fostering a certain degree of sympathy for this ambivalent character, even in the face of an unspeakable crime. This, as it has become clear, cannot be understood as separate from the novel's most interesting feature – its use of unreliable narration in a highly subjective, introspective and frequently self-reflexive account.

In Shiver's novel, the reader is drawn into the abysses of a tortured human mind, while, at the same time, doubts about the degree of candor and the possibility of honesty in the face of this traumatic experience are raised. Despite the unreliability of the narration, *We Need to Talk About Kevin* points toward the extratextual discourse and embeds the diegetic events within greater societal dynamics. Here, the first extratextual function of the novel can be identified: Because the narrative is so bound up with real school shootings within the novel, the act of reading potentially provokes the reader to rethink their reaction to school shootings in the extratextual world. Through its adherence to the epistolary genre and its high degree of subjectivity, Shriver's novel invites the reader to form an empathetic relationship with the ambivalent figure of the mother. However, when her reliability is questioned as her mental state and her underreporting of Franklin's death become clear towards the end of the novel, the reader is prompted to reconsider what they have learned about Kevin and his development. As Eva openly questions her own reliability by commenting on her fallible memory, Kevin's monstrosity becomes an increasingly unlikely possibility. Instead, the reader is confronted with the decision of whom to believe and, eventually, is left with many doubts about the existence of a clear and causal narrative. Even if they believe that Eva has indeed failed as a mother, this alone would not suffice as a valid motive for a school shooting. If this reaction to the narrative of the genesis of a school shooting is then transferred to the extratextual school shooting narrative, the readers of Shriver's novel may be encouraged to questioning the construction of causality and the reductive answers provided to the omnipresent question of 'why?'. Moreover, by presenting a traumatized individual's memory of a school shooting, *We Need to Talk About Kevin* also illustrates the dynamics of the cultural memory of school shootings by frequently relating Eva's process of meaning-making, and of remembering her son's actions and the events that led up to his shooting, to extratextual events. Through genre, narrative technique and the representation of protagonists, the novel thus conveys an emotionally difficult and highly controversial topic to its readers in a way that helps them to understand and critically reflect upon the problems and pitfalls of the school shooting discourse.

The novel's adaptation, on the other hand, does not display these noteworthy qualities to the same extent. As the different media included in this book should already indicate, I do not want to appear 'iconophobic', or suspicious of the visual (cf. Hutcheon 2004: 109). I do, however, aim to emphasize the different possibilities and, consequently, potential functions of the two different media. As Linda Hutcheon puts it, "While no medium is inherently good at doing one thing and not another, each medium (like each genre) has different means of expression and so can aim at certain things better than others" (2004: 109). Ramsay's adaptation fails to present the viewer with a degree of subjectivity that undermines the ability to grasp and order the events. Eva's attempt to construct a congruent and meaningful narrative is hinted at by her memories, which are represented in the form of flashbacks. However, her memories of Kevin lack the degree of subjectivity that would be needed for the audience to critically reflect and question the representation of the child's monstrous demeanor. On the contrary, in some of the scenes that are most significant in terms of Kevin's characterization, spatial point of view shots invite the audience to, quite literally, see Kevin 'through his mother's eyes'. By cinematically underlining the inexplicable bond and similarity between mother and son and by portraying Franklin as a complete outsider, the trustworthiness of Eva's account is bolstered even further. And even though Eva is not an entirely likeable character, the representation of the shooter's mother as a callous woman rather adds to the air of despair and sadness that arouses the audience's sympathy for her. Moreover, as the focalizer of the story, Eva also automatically invites empathy; even though her extreme position differs drastically from those of other mothers, the feelings of maternal regret and struggle with a child to which she cannot relate are likely recognizable emotions for a number of people in the audience. In sum, these aspects of the film lead to a completely different process of reception, as it does not foster as many divergent readings as the novel. Furthermore, since it focuses solely on Eva's individual struggle with her son and later with her son's actions in the aftermath of the school shooting, it does not offer any meta-discursive commentary or reflection and thus remains firmly in the filmic world rather than anchoring itself in the extratextual world of school shootings as the novel does. The novel, in conclusion, has far-reaching extratextual functions, while the film as adaptation presents the audience with just one possible interpretation and limits the ability of the fictional school shooting to influence the audience's engagement in extratextual discourse.

7 Conclusion

While school shootings, as I have stressed time and again, remain an extremely rare phenomenon their presence in popular culture continues to evoke a different impression – not only because of the massive media attention they receive, but also because fictionalizations constantly provide new elements for the cultural imaginary.

Not too long before the 'March for Our Lives' emerged as a reaction to the Marjory Stoneman Douglas High School shooting in 2018, Josh Madden's political thriller *Miss Sloane* (USA 2016) about a gun control lobbyist premiered in the United States. While it is not a school shooting film according to the definition used in this book – a school shooting is not the story's main event – it is a good example of the presence of school shootings in the cultural memory. In telling the story of a lobbyist (Jessica Chastain) who advocates for stricter gun control laws, *Miss Sloane* makes various references to Columbine and other real and fictional school shootings, highlighting how the gun debate is inextricably linked to the fear of mass shootings and, especially, school shootings. *Miss Sloane* thus illustrates how fictional artifacts are important elements in the construction of the school shooting discourse: even though the film acknowledges that school shootings and other incidents of rampage violence are not the most pressing gun control issue, Sloane herself states that her opinion about gun control was formed sometime "between Columbine and Charleston" and blatantly tells her colleague's personal and secret story of surviving a fictional school shooting in the late 1990s. The film depicts school shootings as a highly pressing and topical element of political and media discourse, and illustrates how the public fear of school shootings is used to push political agendas.

"I don't want to live in a society where there's a new school shooting every week", a senator states at a campaign rally in *Miss Sloane*, and a talk-show host starts a gun control debate by claiming that "there were 372 mass shootings last year, and 64 school shootings". As I have argued in this book, these truly astronomical numbers both illustrate and potentially contribute to the public perception of school shootings as a constant threat. But they are also the result of processes of discourse formation, of the 'case-definition-problem' that I described in Chapter 2 and of what has been called the 'Rashomon-effect': what is defined as a school shooting depends on the researcher's or journalist's perspective, intent and aim. Numbers like the ones used in the film are therefore not strictly fictitious, but are merely the result of vague definitions and frequently found in the real world.

Extremely high numbers emerge when gun control activists and organizations, such as *everytownresearch.org*, include cases like that of an unidentified man who fired a gun into the air on a campus parking lot in their school shooting statistics.[1] Despite their best intentions, by using an extremely wide definition of school shootings, gun control lobbyists actively contribute to the construction of a discourse of emergency. By using, further exaggerating and effectively disseminating these numbers, *Miss Sloane* lays open the fear that propels the dynamics of the school shooting discourse and simultaneously shows how this perception can be reinforced by fictional works. Because of the relevance of fiction to the process of discourse formation and due to the continuous presence of school shootings in popular culture, fictionalizations of school shootings remain an important and topical subject for research for the study of culture.

On these last pages, I will briefly summarize what I have described as 'the fictional dimension of the school shooting discourse' and the potential functions that literature and film assume as elements of this dimension. As each analysis chapter already includes a conclusion, this synopsis will not go into great detail. Rather, I will point out the more general findings about the potential functions of literature and film, in order to illustrate why an interdisciplinary approach to school shootings and the analysis of fictional representations in the context of excessive violence is worthwhile.

7.1 The Relevance of Fiction to the School Shooting Discourse

The attempt to describe a specific 'dimension' of a complex discourse is a challenging endeavor. In a discourse that has emerged not only over the last decades, but draws on ancient discourses of excessive violence, as I have shown in Chapter 2, the 'fictional dimension' is understood as a horizontal dimension that can connect the multifarious, interrelated elements of the process of discourse formation. In order to focus on the various ways the school shooting discourse is shaped by and interwoven with different fictional elements – in the construction of its narratives, its performative aspects and fictionalization – a number of other aspects of the school shooting discourse had to be neglected. Nevertheless, my approach connects and combines research from cultural and literary studies

---

[1] For their list of school shootings, see http://everytownresearch.org/school-shootings/. Last retrieved: March 26, 2017.

with findings from sociology, media and communications studies, and thus contributes to an interdisciplinary approach to the contemporary phenomenon.

School shooting novels and films play an important role in the discourse formation, as I show – but, whereas media representations and the influence of fictional works on school shooters have been researched to some extent, novels and films and their relevance to discourse formation as a whole have been largely neglected.

Some of the descriptions of this 'fictional dimension' had to remain rather abstract and theoretical. However, this level of abstraction allowed for more general observations: instead of focusing on selected school shootings and describing them as individual events, as it has already been done, I referred to 'school shootings' more as a social construct. By no means do I want to imply that school shootings are not 'real' – the death and suffering that these crimes bring upon families and communities is horrifyingly real. Nevertheless, it can be observed that these acts of violence would not exist in its current form without the 'fictional dimension' of the school shooting discourse. Neither the definition of school shootings nor the public reaction to them can be understood separately from their discursive dynamics.

School shootings and fiction are inextricably interwoven. In this sense, the fictional dimension permeates the discourse on all levels – and, as I show, school shootings as acts of excessive violence are effectively generated by this constructed discourse. To understand the dynamics of the discourse, it is crucial to realize how fictional representations continually shape and influence the cultural imaginary upon which all communication about school shootings draws. For understanding the 'fictional dimension' and the role that literature and film plays in its emergence, existing observations about the relevance of narratives and the reciprocal relationship between school shootings and fictional artifacts can further be combined with a functional approach to fictional representations of school shootings. Through this approach, this book has shown that analyzing the relevance of fictional elements for the emergence of the school shooting phenomenon and pointing out how literature and film can influence and shape the public perception are inextricably connected. Understanding school shooting novels and films and the processes of their reception, as I have shown, can help to understand the school shooting discourse as such.

The first part of this volume established the relevance of fiction in the genesis of the phenomenon, as well as the construction of the social narratives that try to make sense of it. The second part built upon this observation, focusing on three narrative strategies that illustrate the way school shooting novels and films can participate in the discourse.

The importance of narrative for the construction of the school shooting discourse becomes especially obvious when it comes to attempts at explaining the phenomenon: Every attempt I have shown falls short at some point. Like any form of excessive violence, school shootings confront society with its instability and are therefore met with the desire to construct a narrative that establishes causality. Moreover, because school shootings occur at educational institutions and are committed by adolescents, their symbolic character poses a threat against society as a whole that by far exceeds the actual severity of the attack. The social shock that results has to be countered with attempts to reintegrate the violence into social normalcy by explaining them or, if that fails, by pathologizing or, ultimately, mystifying them (cf. Reemtsma 2012). My approach to the school shooting discourse concerned itself with explaining these dynamics, providing an overview of the attempts at explanation – the results of the human need for creating narratives of causality and efforts toward meaning-making – as well as with providing the very basic and simplified constituents of the school shooting narrative: character, setting and plot. These general observations about the discursive dynamics made it possible to take a closer look at the school shooting phenomenon itself without running the risk of focusing too much on the individual perpetrators, their references to fictional works or their media consumption, and thus contributing to the creation of a causal narrative for explanation – an approach that I consciously rejected. Fictional representations of school shootings, like fictional representations of violence in general, have been hotly debated and often featured in attempts at explanation. Approaches that I have previously outlined, such as that by German scholar Frank J. Robertz, clearly highlight the role of a fantasy that is filled with violent content from fictional works, from which the idea of a school shooting can emerge. On a different note, Katherine S. Newman and colleague's notion of the cultural script of school shootings, which links (fictional) images of masculinity to guns and violence, acknowledges that cultural artifacts do not merely 'invent' potentially dangerous stories and imagery, but draw upon social realities and lifeworlds that adolescents can relate to. Nevertheless, both existing approaches to the relevance of fiction for the school shooting discourse remain on the level of the individual perpetrator and, as such, only want to show how fictional representations can be seen as one of many aspects in the genesis of school shootings.

As I have repeatedly stated, I do not disagree with Newman et al.'s notion. School shooters do obviously refer to a cultural script of school shootings, which is an important notion in regard to the fictional dimension of the school shooting discourse, as it already highlights the complex reception processes involved. Drawing upon these existing notions, I did, however, however, propose a more comprehensive understanding of the role of fiction in the school shooting discourse as I have pointed out that the interrelation of school shootings and fiction can be described as reciprocal and cyclical. This book thus shows that fictional works are not only one element in the genesis of a gruesome crime, but exist in a more dynamic interrelation with the actual events. For a systematic approach to a comprehensive description of the interwovenness of fictional and real school shootings, I have carved out five cyclically connected stages of the 'fictional dimension'. These include (1) the shooter's subject formation; (2) the planning and the staging and the actual attack as a performative act, in which the later fictionalization is already anticipated; (3) the way in which the process of discourse formation includes the fictional elements incorporated by the school shooters prior and during their attack; (4) the fictionalization of the actual school shootings and (5) the way the reception of these fictionalizations can shape the public perception and understanding of actual school shootings (see Chapter 3).

Throughout this volume, I have frequently emphasized that, although hardly anyone will ever experience a school shooting, almost everybody has an idea about the way that school shooters look and behave, and about what happens during a school shooting and its aftermath. Naturally, many of the images have been provided by extensive news media coverage, especially of the Columbine High School shooting. However, these images have been constantly remediated, fictionalized, disseminated and archived and archived by school shooting films and novels, and this remediation therefore still contributes to the popular understanding of school shootings.

I have illustrated this observation with Matt Johnson's The Dirties which is an effective meta commentary on the interwovenness of fact and fiction in the genesis of a school shooting. Furthermore, the film draws upon a number of fictional and real elements available in the discourse, illuminating the ways in which these elements are interrelated. Just as school shooters do not distinguish between their real lives and their fictional idols, *The Dirties* does not distinguish between real and fictional school shootings in its representation: while its grainy, hand-held camera, amateur look remediates videos like the Columbine shooter's school project *Hitmen for Hire*, the look of the shooter's room in the basement clearly refers to the way that Gus Van Sant's *Elephant* imagined Harris' and Klebold's rooms. Thus, *The Dirties* not only illustrates but actually *fictionalizes* the fictional dimension of the school shooting discourse – at least on the level of the perpetrator and the genesis of the school shooting.

Different concepts helped to show how fictional representations of school shootings become effective elements of the discourse, and were explained by using the example of Johnson's film. In addition to demonstrating a general tendency in school shooting fiction to employ strategies of authentication, *The Dirties* also provides a good example of the concepts of pre- and remediation. Pre-

and remediation were used here to approach the fictional dimension of the school shooting discourse in relation to the emergence of the cultural memory of school shootings. They make it possible to describe the media schemata used to represent the events and to understand how mediatized violence is gradually engrained in the collective memory.

Drawing attention to the remediated elements in *The Dirties* further helped to describe what I have called the 'look of school shootings', as well as to show how this 'look of school shootings' is connected to fictional representations of school shootings. The rooms in the basements, the scenes of target practice, the empty high school hallways, the shooters' home videos and the surveillance camera imagery have all been remediated in various ways.

7.2 Potential Functions of School Shooting Novels and Films

As the different stages of the reciprocal, cyclical relationship between fiction and school shootings show, fictional representations of school shootings clearly have the potential to inspire future perpetrators. However, they are read and watched by many who are not potential school shooters – a fact that is frequently neglected. For this majority, fictional representations, I have shown, can fulfill important potential functions. Analyzing various fictional works provided highly valuable insights into the dynamics of the school shooting discourse, as well as into the societal practices of approaching the phenomenon.

By considering the novels' and films' narrative structures and the reception processes, I showed that the fictional representations of school shooting can be ascribed a specific and relevant role as an element that shapes the school shooting discourse. Drawing mainly from theories by Wolfgang Iser and Winfried Fluck, and partially from findings from cultural memory studies and cognitive and intermedial narratology, I showed how the act of reading and of watching films and the aesthetic experience has the ability to change the recipient's understanding of the world around her or him. The three major functions that the fictional works assume can be summarized as a) creation of an archive of a contemporary phenomenon and the way society approaches and communicates it, b) mirroring the dynamics and constructedness of the school shooting discourse and prompting the recipients to reflect upon their own position in the school shooting discourse, and c) confronting the recipients with the ambiguity, polyvalence and, ultimately, the inexplicability of the events. Each of these is detailed in the following paragraphs.

a) All fictional works analyzed here employ highly realistic narrative modes and include authenticating features, modes, or narrative techniques – for example, remediation in the multimodal novel. Through frequent overt or subtle references to extratextual school shootings, the novels and films ensure that the recipients can draw a connection between the fictional and actual school shootings, and thus actively contribute to the collective memory of school shootings. Due to these references, the novels and films create archives of the contemporary phenomenon – a fact that is further enhanced by the integration of other elements of popular culture, news media or communicative practices.

Furthermore, all the novels and films examined here clearly draw upon the school shooting narrative as it has been outlined in this book and include many of the popular attempts at explanation, albeit with varying emphases: gun control, bullying, media violence and the debate about family background and nature vs. nurture. The works from the early 2000s, as well as the more recent novels and films, clearly refer to Columbine and, in some cases, appear to expect the readers to remember aspects from the shooting or its aftermath. By doing so, school shooting fiction exemplifies how fictional works simultaneously draw upon and contribute to the cultural imaginary – as, for example, when Walter Dean Myer's *Shooter* refers to the Goth subculture and fictionalizes Columbine's 'Trenchcoat Mafia'. Even though *Shooter* problematizes the connection made by the media in the wake of Columbine and can thereby prompt critical debate, the connection between school shootings and Goth subculture is still fictionally reinforced.

School shooting novels and films can further have the potential to *expand* the school shooting discourse. As one discursive element among others, fictional representations of school shooting participate in societal processes of discourse formation, providing imagery, reinforcing or questioning established narratives of explanation. All this, as I have shown, happens via the complex reception process in which the recipient uses her or his knowledge to actualize what the text or film shows, while the recipient's knowledge of the extratextual world is changed in the same process. It is the reception process that endows novels and films with possibilities that differ significantly from those offered by news media or academic publications.

All of the fictional works analyzed in this book refer to the various attempts at explanation that were summarized in Chapter 2. Moreover, they dramatize the societal efforts to restore 'normality' by finding answers to the question 'why?', and thereby contribute to a fictional repository of societal coping mechanisms. However, the aesthetic constructedness of fictional representations sets the fictional works apart from other forms or representations, such as documentaries, journalistic reports or photography and newspapers. Even though the boundaries between fiction and fact are constantly blurred in the construction of the school shooting narrative, as I have shown, school shooting novels and films have different possibilities for communicating, commenting on and helping the readers to 'experience' the events described. As recognizably fictional works, novels and films may reference actual school shootings and re-tell and remediate the school shooting narrative. They do, however, have the aesthetic freedom to confront their recipients with the nature of the cultural imaginary and, by various self-reflexive modes, can engage the recipients in reflecting upon both the fictional and actual world. In my analysis of these potential functions, I was particularly interested in strategies that are seen as particularly prone to challenge the semantic closeness of narrative and, at the same time, require a high degree of active participation from the recipients: multimodality, multiperspectivity and unreliable narration.

b) However, as I have shown, the potential functions of school shooting novels and films go beyond the function of creating an archive of the phenomenon or its discourse. All the works aesthetically *mirror* and illustrate the dynamics of the school shooting discourse and thus prompt the reader to reflect upon these dynamics and upon her own position in the discourse. Just as the media coverage in the aftermath of a school shooting confronts the public with various pieces of information that are conflicting, unreliable or untrustworthy and frequently incongruent, multimodal and multiperspectival works challenge their reader or recipient to weigh and order diverging and sometimes even conflicting data. As the readers find themselves in the position of trying to construct a consistent and causal narrative out of multiple accounts of a school shooting, fictional newspaper clippings, interviews and police reports, they are prompted to recognize their similar position in the extratextual discourse. Thus, these narratives strategies not only make the readers realize the constructedness of the school shooting narrative upon which the texts draw, but also highlight the partiality and incompleteness of all the information they receive, as *Elephant* most impressively exemplifies.

In the process of weighing information, the role of empathy also becomes relevant. Multiperspectival novels especially foster perspective taking and challenge the reader by providing shifting perspectives. While none of the young adult school shooting novels enabled a lasting empathetic connection with the perpetrators, *Violent Ends* in particular challenges its readers to empathize with various characters. In the realm of the fictional, this empathic connection is much easier than in real life, where insight into other people is much more restricted. In news coverage, too, the possibility of empathically sharing the experience of others is not guaranteed. In the novels analyzed here, the opportunity to 'practice' empathy with other people and to imagine the perspective of people affected by school shootings – such as officials, or the parents of shooters – was also found to be an important effect of these narrative strategies.

In this regard, I found that the narrative strategies employed in the fictional works can be seen in a close interrelation with the intended readership. This notion may not be particularly important in studies based on reception theory, where the concept of the implied reader as a construct is not to be confused with the real, flesh-and-blood reader (cf. Iser 1980). However, as I have analyzed five novels written for young adults, the intended readership has in fact gained a certain degree of relevance and therefore had to be considered.

Naturally, young adults' position in the school shooting discourse, their ways of being confronted with the events and their perceptions of them all differ significantly from those of adults. For young adults, school shootings are intimately related to their own lifeworld and therefore possess an even higher degree of recognizablity than they do for adults. Young adults are affected by school shootings in a much more direct way, and are frequently seen not only as the victims, but, especially when bullying is given as an explanation, as the reasons for the attack. Thus, the position of young adults in the school shooting discourse is a highly ambiguous one: they are victims, potential victimizers, and potential preventers. This ambiguity could clearly be observed in the narrative construction of the novels, which mainly focus on bullying as the aspect of the school shooting narrative that affects the readers most, which is, of course, also due to the didactic stance that the novels take. In order to establish an immediate connection between the fictional world and the intended readership's actual lifeworld, the novels draw upon images and communicative practices from teenage experience. Most importantly, however, they engage their readers in a particularly intense interaction with the text, presenting different perspectives on the genesis of the school shooting or the perpetrator which readers have to prioritize or combine (e. g., *Give a Boy a Gun*, *Violent Ends*), or prompting the readers to arrange, weigh and order different discursive elements (e. g., *Shooter*), or to imagine the perspective of others. Nevertheless, YA school shooting fiction is also valuable for adult readers: it can help them to imagine the teenage lifeworld from which school shootings emerge, and multimodal YA novels especially can provide insight into the contemporary communicative practices of teenagers. Furthermore, reading YA school shooting novels can prompt the adult reader to reflect upon her or his idea about teenagers and, consequently, upon the ways in which school shooters are perceived, depicted and debated.

c) The way the three narrative strategies that I focus on represent, re-tell and fictionalize the school shooting narrative mirrors how the contingencies in the genesis of a school shooting make the process of creating meaning and making sense highly difficult. As I have shown, the school shooting narrative – even though it is meant to make sense of the events and create causality – is extremely challenging because the event defies rational explanation. Instead of being provided with the solace of causality, the people who 'experience' or 'witness' a school shooting in the media are confronted with conflicting reports and with incongruent or inconsistent narratives. The school shooting narrative aims to resolve the threat that school shootings pose by providing explanations or reassuring society of its self-declared peacefulness by juxtaposing the narrative of peacefulness with a narrative of abnormality. In some of the fictional works, especially *Shooter*, *Violent Ends*, *Elephant* and Shriver's *We Need To Talk About Kevin*, the problematic effects of school shootings are represented and mirrored. These works confront their readers and spectators with an unsettling narrative, withholding both the possibility of causality and a sense of closure.

As readers, Wolfgang Iser writes, "we organize and reorganize the various data offered us by the text" (1974: 288) in a process of trial and error: "We look forward, we look back, we decide, we change our decisions, we form expectations, we are shocked by their nonfulfillment, we question, we muse, we accept, we reject" (ibid.). Multimodal, multiperspectival and unreliable texts enhance this active engagement with the text and thus make the experience of the fictional world an even more active, immediate and relatable one. The connection that the references to extratextual school shootings and the active reading process establish between the fictional and actual school shooting discourse can result in affective reactions of insecurity, distrust or confusion. School shooting fiction can therefore be seen as a productive vehicle through which to deal with the inexplicable. While the entire school shooting discourse aims to annihilate the notion of inexplicability by constructing causality to cope with the contingencies of the events, the aesthetic constructedness of the novels and films allows the works to question these discursive dynamics – even though they are an elemental part of it.

For assuming these potential functions, the three specific narrative strategies are the most valuable and effective ones. Multimodality and multiperspectivity reflect the discursive quest for explanations; they can highlight the partiality of all perspectives, the 'Rashomon-effect', and can confront the reader or spectator with various aspects of the school shooting narrative, putting her or him in charge of constructing an ultimate conclusion and explanation. These narrative techniques highlight the constructedness of the discourse and the relativity of all knowledge. Unreliability, as in Shriver's novel, forces the recipient to question what she or he has perceived as true and highlights the subjectivity that shapes the emotional school shooting discourse. Shriver's novel shows – especially in regard to the questions of nature vs. nurture and the role of the mother – that unreliable narratives not only have the potential to deny an easy answer, but can also highlight the general impossibility of coming to a definite conclusion, even within the extratextual debate.

In sum, these three narrative strategies confront the recipient with a denial of closure that is inacceptable in the extratextual school shooting discourse. Only in the safety of the realm of the fictional can the possibility that some acts of violence defy any rational explanation be endured. Due to the interwovenness of fictional and real events, which is further underlined in the narrative structure of the novels and films, the recipients' experiences of reading or watching are connected to their extrafictional and mediatized experience of school shootings. Whereas reintegrating school shootings usually requires either explanation or denormalisation, fictional representations that employ narrative strategies of disruption, polyvalence and ambiguity can serve as alternative approaches. In the reception process, the experience of an ultimate inexplicability becomes tangible. If readers and spectators transfer this experience to their actual lifeworld, they may approach actual school shootings with an openness to contingencies, which may eventually lead to a constructive way of dealing with them.

No civilization will be able to fully rid itself of excessive violence. Even though certain concepts for prevention have shown some success, school shootings will never be fully preventable and therefore have to be incorporated into society's understanding of itself. Social stability requires the reintegration of excessive violence; the narratives of causality and the attempts for explanations are therefore as useful as they are legitimate. Naturally, a peaceful society cannot and should not legitimize excessive violence and hateful acts committed inside and against it – and yet, it has to come to terms with a certain degree of inexplicability and with being reminded of its own volatility through these acts of violence. As this reminder, excessive violence as the 'abnormal' crime can productively reinforce the societal notions of peacefulness and non-violence. In order to help understand the societal reactions to school shootings, School shooting fiction can represent these acts with greater semantic openness than non-fiction. By making the recipient reflect upon processes of othering the perpetrator (as in *Shooter, Violent Ends,* or *We Need to Talk About Kevin*), by exposing stereotypes that further marginalize people (as in *Shooter* or, to some extent, *Elephant*), or by critically illustrating the effects of the discourse of emergency (as in *Big Mouth & Ugly Girl*), school shooting fiction simultaneously contributes to the construction of the school shooting discourse and interrogates it.

In this respect, this book can be understood as a proclamation of the positive functions of literature and film in a discourse of excessive violence. As I have shown, the way the narrative strategies are activated depends on the degree to which they allow for semantic openness, polyvalence and ambiguity. *Shooter, Violent Ends, Elephant* and Shriver's *We Need To Talk About Kevin* require the recipients to fill in gaps in the narrative, and thus have a rather high potential to transfigure and change the reader's or spectator's perception of actual school shootings. *Give a Boy a Gun, This is Where it Ends* and Ramsay's adaptation of *We Need To Talk About Kevin,* on the other hand, employed narrative strategies that allow for polyvalence and a denial of closure – however, they do not use this potential that is inherent to the respective narrative strategy but instead choose to reduce complexity.

7.3 Contributions, Limitations and Topics for Further Research

Clearly, this book should be read as a proclamation of the social relevance of novels and film. However, as an interdisciplinary approach to a contemporary phenomenon of violence, it is also more than that. Instead of only pointing out the various ways in which fictional representations may influence the understanding and perception of a rare event, I have also examined how the construction of a discourse of violence is inextricably interwoven with fictional elements.

While it may be stated that any construction of a social discourse incorporates elements of fiction – even if it is 'only' in the process narrating of actual events – this connection is especially noteworthy in the school shooting discourse. School shootings are 'mediatized violence' (Muschert/Sumiala 2012), 'media spectacles' (Kellner 2008) and 'media events' (Erll 2007), and have already been approached as such. However, in all but a few studies, fictional media representations have been ignored – even though a connection between the actual events and their fictional representations has been rather widely acknowledged, at least in the notion of the copycat crime and the cultural script.

Although I have focused solely on American fiction, throughout the study I have combined international research perspectives. While this proved to be challenging at times, I believe that it is the best approach. As the references to American and German school shootings have shown, school shootings are an international phenomenon – the fictional dimension also served as a transnational link here. In my own analysis, I have combined German constructivist approaches with American research from the social sciences and media and communication studies. Consequently, this book has the theoretical background to consider the role of the blurred boundaries between the fictional and the real, not only on the level of the school shootings and perpetrators, but also on that of the public and even academic discourse. Even though the creation of causal narratives to make sense of school shootings has garnered some attention over the last few years, the role that fictional elements play in these narratives has thus far been neglected. I have therefore connected the general processes of narrativization to the discursive attempts at meaning-making, and have linked those to the fictional works as elements of an overarching fictional dimension.

Furthermore, instead of simply ascribing certain social effects or functions to fictional representations of school shootings, this books provides an approach for describing the role and functions of literature and film that is theoretically grounded in literary studies, media studies and narratology. By using these theories to explicate my understanding and approach to fictional works, this book shows how thorough analyses of literature and film can contribute to a better understanding of the discursive dynamics and, consequently, of the mediatized phenomenon as such.

In this regard, my approach and the model devloped in this book can also be used to analyze other forms of excessive violence – modern forms of terrorism and the mediatization of terror attacks come to mind. Future research could explore on which levels and, importantly, by which narrative means in fictional representations can influence both actions in the actual world and social ways of perceiving and understanding the extratextual world. Considering narrative practices of meaning-making and the role that fictional representations can play in these societal efforts – whether the narratives strategies disrupt or reinforce prevalent narratives – could prove effective in regard to other forms of mediatized violence.

Due to the scope of this book, I had to ignore a number of highly interesting fictional works. While I have analyzed some works that have not previously been researched at all, and have analyzed others from a perspective that has not yet been employed, quite a number of school shooting novels and films had to be left out. Analyses of autobiography and autofiction could prove extremely fruitful in further exploring the connection between school shootings and fiction. Another highly interesting topic for research is the question of genre: while I have focused on narrative strategies and their potential functions, asking which functions specific genres assume in the school shooting discourse could provide interesting insight into discursive dynamics. For example, an investigation of school shooting fiction from genres like fantasy (e.g., *Buffy the Vampire Slayer* or *American Horror Story*), murder mysteries (e.g., *School Days*) or comedy (e.g., *Vernon God Little*) could reveal a lot about possible approaches to the inexplicable. An in-depth analysis of the contribution of films, from *Bowling for Columbine* to the recently released *Newtown* (Kim A. Snyder, USA 2016), to the school shooting narrative and the emerging cultural memory would also be a very worthy topic for further research.

Since the functional approach employed here was originally developed to analyze the changing functions of literature over time, revisiting school shooting novels and films over the next few years or decades will be very interesting as it can help to find out how the discourse and the phenomenon have changed and how this is connected to cultural, technological and communicative transformations. The multimodal school shooting novels would be especially interesting to consider in this respect.

As this book has contributed to a general discussion about the social and media construction of excessive violence, it would be interesting to transfer these findings to other related forms of mediatized violence. It has recently been underlined, for example, how school shootings and contemporary forms of terrorism are connected (cf. Sandberg et al. 2014). While the effect that films and literature have on the public perception of the threat of terrorism has been thoroughly analyzed since 9/11 in the field of cultural memory studies, comparing the fictional dimensions of both discourses might provide valuable insights into our understanding of contemporary forms of terrorism.

Even though school shootings remain extremely rare events, some tragic incidents made the headlines while this book was being written, such as a shooting committed by an adolescent boy at an elementary school in Townsville, North Carolina in September 2016, and one at Umpqua College in Roseburg, Oregon in October 2016 (cf. Revesz 2016). In Europe, a school shooting in the town of Grasse, France garnered some international media attention (cf. Chrisafis 2017), while rampage violence was hotly debated in the aftermath of the massacre at the Emanuel African Methodist Episcopal Church in Charleston, South Carolina, on June 17, 2015. The shooting at a mall in Munich in July 2016 has the potential to once more challenge the definition of 'school shootings'. The most significant event, however, was the Stoneman Douglas High School shooting in Parkland, Florida, on February 14, 2018. Not only was the shooting shockingly deadly, but the mass protests by students and educators that this particular shooting sparked received extensive international news coverage. Of course, these protests – called "March for Our Lives" – exist in direct connection to the politics of President Donald Trump and will surely be the topic of interesting research concerning contemporary protest cultures among youths (cf. Holpuch 2018).

While these cases have not yet been researched extensively, they show that school shootings are constantly emerging and being transformed, as they are inextricably connected to the available media, imagery and modes of communication. Whether my observations about the media dynamics, the fictional dimension of the school shooting discourse, and the reciprocal relationship between fiction and real events apply to these cases remains to be seen. But whether or not the recent mass shootings would support the observations about the dynamics of excessive violence, and despite the fact that media coverage has clearly changed over the years (cf. Schildkraut/Muschert 2014), the discursive dynamics in the aftermath of these acts remained highly recognizable and appeared to be more and more ritualized. This ritualization is supported by reports that the shooter from Grasse "had watched videos of mass shootings" (Chrisafis 2017), and that a copy of Larkin's *Comprehending Columbine* was found in the Munich shooter's room.

While these recent events may differ from previous school shootings, they remain connected to Columbine and their other predecessors by the fictional dimension of the school shooting discourse, by the act of their definition, by the fictional remediation of Columbine images, and by the recurring dramatization and fictionalization of the school shooting narrative. How the school shooting phenomenon will develop in the future is unclear; one can only hope that excessive violence at schools will decline and eventually cease to exist in today's form. If this should one day be the case: In its fictional representations, in books like this one, and in countless news media articles that contribute to the construction of the school shooting discourse, however, this contemporary phenomenon and the way societies attempt to deal with it, is already thoroughly archived.

Referenced School Shootings and Mass Shooting Incidents

The list below provides the basic facts of all school shootings and mass shooting incidents that were referenced throughout this book.

The list includes: Name of the Perpetrator, Age at time of the shooting, Date of the shooting, Place of the shooting, Number of people dead or injured, Information regarding the outcome for the perpetrator, Reference for information.

School Shootings Referenced by Name of Perpetrator(s)

Auvinen, Pekka-Eric (18): Killed eight people at Jokela upper secondary school in Jokela, Finland. 2007. Suicide. (Kiilakoski/Oksanen 2011b: 31).

Bosse, Sebastian (18). November 20, 2006. Severely injured at least six people by shooting and firing home-made bombs at Geschwister-Scholl-Realschule in Emsdetten, Germany. Suicide. (Grzeszyk 2012, Paton 2012).

Carneal, Michael (14). Killed three and injured five at Heath High School in West Paducah, KY, USA. Arrested. (Newman et al. 2005).

Castillo, Alvaro Rafael (18). August 30, 2006. Killed his father and injured two at Orange High School, Hillsborough, NC. USA. Arrested. (Newman/Fox 2009).

Cho, Seung-Hui (23). April 16, 2007. Killed 32, injured 17 at Virginia Tech University in Blacksburg, VA, USA. Suicide (Newman/Fox 2009, Kellner 2008).

Golden, Andrew / Mitchell Johnson (11 and 13). March 24, 1998. Killed five, wounded ten people at Westside Middle School near Jonesboro, AR, USA. Arrested. (Newman et al. 2005).

Harris, Eric / Dylan Klebold (18 and 17). April 20, 1999. Killed 13 and injured 21 people at Columbine High School near Littleton, CO, USA. Suicide. (Larkin 2007).

Kinkel, Kipland Philip (16). May 20 – 21, 1998. Killed his parents and then shot two and injured 25 students at Thurston High School in Springfield, OR, USA. Arrested. (Fast 2008, Langman 2009).

Kretschmer, Tim (17). March 11, 2009. Killed 15, injured 11 at Albertville Realschule in Winnenden, Germany and during his escape. Shot by police. (Ahrens 2015).

Lanza, Adam (20). December 14, 2012. Shot his mother and 26 people at Sandy Hook Elementary School in Newtown, CT, USA. (Schildkraut/Muschert 2014, Fox/DeLateur 2013).

Loukaitis, Barry (14). February 2, 1996. Killed three people at Frontier Middle School in Moses Lake, WA, USA. Arrested. (Fast 2008, Coleman 2004).

Saari, Matti (22): Shot ten people at a vocational college in Kauhajoki, Finland. 2008. Suicide. (Kiilakoski/Oksanen 2011b: 31, Paton 2012).

Spencer, Brenda Ann (16). January 29, 1979. Shot two people at Cleveland Elementary School in San Diego, CA, USA. Arrested. (Fast 2013).

Steinhäuser, Robert (19). April 26, 2002. Killed 17 at Johann Gutenberg Gymnasium in Erfurt, Germany. Suicide (Ahrens 2015).

Weise, Jeffrey (16). March 21, 2005. Killed his grandfather and his grandfather's female companion, then shot seven people at Red Lake Senior High School. Suicide. (Newman/Fox 2009, O'Toole 2013).

Williams, Latina (23). February 8, 2008. Killed two people at Louisiana Technical College in Baton Rouge, LA, USA. Suicide. (Newman/Fox 2009).

Woodham, Luke (16). October 1, 1997. Killed his mother and two students at Pearl High School in Pearl, MS, USA. (Fast 2008)

School Shootings Referenced by Place

Bethel, AK, USA. February 19, 1997. Evan Ramsey (16) killed two and wounded two more at Bethel Regional High School. Arrested. (Fast 2008).

Grasse, France. March 16, 2007. Student (approx. 17) wounded four people at Alexis de Tocqueville high school with guns and grenades. Arrested. (Christafis 2017)

Townville Elementary School, Townville, SC, USA. September 28, 2016. Jesse Osborne (14) killed his father and one student, injured two more. Arrested (Revesz 2016).

Umpqua Community College, near Roseburg, OR, USA. October 1, 2015. Chris Harper Mercer (26) killed nine and injured seven to nine other people. Suicide. (Revesz 2016).

Stoneman Douglas High School, Parkland, FL. February 14, 2018. Nicolaz Cruz (19) killed 17 and injured 15 others. Arrested. (Holpuch 2018)

Other Mass Shooting Incidents Referenced by Name or Place

Breivik, Anders Bering (32). July 22, 2011. In two sequential attacks, the perpetrator killed at least 77 people and injured at least 319 people, almost 70 severely. After a car bomb explosion in Oslo, Norway, Breivik committed a mass shooting on the island of Utoya, Norway. Arrested. (Sandberg 2014).

Whitman, Charles Joseph (25). August 1, 1966. Killed his mother and wife, then killed 17 and injured 32 at the campus of the University of Austin, TX, USA. Shot by police (Grzeszyk 2012).

Charleston, SC, USA. White supremacists Dylann Roof (21) shot nine people at the Emanuel African Methodist Episcopal Church. Arrested.

Munich, Germany. July 22, 2016. Ali David Sonboly (18) killed nine people and wounded 36 in and around a mall (*Olympia Einkaufszentrum*). Suicide. (Braselmann/Ahrens 2017).

Bibliography

Primary Works

Novels

Brown, Jennifer. *Hate List*. New York: Hachette, 2010 [2009].
Foer, Jonathan Safran. *Extremely Loud & Incredibly Close*. London: Penguin, 2006 [2005].
Golding, William. *Lord of the Flies*. London: Penguin, 2016 [1954].
Guilleragues, Gabriel de. *Letters of a Portuguese Nun*. 1669.
Harnum, Robert. *Exile in the Kingdom*. Hanover: University of New England Press, 2001.
Hutchinson, Shaun David / Neal and Brendan Shusterman / Beth Revis / Cynthia Leitich Smith / Courtney Summers / Kendare Blake / Delilah S. Dawson / Steve Brezenoff / To Leeven / Hannah Moskowitz / Blythe Woolston / Trish Doller/ Mindi Scott / Margie Gelbwasser / Christine Johnson / E.M. Kokie / Elisa Nader. *Violent Ends* (ed. Shaun David Hutchinson). New York et al.: Simon Pulse, 2015.
King, Stephen. *Rage*. New York: Signet, 1977.
Knoll, Jessica. *Luckiest Girl Alive*. London: Simon and Schuster, 2016 [2015].
Lessing, Doris. *The Fifth Child*. London: Harper Perennial, 2007 [1988].
Myers, Walter Dean. *Shooter*. New York: Harper Tempest, 2004.
Nijkamp, Marieke. *This is Where It Ends*. Naperville: Sourcebooks, 2016
Oates, Joyce Carol. *Big Mouth & Ugly Girl*. London: Harper Collins 2003 [2002].
Parker, Robert B. *School Days. A Spenser Novel*. New York: Penguin, 2006 [2005].
Picoult, Jodi. *Nineteen Minutes*. London: Atria, 2007.
Pierre, DBC. *Vernon God Little*. London: Faber and Faber, 2003.
Russo, Richard. *Empire Falls*. London: Vintage, 2002 [2001].
Salinger, J.D. *The Catcher in the Rye*. London: Penguin, 1994 [1951].
Shriver, Lionel. *We Need to Talk About Kevin*. London: Serpent's Tail, 2010 [2003].
Strasser, Todd. *Give a Boy a Gun*. New York et al.: Simon Pulse, 2002 [2000].

Films

Blair Witch Project. Dir. Daniel Myrick / Eduardo Sanchez. Artisan Entertainment, 1999.
Borat! Cultural Learnings of America for Make Benefit Glorious Nation of Kazakhstan. Dir. Larry Charles. 20th Century Fox, 2006.
Elephant. Dir. Alan Clarke. BBC Northern Ireland, 1989.
Elephant. Dir. Gus Van Sant. HBO, 2003.
Gerry. Dir. Gus Van Sant. THINKFilm, 2002.
Last Days. Dir. Gus Van Sant. HBO Films, 2005.
Natural Born Killers. Dir. Oliver Stone. Warner Bros., 1994. 20th Century Fox, 2006.
O. Dir. Tim Blake Nelson. Lionsgate, 2001.
Rashomon. Dir. Akira Kurosawa. Daiei Film, 1950.
The Basketball Diaries. Dir. Scott Kalvert. New Line Cinema, 1994.
The Dirties. Dir. Matthew Johnson. Phase 4 Films, 2013.

This is Spinal Tap. Dir. Rob Reiner. Embassy Pictures, 1984.
We Need to Talk About Kevin. Dir. Lynne Ramsay. Oscilloscope Laboratories, 2011.
Zero Day. Dir. Ben Coccio. Avatar Films, 2003.
Beautiful Boy. Dir. Shawn Ku. Anchor Bay, 2010.
April Showers. Dir. Andrew Robinson. Indieflix, 2009.
Miss Sloane. Dir. John Madden. EuropaCorp, 2016.

TV Productions

"Earshot" (TV Episode, *Buffy the Vampire Slayer*, Season 3, Episode 18). Dir. Regis B. Kimble. 20th Television, 1999.
"With Tired Eyes, Tired Minds, Tired Souls, We Slept" (TV Episode, *One Tree Hill*, Season 3, Episode 16). Dir. Mark Schwahn. Warner Bros., 2006.
Bang Bang You're Dead. Dir. Guy Ferland. Showtime, 2002.
DC Sniper. 23 Days of Fear in Washington DC. Dir. Tom McLoughlin. USA Network, 2003.
Empire Falls (miniseries). Dir. Fred Schepisi. HBO, 2005.
Zero Hour: Massacre at Columbine High. Dir. David Hinckman. BBC, 2004.
"Piggy, Piggy" (TV Episode, *American Horror Story*, Season 1, Episode 6). Dir. Michael Uppendahl. 20th Television, 2011.

Secondary Literature

Adler, Lothar. 2000. *Amok. Eine Studie*. München: Belleville.
Ahrens, Jörn. 2011. "Anthropologie als Störfall. Gesellschaftliche Bearbeitung von Gewalt". In: Lars Koch / Christer Petersen / Joseph Vogl (eds.). *Zeitschrift für Kulturwissenschaft. Thema: "Störfälle"*. Bielefeld: Transcript.
Ahrens, Jörn. 2015. "German Rampage: Social Discourse and the Emergence of a Disturbing Phenomenon". In: Daniel Ziegler / Marco Gerster / Steffen Krämer (eds.). *Framing Excessive Violence. Discourse and Dynamics*. New York: Palgrave Macmillan. 137–159.
Ahrens, Jörn. 2015a. "Filmische Images, Subjektstrategien der Moderne und Visuelle Kultur". In: Jörn Ahrens / Lutz Hieber / York Kautt (eds). *Kampf um Images. Visuelle Kommunikation in gesellschaftlichen Konfliktlagen*. Wiesbaden: Springer VS. 295–311.
Ahrens, Jörn. 2017. "Tätersubjekte. Zur sozialen und medialen Konstruktion von Identität nach Amokläufen". In: Silke Braselmann / Jörn Ahrens. *Vermittlungskulturen des Amoklaufs. Zur medialen Präsenz spektakulärer Gewalt*. Wiesbaden: Springer VS, 2017. 13–32.
Ahrens, Jörn. 2017a. *Die unfassbare Tat. Gesellschaft und Amok*. Frankfurt a. M.: Campus.
Ahrens, Jörn. 2017b. *Einbildung und Gewalt: Film als Medium gesellschaftlicher Konfliktbearbeitung*. Berlin: Bertz+Fischer.
Altman, Janet. 1982. *Epistolarity*. Columbus: Ohio State UP.
Andree, Martin. 2006. *Archäologie der Medienwirkung. Faszinationstypen von der Antike bis Heute (Simulation, Spannung, Fiktionalität, Authentizität, Unmittelbarkeit, Geheimnis, Ursprung)*. München: Wilhelm Fink.
Andree, Martin. 2006a. *Wenn Texte töten. Über Werther, Medienwirkung und Mediengewalt*. München: Fink.

Anonymous. n.d. "11,000 Page Report". Online: http://www.acolumbinesite.com/reports/report.html. Last Retrieved: April 2, 2019.
Anonymous. 2006. "Ich will R.A.C.H.E". *Heise.de*. November 21, 2006. Online: http://www.heise.de/tp/r4/artikel/24 /24032/1.html. Last Retrieved: April 2, 2019.
Arnold, Sarah. 2013. *Maternal Horror Film. Melodrama and Motherhood*. London: Palgrave Macmillan.
Assmann, Aleida. 1995. "Was sind kulturelle Texte?" In: Andreas Poltermann (ed.). *Literaturkanon – Medienereignis – kultureller Text: Formen interkultureller Kommunikation und Übersetzung*. Berlin: Erich Schmidt. 232–244.
Assmann, Aleida. 2010. "Canon and Archive". In: Astrid Erll / Ansgar Nünning (eds.). *A Companion to Cultural Memory Studies*. Berlin / New York: De Gruyter. 97–107.
Auslander, Philip. 2001. "Liveness, Mediatization, and Intermedial Performance". In: *Degrés: Revue de synthèse à orientation sémiologique* No. 101 (2000). 1–12. Online: homes.lmc.gatech.edu / ~auslander / publications / liveness.pdf. Last Retrieved: March 26, 2019.
Bakthin, Mikhail Mikhailovich. 1983. *The Dialogic Imagination. Four Essays by M.M. Bakthin*. Ed. by Michael Holquist. Austin / London: University of Texas Press.
Bal, Mieke. 1994. *On Meaning-Making: Essays in Semiotics*. Sonoma: Polebridge Press.
Bal, Mieke. 1999. "Introduction". In: Mieke Bal / Jonathan Crewe / Leo Spitzer. *Acts of Memory: Cultural Recall in the Present*. Hanover, NH: University Press of New England. vii-xvii.
Bannenberg, Britta. 2010. *Amok. Ursachen erkennen – Warnsignale verstehen – Katastrophen verhindern*. Gütersloh: Gütersloher Verlagshaus.
Baroni, Raphaël. 2014. "Tellability". In: Peter Hühn / Jan Christoph Meister / John Pier / Wolf Schmid (eds.). Handbook of Narratology. 2nd rev. and exp. edition. Vol 1. Berlin / Boston: De Gruyter. 836–845.
Barron, James. 2012. "Nation reels after Gunman Massacres 20 Children at School in Connecticut". New York Times. Nytimes.com. December 14, 2012. Online: http://www.nytimes.com/2012/12/15/nyregion/shooting-reported-at-connecticut-elementary-school.html?pagewanted=all&_r=0. Last Retrieved: March 3, 2019.
Barthes, Roland. 1975 [1966] "An Introduction to the Structural Analysis of Narrative". In: *New Literary History*, Vol. 6, No. 2 (1975). 237–272.
Bartz, Christina. 2007. "'Mike Mendez Killers-Coolness-Faktor'. Warum Robert Steinhäuser Amok läuft". In: Irmela Schneider / Christina Bartz (eds.). *Formationen der Mediennutzung I – Medienereignisse*. Bielefeld: Transcript. 229–243.
Bateman, John. 2008. *Multimodality and Genre. A Foundation for the Systematic Analysis of Multimodal Documents*. Basingstoke: Palgrave Macmillan.
Bateman, John. 2014. *Text and Image: A Critical Introduction to the Visual/Verbal Divide*. London: Routledge.
Bauman, Richard. 1986. *Story, Performance, and Event: Contextual Studies of Oral Narrative*. Cambridge: Cambridge UP.
Beaver, Frank. 1994. *Dictionary of Film Terms. The Aesthetic Companion to Film Analysis*. New York: Twayne Publishers.
Beebee, Thomas O. 1998. "Epistolary Novel". In: Paul Schellinger (ed.). *Encyclopedia of the Novel*. Chicago: Dearborn. 384–388.

Belluck, Pam / Wilgoren, Jodi. 1999. "Shattered Lives – A special report: Caring Parents, No Answers, In Columbine Killers' Pasts". *New York Times*, 29. June 1999. Online: http://www.nytimes.com/1999/06/29/us/shattered-lives-special-report-caring-parents-no-answers-columbine-killers-pasts.html. Last Retrieved: March 3, 2019.

Benson, Thomas W. / Snee, Brian J. 2015. "Michael Moore and the Rhetoric of Documentary: Art, Argument, Affect". In: Benson, Thomas W. / Snee, Brian J. / Borda, Jennifer L. / Harold, Christine / Ott, Brian L. / Sci, Susan (eds.). *Michael Moore and the Rhetoric of Documentary*. Carbondale: Souther Illinois University Press. 1–24

Berardi, Franco 'Bifo'. 2015. *Heroes. Mass Murder and Suicide*. London / New York: Verso.

Berns, Ute. 2014. "Performativity". In Peter Hühn / Jan Christoph Meister / John Pier / Wolf Schmid (eds.). *Handbook of Narratology*. 2nd rev. and exp. edition. Vol 1. Berlin / Boston: De Gruyter.

Birke, Dorothee / Butter, Stella. 2013. "Introduction" In: Dorothee Birke / Stella Butter (eds.). *Realisms in Contemporary Culture: Theories, Politics, and Medial Configurations*. Berlin: De Gruyter. 1–12.

Bishop, Ryan. 2013. *Comedy and Cultural Critique in American Film*. Edinburgh: Edinburgh University Press.

Bläss, Ronny. 2005. "Der Tabubruch in der Literatur: Die Funktionalisierung von literarischer Unzuverlässigkeit zur Inszenierung moralischer Grenzüberschreitung am Beispiel von Vladimir V. Nabokovs Lolita". In: Marion Gymnich / Ansgar Nünning (eds.). *Funktionen von Literatur. Theoretische Grundlagen und Modellinterpretationen*. Trier: WVT. 215 – 231.

Böckler; Nils / Seeger, Thorsten. 2010. *Schulamokläufer. Eine Analyse medialer Täter-Eigendarstellungen und deren Aneignung und jugendliche Rezipienten*. Weinheim / München: Juventa, 2010.

Böckler, Nils / Seeger. Thorsten. 2013. "Revolution of the Dispossessed: School Shooters and their Devotees on the Web". In: Böckler, Nils / Seeger Thorsten / Sitzer Peter / Heitmeyer, Wilhelm (eds.). School Shootings: International Research, Case Studies and Concepts for Prevention. New York: Springer, 2013. 309–339.

Böckler, Nils / Seeger, Thorsten / Sitzer, Peter. 2012. "Media Dynamics in School Shootings: A Socialization Theory Perspective". In: Glenn W. Muschert / Johanna Sumiala (eds). *School Shootings: Mediatized Violence in a Global Age*. Bingley: Emerald. 25–46.

Böckler, Nils / Seeger, Thorsten / Sitzer, Peter / Heitmeyer, Wilhelm. 2013. "School Shootings: Conceptual Framework and International Empirical Trends". In: Nils Böckler / Thorsten Seeger et.al. (eds.). *School Shootings: International Research, Case Studies and Concepts for Prevention*. New York: Springer. 1–26.

Bode, Christoph. 2011. *The Novel*. Oxford: Wiley-Blackwell.

Bolter, Jay David. 2008. "Digital Media and the Future of Filmic Narrative". In: Robert Kolker (ed.). The Oxford Handbook of Film and Media Studies. Oxford / New York: Oxford University Press, 2008. 21–37.

Bolter, Jay David / Grusin, Richard. 2000. *Remediation. Understanding New Media*. Cambridge, Mass.: MIT Press.

Bondü, Rebecca. 2012. *School Shootings in Deutschland. Internationaler Vergleich, Warnsignale, Risikofaktoren, Entwicklungsverläufe*. Berlin: Freie Universität Berlin, 2012. Online. http://www.diss.fu-berlin.de/diss/receive/FUDISS_thesis_000000037683. Last Retrieved: April 11, 2019.

Bondü, Rebecca / Cornell, Dewey G. / Scheithauer, Herbert. 2011. "Student homicidal violence in schools: An international problem". In: *New Directions for Youth Development*. 129 (2011). 13–30.

Bondü, Rebecca / Beier, Sophia. 2015. "Two of a Kind? Differences and Similarities of Attacks in Schools and in Institutes of Higher Education". In: *Journal of Interpersonal Violence* Vol. 30 No. 2 (2015). 253–271.

Bordwell, David. 1985. *Narration in the Fiction Film*. Madison: University of Wisconsin Press, 1985.

Bordwell, David. 2012. "Observations on film art: Return to Paranormalcy". *Davidbordwell.net*. Online: http://www.davidbordwell.net/blog/2012/11/13/return-to-paranormalcy/. Last Retrieved: May 15, 2019.

Bordwell, David / Thompson, Kristin. 2008. *Film Art. An Introduction*. 8th edition. New York: McGrawHill Higher Education.

Braselmann, Silke. 2016. "Schools under Fire? School Shootings and the Construction of a Cultural Discourse of Emergency". In: *On_Culture* Issue 1 (2016). Online. http://www.on-culture.org/journal/issue-1/schools-shootings-emergency/. Last Retrieved: April 5, 2017.

Braselmann, Silke. 2017 . "Losing the Reality Test: Fiktionalität und narrative Erklärungsstrategien für *school shootings* in Matt Johnsons *The Dirties*". In: Silke Braselmann / Jörn Ahrens (eds.). *Vermittlungskulturen des Amoklaufs. Zur Medialen Präsenz Spektakulärer Gewalt*. Wiesbaden: Springer VS.

Braselmann, Silke / Ahrens, Jörn (2017). "Vermittlungskulturen von Amokläufen. Eine Einleitung". In: Silke Braselmann / Jörn Ahrens. *Vermittlungskulturen des Amoklaufs. Zur medialen Präsenz spektakulärer Gewalt*. Wiesbaden: Springer VS. 1–12.

Brumme, Robert. 2011. *School Shootings. Soziologische Analysen*. Wiesbaden: Springer VS.

Burger, Alissa. 2016. *Teaching Stephen King. Horror, The Supernatural, and New Approaches to Literature*. New York: Palgrave.

Butler, Judith. 2006 [1990]. *Gender Trouble. Feminism and the Subversion of Identity*. 2nd ed. New York: Routledge.

Caracciolo, Marco. 2014. "Experientiality". In: *The Living Handbook of Narratology*. University of Hamburg. Online. http://www.lhn.uni-hamburg.de/article/experientiality. Last Retrieved: April 11, 2019.

Cart, Michael. 2001. "From Insider to Outsider: The Evolution of Young Adult Literature". In: *Voices from the Middle* Vol. 9 No. 2 (2001). 95–97.

Cavell, Stanley. 1979. *The World Viewed. Reflections on the Ontology of Film*. Cambridge: Cambridge University Press.

Christafis, Angelique. 2017. "Armed Teenager Arrested after School Shooting in French Town of Grasse". *The Guardian*. March 16, 2017. Online: https://www.theguardian.com/world/2017/mar/16/school-shooting-in-french-town-of-grasse-sparks-terror-alert. Last Retrieved: March 26, 2019.

Christians, Heiko.2008. *Amok. Geschichte einer Ausbreitung*. Bielefeld: Aisthesis.

Christopher J. Ferguson / Ivory, James D. 2012. "A Futile Game: On the Prevalence and Causes of Misguided Speculation About the Role of Violent Video Games in Mass School Shootings". In: Glenn W. Muschert / Johanna Sumiala (eds.). *School Shootings: Mediatized Violence in a Global Age*. Bingley: Emerald. 47–68

Coats, Karen. 2011. "Young Adult Literature: Growing Up, In Theory". In: Shelby A. Wolf / Karen Coats / Christine A. Jenkins (eds.). *Handbook of Research on Children's and Young Adult Literature*. New York: Routledge. 315–329.

Cohen, Stanley. 2002 [1972]. *Folk Devils and Moral Panics. The Creation of Mods and Rockers*. 3rd ed. New York: Routledge, 2002.

Coleman, Loren. 2004. *The Copycat Effect: How the Media and Popular Culture Trigger the Mayhem in Tomorrow's Headlines*. New York: Paraview Pocket.

Colón-Sermeza, Gregory M. 2005. "Shakespeare after Columbine. Teen Violence in Tim Blake Nelson's 'O'". In: *College Literature*. Vol 32. No. 4 (2005). 99–124.

Cullen, Dave. 2009. *Columbine*. Devon: Old Street.

De Bruyn, Ben. 2012. *Wolfgang Iser. A Companion*. Berlin: De Gruyter.

Deleyto, Celestino. 1996 [1991]. "Focalization in Film Narrative". In: Susanna Onega (ed.). *Narratology. An Introduction*. London: Longman. 217–233.

Dernbach, Beatrice. 2015. "(Un)reliable Narration in Journalism: The Fine Line Between Fact and Fiction". In: Vera Nünning (ed.). Unreliable Narration and Trustworthiness. Intermedial and Interdisciplinary Perspectives. Berlin / Munich / Boston: Walter de Gruyter. 305–328.

Diehl, Felix. 2014. "Einfache Erklärungen von Amokläufen sind gefährlich. Eine Buchbesprechung von Jonathan Fasts *Ceremonial Violence – Understanding Columbine and other School Rampage Shootings*". In: *Zeitschrift für Internationale Strafrechtsdogmatik* No. 13 (2014). 728–736. Online: http://www.zis-online.com/dat/artikel/2014_13_884.pdf. Last Retrieved: May 15, 2019. n.pag.

Eagleton, Terry. 2010. *On Evil*. New Haven / London: Yale University Press.

Eberwein, Robert. 2010. *The Hollywood War Film*. Malden, MA: Wiley-Blackwell.

Elias, Caroline / Weber, Thomas. 2009. "Defekt als Referenz. Von neuen Hybrid-Formaten zum Verfall der Doku-Kultur". In: Harro Seegeberg (ed.) *Referenzen*. Marburg: Schüren. 177–197.

Emmott, Catherine / Alexander, Marc. 2014. "Schemata". In: *The Living Handbook of Narratology*. University of Hamburg. Online: http://www.lhn.uni-hamburg.de/article/schemata. Last Retrieved: April 11, 2019. n.pag.

Erll, Astrid. 2002. "Literatur und kulturelles Gedächtnis: Zur Begriffs- und Forschungsgeschichte, zum Leistungsvermögen und zur literaturwissenschaftlichen Relevanz eines neuen Paradigmas der Kulturwissenschaft". In: *Literaturwissenschaftliches Jahrbuch* 43 (2002). 249–276.

Erll, Astrid. 2007. *Prämediation – Remediation. Repräsentationen des indischen Aufstands in imperialen und post-kolonialen Medienkulturen (von 1857 bis zur Gegenwart)*. Trier: WVT, 2007.

Erll, Astrid. 2008. "'Bringing War Home': *Jarhead* und die Kriegserinnerung *made in Hollywood*". In: Astrid Erll / Stephanie Wodianka (eds.). *Film und Kulturelle Erinnerung. Plurimediale Konstellationen*. Berlin: De Gruyter. 139–170.

Erll, Astrid. 2010. "Literature, Film, and the Mediality of Cultural Memory". In: Astrid Erll / Ansgar Nünning (eds.). *A Companion to Cultural Memory Studies*. Berlin / New York: De Gruyter. 389–397.

Erll, Astrid / Nünning, Ansgar. 2006. "Concepts and Methods for the Study of Literature and / as Cultural Memory". In: Ansgar Nünning / Marion Gymnich / Roy Sommer (eds.).

Literature and Memory. Theoretical Paradigms – Genres – Functions. Tübingen: Francke. 11–28.

Erll, Astrid / Wodianka, Stephanie. 2008. "Einleitung: Phänomenologie und Methodologie des ‚Erinnerungsfilms'". In Astrid Erll / Stephanie Wodianka (eds.). *Film und Kulturelle Erinnerung. Plurimediale Konstellationen*. Berlin: De Gruyter. 1–20.

Erll, Astrid / Rigney, Ann. 2009. "Introduction: Cultural Memory and its Dynamics". In: Astrid Erll / Ann Rigney (eds.). *Mediation, Remediation, and the Dynamics of Cultural Memory*. New York: De Gruyter. 1–11.

Erll, Astrid. "Literature, Film, and the Mediality of Cultural Memory". In: Astrid Erll / Ansgar Nünning (eds.). *A Companion to Cultural Memory Studies*. Berlin / New York: De Gruyter, 2010. 389–397.

Evans, Richard T. 2016. "'Faggots, Fame and Firepower': Teenage Masculinity, School Shootings, and the Pursuit of Fame". In: Canadian Review of American Studies Vol 46, No. 1 (2016). 1–21.

Farrell, Kirby. 2016. "Killing the Killer. Rampage and Gun Rights as a Syndrome". In: Yochai Ataria / David Gurevitz / Haviva Pedaya / Yuval Neria (eds.). *Interdisciplinary Handbook of Trauma and Culture*. Cham: Springer Switzerland. 353–564.

Fast, Jonathan. 2008. *Ceremonial Violence. Understanding Columbine and other School Shootings*. New York: Overlook Press.

Fast, Jonathan. 2013. "Unforgiven and Alone: Brenda Spencer and Secret Shame". In: Nils Böckler / Thorsten Seeger / Peter Sitzer / Wilhelm Heitmeyer (eds.). *School Shootings: International Research, Case Studies and Concepts for Prevention*. New York: Springer. 245–261.

Fluck, Winfried. 1996. "The American Romance and the Cultural Imaginary". In: *New Literary History* Vol. 27 No.1 (1996). 415–457.

Fluck, Winfried. 1997. *Das kulturelle Imaginäre. Eine Funktionsgeschichte des amerikanischen Romans 1790–1900*. Frankfurt a.M.: Suhrkamp, 1997.

Fluck, Winfried. 2002. "The Role of the Reader and the Changing Functions of Literature: Reception Aesthetics, Literary Anthropology, Funktionsgeschichte". In: *European Journal of English Studies* Vol.6 No.3 (2002) 253–271.

Fluck, Winfried. 2005. "Funktionsgeschichte und Ästhetische Erfahrung". In: Marion Gymnich / Ansgar Nünning (eds.). *Funktionen von Literatur. Theoretische Grundlagen und Modellinterpretationen*. Trier: WVT, 2005. 29–54.

Fludernik, Monika. 1996. *Towards a 'Natural' Narratology*. London: Routledge.

Foucault, Michel. 1995 [1977]. Transl. by Alan Sheridan. *Discipline and Punish*. New York: Vintage.

Foucault, Michel. 2002 [1972]. Transl. by A.M. Sheridan Smith. *The Archeology of Knowledge*. New York: Routledge.

Fox, James Alan / Levin, Jack. 1999. "Serial Murder: Popular Myths and Empirical Realities". In: M. Dwayne Smith / Margaret A. Zahn (eds.). *Homicide: A Sourcebook of Social Research*. Thousand Oaks / London / New Delhi: Sage. 165–176.

Fox, James Alan / Levin, Jack. 2003. "Mass Murder: An Analysis of Extreme Violence". In: *Journal of Applied Psychoanalytic Studies* Vol. 5 Issue 1 (2003). 47–63.

Fox, James Alan / DeLateur, Monica J. 2014. "Mass Shootings in America: Moving Beyond Newtown". In: *Homicide Studies* Vol. 18 No. 1 (2014). 125–145.

Franzak, Judith / Noll, Elizabeth. 2006. "Monstrous Acts: Problematizing Violence in Young Adult Literature". In: *Journal of Adolescent & Adult Literacy (JAAL)* Vol. 49 No. 8 (2006). 662–672.

Frizzoni, Brigitte. 2015. "Der 'Amok-Opa'. Populärkulturelle Deutungsmuster in der Darstellung von Gewalttaten". In: Isabella von Treskow / Ralf Junkerjürgen (eds.). *Amok und Schulmassaker. Kultur- und Medienwissenschaftliche Annäherungen*. Bielefeld: Transcript, 2015. 121–141

Fulton, Helen. 2005. "Film Narrative and Visual Cohesion". In: Helen Fulton / Rosemary Huisman / Julian Murphet / Anne Dunn (eds.). *Narrative and Media*. Cambridge: Cambridge UP. 108–22.

Garry III, John P. 2004. "Elephant. An Ordinary High School Moive. Except That It's Not". In: *Jump Cut. A Review of Contemporary Media*. Nr. 46 (2004). Online: http://ejumpcut.org/archive/jc47.2005/elephant/index.html. Last Retrieved: May 15, 2019. n.pag.

Gavins, Joanna. 2008. "Scripts and Schemata". In: David Herman / Manfred Jahn / Marie-Laure Ryan. *Routledge Encyclopedia of Narrative Theory*. London / New York: Routledge. 520–521

Gaw, Albert C. / Bernstein, Ruth L. 1992. "Classification of Amok in DSM-IV". In: *Hospital & Community Psychiatry*, Vol. 43 No. 8 (1992). 789–793.

Gerster, Marco. 2017. "Symbole des Bösen und Enthymeme des Guten. Über die kollektive Bewältigung von Amokläufen". In: Silke Braselmann / Jörn Ahrens. *Vermittlungskulturen des Amoklaufs. Zur medialen Präsenz spektakulärer Gewalt*. Wiesbaden: Springer VS. 33–52.

Gerster, Marco 2016. *Gewalt ohne Grund. Über die Narrative Bewältigung von Amokläufen*. Weilerswist: Velbrück Wissenschaft.

Gerster, Marco / Krämer, Steffen / Ziegler, Daniel. 2015. "Introduction". In: Ziegler, Daniel / Gerster, Marco / Krämer, Steffen (eds.). *Framing Excessive Violence. Discourse and Dynamics*. New York: Palgrave McMillan. 1–13.

Gibbons, Alison. 2008. "Multimodal Literature 'Moves Us': Dynamic Movement and Embodiment in *VAS: An Opera in Flatland*". In: *Hermes – Journal of Language and Communication Studies*. No. 41 (2008). 107–124.

Gibbons, Alison. 2014. *Multimodality, Cognition, and Experimental Literature*. New York: Routledge.

Godfrey, Alex. 2014. "The Dirties Director Matt Johnson on Fame and High School Shootings". The Guardian. 2 June 2014. Online: https://www.theguardian.com/film/2014/jun/02/matt-johnson-the-dirties-director. Last Retrieved: March 3, 2019.

Green, Melanie C. / Brock, Timothy C. 2000. "The Role of Transportation in the Persuasiveness of Public Narratives". In: *Journal of Personality and Social Psychology* Vol. 79 No.5 (2000). 701–721.

Griem, Julika. 2000. "Mit den Augen der Kamera? Aspekte filmischer Multiperspektivität in Bryan Singers *The Usual Suspects*, Akiro Kurosowas *Rashomon* und Peter Weirs *The Truman Show*". In: Vera Nünning / Ansgar Nünning (eds.). *Multiperspektivisches Erzählen. Zur Theorie und Geschichte der Perspektivenstruktur im englischen Roman des 18. bis 20. Jahrhunderts*. Trier: WVT. 307–322.

Griem, Julika / Voigts-Virchow, Eckart. 2002. "Filmnarratologie: Grundlagen, Tendenzen und Beispielanalysen". In: Vera Nünning / Ansgar Nünning (eds.). *Erzähltheorie transgenerisch, intermedial, interdisziplinär*. Trier: WVT.

Grodal, Torben. 2008. "Film Narrative". In: David Herman / Manfred Jahn / Marie-Laure Ryan (eds.). *Routledge Encyclopedia of Narrative Theory*. London / New York: Routledge. 168–172.

Grusin, Richard. 2010. *Premediation: Affect and Mediality after 9 / 11*. Basingstoke: Palgrave Macmillan.

Grzeszyk, André. 2012. *Unreine Bilder. Zur medialen (Selbst-)Inszenierung von School Shootern*. Bielefeld: Transcript.

Hallet, Wolfgang. 2008. "The Multimodality of Cultural Experience and Mental Model Constructions of Textual Worlds". In: Jürgen Schlaeger / Gesa Stedmann (eds.). *The Literary Mind. REAL. Yearbook of Research in English and American Literature 24*. Tübingen: Narr. 233–250.

Hallet, Wolfgang. 2008a. "Can Literary Figures Serve as Ethical Models?" In: Astrid Erll / Herbert Grabes / Ansgar Nünning (eds.). *Ethics in Culture. The Dissemination of Values through Literature and Other Media*. Berlin / New York: De Gruyter. 195–215.

Hallet, Wolfgang. 2009. "The Multimodal Novel. The Integration of Modes and Media and Novelistic Narration". In: Sandra Heinen / Roy Sommer. *Narratology in the Age of Cross-Disciplinary Narrative Research*. Berlin / New York: De Gruyter. 129–153.

Hallet, Wolfgang. 2014. "The Rise of the Multimodal Novel. Generic Change and its Narratological Implications". In: Marie-Laure Ryan / Jan Noel Thon. *Storyworlds Across Media. Towards a Media Conscious Narratology*. Lincoln / London: University of Nebraska Press. 151–172.

Hallet, Wolfgang. 2015. "Non-verbal Semiotic Modes and Media in the Multimodal Novel". In: Gabriele Rippl (ed.). *Handbook of Intermediality. Literature – Image – Sound – Music*. Berlin: De Gruyter Mouton. 637–651

Hansen, Per Krogh. 2007. "Reconsidering the Unreliable Narrator". In: *Semiotica* No. 165 (2007). 227–246.

Harding, David J. / Fox, Cybelle / Mehta, Jal D. 2002. "Studying Rare Events Through Qualitative Case Studies: Lessons from a Study of Rampage School Shootings". In: *Sociological Methods&Research* No. 31 (2002). 174–217.

Hartner, Marcus. 2008. "Narrative Theory Meets Blending: Multiperspectivity Reconsidered". In: Jürgen Schläger / Gesa Stadmann (eds.). *The Literary Mind. REAL. Yearbook of Research in English and American Literature 24*. Tübingen: Narr. 181–194.

Hartner, Marcus. 2012. *Perspektivische Interaktion im Roman. Konzeption, Rezeption, Interpretation*. Berlin / Boston: De Gruyter.

Hartner, Marcus. 2014. "Multiperspectivity". In: Peter Hühn / Jan Christoph Meister / John Pier / Wolf Schmid (eds.). *Handbook of Narratology*. 2nd rev. and exp. edition. Vol 1. Berlin / Boston: De Gruyter. 354–363.

Heath, Shirley Brice / Wolf, Jennifer Lynn. 2012. "Brain and Behaviour: The Coherence of Teenage Responses to Young Adult Literature". In: Mary Hilton / Maria Nikolajeva (eds.). *Contemporary Adolescent Literature and Culture*. Farnham / Burlington: Ashgate. 139–154.

Heitmeyer, Wilhelm / Böckler, Nils / Seeger, Thorsten. 2013. "Social Disintegration, Loss of Control, and School Shootings". In: Nils Böckler / Thorsten Seeger et al. (eds.). *School Shootings: International Research, Case Studies and Concepts for Prevention*. New York: Springer. 27–54

Herman, David. 2009. *Basic Elements of Narrative*. Chichester: Wiley-Blackwell, 2009.

Herman, David. 2013. "Cognitive Narratology". In: *The Living Handbook of Narratology*. Hamburg University. Online: http://wikis.sub.uni-hamburg.de/lhn/index.php/Cognitive_Narratology. Last Retrieved: March 26, 2019. n.pag.

Heyd, Theresa. 2006. "Understanding and handling unreliable narratives: A pragmatic model and method". In: *Semiotica* No. 162 (2006). 217–243.

Hill, Alexandra Merley. 2011. "Motherhood as Performance. (Re)Negotiations of Motherhood in Contemporary German Literature". In: *Studies in Twentieth & Twenty-First Century Literature* Vol. 35 No. 1 (2011). 74–94.

Hillebrandt, Claudia.2011. "Emotional Functions of Unreliable Narratives. An Outline for Future Research". In: *Journal of Literary Theory*, Vol. 5 No.1 (2011). 19–36.

Hilton, Mary / Nikolajeva, Maria. 2012. "Introduction: Time of Turmoil". In: Mary Hilton / Maria Nikolajeva (eds.). *Contemporary Adolescent Literature and Culture*. Farnham / Burlington: Ashgate. 1–16.

Hjorth, Larissa. 2014. "Cell Phone Novel". In: Marie Laure Ryan / Lori Emerson / Benjamin J. Robertson (eds.). *The Johns Hopkins Guide to Digital Media*. Baltimore: Johns Hopkins University Press. 52f.

Hoffmann, Jens. 2007. "Tödliche Verzweiflung – der Weg zu zielgerichteter Gewalt an Schulen". In: Jens Hoffmann / Isabel Wondrak (eds.): *Amok und zielgerichtete Gewalt an Schulen. Früherkennung / Risikomanagement / Kriseneinsatz / Nachbetreuung*. Frankfurt a.M.: Verlag für Polizeiwissenschaft. 25–34.

Holpuch, Amanda. "Post-Columbine generation demands action on guns: 'We don't deserve this'". *The Guardian*. February 17, 2018. Online: https://www.theguardian.com/us-news/2018/feb/17/florida-school-shooting-columbine-generation-gun-control. Last Retrieved: May 15, 2019.

Howells, Stephanie. 2012. "Making Headlines: A Quarter Century of the Media's Characterization of Canadian School Shootings". In: Glenn W. Muschert / Johanna Sumiala (eds). *School Shootings: Mediatized Violence in a Global Age*. Bingley: Emerald. 91–116.

Hubmann, Philipp. 2012. "Dokumente des Amoks. Literarische Montage als narrative Authentifizierungsstrategie am Beispiel von Joachim Gaertners Roman Ich bin voller Hass – und das liebe ich!". In: Antonius Weixler (ed.). *Authentisches Erzählen: Produktion, Narration, Rezeption*. Berlin: de Gruyter. 145–175.

Hutcheon, Linda. 2004. "On the Art of Adaptation". In: *Daedalus*, Vol. 133, Issue 2 (2004). 108–111.

Hutcheon, Linda. 2006. *A Theory of Adaptation*. London: Routledge, 2006.

Iser, Wolfgang. 1974. *The Implied Reader. Patterns of Communication in Prose and Fiction from Bunyan to Beckett*. Baltimore / London: The Johns Hopkins University Press.

Iser, Wolfgang. 1980 [1976]. *The Act of Reading: A Theory of Aesthetic Response*. Baltimore: Johns Hopkins University Press.

Iser, Wolfgang. 1989. *Prospecting: From Reader Response to Literary Anthropology*. Baltimore: Johns Hopkins University Press.

Iser, Wolfgang. 1993. *The Fictive and The Imaginary: Charting Literary Anthropology*. Baltimore: Johns Hopkins University Press.

Iser, Wolfgang. 1996. "Why literature matters". In: Rüdiger Ahrens / Laurenz Volkmann (eds.). *Why Literature Matters. Theories and Functions of Literature*. Heidelberg: Winter. 13–22.

Jahn, Manfred. 2008. "Focalization". In: David Herman / Manfred Jahn / Marie-Laure Ryan (eds.). *Routledge Encyclopedia of Narrative Theory*. London / New York: Routledge. 173–177

Jeremiah, Emily. 2010. "We Need to Talk about Gender: Mothering and Masculinity in Lionel Shriver's *We Need to Talk about Kevin*". In: Elizabeth Podnieks / Andrea O'Reilly (eds.). *Textual Mothers / Maternal Texts. Motherhood in Contemporary Women's Literatures*. Waterloo: Wilfrid Laurier Univ. Press. 169–184.

Johnson, Matthew. 2013. "One-man Band. A Conversation with Matt Johnson about The Dirties". Interview by Calum Marsh. *Cinema-Scope* Vol. 55 (2013). Online: http://cinema-scope.com/features/one-man-band-a-conversation-with-matt-johnson-about-the-dirties-by-calum-marsh/. Last Retrieved: May 15, 2019.

Johnston, Chris. 2016. "Munich gunman had book about Columbine and Virginia Tech killers". July 23, 2016. https://www.theguardian.com/world/2016/jul/23/munich-gunman-book-columbine-virginia-tech-killers. Last Retrieved: March 3, 2019.

Jostock, Simone. 1999. *Kindheit in der Moderne und Postmoderne. Eine bildungstheoretische und sozialwissenschaftliche Untersuchung*. Opladen: Leske+Budrich.

Kauffman, Linda. 1988. *Discourses of Desire. Gender, Genre, and Epistolary Fiction*. Ithaca: Cornell UP.

Kauffman, Linda. 1992. *Special Delivery: Epistolary Modes in Modern Fiction*. Chicago: University of Chicago Press.

Keen, Suzanne. 2006. "A Theory of Narrative Empathy". In: *Narrative* Vol. 14 No. 3 (2006). 207–236.

Kellner, Douglas. 2008. *Guys and Guns Amok: Domestic Terrorism and School Shootings from the Oklahoma City Bombing to the Virginia Tech Massacre*. London: Boulder, 2008.

Kellner, Douglas. 2012. "School Shootings, Crises of Masculinity, and Media Spectacle: Some critical Perspectives". In: Glenn W. Muschert / Johanna Sumiala (eds). *School Shootings: Mediatized Violence in a Global Age*. Bingley: Emerald. 299–332.

Kidd, Scott T. / Meyer, Cheryl L. 2002. "Similarities of School Shootings in Rural and Small Town Communities". In: *Journal of Rural Community Psychology* Vol 5 Issue 1 (2002). Online: http://corescholar.libraries.wright.edu/sopp/3. Last Retrieved: April 11, 2019. n.pag.

Kiilakoski, Tomi / Oksanen, Atte. 2011. "Soundtrack of the School Shootings: Cultural Script, Music and Male Rage". In: *Young* Vol. 19 No. (2011). 247–269.

King, Stephen. 1999. "The Bogeyboys. Keynote Address at the Vermont Library Conference. 26. May 1999". Online: http://www.stephen-king.de/stephen-king/interviews/28-stephen-kings-keynote-address.html. Last Retrieved: April 11, 2019.

Klebold, Susan. 2009. "I will never know why". *O. The Oprah Magazine*. Online: http://www.oprah.com/omagazine/Susan-Klebolds-O-Magazine-Essay-I-Will-Never-Know-Why. Last Retrieved: April 11, 2019.

Klebold, Susan. 2016. *A Mother's Reckoning: Living in the Aftermath of Tragedy*. London: Penguin.

Koch, Jonas. 2011. "Unreliable and Discordant Film Narration". In: *Journal of Literary Theory* Vol. 5 No. 1 (2011). 57–80.

Koss, Melanie D. 2009. "Young Adult Novels with Multiple Narrative Perspectives: The Changing Nature of YA Literature". In: *The ALAN Review*. Vol. 36 No. 3 (2009). Online:

https://scholar.lib.vt.edu/ejournals/ALAN/v36n3/koss.html. Last Retrieved: 3. March 2019.
Kress, Gunther R. 2010. *Multimodality: A Social Semiotic Approach to Contemporary Communication*. London: Routledge.
Kress, Gunther R. / van Leeuwen, Theo. 2001. *Multimodal Discourse: The Modes and Media of Contemporary Communication*. London: Arnold.
Kuhn, Markus. 2009. "Film Narratology: Who Tells? Who Shows? Who Focalizes? Narrative Mediation in Self-Reflexive Fiction Films". In: Peter Hühn / Wolf Schmid / Jörg Schönert (eds). *Point of View, Perspective, and Focalization. Modeling Mediation in Narrative*. Berlin / New York: De Gruyter. 260–278.
Kuhn, Markus / Schmidt, Jonas N. 2014. "Narrative in Film". In: Peter Hühn / Jan Christoph Meister / John Pier / Wolf Schmid (eds.). *Handbook of Narratology*. 2nd rev. and exp. edition. Vol 1. Berlin / Boston: De Gruyter. 384–405.
Kümmerling-Meibauer, Bettina. 2012. "Emotional Connection: Representations of Emotions in Young Adult Literature". In: Mary Hilton / Maria Nikolajeva (eds.). *Contemporary Adolescent Literature and Culture*. Farnham / Burlington: Ashgate.
Kunczik, Michael / Zipfel, Astrid. 2006 [1986]. *Gewalt und Medien. Ein Studienhandbuch*. 5. überarb. Ausg. Köln: Böhlau.
Langman, Peter. 2009. *Why Kids Kill – Inside the Mind of School Shooters*. New York: St. Martin's Press.
Langman, Peter. 2009a. "Rampage School Shooters: A Typology". In: *Aggression and Violent Behavior* 14 (2009). 79–86.
Langman, Peter. 2012. "School Shooters Who Are Not White Males". *Psychology Today*. December 23, 2012. Online: https://www.psychologytoday.com/blog/keeping-kids-safe/201212/school-shooters-who-are-not-white-males. Last Retrieved: March 3, 2019.
Langman, Peter. 2014. "*Eric Harris's Journal*". Vol. 1. No. 3. Online: https://schoolshooters.info/eric-harris. Last Retrieved: May 15, 2019.
Langman, Peter. 2014b. "Transcript of the Columbine Basement Tapes Vs.1.0. July 2014". Online: https://schoolshooters.info/transcript-columbine-basement-tapes. Last Retrieved: April 11, 2019.
Langman, Peter. 2016. "JCSO Columbine Documents Organized by Theme. Vs. 1.5. January 2016". Online: https://schoolshooters.info/eric-harris. Last Retrieved: April 11, 2019.
Larkin, Ralph W. *Comprehending Columbine*. Philadelphia: Temple University Press, 2007.
Larkin, Ralph W. 2013. "Legitimated Adolescent Violence: Lessons from Columbine". In: Nils Böckler/Thorsten Seeger et.al. (eds.) *School Shootings: International Research, Case Studies and Concepts for Prevention*. New York: Springer. 159–176.
Latham, Monica. 2009. "Breaking the Silence and Camouflaging Voices in Lionel Shriver's We Need to Talk about Kevin". In: Vanessa Guignery (ed.). *Voices and Silence in the Contemporary Novel in English*. Newcastle: Cambridge Scholars. 130–147.
Lempp, Reinhart. 2006. "Mörderische Fantasien und Wirklichkeit – Die kriminologische Bedeutung der Nebenrealität". In: *Forensische Psychiatrie und Psychotherapie* Vol 13 No 3 (2006). 17–4.
Lenk, Hans. 2004. *Bewusstsein als Schemainterpretation: Ein methodologischer Integrationsansatz*. Paderborn: Mentis.
Lieberman, Joseph A. 2008. *School Shootings. What every Parent and Educator Needs to Know to Protect our Children*. New York: Citadel.

Linder, Kathryn E. 2014. *Rampage Violence Narratives. What Fictional Accounts of School Shootings Say About The Future of America's Youth*. Lanham / Boulder / New York: Lexington.

Lindgren, Simon. 2012. "Collective Coping Through Networked Narratives: Youtube Responses to the Virginia Tech Shooting". In: Glenn W. Muschert / Johanna Sumiala (eds.). *School Shootings: Mediatized Violence in a Global Age*. Bingley: Emerald. 279–298.

Lohr, David. 2012. "Sandy Hook Blame Game: 'Eeny, Meeny, Miny, Moe". *The Huffington Post*. December 18, 2012. Online: http://www.huffingtonpost.com/2012/12/17/sandy-hook-blame-game_n_2318334.html. Last Retrieved: March 3, 2019.

Luhmann, Niklas. 2000. Transl. by Kathleen Cross. *The Reality of Mass Media*. Cambridge: Polity Press, 2000.

MacLeod, Lewis. 2011. "'A Documentary Style Film': 'Borat' and the Fiction / Nonfiction Question". In: *Narrative* Vol. 19 No. 1 (2011). 111–132.

Manch, Rob. 2016. "Virginia Tech Student Protesting to Bring Concealed Weapons to Campus". WSLS10. September 30, 2016. Online: http://wsls.com/2016/09/30/virginia-tech-protests-weapon-policy/. Last Retrieved: February 22, 2017.

McRobbie, Angela / Thornton, Sarah L. 1995. "Rethinking 'Moral Panic' for Multi-Mediated Social Worlds". In: *The British Journal of Sociology* Vol. 46 No.4 (1995), 559–574.

Meloy, J. Reid / Hempel, Anthony G. / Mohandie, Kris / Shiva, Andrew / Gray, Thomas. 2001. "Offender and Offense Characteristics of a Nonradnom Sample of Adolescent Mass Murderers". In: *Journal of American Academy of Child and Adolescent Psychiatry* Vol. 40 No. 6 (2001). 719–781.

Menhard, Felicitas. 2009. *Conflicting Reports. Multiperspektivität und Unzuverlässiges Erzählen im Englischsprachigen Roman seit 1800*. Trier: WVT.

Mitchell, Elvis. 2003. "Film Festival Review: 'Normal' High School on the Verge". *New York Times*. October 10, 2003. Online: http://www.nytimes.com/movie/review?res=980CEED6163FF933A25753C1A9659C8B63. Last Retrieved: March 25, 2019.

Mosel, Michael / Waldschmidt, Christian. 2010. "…und wir sagen immer noch ‚Killerspiele'. Der Diskurs um Computerspiele im Zusammenhang mit school shootings". In: *AugenBlick. Marburger Hefte zur Medienwissenschaft* 46 (2010). 86–99.

Müller, Marion G. / Seizov, Ognyan / Wieneck, Florian. 2012. "Analyzing Visual Media Coverage of Amok School Shootings – A Novel Iconographic Approach". In: Glenn W. Muschert / Johanna Sumiala (eds). *School Shootings: Mediatized Violence in a Global Age*. Bingley: Emerald. 117–140.

Muschert, Glenn W. 2002. *Media and Massacre: The Social Construction of the Columbine Story*. Dissertation: 2002. Online: www.users.miamioh.edu/muschegw/Muschert-Dissertation.pdf. Last Retrieved: March 3, 2017.

Muschert, Glenn W. 2007. "Research in School Shootings". In: *Sociology Compass* 2007 (1). 60–80.

Muschert, Glenn W. 2007a. "The Columbine Victims and the Myth of the Juvenile Superpredator". In: *Youth Violence and Juvenile Justice* Vol. 5 No. 4 (2007). 351–366.

Muschert, Glenn W. 2013. "School Shootings as Mediatized Violence". In: Nils Böckler / Thorsten Seeger et.al. (eds.) *School Shootings: International Research, Case Studies and Concepts for Prevention*. New York: Springer, 2013. 265–281.

Muschert, Glenn W. / Ragnedda, Massimo. 2011. "Media and Control of Violence: Communication in School Shootings". In: Wilhelm Heitmeyer / Heinz-Gerhard Haupt /

Stefan Malthaner / Andrea Kirschner (eds.). *Control of Violence. Historical and International Perspectives on Violence in Modern Societies.* New York: Springer. 345–361.

Muschert, Glenn W. / Sumiala, Johanna. 2012. "Introduction: School Shootings as Mediatized Violence". In: Glenn W. Muschert / Johanna Sumiala (eds.). *School Shootings: Mediatized Violence in a Global Age.* Bingley: Emerald. xv-xxix.

Muschert, Glenn. W. / Janssen, Leah. 2012. "Deciphering Rampage: Assigning Blame to Youth Offenders in News Coverage of School Shootings". In: Glenn W. Muschert / Johanna Sumiala (eds.). *School Shootings: Mediatized Violence in a Global Age.* Bingley: Emerald. 161–180.

Neumann, Birgit. 2010. "The Literary Representations of Memory". In: Astrid Erll / Ansgar Nünning. A *Companion to Cultural Memory Studies.* Berlin / New York: De Gruyter. 333–343.

Newman, Katherine S. / Fox, Cybelle. 2009. "Repeat Tragedy: Rampage Shootings in American High School and College Settings, 2002–2008". In: *American Behavioral Scientist* Vol. 52 No. 9 (2009). 1286–1308.

Newman, Katherine S. / Fox, Cybelle / Harding, David J. / Mehta, Jal / Roth, Wendy. 2005. *Rampage. The Social Roots of School Shootings.* New York: Basic Books.

Nichols, Bill. 1994. *Blurred Boundaries: Questions of Meaning in Contemporary Culture.* Bloomington / Indianapolis: Indiana University Press: 1994

Nichols, Bill. 2001. *Introduction to Documentary.* Bloomington: Indiana Univ. Press.

Nünning, Ansgar (2010). "Making Events – Making Stories – Making Worlds: Ways of Worldmaking from a Narratological Point of View". In: Vera Nünning / Ansgar Nünning / Birgit Neumann (eds.). *Cultural Ways of Worldmaking. Media and Narratives.* Berlin / New York: De Gruyter, 2010. 191–214

Nünning, Ansgar. 1992. "Narrative Form und fiktionale Wirklichkeitskonstruktion aus der Sicht des New Historicism und der Narrativik: Grundzüge und Perspektiven einer kulturwissenschaftlichen Erforschung des englischen Romans im 18. Jahrhundert". In: *Zeitschrift für Anglistik und Amerikanistik: A Quarterly of Language, Literature and Culture* (ZAA) Vol. 40 No. 3 (1992). 197–213.

Nünning, Ansgar. 2001. "On the Perspective Structure of Narrative Texts: Steps Toward a Constructivist Narratology". In: Willie van Peer / Seymour Chatman (eds.). *New Perspectives on Narrative Perspective.* Albany: State University of New York Press. 207–224.

Nünning, Ansgar. 2005. "Reconceptualizing Unreliable Narration: Synthesizing Cognitive and Rhetorical Approaches". In: James Phelan / Peter J. Rabinowitz. *A Companion to Narrative Theory.* Oxford: Blackwell. 89–107.

Nünning, Vera. 2014. *Reading Fictions, Changing Minds. The Cognitive Value of Fiction.* Heidelberg: Winter.

Nünning, Vera. 2015. "Conceptualizing (Un)reliable Narration and (Un)trustworthiness". In: Vera Nünning (ed.). *Unreliable Narration and Trustworthiness. Intermedial and Interdisciplinary Perspectives.* Berlin / Munich / Boston: De Gruyter. 1–30.

Nünning, Vera. 2015a. "Reconceptualizing Fictional (Un)reliability and (Untrustworthiness form a Multidisciplinary Perspective: Categories, Typology and Function. In: Vera Nünning (ed.). *Unreliable Narration and Trustworthiness. Intermedial and Interdisciplinary Perspectives.* Berlin / Munich / Boston: De Gruyter, 2015b. 83–108.

Nünning, Vera (2014). *Reading Fictions, Changing Minds. The Cognitive Value of Fiction.* Heidelberg: Winter.
Nünning, Vera / Nünning, Ansgar. 2000. "Multiperspektivität aus Narratologischer Sicht: Erzähltheoretische Grundlagen und Kategorien zur Analyse der Perspektivenstruktur Narrativer Texte". In: Vera Nünning / Ansgar Nünning (eds.). *Multiperspektivisches Erzählen. Zur Theorie und Geschichte der Perspektivenstruktur im englischen Roman des 18. bis 20. Jahrhunderts.* Trier: WVT. 39–78.
Nünning, Vera / Nünning, Ansgar 2000a. "Von 'der' Erzählperspektive zur Perspektivenstruktur Narrativer Texte: Überlegungen zu Definition, Konzeptualisierung und Untersuchbarkeit von Multiperspektivität". In: Vera Nünning / Ansgar Nünning (eds.). *Multiperspektivisches Erzählen. Zur Theorie und Geschichte der Perspektivenstruktur im englischen Roman des 18. bis 20. Jahrhunderts.* Trier: WVT. 3–38.
O'Toole, Mary Ellen. 2013. "Jeffrey Weise and the Shooting at Red Lake Minnesota High School: A Behavioral Perpective". In: Nils Böckler / Thorsten Seeger et.al. (eds.) *School Shootings: International Research, Case Studies and Concepts for Prevention.* New York: Springer. 177–188.
Oksanen, Atte / Hawdon, James E. / Räsänen, Pekka. 2016. "Der schmale Grat zwischen Leid und Entertainment – Berichterstattung finnischer Massenmedien nach schweren Gewalttaten". In: Frank J. Robertz / Robert Kahr (eds.). *Die mediale Inszenierung von Amok und Terrorismus. Zur medienpsychologischen Wirkung des Journalismus bei exzessiver Gewalt.* Wiesbaden: Springer.
Oliveira Jr., Pedro. 2014. "Anorexic, unmedicated and obsessed with a murder-mad cyber world: Adam Lanza's mental issues went untreated by officials who allowed Sandy Hook shooter's mother to overpower them, probe finds". *Daily Mail.* November 21, 2014. Online: http://www.dailymail.co.uk/news/article-2843674/New-report-details-schools-health-officials-repeatedly-appeased-Sandy-Hook-shooter-Adam-Lanza-s-mom-addressing-crippling-mental-health-issues.html#ixzz4dlsKoZ69. Last Retrieved: May 15, 2019.
Olson, Greta. 2003. "Reconsidering Unreliability: Fallible and Untrustworthy Narrators". In: *Narrative* Vol. 11 No. 1 (2003). 93–109.
Otto, Isabell. 2008. *Aggressive Medien. Zur Geschichte des Wissens über Mediengewalt.* Bielefeld: Transcript.
Page, Ruth. 2010. "Introduction". In: Ruth Page (ed.): *New Perspectives on Narrative and Multimodality.* New York / London: Routledge. 1–14
Paget, Derek. 2012. "Docudrama: A Format of Last Resort?" In: Kay Hoffmann / Richard Kilborn / Werner C. Barg (eds.). *Spiel mit der Wirklichkeit.* Konstanz: UVK Verlagsgesellschaft. 241–255.
Paton, Nathalie E. 2012. "Media Participation of School Shooters and their Fans: Navigating Between Self-Distinction and Imitation to Achieve Individuation". In: Glenn W. Muschert / Johanna Sumiala (eds). *School Shootings: Mediatized Violence in a Global Age.* Bingley: Emerald. 203–230.
Paton, Natalie / Figeac, Julien. 2015. "Expressive Violence: The Performative Effects of Subversive Participatory Media Use". In: *ESSACHESS. Journal for Communication Studies.* Vol 8, No. 1 (2015). 231–256.
Phelan, James. 2005. *Living to tell about it. A Rhetoric and Ethics of Character Narration.* Ithaca / London: Cornell UP.

Phelan, James. 2007. "Estranging Unreliability, Bonding Unreliability, and the Ethics of *Lolita*". *Narrative* 15 (2007). 222–38.
Phelan, James / Martin, Mary Patricia. 1999. "The Lessons of 'Weymouth': Homodiegesis, Unreliability, Ethics, and the *Remains of the Day*". In: Herman, David (ed.). *Narratologies: New Perspectives on Narrative Analysis*. Columbus: Ohio State UP. 88–109.
Philipps, Kendall R. 2008. *Controversial Cinema. The Films that Outraged America*. Westport: Praeger.
Pinker, Steven. 1997. *How the Mind Works*. New York / London: Norton.
Prokop, Andreas. 2015. *Gewalt und Mimikry. Vom Frühen Trauma zum Amoklauf*. Wiesbaden: Springer VS.
Quinn, Naomi / Holland, Dorothy. 1987. "Culture and Cognition". In: Dorothy Holland / Naomi Quinn (eds.). *Cultural Models in Language and Thought*. Cambridge: Cambridge UP. 3–42.
Reemtsma, Jan Philipp. 2012. *Trust and Violence. An Essay on a Modern Relationship*. Princeton: Princeton University Press.
Regener, Susanne. 2017 (in press). "Attentat mit Maske – Die öffentliche Suche nach dem bösen Gesicht". In: Silke Braselmann / Jörn Ahrens. *Vermittlungskulturen des Amoklaufs. Zur medialen Präsenz spektakulärer Gewalt*. Wiesbaden: Springer VS, 2017 (in press). 91–104.
Reimer, Mavis. 2000. "Traditions of the School Story". In: M.O. Grenby / Andrea Immel. *The Cambridge Companion to Children's Literature*. New York: Cambridge University Press. 209–225.
Reinfandt, Christoph 1997. *Der Sinn der fiktionalen Wirklichkeiten. Ein systemtheoretischer Entwurf zur Ausdifferenzierung des englischen Romans von 18. Jahrhundert bis zur Gegenwart*. Heidelberg: Winter.
Rettberg, Jill Walker 2014. "E-mail Novel". In: Marie Laure Ryan / Lori Emerson / Benjamin J. Robertson (eds.). *The Johns Hopkins Guide to Digital Media*. Baltimore: Johns Hopkins University Press. 178 f.
Revesz, Rachael. 2016. "School and College Campus Shootings Timeline: These are all the mass shootings in 2016". *The Independent*. November 28, 2016. Online: https://www.in dependent.co.uk/news/world/americas/ohio-state-university-mass-shooting-injured-time line-schools-colleges-last-12-months-a7444001.html. Last retrieved: May 15, 2019.
Rich, Jeniffer A. 2012. "Shock Corridors: The New Rhetoric of Horror in Gus Van Sant's Elephant" In: *The Journal of Popular Culture* Vol. 45 No. 6 (2012). 1310–1329
Ricœur, Paul. 1984. *Time and Narrative*. Volume 1. Chicago / London: University of Chicago Press.
Ricœur, Paul. 1988. *Time and Narrative*. Volume 3. Chicago / London: University of Chicago Press.
Rimmon-Kenan, Shlomith. 2002 [1983]. *Narrative Fiction. Contemporary Poetics*. London: Routledge.
Robbins, Ruth. 2009. "(Not Such) Great Expectations: Unmaking Maternal Ideals in *The Fifth Child* and *We Need to Talk about Kevin*". In: Alice Ridout / Susan Watkins (eds.). *Doris Lessing. Border Crossings*. London / New York: Continuum. 93–106.
Robertz, Frank J. 2004. *School Shootings. Über die Relevanz der Phantasie für die Begehung von Mehrfachtötungen durch Jugendliche*. Frankfurt a.M.: Verlag für Polizeiwissenschaft.

Robertz, Frank J. 2007. "Erfurt – 5 Jahre danach". In: Hoffmann, Jens / Wondrak, Isabel (eds.): *Amok und zielgerichtete Gewalt an Schulen. Früherkennung / Risikomanagement / Kriseneinsatz / Nachbetreuung*. Frankfurt a.M.: Verlag für Polizeiwissenschaft. 9–23.

Robertz, Frank J. 2013. "On the Relevance of Phantasy for the Genesis of School Shootings". In: Nils Böckler / Thorsten Seeger et.al. (eds.) *School Shootings: International Research, Case Studies and Concepts for Prevention*. New York: Springer. 105–129.

Robertz, Frank J. / Kahr, Robert. 2016. "Phantasien absoluter Gewalt – Ein kriminologischer Blick auf Berichterstattunga ls Anregung zur Nachahmung". In: Frank J. Robertz / Robert Kahr (eds.). *Die mediale Inszenierung von Amok und Terrorismus. Zur medienpsychologischen Wirkung des Journalismus bei exzessiver Gewalt*. Wiesbaden: Springer.

Robertz, Frank J. / Wickenhäuser, Robert. 2007. *Der Riss in der Tafel. Amoklauf und schwere Gewalt in der Schule*. Heidelberg: Springer.

Rousseau, Jean Jacques. 1921 [1762]. Transl. by Barbara Foxley. *Emile, or Education*. Online: http://oll.libertyfund.org/titles/rousseau-emile-or-education. Last retrieved October 1, 2104.

Ryan, Marie-Laure. 2004. "Introduction". In: Marie-Laure Ryan (ed.). *Narrative Across Media. The Languages of Storytelling*. Lincoln / London: University of Nebraska Press. 1–40.

Ryan, Marie-Laure. 2014. "Story / Worlds / Media. Tuning the Instruments of a Media-Conscious Narratology". Marie-Laure Ryan / Jan Noel Thon (eds.). *Storyworlds Across Media. Towards a Media Conscious Narratology*. Lincoln / London: University of Nebraska Press. 25–49.

Saint Martin, Manuel L. 1999. "Running Amok: A Modern Perspective on a Culture-Bound Syndrome". In: *Journal of Clinical Psychiatry* Vol. 1 No. 3 (1999). Online: https://www.ncbi.nlm.nih.gov/pmc/articles/PMC181064/. Last Retrieved: May 15, 2019. 66–70.

Sandberg, Sveinung / Oksanen, Atte / Berntzen, Lars Erik / Kiilakosi, Tomi. 2014. "Stories in action: the cultural influences of school shootings on the terrorist attacks in Norway". In: *Critical Studies on Terrorism* Vol. 7 NO. 2 (2014). 277–296.

Schank, Roger C. / Abelson, Robert P. 1977. *Scripts, Plans, Goals and Understanding: An Inquiry into Human Knowledge Structures*. New York: Erlbaum.

Schildkraut, Jaclyn. 2012. "The Remote is Controlled by the Monster: Issues of Mediatized Violence and School Shootings". In: Glenn W. Muschert / Johanna Sumiala (eds.). *School Shootings: Mediatized Violence in a Global Age*. Bingley: Emerald. 231–254.

Schildkraut, Jaclyn / Glenn W. Muschert. 2014. "Media Salience and the Framing of Mass Murder in Schools: A Comparison of the Columbine and Sandy Hook Massacres". In: *Homicide Studies* Vol. 18 No. 1 (2014). 23–43.

Schlickers, Sabine. 2009. "Focalization, Ocularization and Auricularization in Film and Literature". In: Peter Hühn / Wolf Schmid / Jörg Schönert (eds). *Point of View, Perspective, and Focalization. Modeling Mediation in Narrative*. Berlin / New York: De Gruyter. 243–258.

Scott, Neera. 2005. "Sublime Anarchy in Gus van Sant's Elephant". In: *Sense of Cinema*. No. 36 (2005). Online: http:// senseofcinema.com/2005/36/elephant-2. Last Retrieved: March 25, 2015. n. pag.

Serazio, Michael. 2009. "Shooting for Fame: The (Anti-)Social Media of a YouTube-Killer". In: *Flow Journal* 9.14 (2009). http://www.flowjournal.org/2009/05/shooting-for-fame-the-anti-social-media-of-a-youtube-killer-michael-serazio-university-of-pennsylvania/. Last Retrieved: April 11, 2019. n.pag.

Shepard, C. n.d. *A Columbine Site*. Online: http://www.acolumbinesite.com/about.php. Last Retrieved: April 11, 2019.

Shriver, Lionel. 2005. "We need to talk about Kevin – Lionel Shriver in Interview". Interview by Andrew Lawless. *Three Monkey Online*. Online: http://www.threemonkeysonline.com/we-need-to-talk-about-kevin-lionel-shriver-in-interview/. Last Retrieved: May 15, 2019.

Sitzer, Peter. 2013. "The Role of Media Content in the Genesis of School Shootings: The Contemporary Discussion". In: Nils Böckler/Thorsten Seeger et al. (eds.) *School Shootings: International Research, Case Studies and Concepts for Prevention*. New York: Springer. 283–308.

Solomon, Andrew. 2013. *Far from the Tree: Parents, Children and the Search for Identity*. New York: Scribner.

Spores, John C. 1988. Running *Amok: An Historical Inquiry*. Athens, OH: Ohio University Center for International Studies.

Sternberg, Meir / Yacobi, Tamar. 2015. "(Un)Reliability in Narrative Discourse: A Comprehensive Overview". In: *Poetics Today* Vol. 36 Issue 4 (2015). 327–498.

Stratmann, Gerd. 1984. "The Contextual Functions of Literature: The Concept and its Prophet". In: Ulrich Broich / Theo Stemmler / Gerd Stratmann. *Functions of Literature, Essays presented to Erwin Wolff on his Sixtieth Birthday*. Tübingen: Niemeyer. 1–19

Surkamp, Carola. 2003. *Die Perspektivenstruktur Narrativer Texte. Zur Ihrer Theorie und Geschichte im englischen Roman zwischen Viktorianismus und Moderne*. Trier: WVT.

The White House. "President Obama Makes a Statement on the Shooting in Newtown Connecticut". December 14, 2012. https://obamawhitehouse.archives.gov/photos-and-video/video/2012/12/14/president-obama-makes-statement-shooting-newtown-connecticut. Last Retrieved: February 22, 2017.

The White House. "Remarks by the President at Sandy Hook Interfaith Prayer Vigil". December 16, 2012. https://obamawhitehouse.archives.gov/the-press-office/2012/12/16/remarks-president-sandy-hook-interfaith-prayer-vigil. Last Retrieved: February 22, 2017.

Thon, Jan-Noël. 2014. "Subjectivity across Media. On Transmedial Strategies of Subjective Representation in Contemporary Feature Films, Graphic Novels, and Computer Games". In: Marie-Laure Ryan / Jan-Noël Thon (eds.). *Storyworlds across Media. Toward a Media-Conscious Narratology*. Lincoln / London: University of Nebraska Press. 67–102.

Tjupa, Valerij. 2014. "Narrative Strategies". In: Peter Hühn / Jan Christoph Meister / John Pier / Wolf Schmid (eds.). *Handbook of Narratology*. 2nd rev. and exp. edition. Vol 1. Berlin / Boston: De Gruyter. 564–574.

Tonso, Karen L. 2009. "Violent Masculinities as Tropes for School Shooters: The Montréal Massacre, the Columbine Attack, and Rethinking Schools". In: *American Behavioral Scientist* Vol. 52 No. 9 (2009). 1266–1285.

Van Sant, Gus. 2003. "Gus van Sant – Elephant". Interview by Gerald Peary. Online: http://www.geraldpeary.com/interviews/stuv/van-sant-elephant.html. Last Retrieved: March 25, 2019.

Van Sant, Gus. 2006. "Van Sant on Elephant". Interview by Emanuel Levy. January 31, 2006. Online: http://emanuellevy.com/comment/gus-van-sant-on-elephant-2/. Last Retrieved: March 25, 2019.

Verhovnik, Melanie. 2015. *School Shootings. Interdisziplinäre Analyse und empirische Untersuchung der journalistischen Berichterstattung.* Baden-Baden: Nomos.
Verlinden, Stephanie / Hersen, Michel / Thomas, Jay. 2000. "Risk Factors in School Shootings". In: *Clinical Psychology Review* Vol. 20 No. 1 (2000). 3–56.
Vogl, Joseph. 2003. "Beliebige Feindschaft. Zur Epoche des Amok". In: Medardus Brehl / Kristin PlattVos (eds.). *Feindschaft.* München: Fink. 211–225.
Vogl, Joseph. 2014. "Der Amokläufer". In: Lars Friedrich / Karin Harasser / Daniel Tyradellis / Joseph Vogl (eds.). *Figuren der Gewalt.* Zürich / Berlin: Diaphenes. 13–18.
Von Treskow, Isabella. 2015. "First Person Shooter. Täterprofilierungen in Amok-Darstellungen von E. Carrére, M. Rhue, N. Niemann und C. Meyer". In: Isabella von Treskow / Ralf Junkerjürgen. *Amok und Schulmassaker. Kultur- und Medienwissenschaftliche Annäherungen.* Bielefeld: Transcript. 211–252.
Von Treskow, Isabella. 2017. "Amok als Antwort: Geschlechter-Antagonismen in ausgwählter Literatur zu Amokläufen (1911–2011)". In: Silke Braselmann / Jörn Ahrens. *Vermittlungskulturen des Amoklaufs. Zur medialen Präsenz spektakulärer Gewalt.* Wiesbaden: Springer VS. 123–148.
Vossekuil, Bryan / Fein, Robert A. / Reddy, Marisa / Borum, Randy / Modzeleski, William. 2002. *The Final Report and Findings of the Safe School Initiative. Implications for the Prevention of School Attacks in the United States.* Washington, D.C.: United States Secret Service and United States Department of Education.
Weber, Christian. 2015. *Gus Van Sant. Looking for a Place Like Home.* Berlin: Bertz+Fischer.
White, Hayden. 1980. "The Value of Narrativity in the Representation of Reality". In: *Critical Inquiry* Vol. 7 No. 1 (1980). 5–27.
Wolf, Werner. 2000. "Multiperspektivität: Das Konzept und seine Applikationsmöglichkeiten auf Rahmungen in Erzählwerken". In: Vera Nünning / Ansgar Nünning. *Multiperspektivisches Erzählen. Zur Theorie und Geschichte der Perspektivenstruktur im englischen Roman des 18. bis 20. Jahrhunderts.* Trier: WVT. 79–132.
Young, Peter. 2008. "Film Genre Theory and Contemporary Media: Description, Interpretation, Intermediality". Oxford Handbook. In: Robert Kolker (ed.). *The Oxford Handbook of Film and Media Studies.* Oxford / New York: Oxford University Press. 224–259.
Zapf, Hubert. 2002. *Literatur als kulturelle Ökologie: Zur kulturellen Funktion imaginativer Texte an Beispielen des amerikanischen Romans.* Tübingen: Niemeyer.
Zerweck, Bruno. 2001. "Historicizing Unreliable Narration: Unreliability and Cultural Discourse in Narrative Fiction" In: *Style* No. 35 (2001). 151–78.

Index

Abject hero 201, 205
Accomplice 112, 158, 160, 174f., 181, 192, 198, 201f., 204, 207, 220, 239, 244, 253, 291
Active reading process 15, 157, 187, 190, 204, 233, 324
Adaptation 11, 16, 265, 267f., 300–308, 310–312, 314, 326
Adolescent reader 150, 163–167, 169, 171, 177, 185, 188, 190–192, 196, 199, 203–205, 214, 226, 230, 233
Aesthetic experience 12, 15f., 135–137, 139f., 142, 157, 167–169, 236, 241, 261f., 264, 266, 320
Aesthetic freedom 7, 236, 322
Ambivalence 200f., 234–236, 251, 255, 257, 261f., 280f., 285f., 289f.
Amok 11, 19f., 22, 24–34, 38f., 41–43, 52f., 69, 73, 77, 89, 113, 124, 127, 185, 187, 191, 287
Amok-persona 113, 115, 254
Archive 50, 143, 160, 177–179, 181, 183, 265, 297f., 320–322
Artifact 7f., 10, 12, 58, 60, 64–66, 70, 74, 89f., 92, 115, 118, 123, 140, 143f., 149, 267f., 315, 317
– Cultural artifact 3f., 6, 65, 73–75, 90, 92–94, 107, 111f., 117, 155f., 318
– Multimodal artifact 155
Authenticity 15, 95–99, 101, 104, 144, 153, 161f., 176, 184, 189, 244
– Authentication 9, 101, 103, 105f., 176, 181, 183f., 188, 194, 207, 319
Auvinen, Pekka-Erik 64, 107, 112, 119, 122, 187

Basement Tapes 63, 83, 105, 128, 252
Blending 228, 307, 309
Bosse, Sebastian 48, 107, 112, 117f., 122, 127f., 187
Breivik, Anders Bering 113, 120
Bullying 2, 31f., 38f., 41, 47–49, 61, 94f., 100, 106, 117, 163–165, 172, 174, 177, 189–191, 193, 201f., 206, 208, 219f., 223, 228, 233–236, 249, 253, 255f., 299, 321, 323

Carneal, Michael 44, 62, 64f., 282, 296
Case-definition-problem 33f., 315
Causality 5, 11, 13, 22, 32, 39, 41f., 46, 52, 71f., 74, 79f., 87–90, 124, 129–131, 141f., 164f., 174, 191, 208, 211, 223, 239, 250–252, 255f., 261, 265f., 274, 288, 297, 313, 318, 323–325
Character-perspective 214–216, 219, 222, 226f., 229, 231, 242, 248, 250, 263
Cho, Seung-Hui 34, 48, 68, 107, 112–115, 119, 122, 127f., 130, 187, 220
Closure 63, 80, 87, 213, 226, 233–237, 251, 255, 257, 261, 264, 273, 279, 324–326
Cognitive narratology 71, 78f., 145, 171
College Rampage Shooting 34
Communication 6, 75, 132, 136f., 153, 155–158, 161, 164f., 167, 177–180, 183, 187f., 206f., 215, 217, 225, 271, 286, 303, 317, 326, 328
Community 13, 22–24, 36, 38, 46f., 64, 83, 85, 107, 121, 129, 143, 152, 163, 193–195, 201, 214, 231, 234, 253, 282, 291
Constructivist approach 9, 326
Copycat crimes 58f., 62, 268
Cultural Memory 82, 102f., 141–145, 206, 292, 294, 313, 315, 320, 327
– Cultural Memory Studies 12, 14, 93, 102, 125, 134, 140, 320, 328
Cultural Script 35, 64, 66, 70–76, 88–90, 92f., 107, 111, 115, 117, 119f., 149, 198, 209, 238, 318, 326

Diary 48, 83, 100, 113, 160f., 176, 185–187, 200f., 204f., 233, 245, 272

352 — Index

Discourse formation   6, 12, 81, 91, 106, 124–128, 133, 135, 144 f., 149, 166, 190, 208, 239, 262, 292, 315–317, 319, 321
Drugs   64, 187, 200, 204

Empathy   164 f., 170–175, 187, 190 f., 202, 212, 222, 224–226, 246, 248, 261, 263, 280, 296, 304 f., 312, 314, 322
Epistolarity   269, 271 f.
Evil   5, 16, 84, 127, 131, 165, 266, 286 f., 289, 306–308
Experientiality   80 f., 85, 104, 106, 150, 163, 167 f., 172, 179, 189, 275

Fallible narrator   280 f.
Fictional Dimension   6 f., 10, 19–22, 25, 28, 35 f., 77, 86, 88–90, 93 f., 106, 108, 112, 115, 118, 121 f., 124 f., 128, 130–132, 138, 142, 144, 149, 166, 168, 196, 237 f., 250, 252, 265, 316–320, 326–329
Filmic narration   242
Fluck, Winfried   7, 12, 19, 77, 93, 134, 136–141, 167, 282, 320
Focalization   240–242
Frame   2, 24, 28, 32, 35 f., 39, 71, 95, 98, 113, 145, 156, 181, 199, 219, 222, 243 f., 256, 259
– Framing perspective   222
Functional Approach   11 f., 14, 93, 317, 327
Fundamental Attribution Error   226, 229
Funktionsgeschichte   134, 138

Golden, Andrew   252, 282, 296
Goth culture   40, 65, 198 f.
Gun control   49, 51, 208, 220 f., 299, 315 f., 321

Harris, Eric   3, 42, 45, 48, 60 f., 63–65, 68, 75, 82–84, 86–88, 94 f., 105–107, 110, 112 f., 115 f., 118, 122 f., 172, 180, 185–187, 197 f., 200, 205, 207, 245, 249, 252, 254, 276, 319
Hierarchy   169, 218, 222, 227, 248, 250
– Hierarchization   222
Homodiegetic narrator   225, 277–279

Identity formation   75, 91, 93, 108, 111 f., 118, 123–125, 127, 144, 155, 178, 198, 208 f.
IHE shooting   34
Imaginary   7, 29, 31, 61, 77, 94, 98, 101, 121, 136–138, 140 f., 245, 257, 282, 294
– cultural imaginary   3, 7, 12 f., 15, 19, 60, 75, 77, 85, 88, 90, 106, 126–128, 137 f., 141, 144, 149, 151, 167, 209, 212, 231, 237, 250, 252, 257, 282, 315, 317, 321 f.
Intermedial narratology   320
Iser, Wolfgang   7, 12, 93, 101, 114, 121, 134–140, 168, 171, 175, 228, 241, 320, 323 f.

JCSO Documents   82 f., 180–182, 184, 186
Johnson, Mitchell   302

Kinkel, Kip   36
Klebold, Dylan   3, 45 f., 60 f., 63–65, 68, 75, 82–84, 94 f., 105 f., 110, 112, 115 f., 118 f., 122 f., 180, 185, 187, 197 f., 207, 254, 276, 291, 319

Lanza, Adam   20, 34, 36, 43 f., 51, 60, 113, 115
Loukaitis, Barry   62

Marginalization   47–49, 53, 66 f., 73, 163 f., 174, 188–194, 199, 203, 205–207, 209, 222 f., 235
Mass media   2 f., 7, 19, 21, 29, 37 f., 52, 54 f., 61, 104, 126, 128, 131
Maternal   266, 269, 283–286, 289, 308–310, 314
– Maternal ambivalence   283
– Maternal guilt   291
– Maternal love   283, 292
Meaning-making   6 f., 11, 22, 77 f., 89, 124, 151, 154 f., 161, 165–167, 175, 185, 188, 190, 196, 215, 222, 224, 251, 272, 282, 288, 295, 297, 313, 318, 327
Media dynamics   9, 30, 38, 40, 83, 89, 107, 193, 197, 207, 328
Media event   3, 131, 133, 267, 326
Media spectacle   3, 21, 75, 89, 129, 142, 326

Memorial media   103
Mental Illness   40–44, 74, 87, 129, 185, 204, 208 f.
Mockumentary   96–100
Model   53, 61, 69 f., 72, 90 f., 111, 114 f, 128, 136, 173, 175, 212, 216 f., 282, 230, 235, 241, 242, 277, 288, 294, 327
Modus Operandi   20, 61, 74–76, 90, 112, 120, 149, 191, 209
Monstrosity   5, 84, 86, 287, 308, 311, 313
Moore, Michael   12, 239, 253
Moral panic   37 f., 57, 150, 189, 193
Multicausality   71, 226, 262
Music   6, 40, 55, 57, 61 f., 74, 94, 108, 110, 113, 140, 156, 166, 196, 198 f., 301

Narrative structure   12, 14, 82, 87, 131, 142, 196, 212, 215 f., 222, 228, 237, 240 f., 243, 248, 251 f., 257, 268, 270, 278, 292, 300, 320, 325
Natural Born Killers   62, 64 f., 69 f., 118 f., 132
Notoriety   59, 73, 75, 87, 93, 115, 117 f.

Othering   5, 16, 44, 79, 84, 127–131, 142, 231, 267, 287, 305, 307, 310, 312, 325
Over-Identification   66

Performativity   74, 286
– Performative act   6, 12, 91, 93, 107, 120 f., 126–128, 319
Perspective structure   212, 214–219, 221–224, 226–228, 232 f., 235 f., 248 f.
Perspective taking   172, 174, 212, 214 f., 223–226, 246 f., 322
Polyvalence   175, 226, 230, 235 f., 261, 320, 325 f.
Potential Effect   139–141,
Premediation   12, 131–133, 142
Prevention   8 f., 39, 43, 49, 51 f., 67, 130 f., 150, 152, 163, 170, 174, 187, 189, 195 f., 205, 207, 210, 226, 235 f., 256 f., 299, 325
Pseudo-Documentary   92, 95–97, 99–102

Rashomon-Effect   210

Reception Aesthetics   12, 14, 93, 125, 134, 136 f., 145
Reciprocity   12, 75, 90 f., 93 f., 106, 133, 299
Recognizablity   323
Remediation   12, 93, 95, 102–106, 123, 132, 135, 142, 153, 175–177, 183 f., 206, 209, 237, 249 f., 253, 267, 319–321, 329
Revenge   23, 39, 47 f., 68, 83, 87, 95, 105, 111 f., 117, 132, 164, 191, 193, 198, 200, 204, 218, 259, 290
Ricœur, Paul   5, 121, 130 f., 234, 297

Sandy Hook Elementary School   2, 15, 20, 34, 36, 43, 49 f, 53, 60
Schema   71, 74, 76 f.
– Schemata   71 f., 76 f., 133, 168, 215, 320
– Schematizing   76
Schulamoklauf   24
Self-reflexive   103, 105, 188, 249, 313, 322
– Self-reflexivity   103
Semantic openness   325
Semiotic modes   150, 152–159, 161, 165–167, 171 f., 176, 179, 183, 188, 193, 217
Social effect   139, 327
Spencer, Brenda Ann   73
Steinhäuser, Robert   107, 122, 187
Stone, Oliver   62, 64, 159, 220

Terror   78, 103, 132, 158, 257, 260, 305, 327
– Terrorism   74, 151, 327 f.
Travel report   29 f.
Trenchcoat Mafia   83, 198 f., 321
Trust   36, 46, 79, 109, 124, 265, 291, 297

Unreliable Narrator   280 f, 287, 290

Victimization   38, 66, 85, 163 f., 173, 201 f., 206
Violence
– Autotelic Violence   4 f., 81
– Excessive violence   4, 9–11, 19 f., 22, 24 f., 27, 29, 31, 35–38, 42–44, 47, 52 f., 55, 59, 61 f., 65 f., 68–71, 74, 77, 82, 89 f., 103, 124–126, 128, 130–132, 145,

152, 185, 225, 259, 264–266, 269, 271, 287f., 316–318, 325, 327–329
– Media violence   9, 11, 21f., 53, 55–58, 61f., 65f., 68, 106, 134, 151, 208, 268, 321
– Youth violence   10, 50, 57f., 90, 116, 130, 149f., 158, 167, 189, 193, 203, 212
Voyage narrative   29, 38, 124

Weise, Jeffrey   32, 69, 111, 129, 252
Werther Effect   58, 65, 139
Whitman, Charles   30, 34, 42
Williams, Latina   73, 295
Winnenden   51, 122
Woodham, Luke   47f., 67, 73, 296

www.ingramcontent.com/pod-product-compliance
Lightning Source LLC
Chambersburg PA
CBHW031752220426
43662CB00007B/378